SOCIETAL PROBLEMS AS PUBLIC BADS

Corruption, crime, economic inequality, religious fundamentalism, financial crises, environmental degradation, population ageing, gender inequality, large-scale migration . . . This book tackles many of the most pressing problems facing societies today. The authors demonstrate that similar social mechanisms lie behind many of these seemingly disparate problems. Indeed, many societal problems can be traced back to behaviours that are perfectly rational and often well-intended from an individual perspective. Yet, taken together these behaviours can – paradoxically – give rise to unintended and undesirable outcomes at the society level.

In addition to addressing the causes of societal problems, the book explains why some problems rank higher on the public agenda than others. Moreover, it is shown how government intervention may sometimes provide a cure, yet other times exacerbate existing problems or create new problems of its own. This book includes an extensive amount of data on trends and geographic variation in the prevalence of different problems, as well as telling examples – both recent and historical – from a variety of countries to support its key arguments.

Employing a bold multidisciplinary approach, the authors draw on insights from across the social sciences, including sociology, economics, anthropology, criminology, and psychology. Throughout the book, students are introduced to analytical concepts such as free-riding, herding behaviour, principal-agent relations and moral hazard. These concepts are essential tools for better understanding the roots of many societal problems that regularly make headlines in the news. This improved understanding will, in turn, be critical for ultimately finding solutions to these problems.

Nan Dirk de Graaf is an Official Fellow at Nuffield College and Professor of Sociology at the University of Oxford. His research interests include social stratification – especially educational attainment and how social mobility affects political preferences, health and attitudes, sociology of religion, pro-social behaviour, and political sociology.

Dingeman Wiertz is a Lecturer in Social Science and British Academy Postdoctoral Fellow at University College London. Having received training in economics as well as sociology, his research interests include civic engagement, inter-ethnic relations, social networks, economic hardship, political attitudes, school choice, and residential segregation.

SOCIETAL PROBLEMS AS PUBLIC BADS

Nan Dirk de Graaf and Dingeman Wiertz

Routledge
Taylor & Francis Group
LONDON AND NEW YORK

First published 2019
by Routledge
2 Park Square, Milton Park, Abingdon, Oxon OX14 4RN

and by Routledge
52 Vanderbilt Avenue, New York, NY 10017

Routledge is an imprint of the Taylor & Francis Group, an informa business

British Library Cataloguing-in-Publication Data
A catalogue record for this book is available from the British Library

Library of Congress Cataloging-in-Publication Data
Names: Graaf, N. D. de. (Nan Dirk), author. | Wiertz, Dingeman, 1988- author.
Title: Societal problems as public bads / Nan Dirk de Graaf and Dingeman Wiertz.
Description: Abingdon, Oxon ; New York, NY : Routledge, 2019. | Includes bibliographical references and index.
Identifiers: LCCN 2018060678| ISBN 9781138480209 (hardback) | ISBN 9781138480216 (pbk.) | ISBN 9781351063463 (ebook)
Subjects: LCSH: Social problems. | Social policy.
Classification: LCC HN18.3 .G73 2019 | DDC 306—dc23
LC record available at https://lccn.loc.gov/2018060678

ISBN: 978-1-138-48020-9 (hbk)
ISBN: 978-1-138-48021-6 (pbk)
ISBN: 978-1-351-06346-3 (ebk)

Typeset in Sabon
by Swales & Willis Ltd, Exeter, Devon, UK

CONTENTS

ILLUSTRATIONS

Figures

Tables

PREFACE

Economic inequality, environmental degradation, large-scale migration, crime, corruption, religious fundamentalism, financial crises, gender inequality, population ageing . . . In this book we tackle several of the most pressing problems facing societies today. In particular, we aim to improve readers' understanding of the features, causes and implications of these problems.

Crucially, we do not analyse these problems through the lens of a particular discipline, but rather employ a multidisciplinary approach, drawing on insights from across the social sciences, including sociology, economics, psychology, criminology and anthropology. We argue that such a multidisciplinary perspective is indispensable for gaining a comprehensive appreciation of how these problems are embedded in society. Different disciplines have different things to say in this regard and, therefore, it is critical to let them speak to and complement one another. This strongly reflects our philosophy in relation to social science, whereby the empirical realities of key societal problems take centre stage, with the insights from various disciplines being servants to a better understanding of these problems.

A fundamental element of our analytical approach is that we relate any observed society-level phenomena to the individual-level behaviours underlying them. We consider how society-level circumstances shape the behaviour of individual actors in concrete situations, and how the aggregation of these individual-level actions subsequently give rise to society-level outcomes. In doing so, we demonstrate that similar social mechanisms lie behind seemingly disparate societal problems. We especially highlight that many societal problems can be traced back to behaviours that are perfectly rational and often well-intended from an individual perspective. Yet, taken together these individual-level behaviours can paradoxically give rise to unintended and undesirable societal outcomes.

Throughout the book we provide many telling examples of such dynamics, whether related to the origins of environmental problems, the persistence of corruption, or the unfolding of stock market crashes. Moreover, we show how government intervention may sometimes provide a cure to societal problems, yet other times exacerbate existing problems or create new problems of its own. We illustrate our discussions with an extensive amount of figures and tables on trends and cross-country variation in the prevalence of different problems. Furthermore, we introduce readers to analytical concepts such as free-riding, herding behaviour, principal-agent relations, moral hazard, self-fulfilling prophecies and critical mass models. As will become clear, these concepts are essential tools for better understanding the roots of societal problems that continually make headlines in the news and, ultimately, for finding solutions to them.

This book is the result of a long process, which goes back to when Nan Dirk, together with Willem Wolters, started teaching on societal problems in the early 1990s. Based on their teaching they wrote a book in Dutch: *Maatschappelijke Problemen* (Societal Problems), published with Boom in 2005. Nevertheless, Nan Dirk always maintained the idea to write another book on this topic for a broader international audience. These plans gained momentum after Dingeman arrived in Oxford in 2010, driven by a similar passion for understanding societal problems and equally committed to a multidisciplinary social science approach.

While it is an understatement that the scope of our book is highly ambitious – dealing with a wide variety of societal problems and doing so from a multidisciplinary perspective – Nuffield College has provided the ideal breeding ground to develop this challenging project. Indeed, founded by Lord Nuffield to enhance cooperation between the academic and non-academic worlds in order to address social, economic and political problems, Nuffield College and our book very much share the same DNA and mission. When it comes to the social sciences, Nuffield provides an unsurpassed intellectual climate in the broadest sense of the term and reflecting this, many Nuffield colleagues have provided key input on our book.

In this context, we cannot stress enough how much we have benefited from the advice and support of many people in preparing this book. We especially would like to thank Noah Carl and Andreas Flache, who have both provided extensive comments on most chapters while these were still in an early stage of development. We are also indebted to Ask Neve for his excellent support in preparing the figures in this book and tracking down the underlying data. Furthermore, since our work is inspired by the earlier mentioned Dutch book on societal problems, Willem Wolters deserves great credit as co-author of that book. Finally, we wish to express our gratitude for feedback, discussions and assistance to Charlotte Baarda, Fleur Dinjens, René Hesseling, David Kirk, Fijnanda van Klingeren, Ariana Need, Menno Rol, Jörg Stolz, Belinda Tracey, Federico Varese, Laurin Weissinger, Annette Wiertz, as well as our copy editors Cherry Mosteshar and Ashley Thorpe, our editorial assistant Mihaela Diana Ciobotea, and our publisher Gerhard Boomgaarden.

1 Introduction

Chapter overview

In this chapter we introduce our approach to societal problems. Importantly, we draw a distinction between societal problems and social problems. The latter refers to problems occurring in social life – that is, in relations and interactions between people. These social problems only become societal problems if they are experienced by a large group of people and leave their mark on society as a whole. We begin this chapter with a historical overview of how societal problems have been approached over the past centuries by public thinkers as well as governments. We then discuss the process through which societal problems arrive onto the public agenda and eventually become targets for government policy. We also address the philosophical underpinnings of social norms, present a simple model of the structure of society, and provide a justification for our selection of societal problems. In particular, we focus on problems that emerge at the societal level from the aggregation of many individual actions. These problems can be viewed as public bads, which stand in contrast to their well-known counterpart, public goods.

Societal problems as public bads

This book deals with a number of pressing societal problems. The first chapter addresses the question of what societal problems are, and the second chapter explains how we approach these problems in this book. The third chapter considers the opportunities and limits of government intervention as a solution to societal problems. The following ten chapters are then devoted to the study of specific societal problems.

In a very general sense, there is a societal problem when a substantial group of citizens perceives a certain state of affairs as problematic. Importantly, we make a distinction here between *societal problems* and *social problems*. The latter refer to problems occurring in relations or interactions between people. However, social problems only become societal problems if they are shared by a large group of people and leave their mark on society as a whole. For example, an occasional case of theft or corruption does not necessarily constitute a societal problem.

Certainly, there will be victims in those cases, but the phenomenon only becomes a societal problem once it is so widespread that it reduces social trust across large swathes of society. In such cases, corruption will also undermine the legitimacy of the government and harm the economy. More generally, societal problems will often have clear political and economic implications in addition to the social.

In this book, we view societal problems as *public bads*, which stand in contrast to their well-known counterpart, *public goods*. Indeed, some public bads concern the under-provision of public goods. Within this framework, societal problems are the unintended society-level consequences of numerous acts by individual actors. These individual actors could be actual individuals but also individual firms or states, and they do not usually intend to cause any harm with their behaviour. Indeed, the true origin of societal problems does not generally lie in the intentions of individuals, but rather in the aggregation of individual actions into society-level phenomena. The crucial aspect is that individual actors do not take into account the effects of their behaviour on others. In economics, these effects – which may be positive or negative – are called *externalities*. As a result of these externalities, together all individual actors produce too much of what is bad for society in the case of negative externalities; or too little of what is good for society in the case of positive externalities. Later in this chapter we present a typology of public bads, but first we turn to some background on how societal problems have been perceived in the past.

A brief history of the problematic society

Only fairly recently have societal problems become an issue of major public concern. While for many centuries societal problems had simply been perceived as a given, an inherent and unavoidable part of any society, this changed in the seventeenth and eighteenth centuries. This trend break was put in motion by philosophers of the Enlightenment such as John Locke, Immanuel Kant, Cesare Beccaria, and Jean-Jacques Rousseau, who began to think critically about the state and society. These philosophers started to develop theories in response to the question of why the circumstances in which people lived were often not in accordance with important moral principles such as liberty and equality.

The term *society* acquired its modern meaning after being used by these thinkers as the opposite to the term *state*. Whereas the state was seen as an institution of power based on hierarchy, society was considered to be an association of free people. In this light, the 1789 French Revolution was perceived as a revolt by society against the state – and against absolutist monarchy in particular. Ever since, the relationship between the state and society has remained subject to tension and change (see also the section "Social norms and the organization of society").

Many Enlightenment philosophers, such as Rousseau and Baron de Montesquieu, had an optimistic view of society. They expected that if individuals surrendered to reason as a guideline for their behaviour, they would collectively be able to redesign society for the better. This spirit is clearly visible in Montesquieu's theory of the *trias politica* (the separation of powers). According to this vision, the administrative powers of governments should be divided into three separate branches: executive, legislative and judicial. These three branches should be independent and thus balance each other in such a way that none of them could over-rule the others. This would in turn protect society against despotism.

The idea that society could be designed according to people's preferences was put into practice by the rebels during the French Revolution. They tried to create a society founded upon the principles of liberty, equality and fraternity. However, it turned out that the rebels had to resort to force and violence in order to achieve their goals. Their attempt to achieve liberty, equality and fraternity had thus led to tyranny. Reflecting on this revolution, the eighteenth century British philosopher Edmund Burke (2003[1790]:51) made his famous statement about *perverse consequences*, namely that "very plausible schemes, with very pleasing commencements, have often shameful and lamentable conclusions". Throughout this book, we present many examples of how innocent or even noble intentions can give rise to undesirable outcomes.

During the twentieth century, social science became firmly established as an area of academic inquiry that aims to increase our understanding of societal problems. The underlying goal is to ultimately help solve these problems. At the same time, social science has become increasingly associated with government policy. In the 1940s and 1950s, social scientists were, for example, actively involved in the development of Western welfare states. In the United Kingdom, the *Beveridge Report* (Beveridge 1942) laid the foundations of the welfare state as it was erected after the Second World War. The report identified five "Giant Evils" (want, disease, ignorance, squalor, and idleness) and outlined a range of social reforms to address these problems.

Since the 1950s, governments have increasingly consulted social scientists on questions such as: How can economic growth be stimulated? How can we safeguard a satisfactory standard of living for the elderly? How should we tackle climate change? What is the best strategy to diminish crime or inter-ethnic conflicts? In short, as the state has become more involved in the organization of society (see also Chapter 3), this has generated an increased need for social scientific knowledge about society. More generally, it is the societal problems themselves that call for the development of theories and the acquisition of empirical insights on why and how such problems occur. Therefore, societal problems constitute the ultimate reason for the existence for social science.

When does a problem become a societal problem?

There will always be a certain level of disagreement among citizens on whether something constitutes a societal problem or not. As soon as one begins to discuss particular societal problems, opinions on their severity and whether any sort of corrective action is needed will differ. Some problems will be immediately recognized as such, whereas others will provoke fearsome debate. In addition, people may have mixed feelings about certain societal problems.

Take, for example, the case of greenhouse gas emissions. These emissions have skyrocketed during the past century, carrying "risks of severe, pervasive, and irreversible impacts for people and ecosystems, and long-lasting changes in all components of the climate system" according to the Intergovernmental Panel on Climate Change (IPCC 2015:v). Moreover, the IPCC (2015:v) concludes that it "is now 95 percent certain that humans are the main cause of current global warming". From this perspective, few rational people would disagree that rising greenhouse gas emissions are an important cause for concern. Nevertheless, many people feel conflicted when it comes to cutting down on emissions.

This can be better understood if we consider the contexts in which individuals act. First, many people work in industries such as manufacturing that contribute strongly to global greenhouse gas emissions. While these people may subscribe to the general opinion that emissions should be reduced, they would probably oppose closing down the factories on which they rely to make a living. Likewise, companies in high-emission industries have set up a powerful lobby aimed at preventing, or slowing down, further environmental regulations. Second, many people have grown accustomed to travelling by car or airplane in their everyday lives. Even though these modes of transport are known to be a major culprit in the recent rise in greenhouse gas concentrations, people are reluctant to give up their habits. As a result, proposals for making these modes of transport more expensive by introducing carbon taxes generally meet fierce public opposition. Third, the fact that alternative energy sources, such as solar energy, are still very expensive leads some people to conclude that we should not throw away our old shoes before we have new ones. Indeed, a certain level of greenhouse gas emissions may, for the moment at least, be efficient – that is to say, the costs of preventing those emissions may exceed the harm done by them to society.

In summary, it is not always evident whether a certain situation constitutes a societal problem and, if so, what should be done about it. Indeed, the process through which societal problems are recognized as such and through which they may eventually bring about collective action inevitably contains elements of contestation. More generally, this process of forming a diagnosis and deciding on a treatment plan consists of several components, as illustrated in Figure 1.1.

The first condition in Figure 1.1 is closely connected to our view of societal problems as public bads. As described in the section "Societal problems as public bads", these problems often originate from an aggregation of individual-level behaviours that generate unintended consequences at the society level. Because individual actors do not take these consequences into account when planning their actions, they end up doing either too much or too little of certain things, compared to what would be optimal from a societal perspective.

The example of greenhouse gas emissions again offers an illustration. After all, when individuals take their petrol or diesel fuelled car to drive somewhere, they are usually primarily concerned with the individual-level target of reaching their destination and only secondarily, if at all, with the environmental consequences of their behaviour at the societal level. As this holds for most individual car drivers, their joint emission of greenhouse gases is much bigger than societally optimal. Similar kinds of problems arise in other life domains. Most Western societies have, for instance, witnessed sharp declines in fertility in recent decades, which together with increases in longevity have resulted in an ageing population. Among other things, this puts pressure on the affordability of the welfare state, including retirement and health care policies. From a societal perspective, there is hence an argument for increases in the number of children that people have, but parents are unlikely to take such concerns into account in their personal family planning. In the financial sphere, problems such as stock market bubbles and bank runs can also be traced back to a collection of individual-level behaviours with unintended consequences. For individual investors it can be wise to retract their savings or sell their stock holdings when they are uncertain whether they will get their money back. However, by doing so, they may stir up similar feelings among other investors, who may follow suit, triggering a bank run or a stock market crash, eventually leaving the whole economy in crisis.

The second condition in Figure 1.1 requires that the society-level situation arising from the collection of individual-level behaviours be recognized as a societal problem. This is a matter of both detection and evaluation: people need to be aware of the situation, as well as consider it to be in conflict with important values. Detecting a societal problem sometimes requires

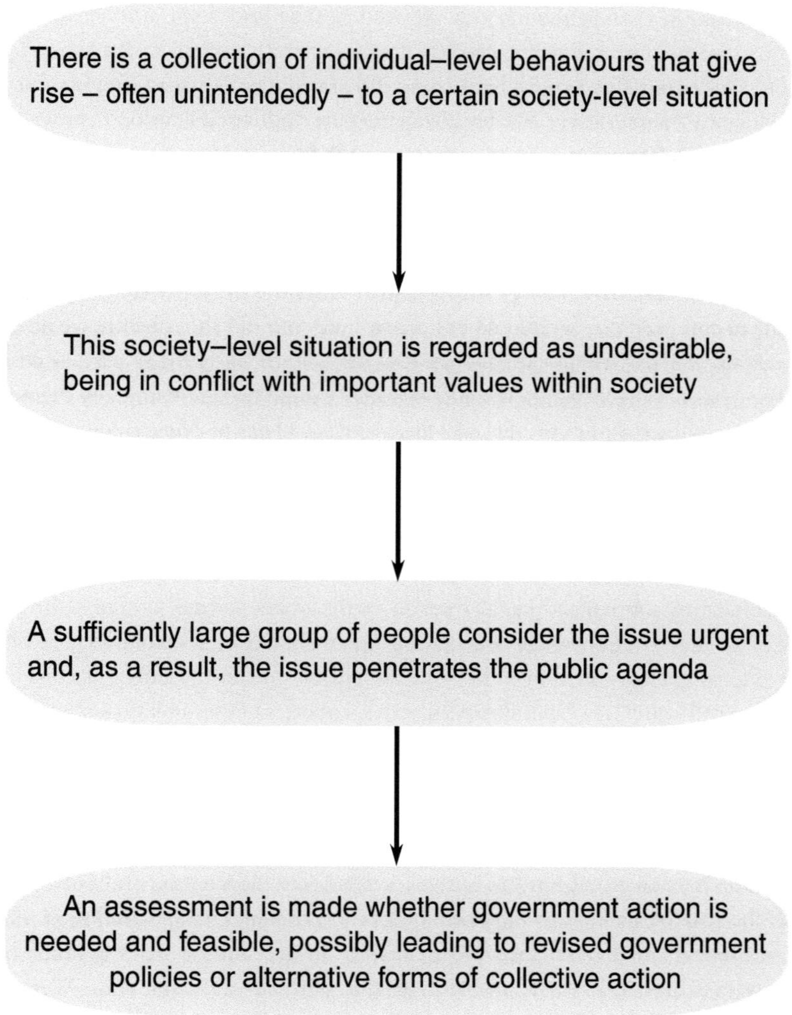

Figure 1.1 How societal problems are recognized and bring about collective action

knowledge and expertise. There are a wide range of problems that resulted in a large-scale public outcry only after first being identified by experts. Many environmental problems can be grouped into this category. Consider, for example, the health risks of chemical pollution, the risks of nuclear power plants, the degradation of the ozone layer, the greenhouse effect, or the exhaustion of fish stocks and other natural resources. Ordinary citizens cannot directly observe these problems. They only become anxious when there is a substantial rise in fish prices, when the supply of drinking water is disrupted, or when experts explain that people face increased risks of skin cancer due to the hole in the ozone layer.

After detecting a problematic situation, the phenomenon also needs to be evaluated as a critical issue rather than just an innocent imperfection. This can sometimes take a long time. For example, while many people today complain about low levels of air quality, air pollution actually occurred on a much greater scale in the nineteenth century. Families living in densely populated working-class neighbourhoods suffered heavily and respiratory diseases were very common. Yet, air pollution was not identified as a societal problem at the time. Writers who lamented the degradation of natural landscapes did not find widespread support; they were dismissed as romantic conservatives who idealized the past. Industrial development was considered necessary: industrial plants produced goods for the modern world, and workers earned their living from these plants. Pollution was seen as a price that had to be paid. It took until the 1960s for air pollution to be seriously addressed by governments in the Western world. For example, in the United States the Clean Air Act of 1963 represented the first federal law on air pollution control, with the Clean Air Act of 1970 subsequently setting up concrete programmes to regulate emissions from both stationary (e.g., factories) and mobile (e.g., cars) sources.

This story demonstrates that the prevailing values within society play a key role in whether or not a certain society-level phenomenon is regarded as undesirable. Only when there is a sharp conflict with dominant values, can there be a societal problem. In this context, even widespread human suffering is not necessarily a societal problem. Only when human suffering is considered to be a moral problem – when it is perceived as irreconcilable with prevailing ethical principles – does it turn into a societal problem. In this sense, the process by which phenomena are recognized as societal problems is as much about normative debates as it is about the observation of reality.

For a problem to subsequently gain traction in the public debate, it should be perceived as important by a large portion of the population: there should be a certain degree of consensus that there is an urgent problem and the issue should be put on the public agenda. This is the third condition in Figure 1.1. From this perspective, expert analyses pointing at certain problems are by themselves insufficient for these problems to be regarded as societal problems. One of the reasons for this is that experts often do not agree in their analyses. Examples abound of longstanding debates among scientists over the meaning of observed phenomena, and the existence of any trends over time. Some problems are so highly disputed that one group of scientists is extremely concerned about it while another group systematically denies the mere existence of a problem. This clearly applies to issues such as the dangers of nuclear energy and the integration of immigrants.

In order to put the problem on the public agenda influence is needed. Even when feelings of discontent and concern are widely shared, nothing will happen in the absence of an engaged group of people who will stand up and raise the alarm. If such an engaged group exists, it needs to be capable of exerting societal influence. If the group has insufficient material resources or social status, and no contacts with any political authorities, the likelihood is that it will fail to bring the problem to public attention. This is particularly true given that any such group will usually also face opposition.

Indeed, there are numerous phenomena that are considered to be societal problems by one group of people, but that are dragged down on the public agenda due to counterforces. To mention one example, many people regard the easy access to guns in US as a societal problem that contributes to the country's high murder rate. However, advocates of gun control are opposed by a large number of their fellow citizens as well as the politically influential National Rifle Association. Those parties retort that gun ownership is a constitutional right and that gun control measures will disarm law-abiding people rather than criminals. The strength of these sentiments – undeniably influenced by the strong gun lobby – has so far prevented any legislation that would seriously restrict gun ownership in the US. This example underscores that penetrating the public agenda is not merely a social or political battle, but also has a strong moral component. It has to be shown that the contested situation clashes with the values that a society adheres to, but since different groups in society may have different priorities in this regard (e.g., freedom versus security), normative debates are an essential part of getting an issue on to the public agenda.

Similarly, it took many hard-fought moral battles before poverty eradication gained a prominent spot on the public agenda. For centuries poverty was not seen as a problem but simply as an unfortunate fact of life. It was believed that a certain part of the population would inevitably live in a state of privation, and that this could not be changed. According to the dominant view at the time, the most that could be done were small reliefs by way of private charity to especially disadvantaged persons such as widows and orphans. The poor tried to find solutions for their problems on an individual basis, within their families or via mutual associations whereby individuals paid a small fee in exchange for protection and monetary assistance in times of hardship. In the end, it took until the second half of the nineteenth century, when a labour movement that did not accept poverty as a fact of life gained momentum. They fought for improvements in the living conditions of the poor and even threatened with revolution for the "social issue" to be put on the public agenda by the middle classes and the government.

Arguably, in this age of social media, it is easier for individuals or small groups to elevate issues on to the public agenda. Quite often, a simple Facebook or Twitter post by an ordinary citizen or small action group addressing a social issue turns viral, resulting in thousands of likes or retweets. Thus a piece of information enters the public domain and can no longer be ignored by political elites. As such, the agenda-setting process has undergone democratization. However, at the same time, resources and social status continue to play an important role. Many social media posts that turn viral, for instance, only do so after a celebrity or opinion leader has picked up and drawn attention to the original post. Furthermore, whereas social media has made it easier to gain momentum for a given issue, the abundance of information shared through these networks on a daily basis implies it has also become more difficult to maintain this momentum. There seems to be ever-increasing competition for people's attention.

When a sufficiently large group of people agrees that there is a societal problem, and when this problem finds its way up on to the public agenda, the key question that remains is what to do about it. This brings us to the final component of Figure 1.1. While the existence of the problem indicates that there is some kind of *market failure* (the outcome arising from individual actors interacting without any restrictions is not satisfactory from the point of view of society), this does not necessarily imply that government intervention is needed. Whether or not such intervention is needed very much depends on the nature of the problem in question.

Some problems can be resolved satisfactorily by collective action and coordination among private actors and non-government parties – for example, via covenants and self-regulation. In the section "A typology of goods", it will become clear for which types of problems such solutions may be viable. Throughout the book we also give examples of collective action without government intervention – as in Chapter 12 on environmental problems, where we discuss self-organized irrigation schemes were communities have successfully managed their limited water resources for centuries.

That said, many societal problems have certain characteristics that make it difficult to tackle them while bypassing the government. In such cases there is an evident need for government action. Moreover, collective action in the form of individual actors cooperating with each other is often hard to sustain for a prolonged time. Sooner or later, *free rider problems* may show up, whereby certain actors stop contributing to the collectively produced public good while still reaping the benefits of it. Such problems can easily trickle down, leading to the collapse of the cooperation structure. For this reason, societal concerns that are successfully championed by social movements are often taken over by governments. A by-product is that influencing government policies has increasingly become the aim of collective action. This also relates to the fact that government intervention has vastly expanded over the last century, so that we now speak of *interventionist states* (see Chapter 3).

However, even when addressing a societal problem requires government involvement, it may actually not always be optimal for the government to step in. Ideally, there needs to be evidence that the government has the tools and resources to outperform the market and contribute to an improved situation. It is important in this context to realize that government intervention can have enormous benefits, but may also be extremely expensive in itself. While one could easily identify numerous areas where governments could possibly make a difference, there are limits to what they can do given restricted resources. In this sense, any decision to focus governmental resources on one particular problem inevitably comes at the expense of dealing with other problems. Hence, some sort of cost-benefit trade-off and prioritization is necessary to determine whether the societal problem justifies the costs that would be incurred by the government stepping in. Moreover, as we discuss more extensively in Chapter 3, government intervention can, in some cases, aggravate existing problems or itself be the source of new societal problems.

A telling example is the case of the generous welfare state systems established in many Western countries in the 1950s and 1960s. Following the miseries of the Second World War, and facilitated by the economic recovery that took place afterwards, people were attracted to the reassuring idea of the state protecting its citizens against the risks of unemployment, disability, and old-age poverty. The expectation was that such social protection would give rise to popular gratitude, and that individuals would be prudent and economical in claiming the relevant benefits. However, around 20 years later, it became clear that this expectation was perhaps founded on an overly optimistic vision of human behaviour, as the perverse incentives offered by the generous welfare schemes were revealed. Generous unemployment benefits discouraged the unemployed from finding new jobs. Disability acts were exploited by employers to lay off older employees in exchange for financial compensation from the state. Early retirement schemes permitted older employees to end their careers early on financially attractive terms. By the 1980s, all of this had gradually led to substantial reductions in employment rates and an explosive rise in government expenditures, threatening economic growth and the public treasury in the longer run. Chapter 4 discusses problems related to the welfare state in greater detail.

The welfare state example demonstrates that cost-benefit analyses of government action can be very complicated. The potential consequences of government action can run far into the future, and many of them may not even be on the radar when deciding whether or not to intervene. Furthermore, the very act of intervening may change the incentives and constraints faced by individual actors, thus changing the "rules of the game", and making the eventual outcomes even harder to predict. Finally, the assumptions on which the cost-benefit analyses are based might be wrong, such as the overly optimistic vision of human behaviour in the previous example. This also goes to show how ideology plays an important role in explaining governmental action, shaping the assumptions on which cost-benefit analyses are based as well as the weights attached to different types of costs and benefits.

Politicians also sometimes push aside societal cost-benefit trade-offs in favour of electoral considerations – thinking primarily about what would get them (re-) elected, rather than about what would be optimal for society. This often leads to *short-termism* and a relative neglect of longer-term issues. It is, for instance, well known that incumbent governments often aim to stimulate the economy just before a general election in order to maximize their chances of getting re-elected, thus creating a *political business cycle*: fluctuations in economic performance that hinge on the timing of elections (Nordhaus 1975). Another example concerns many governments' reluctance to increase taxes on cars and fuel for fear that this would alienate potential voters, even though such taxation would clearly help to alleviate environmental problems. In the welfare state example, electoral considerations also play a prominent role: expansions of social protection are popular among many voters, while reductions of entitlements tend to elicit the opposite response. In this case, it is furthermore relevant that those people with a vested interest in maintaining generous welfare state policies – such as pensioners – tend to be more likely to turn out to vote than the average citizen. Politicians interested in clinging on to their power thus have a strong interest in keeping these people happy and may therefore postpone decisions that would benefit society more broadly – for example, a reduction in old age benefits to keep them affordable in the long run.

Social norms and the organization of society

In the previous section we argued that a certain society-level phenomenon can only be regarded as a societal problem if it stands in sharp contrast with the values that society adheres to. However, as already demonstrated by the example of gun control laws in the United States, the existence of a generally shared set of values cannot be taken for granted. In practice, different groups within society often clash horns on what they find (most) important. People's views also tend to change over time, as could be seen on the issues of air quality and poverty. Here we further explore this idea, focusing especially on *social norms* as the more concrete behavioural rules and expectations derived from people's values. In addition, we discuss the organization of society as the structure in which social norms are embedded.

Social norms can be considered a public good. In this context, the sociologist James Coleman (1990) portrays social norms as a form of *social capital*: a productive asset for a group, from which each individual member of the group may benefit. After all, because social norms make the behaviours of others more predictable, fewer problems will arise in people's everyday interactions and it becomes easier to trust one another. In this sense, social norms act as a lubricant for social interactions (see also our discussion of social capital as a public good in the section "A typology of goods").

However, are there in real life any generally accepted norms that are shared across all members of society or even across societies? One obvious candidate would be the system of *universal human rights*, recorded in the *Universal Declaration of Human Rights* adopted by the United Nations in 1948. This declaration represented a huge step forward in the recognition of individuals' human rights. Before the Second World War, only sovereign states had rights according to international law. The significance of the Universal Declaration of Human Rights is thus that – for the first time in history – the rights of individuals in relation to the state were recognized in international law. Since the adoption of the Universal Declaration, the UN has adopted a number of additional covenants, declarations and protocols for securing the rights of, among others, women, children, stateless persons and prisoners. Nevertheless, the Universal Declaration arguably still falls short of setting out a truly universal set of social norms. Indeed, while some commentators criticize the declaration for not going far enough, or not being sufficiently enforceable, others criticize it for being a form of Western imperialism, imposing secular-liberal norms that clash with prevailing social structures in other parts of the world.

The philosophical underpinnings of social norms

Aside from the question of whether there *are* any generally accepted social norms, it is useful to take a step back and consider what those norms *should be*. For this purpose, we turn to the work of political and moral philosophers, who have studied what constitutes a just and ethically defensible society.

One way to evaluate this question is from an individual perspective, as embodied in Immanuel Kant's *categorical imperative*: the notion that one should behave in such a way that one's behaviour could serve as the basis for general legislation. This imperative will often lead to the adoption of the Golden Rule that can be found in many religions that one should treat others as one would like others to treat oneself. However, another way to approach the question of what is a just and ethically defensible society is from the perspective of society as a whole, as seen in the work of the American moral philosophers John Rawls (1971) and Robert Nozick (1974). These thinkers pose the question of what would be a just distribution of rights and resources among members of society. They offer answers that are bolstered by abstract arguments as opposed to positive, empirically testable conjectures about human behaviour and society.

Rawls and Nozick address the question of how society should be organized, and what principles collective institutions like the state should be founded upon. They begin their reasoning from an imaginary *state of nature*. This state of nature can be seen as a clean slate – a situation which, so to speak, has just come into existence, and where people are thus unrestrained by any pre-existing rules or institutions. Rawls and Nozick argue that in the state of nature individuals do not know what the future will bring, but that they are aware of various risks and dangers that they cannot deal with on their own. Sensible people will, therefore, establish collective provisions that can offer a certain amount of security, such as an army for protection against enemies, a bureaucracy to provide stable administration, legislation that regulates the relations between members of society, a judiciary that punishes those who misbehave, and a police service that maintains public order. These provisions require citizens to hand over some of their rights to the state as a coordinating actor. This also means that they voluntarily submit themselves to obligations imposed by the state, such as paying taxes and serving in the army.

What rights should individuals then keep for themselves and what rights should they hand over to the state? Rawls and Nozick both believe that the community of individuals has to reach a consensus on this question if it is to maintain a functioning society, yet their views diverge on what this consensus should look like. The two philosophers advocate markedly different principles for the hypothetical society to adopt, which in turn lead to very different rights and obligations for the citizens of this society. Rawls argues that the state should play a major coordinating role, whereas according to Nozick, the power and scope of the state should be strictly limited.

In his book *A Theory of Justice* (1971), Rawls advances the so-called *original position* thought experiment. One way to think of the original position is to imagine yourself before you were born into this world. Rawls argues that the fairest and therefore most just principles for governing society are the ones that would be selected by rational citizens reasoning from the original position. Importantly, in the original position citizens do not yet know the characteristics they would have once the original position has been superseded. They would not know their gender, ethnicity, height, strength, or talents, nor would they know where in society they will end up – in terms of geographic location, social class and so on. In this sense, people in the original position are situated behind a "veil of ignorance". This is a crucial element of Rawls's reasoning: given this veil of ignorance regarding one's own position in society, what would one want society to look like? The reason for assuming a veil of ignorance is that without one, the taller, stronger or more intelligent citizens would have an incentive to choose principles that would benefit them at the expense of their shorter, weaker or less intelligent rivals. We have an intuitive sense that these sorts of principles would be unfair.

According to Rawls, rational citizens deliberating from behind a veil of ignorance would select the following principles. First, the *principle of equal liberty* posits that every citizen should be guaranteed a set of basic liberties, including protection from violence, freedom of conscience, and equal opportunity within the marketplace. Second, there is the *difference principle*, which contains two subcomponents and follows from Rawls's premise that citizens who are reasoning from behind a veil of ignorance would be averse to risk. According to this principle, inequalities among citizens should be permitted so long as everyone faces equal opportunities to access different positions (the *fair equality of opportunity principle*), and so long as they are advantageous to those who are least well off (the *maximin principle*, as it involves the maximization of the outcomes for those at the bottom of the distribution).

Based on these rules, a doctor or pilot is in principle allowed to earn more than an unskilled worker. After all, if there was no difference in income, there would be hardly any doctors or pilots as hardly anyone would take the trouble of going through the long and expensive education required to become a doctor or pilot. This would, in turn, threaten the health of all members of society or seriously limit their mobility. Hence, Rawls argues, the incentives offered by the higher salaries of doctors and pilots serve society as a whole, and thereby also the unskilled worker. Therefore, as long as everyone in society has equal opportunities to become a doctor, higher salaries for doctors would be justified. Another implication of Rawls's second principle is that if a certain policy leads to the middle class getting massively richer, and the poor getting slightly poorer, then it would not be permissible. However, if it leads to the middle class getting massively richer and the poor getting slightly richer, then it would be permissible, as it would improve the situation of the most disadvantaged in society. We return to these arguments in Chapter 7 on economic inequality.

On the basis of the preceding principles of justice, Rawls advocates a society in which the state assumes a number of functions over and above guaranteeing citizens' fundamental rights. These additional responsibilities include mandating that businesses do not discriminate against minority groups when hiring workers, investing in public education and training so as to ensure that the rich cannot unduly advantage their own children, and redistributing income from those who are comparatively wealthy to those who are comparatively poor. Rawls's arguments represent a progressive or egalitarian variant of liberal social theory.

In his book *Anarchy, State and Utopia* (1974), Robert Nozick advances an alternative model of society. In particular, he argues that the most just principles for governing society are those that maximise the liberty of the individual to live by his own values and pursue his own goals. Citizens living in the state of nature are assumed to possess certain natural rights, all of which concern non-interference by outsiders. They are therefore sometimes termed *negative liberties*: private property rights, the right to freedom from violence, the right to freedom of speech, and so on. In making this argument, Nozick invokes the so-called *non-aggression principle*, which states that it is fundamentally immoral to use force against another person. In this context, the use of force against another person encompasses such acts as stealing from them, vandalizing their property and assaulting them physically. Critically, as long as there is no coercion or force involved, everything is allowed. This even includes enslavement contracts, as long as people voluntarily enter into these contracts.

In Nozick's view, citizens do not possess any so-called *positive liberties* – the right to health care, the right to a home, the right to a certain standard of living – since all of these entitlements would entail other members of society being subject to the use of force. For example, if every citizen had a right to health care, and one particular citizen could not provide it for themself, then their fellow citizens would need to provide it for them. Since health care must be produced before it can be provided to someone, their fellow citizens would be forced to work to produce that health care for them. While rejecting such use of force, Nozick argues that citizens have an absolute right of ownership over private property, so long as they have acquired it in a just way (without the use of force against others). Those whose property has been taken from them unjustly are entitled to compensation. It is subsequently entirely up to citizens themselves to voluntarily transfer or exchange their property with other citizens.

On the basis of the preceding principles of justice, Nozick advocates a society with a *night-watchman state*, which only assumes the very basic functions of defending the society from external threats, enforcing freely negotiated contracts between individual actors, and protecting citizens from violence against themselves or their property. Nozick's arguments represent the quintessence of libertarian social theory, which is sometimes termed classical liberalism – in contrast to Rawls's progressive liberalism.

Socialists, liberals, and conservatives

Most people in modern Western societies primarily identify with one of three political ideologies, namely *socialism, liberalism*, or *conservatism*. However, these schools of thought are not entirely mutually exclusive and some people may feel closer to a certain ideology on one particular topic (such as government intervention in the economy) yet closer to another ideology as far as another topic is concerned (such as abortion or euthanasia). Moreover, the salience of each of these ideologies varies from country to country. For instance, while socialism, liberalism, and conservatism provide a comprehensive summary of the political landscape in most European countries, the American political landscape is more aptly described as a division between *progressivism, libertarianism*, and *conservatism* (Kling 2017).

Socialists and liberals can be quite straightforwardly contrasted with one another. Liberals, to start with, tend to treat the individual as focal point. They generally view individual rights and freedoms as the greatest good, and believe that these can only be constrained in exceptional circumstances (for example, when someone else's freedom is at stake). A concrete corollary is that liberals prefer the state to intervene as little as possible in the market outcomes that arise from interactions between free individuals. On the other hand, socialists advocate a larger role for the state, not just respecting and protecting individuals' freedoms, but also facilitating improvements in individuals' living conditions. They view the state as facilitator for human advancement. Socialists thus support state intervention in markets if this helps individuals to develop and reach their full potential. As such, they are in favour of economic redistribution to help the poor in society live a more dignified life.

Compared to socialists and liberals, conservatives attach more value to pragmatic rather than abstract arguments and to experience rather than reason. They reject both *rationalism* – the presumption that humans can reason their way to the most just social institutions – and its close cousin *universalism* – the presumption that it is possible to design a blueprint for society ungrounded in concrete particulars.

Instead, conservatives emphasise the wisdom and experience embodied in long-standing social institutions such as laws and informal norms. They argue that such social intuitions often serve important functions that their original designers may not have intended, and that their current custodians may not understand. For example, laws protecting intellectual property may serve to encourage technological innovation by offering inventors the opportunity to profit from their discoveries; laws proscribing sex before marriage may serve to reduce child poverty by curtailing the number of unwanted children; laws dictating monogamy may serve to keep criminality down by limiting the pool of unmarried men, as the latter is a well-known predictor of crime levels.

Conservatives additionally argue that social institutions generally take many decades or even centuries to build up, through incremental changes that bring about further changes. Insofar as this is the case, conservatives caution against rapid social change, preferring gradual reform – even in relation to institutions that appear grossly unfair or utterly anachronistic such as colonial government or hereditary monarchy. They prioritize order and stability over equality or liberty. Where order and stability are deemed to have broken down, conservatives often favour returning to the tried and tested institutions that preceded that turmoil.

This discussion demonstrates that the answer to the question to what extent the state should take responsibility for resolving societal problems very much depends on the political ideology one adheres to – that is, socialism, liberalism or conservatism. Therefore, in later chapters we regularly refer back to these three ideologies when discussing whether the state should intervene with respect to specific societal problems.

The state versus the other spheres of society

Our review of these different ideologies has demonstrated that there exist markedly different views on what is a fair society and what is the role of the state in attaining and maintaining such a society. In general, the state comprises the legislative, administrative and judicial organizations that are supposed to execute public tasks. As such, it includes, among other things, the national parliament, ministries of state, local governments, courts, the police, the army, and the educational system. Aside from the state, we can distinguish three main spheres of society: the *market sphere*, the *civic sphere*, and the *private sphere*. Rather than each covering exclusive territory, the four spheres of society are to some degree connected to one another, having blurred boundaries. Sometimes these interconnections have the character of peaceful co-existence, other times of fierce competition. Figure 1.2 offers a visualization of how the different spheres of society intersect and overlap. This visualization is approximate insofar as the market and civic sphere can in reality also overlap (e.g., social enterprises). What is more, in some cases there can be overlap between more than two spheres at the same time, and the exact position of some of the examples included in Figure 1.2 may vary across countries (see our discussion of religious organizations).

Tension arises at many points in Figure 1.2. For instance, while all market parties are required to operate within the legal boundaries set by the state, many private companies – including big multinationals such as Starbucks and Amazon – go to great lengths to avoid paying taxes and circumvent other restrictive regulations. Similarly, while what people do in their own time is largely protected by the right to privacy, the right to privacy is not an absolute entitlement. If there are, for example, indications that children are mistreated by their parents, the state can intervene. However, in intervening in the private sphere, the state has to walk a thin line, making sure to also respect citizens' fundamental freedoms. This is clearly apparent in recent debates in Western Europe around the dress style of Muslim women, which some politicians want to curtail via burqa bans and headscarf taxes. At the same time, the leaks by Edward Snowden in 2013 have revealed that many state intelligence services, such as the National Security Agency (NSA) in the US, have become increasingly involved in large-scale surveillance programs of politicians and other citizens that extend well beyond direct threats to state security.

The media take a special place in Figure 1.2, covering multiple spheres of society. To a large degree, media consumption takes place in the private sphere, but many media companies are

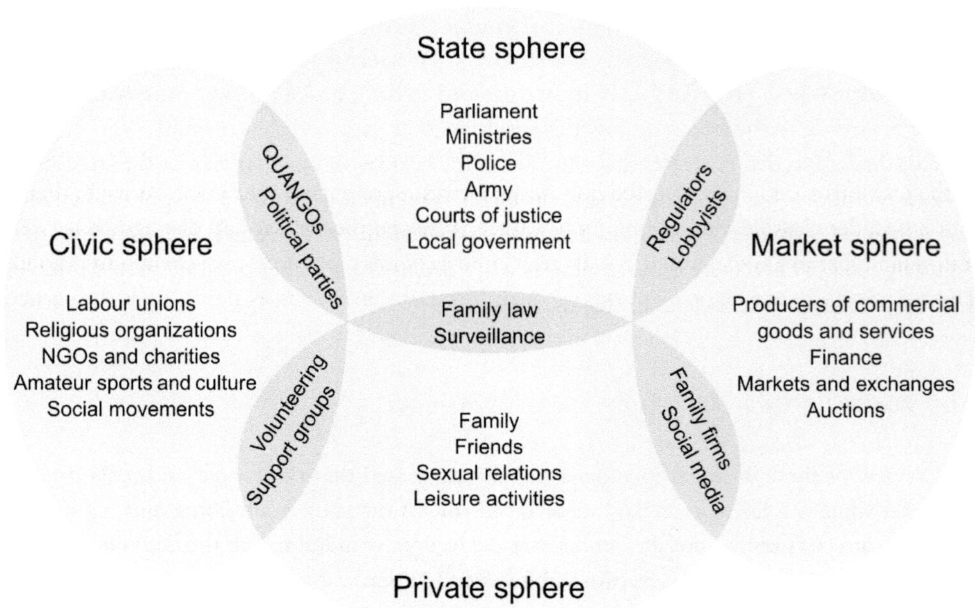

Figure 1.2 The four spheres of society

Note: This chart is an adapted version of Thomas Janoski's conceptual diagram (Figure 1.1 in Janoski 1998).

private corporations and thus part of the market sphere, while state-owned or heavily subsidized television networks belong at least partly to the state. Numerous problems can arise in this context, such as when the media outlets use their influence on public opinion to promote the interests of incumbent political groups or private businesses. There have been long-standing concerns about such conflicts of interests in many countries. Former Italian Prime Minister Silvio Berlusconi, for example, owned at least half of the Italian national media during his time in office. This led to accusations of misinformation and propaganda, and also to a downgrading of Italy's press freedom rankings by international organizations. The introduction of social media further complicates the position of the media in Figure 1.2, enabling individuals to reach wide audiences while bypassing traditional media outlets. From this perspective, the private sphere is nowadays a domain of media consumption as well as production. Also, politicians eagerly utilize this opportunity, engaging in political debates through private social media accounts. In doing so, they do not only bypass the traditional venues for such debates (e.g., parliament) but also the checks and balances that are built into the way traditional journalists report on these debates.

We can finally add a few remarks about the position of religious organizations within Figure 1.2. As discussed in Chapter 13, in Western Europe Christian churches have become ever more marginalized within society, and religious practices have become increasingly confined to the private sphere. By contrast, other parts of the world have witnessed a revival of the role of religion within public life. Such trends are clearly visible in Turkey, a country that has long prided itself as a secular nation with a strict division between religion and the state. However, under the leadership of Recep Tayyip Erdoğan the ties between the state and Islam have been reinforced. In the United States, evangelical Protestant movements remain a powerful force in politics and have lodged themselves firmly within the public sphere. From this position they exert considerable pressure on state institutions, expressing strong religion-based opinions on socio-legal issues and foreign policy.

A typology of goods

In the previous section we discussed how social norms represent a public good. As such, they fit into a broader classification of objects of value. More specifically, we can distinguish between four main types of goods: private goods, club goods, common pool resources, and public goods. These distinctions are pivotal to our approach to societal problems as public bads. In particular, we do not count problems that purely revolve around private goods as societal problems. We instead only treat phenomena with certain public good elements as societal problems or, in other words, public bads. The distinctions between the different types of goods are based on two characteristics by which goods may vary: excludability and rivalry.

The *excludability* of a good refers to the extent to which it is possible to prevent people from consuming that good. For example, it is straightforward for one individual to prevent another from consuming the good of his house. He simply puts locks on the doors and installs a burglar alarm, which precludes others from entering uninvited. A house is therefore said to be excludable. In contrast, it is complicated and well-nigh impossible for one individual to prevent another from consuming the good of sunlight. There is no feasible way for an individual to prevent others from enjoying the sun's rays, except perhaps by locking those others away in a basement, which would obviously be criminal. Sunlight is therefore said to be non-excludable.

The *rivalry* of a good refers to the extent to which any one person's consumption of that good reduces other people's opportunities to consume it. For example, if one individual catches and then eats a fish, it is impossible for anybody else to catch and eat that same fish. Fish are therefore said to be rival, even though Jesus is said to have fed as many as five thousand people with only two fish (and five loaves of bread). By contrast, if one individual rents a film on the internet, their sitting down to watch it does not prevent anyone else who has rented the same movie from watching it simultaneously. Online films are therefore said to be non-rival.

With reference to the characteristics of rivalry and excludability, Table 1.1 classifies the different types of goods. Those goods that are both excludable and rival, such as houses, are termed *private goods*. Other examples of private goods include food, clothes, electronics and parking spaces. Those goods that are excludable but not rival, such as films on the internet, are termed *club goods*. Other examples of club goods include cinemas, satellite television and gyms. Those goods that are rival but not excludable, such as fish stocks, are termed *common-pool resources*. Other examples of common-pool resources include timber, coal and rare minerals. Finally, those goods that are neither excludable nor rival, such as sunlight, are termed *public goods*. Other examples of public goods include lighthouses, infrastructure, scientific discoveries and national defence.

It is important to stress that public goods need not only comprise physical objects, such as the roads, bridges, railways, and flood protection systems that make up a country's infrastructure, or the soldiers, tanks, planes, and ships that make up its national defence. Public goods also comprise certain types of information, such as scientific discoveries. Unless someone obtains a patent for a scientific discovery they have made, anyone can benefit from that discovery, for example by utilizing it to develop a new technology. For instance, the invention of the World Wide Web by Tim Berners-Lee around 1990 – inspired by earlier systems of networked computers such as ARPANET run by the US Department of Defense – opened the door to a multitude of other inventions and innovations in numerous life domains. In addition, public goods comprise important social institutions, such as courts of law, regulatory systems, and emergency services. Courts allow disputes between parties to be arbitrated impartially and permit citizens who are accused of committing crimes to be tried fairly. They thus fulfil a critical role in facilitating social interaction, protecting everyone in society against unfairness. Finally, public goods also comprise certain states of affairs that are considered desirable by citizens, such as safe neighbourhoods, attractive surroundings, and a clean environment.

If we recall the four spheres of society that we identified in the section "Social norms and the organization of society" (the state, the civic sphere, the market, and the private sphere), the vast

Table 1.1 A typology of goods

	Rival	**Non-rival**
Excludable	Private goods (e.g., food, clothes, electronics, parking spaces)	Club goods (e.g., cinemas, satellite television, gyms)
Non-excludable	Common-pool resources (e.g., timber, coal, rare minerals, fish stocks)	Public goods (e.g., infrastructure, scientific discoveries, national defence)

majority of goods within society are provided through either the state or the market. Nearly all private and club goods – that is, all goods that are excludable – are supplied by the market, except in communist or socialist countries such as Cuba, Venezuela and North Korea. There are several reasons why this is the case. First, in principle, the price system of the market tends to allocate resources efficiently by ensuring that the supply of each good is equal to the demand for it, thereby preventing large surpluses or shortages. If the demand for a good vastly exceeds its supply, for instance, the price of the good will rise, making it more profitable for existing suppliers to increase their production and for other firms to enter the market. In the absence of any market failures – admittedly, a big "if" – these dynamics will eventually restore the balance between supply and demand. Second, competition between firms within the market tends to drive down prices and improve the quality of goods over time, as consumers are generally sensitive to changes in prices and quality. Third, the decentralized nature of the market means that errors and deviations from what is optimal tend to be localized, and that the economic system as a whole can respond adaptively to shocks. However, there are important exceptions to each of these statements, to which we return in subsequent chapters.

The situation is rather different for public goods, which are often – though not always – supplied by the state. Indeed, as the state has expanded over the last few centuries (see Chapter 3), the number of public goods available to citizens has increased correspondingly. The state often steps in to supply public goods, because these goods – despite their societal payoffs – will rarely be supplied by private actors due to their non-excludable character. If it is not possible to restrict access to a certain good, entrepreneurs will not be able to make any money by producing that good, while they will still incur costs in the production process, rendering their business unprofitable. Imagine an entrepreneur who considers whether it is worth his while to build a lighthouse on a particularly dark headland. Passing ships will obviously benefit greatly from the lighthouse as it will illuminate hazardous rocky outcrops. However, since there is generally no feasible way to charge each passing ship for this service, and to restrict non-paying ships from benefitting from the lighthouse, the profit-driven entrepreneur is unlikely to end up building the lighthouse.

In general, the provision of public goods requires collective action – that is, individuals acting in concert to achieve a common objective. However, as we explain in greater detail in Chapter 2, collective action is difficult, or nearly impossible, to achieve without the coercive apparatus of the state, except in small groups with very regular interactions and a large degree of social control (Olson 1965). One reason why it is often difficult for a large number of individuals (e.g., the population of a city or country) to act in concert is coordination failures stemming from incomplete information and communication limitations. For example, it would be problematic for a country to defend itself if its military consisted of a collection of private forces as opposed to a single unified army, where commands are issued from above, and information is relayed from below.

As an additional complication, each individual has an incentive not to participate in the collective action. After all, participation is costly – in terms of money, time, or other resources – and due to the non-excludable character of the public good that is produced through the collective action each individual stands to benefit regardless of whether or not they participate. This kind of non-participation is called *free riding*. Taking the example of taxation, it is unlikely that many people would pay taxes if doing so were entirely voluntary. In that case, most people would rather leave paying taxes to other people, while still benefitting themselves from the services financed from the tax revenues. People would probably also realize that their own tax contributions only represent a tiny portion of all funds needed for producing any public goods. From this viewpoint, their non-participation will only have a negligible impact. Nevertheless, if everyone followed this same line of reasoning, the public coffers would be severely underfunded and, consequently, nobody would have access to crucial public services. The threat of imprisonment or penalization is thus needed to incentivize citizens to pay their taxes, but they are generally better off as a result of it –assuming that the government is not too corrupt (a problem we revisit in Chapter 10).

So far, we have discussed private goods, club goods, and public goods, but we have not yet mentioned common-pool resources. These are managed by the state in some cases (e.g., state-owned energy providers), by local communities or small-scale cooperatives in others (e.g., local water authorities), and by private companies or individual actors in others (e.g., fishing companies). There are also hybrid set-ups, whereby, for example, private companies can extract from the common-pool resource within a framework of quotas stipulated by the state.

In a renowned study, the ecologist Garrett Hardin (1968) explicates the logic of unchecked exploitation of common-pool resources, which he termed the *tragedy of the commons*. Hardin's key example concerns a collection of rational, profit-maximizing herdsmen who have their animals grazing on a piece of common land. These herdsmen will continuously ask themselves the question, "Will I gain anything by increasing my animal stock?" As Hardin explains, the answer will generally be positive, as all of the returns of the additional animals will accrue to the herdsmen, while they will only bear a fraction of the costs in terms of increased overgrazing since these costs are shared among all herdsmen using the land. With all herdsmen applying the same logic, the inevitable outcome is the depletion and eventual exhaustion of the common-pool resource.

For many years, it was widely assumed that the only way to avoid this tragedy was either for the state to assume ownership over the resource or for private property rights to be conferred over it. Either solution would remove the element of competition among private actors that otherwise causes a "race to the bottom". However, the political scientist Elinor Ostrom, a winner of the Noble prize for economics, later demonstrated how small-scale communities often manage common-pool resources quite effectively without recourse to state ownership or privatization (Ostrom 1990). Nevertheless, such solutions are only viable under an extensive set of conditions, such as that we are dealing with a small-scale community with high levels of mutual trust and social control – see Chapter 12 on the environment for an extended discussion of Ostrom's work.

It is important to make two more points regarding the typology of goods in Table 1.1. First, we need to distinguish between public goods on the one hand, and goods provided publicly, such as by the state, on the other. While these two terms may once have been practically synonymous, the distinction between them has grown increasingly blurred over the years. This is partly due to the wave of privatizations in recent decades. Services that had formerly been the purview of the state, including energy, transport and waste collection, were passed into private hands. Although these services still serve the public interest, they are now handled by private companies instead of state-owned enterprises.

Another important point is that the position of any particular good within the typology in Table 1.1 is not fixed. Goods may move between categories, due to changes in cultural norms, regulations or technological innovations. In some big cities, for example, the public good of a safe neighbourhood has been morphed into a club good. Wealthy families living in these cities can buy a house within the safer, but more expensive, areas or even within so-called gated communities. Furthermore, so as to prevent public services from becoming overburdened and overcrowded, governments often convert them from pure public goods into club goods. In Singapore, for example, the government has introduced an intricate system of electronic road pricing, which charges road users to enter the congested parts of the city during peak hours. The price charged varies depending on prevailing traffic conditions and is administered via electronic sensors so vehicles do not have to stop in order to pay.

Social capital as a public good

As mentioned previously, public goods do not only concern physical objects. Moreover, although many public goods are provided or regulated by governments, this is not always the case either. One particular type of non-physical public good that is not provided by the government is *social capital*. The political scientist Robert Putnam (1995:67) defines social capital as referring to "features of social organization such as networks, norms, and social trust that facilitate coordination and cooperation for mutual benefit". Social capital is thus similar to physical or human capital in that it represents a resource of productive value. It facilitates smooth interpersonal contacts, and thereby the achievement of optimal societal outcomes. Social capital is a public good because it meets the criteria of non-excludability and non-rivalry: anyone could in principle draw upon it and its value does not diminish as more people make use of it – if anything, it may become a more valuable resource in that case. In short, social capital can help in producing other public goods but is also a public good in itself.

The sociologist James Coleman (1990) played an important part in introducing the concept of social capital. He explicitly defines social capital by its function as those aspects of social structure that can be used as resources by individual actors to realize their personal interests. As an example, Coleman refers to the central market (*souk*) in Cairo, Egypt. When shopkeepers there are asked about a product they do not sell themselves, they immediately guide the customer to a close associate who does sell it. Similarly, when they do not have the right amount of change in till for a transaction with a customer, they instantly turn into money changers by simply asking to borrow cash from a colleague. Such favours are exchanged without commissions, with merely the creation of an obligation to return the favour in the future. Social control within the network will ensure that everyone lives up to such obligations. Hence, the market can be viewed as consisting of many individual merchants all tied together through an extensive body of social capital. Each individual shopkeeper can draw upon this social capital when they need to, implying that all shopkeepers will ultimately be better off.

Another example provided by Coleman concerns the relationship between doctors and their patients. This relationship has traditionally been characterized by patients placing trust in their doctor and doctors, in turn, using their medical skills in the best interest of their patients. This combination of trust, social norms, and mutual expectations is a form of social capital that facilitates interactions between doctors and patients. However, in the US this social capital has eroded over time, as illustrated by the rise in malpractice suits brought by patients against their doctors. This breakdown of social capital has had grave consequences, including a steep increase in the costs of many medical treatments (since doctors now buy into expensive malpractice insurance schemes) and a substantial number of doctors closing down their practice. Coleman reports that some obstetricians even refuse to treat attorneys or their partners because of the increased risk of facing legal proceedings in these cases. The disappearance of trust has thus led to reduced access to health care.

These examples demonstrate the public good character of social relations and social norms. Individuals can use their social networks for acquiring information, meeting new people, getting promoted, exerting influence, and receiving support in times of misery. In turn, these same individuals also find themselves within other people's networks, where they may serve the interests of those other people. Once firm social relations have been established, individuals can often not break them without incurring costs in the form of social sanctions, distrust, expulsion or reputational damage. In this sense, social networks also put constraints on individual behaviour.

Within networks, social control can be exercised, and norms can be propagated and administered. What a single individual cannot do alone, actors within a social network can do together, while ensuring that others comply with agreements, rules, and norms. How easily this can be achieved depends, however, on the structure of the network. If the network has a relatively closed character – that is, practically all actors are connected through personal relations – it will be very difficult, if not impossible, for a single actor to avoid being influenced by group pressure and social control. Maintaining social norms will be rather simple in that case. On the other hand, in a sparse network with many missing links, individuals can quite easily hide away from social control. There it will be harder to maintain social norms.

The discussion above underscores the positive effects of social capital: if people establish norms of cooperation in organizations and social networks, they will be more likely to succeed in improving safety in their neighbourhoods, protecting the environment, preventing poverty, and achieving other desirable ends. However, social capital can also have a dark side. Within close-knit networks of social relations, individuals may have strongly inward-looking attitudes and approach non-members in an exclusive, or even hostile, way. In this atmosphere, social capital might translate into corruption and nepotism, or social control and the possibility of group sanctioning may give rise to an oppressive environment that is hard to escape. Indeed, networks with a high degree of closure may obstruct individuals in transcending the boundaries of the network – for example, by studying for a degree and establishing a career outside the local neighbourhood. Likewise, while it can be beneficial for immigrants to have many close ties to other immigrants (e.g., earlier immigrants can provide guidance and support to new arrivals), it can also make it harder for them to adopt the language of their host society. Within ethnic enclaves, criminal groups are known to pressure their fellow residents to tolerate their crimes rather than go to the police, exploiting the strong bonds between ethnic group members. In all of these cases, social capital gives rise to public bads.

A selection of ten societal problems

In this book, we examine a number of pressing societal problems. Needless to say, this inevitably involves making a selection. In this regard, we rely on three key criteria. First, we primarily – but not only – deal with societal problems in the industrialized parts of the world. Second, we focus on societal problems that are regarded as important by the general public or that have attracted ample attention in political debates. Third, we concentrate on problems that can be seen as public bads – that is, problems that concern society-level phenomena with public good characteristics and that often arise as unintended consequences of individual-level behaviours.

Our first selection criterion implies that less space is allocated to societal problems specific to the poorest regions of the world, such as sub-Saharan Africa. Due to their political and historical particulars and their low levels of economic development, countries in those regions are confronted with noticeably distinct problems that call for their own explanations. That said, many of the general principles and dynamics discussed in this book are still also relevant to explaining those problems. For example, we explicitly refer to the poorer areas of the world when we consider demographic problems in Chapter 5, international inequality in Chapter 7, corruption in Chapter 10, and environmental problems in Chapter 12.

The second criterion restricts our attention to problems that are viewed as important societal issues by the general public or that feature prominently in political debates. Opinion polls allow us to see how much importance people attach to various problems. The European Commission's Eurobarometer survey, for example, regularly asks citizens of European Union member states which societal issues are the most important ones currently facing their country. In 2017, the three most frequently cited issues across Europe were unemployment, immigration, and health and social security. Taxation, housing and the education system were among the least frequently mentioned issues. However, which issues are considered most important varies strongly from one country to another as well as over time. In Spain, for example, where the unemployment rate is high, unemployment has been cited as the most important issue by well over half of the population for the past decade. In Germany, on the other hand, which has in recent years admitted a large number of asylum seekers, immigration has been topping the ranking for the past few years, with as much as 76 percent of the population considering this the most important issue in November 2015. As to variation over time, about 95 percent of all EU citizens considered unemployment the most urgent problem over the period 2010–2012, but by the end of 2017 this figure had dropped to 25 percent. Conversely, while immigration used to be mentioned by ten percent or less of the EU population, this figure increased to around 20 to 40 percent after the start of the refugee crisis in 2015.

There are also issues that do not usually reach the top of individual's priority lists, but that are the subject of intense campaigns by governments, international institutions and civic organizations. A prominent example is that of discrimination on the grounds of race, ethnicity, gender, and religion. Most Western countries have adopted laws that prohibit such discrimination and violations of these laws result in legal prosecution. In the US, for example, the 1964 Civil Rights Act, adopted after years of campaigning by the civil rights movement, plays an important role in the fight against discrimination. Another problem in this category is corruption. While mass protests against corruption are rare, eliminating corruption is a key priority for international institutions such as the World Bank and the International Monetary Fund, but also the non-governmental organization Transparency International, which publishes annual reports on corruption around the world.

Our third selection criterion concerns a central element of our approach to societal problems, namely that we concentrate on problems that can be seen as *public bads*. Recall in this regard the typology of goods presented in Table 1.1. Problems that relate to private goods, which we could label *private bads*, are not discussed in this book. By contrast, all of the problems that we do address revolve around goods that are non-rival, non-excludable, or both. The links between the problems that we look at and the underlying, pure or imperfect, public goods can be more or less direct. For example, while Chapter 12 is directly linked to the public good of a clean environment, it may not be immediately obvious what public good is at stake in Chapter 5 on demographic trends. However, indirectly, population growth may undermine a number of public goods due to overcrowding, whereas declining fertility threatens the sustainability of various forms of social insurance provided by the state.

It is worth stressing that we do not directly discuss problems that result from the actions of a small number of ill-intentioned individuals (such as genocide, repressive dictatorial regimes, and terrorist attacks), although the ultimate sources of these problems often relate to societal problems that we do study (such as overpopulation, corruption, inequality, and religious fundamentalism). Our book focuses on problems that emerge at the society-level from the aggregation of many individual-level actions that are generally driven by harmless intentions.

Consider, for example, environmental degradation. Air pollution from factories, overabundance of non-degradable waste, and overfishing in the oceans all lead to deteriorations of our environment. However, if one were to ask the individuals involved whether it was ever their intention to destroy the environment, their reply would undoubtedly be in the negative. Likewise, while we noted previously that too much or too little fertility might undermine various public goods, these consequences are certainly not at the top of most young people's minds when they are considering having children. Societal problems can even result from behaviour that is explicitly motivated by good intentions towards society. The perverse incentives that certain welfare state policies may create is a prime example, as is the tension that results from religious adherents attempting to forcibly convert their fellow citizens. For all of these examples, the individual actors by no means want to cause society-wide disasters. The crux, however, is that the aggregation of many individual actions – actions that are not necessarily ill intentioned – can have adverse society-level effects. It is exactly these problems that we focus on.

To outline the remainder of this book, Chapter 2 presents our analytical framework. We describe our analytical approach and various concepts, principles and explanations that are essential to understanding the origins and persistence of societal problems. Later in the book we draw upon this framework when discussing specific societal problems. Chapter 3 elaborates on government intervention as a potential solution to societal problems. We discuss the ideal of an effective government, but also the limits of government intervention, and how government actions may sometimes backfire.

After these chapters that set the scene for the rest of the book, we dig into specific societal problems in the chapters that follow. Chapter 4 concerns the welfare state. We address the perverse incentives generated by this system of social safety nets, and how such incentives threaten to undermine the sustainability of the welfare state. Chapter 5, on demographic problems, discusses population trends across the globe and their societal consequences. We show how in some places population growth puts serious pressure on available resources, while in other places it is mainly changes in the age composition of the population that cause trouble. Chapter 6 considers problems related to migration and multi-ethnic societies. We address explanations for international migration flows, policy reactions in societies receiving migrants, and challenges to the societal integration of migrants, and the peaceful coexistence of different ethnic groups. In Chapter 7 we discuss economic inequality across and within societies. After describing ongoing trends, we consider the relationships between inequality and well-being and economic growth, and how inequality may, among other things, lead to a lack of cooperation in society. In Chapter 8, on gender discrimination, we examine to what degree men and women are treated according to norms of equality. In doing so, we look at both the public and private sphere, covering, for example, not only gender differentials in labour market achievement but also in housework. Chapter 9 addresses trends and spatial variation in crime levels. We discuss how crime threatens security, social trust, and the value of private property, and what actions can be taken to reduce crime, while also taking into account organized crime and cybercrime. Chapter 10 deals with the societal problem of corruption, which makes public governance more inefficient, less reliable and less trustworthy, and which may increase inequality and lower economic growth. We deal with the issue of how to measure corruption and how it can be explained. Chapter 11 is about societal problems originating from the financial system. Drawing a link between the financial crisis of 2008 and historical precedents, we illuminate the social processes that underlie these events. We also address the difficulties faced by supervisory and regulatory authorities in these complex environments. Chapter 12 is devoted to environmental problems. We demonstrate the tension between individual incentives and collective outcomes from which many environment problems originate and consider the hurdles in achieving a more sustainable management of our environmental resources. Chapter 13 zooms in on societal problems that relate to religion. We explain why some areas have experienced secularization whereas others have witnessed a rise in fundamentalism, and we describe the social tensions and human rights dilemmas that may arise as a result.

Bibliography

Beveridge, William H. 1942. *Social Insurance and Allied Services*. London: Report to Parliament. https://archive.org/details/in.ernet.dli.2015.275849.

Burke, Edmund. 2003[1790]. *Reflections on the Revolution in France*, edited by Frank M. Turner. New Haven, CT: Yale University Press.

Coleman, James S. 1990. *Foundations of Social Theory*. Cambridge, MA: The Belknap Press of Harvard University Press.

Hardin, Garrett. 1968. "The Tragedy of the Commons". *Science* 162:1243–1248.

IPCC. 2015. *Climate Change 2014 – Synthesis Report. Contribution of Working Groups I, II and III to the Fifth Assessment Report of the IPCC*, edited by The Core Writing Team, Rajendra K. Pachauri, and Leo A. Meyer. Geneva: IPCC Publication.

Janoski, Thomas. 1998. *Citizenship and Civil Society: A Framework of Rights and Obligations in Liberal, Traditional, and Social Democratic Regimes*. Cambridge: Cambridge University Press.

Kling, Arnold. 2017. *The Three Languages of Politics: Talking Across the Political Divides*. Washington, DC: Cato Institute.

Nordhaus, William D. 1975. "The Political Business Cycle". *Review of Economic Studies* 42:169–190.

Nozick, Robert. 1974. *Anarchy, State, and Utopia*. New York, NY: Basic Books.

Olson, Mancur. 1965. *The Logic of Collective Action*. Cambridge, MA: Harvard University Press.

Ostrom, Elinor. 1990. *Governing the Commons: The Evolution of Institutions for Collective Action*. Cambridge: Cambridge University Press.

Putnam, Robert. 1995. "Bowling Alone: America's Declining Social Capital". *Journal of Democracy* 6:65–78.

Rawls, John A. 1971. *A Theory of Justice*. Cambridge, MA: The Belknap Press of the Harvard University Press.

2 Analytical framework

Chapter overview

This chapter outlines the core tools and concepts that we draw upon when studying specific societal problems. We adopt a macro-micro-macro framework, whereby we take individual actors as the starting point for explanations of phenomena at the societal level. According to this framework, understanding the behaviour of micro-level actors requires us to study the macro-level contexts in which they are embedded and how these contexts shape the incentives and constraints that they face: the macro-to-micro link. Based on certain assumptions on human behaviour, we can subsequently predict how individual actors will behave in concrete micro-level situations. As a final step we can then consider the macro-level outcomes that will result from the aggregation of these micro-level actions: the micro-to-macro link. To further illuminate this framework, we discuss different models of human behaviour as well as the role of social mechanisms in linking the components of the macro-micro-macro model. In particular, we distinguish three types of mechanisms: situational mechanisms, action-forming mechanisms, and transformation mechanisms. We also discuss the principal-agent model and how information asymmetries can lead to moral hazard and adverse selection. Throughout the chapter we demonstrate that individually rational choices do not necessarily lead to desirable outcomes at the society level. We explain this, among other things, with reference to the prisoner's dilemma and the notion of free-riding.

Social scientific explanations

Social scientific analysis aims to shed light on societal realities. There are two parts to this task: *descriptions* and *explanations*. Descriptions comprise statements of a qualitative or quantitative nature that characterize the phenomenon in terms of such things as its distribution within the population and its trend over time, among other factors. For example, descriptions could address in which countries or sectors of the economy there is the biggest pay gap between men and women, or whether corruption has increased over time. The search for explanations, on the other hand, goes beyond simply describing a phenomenon but aims to reveal the underlying determinants and

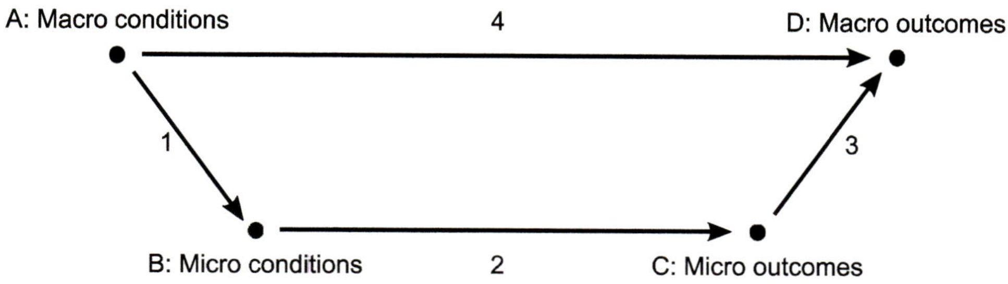

Figure 2.1 The macro-micro-macro model for explaining societal phenomena

causal forces. Explanations thus address questions such as: What are the drivers of the recent growth in international migration? or Why do we fail to prevent financial crises over and over again?

In this book, we follow the explanatory approach advocated by the sociologists Raymond Boudon (1986), James Coleman (1990), and the philosopher Jon Elster (2007). They view any type of society-level (macro-level) phenomenon as being rooted in individual-level (micro-level) behaviours and interactions. Indeed, their explanatory approach broadly focuses on the micro-level social mechanisms that give rise to certain macro-level situations. Recall here that micro-level mechanisms can pertain to actual individuals but also, for example, individual firms. In dissecting these relationships, Boudon, Coleman, and Elster assume that micro-level actors usually behave rationally though subject to limited options and information. This assumption implies that micro-level actors usually exhibit behaviour that makes sense given their objectives and constraints. While Boudon, Coleman, and Elster consider the behaviour of micro-level actors to be at the core of any explanation, they also argue that this behaviour should be understood in the macro-level contexts in which the micro-level actors are embedded. These contexts can shape both their objectives and their constraints. As such, Boudon, Coleman and Elster advocate an *actor-in-context approach* or, more specifically, a *macro-micro-macro model.*

The macro-micro-macro model

The macro-micro-macro model of explanation can be traced back to the work of German, Dutch and French social scientists in the 1970s, and an earlier version can be found in a study, by the American psychologist David McClelland (1961), on the role of the motivation for achievement in shaping economic growth. See also Raub and Voss (2017), who provide a historical overview of the development of this model. Figure 2.1 visualizes the general structure of the macro-micro-macro model. Given the shape of Figure 2.1 and the central role played by Coleman in promoting this explanatory approach, the macro-micro-macro model is also referred to as *Coleman's boat* or *Coleman's bathtub.*

As Figure 2.1 illustrates, the macro-micro-macro model of explanation links conditions and outcomes at the macro and micro level through several steps:

1 Macro-level conditions influence the micro-level conditions in which individual actors operate, shaping, among other things, their opportunity structure.
2 Given these micro-level conditions, as well as their preferences and objectives, individual actors will behave in certain ways, resulting in certain micro-level outcomes.

3 The aggregation of all these micro-level outcomes subsequently gives rise to certain macro-level outcomes. In some cases this aggregation process may concern a simple summation of micro-level behaviours, yet – as we will explain– it often involves complex interactions that may lead to unexpected macro-level outcomes.
4 Through the preceding three steps, we are able to connect macro-level conditions to macro-level outcomes via the underlying micro-level processes. As such, the preceding three steps jointly provide explanations for relationships that we observe between conditions and outcomes at the macro level.

We can demonstrate the logic behind Figure 2.1 by referring to the *hog cycle* phenomenon. This refers to the cyclical patterns in the supply and prices of certain products, which were first observed in pig markets in the 1920s. The dynamics are as follows: the macro-level starting point is that the supply of pork is low and that, accordingly, its price is high (point A in Figure 2.1). At the micro level, individual farmers observe this information and use it as input for decisions about their future behaviour (point B in Figure 2.1). Given that the price of pork is high, each individual farmer will most likely decide to increase their stock of pigs, so they can sell more pigs at this higher price and thus make more profit (point C in Figure 2.1). However, with many farmers applying this same reasoning, soon enough there will be a surplus of pork at the macro level, with a drop in the price of pork as a consequence (point D in Figure 2.1). This, in turn, provides the starting point of a new run through Figure 2.1: the decline in prices at the macro level will cause some farmers to leave the market, or at least decrease their production, which will eventually lead to a shortage of pork and higher prices once again.

Two crucial aspects of these dynamics are that farmers adapt their expectations and determine their behaviour in response to the *current* demand for pork, but that their actual production only responds to this with a delay (because it, after all, takes time to rear pigs). Similar cycles have been observed elsewhere, for example in the supply of different types of professionals, such as engineers, doctors or teachers. If, initially, there is a surplus of these professionals, this discourages young people from embarking on these careers. In due time, this will result in shortages of engineers, doctors or teachers. By that time, the salaries for these jobs may start to increase, but it will still take at least a couple of years before the shortages have been eliminated, as it takes time to study to become an engineer, doctor, or teacher. Hence, we see that an undesirable macro-level phenomenon – namely, regular shortages and surpluses, which ultimately harm both suppliers and consumers – can be explained by micro-level decisions that are themselves perfectly sensible given the situation.

Understanding individual actors

The hog cycle example underscores that in order to understand macro-level phenomena we have to turn to the underlying micro-level behaviours. Putting these micro-level behaviours at the heart of the explanatory process is also referred to as *methodological individualism*. A key tenet of this approach is the idea that only individuals can be considered as beings with a will and a capacity to act purposefully. Aggregations of individuals – such as communities, nations, organizations, or classes – do not possess their own will or their own objectives and thus can only take actions when their members have agreed upon a course to follow.

With this actor-based starting point, we join a longstanding tradition in the social sciences, going back to the German sociologists Max Weber and Georg Simmel. As early as in the late nineteenth and early twentieth century, Weber and Simmel argued that social science should be founded upon individualistic methods in which the "purposeful" actor takes a central place. Importantly, however, the behaviour of individual actors should be interpreted within the context in which it occurs. This context imposes constraints, incentivises choices, and structures actions. By definition, social situations always comprise two or more participants, who interact with each other, try to influence each other, try to outsmart each other, or who adapt their decisions to those of the other. Contextual influences thus shape people's motives, desires, and preferences, as well as people's opportunities to act on these motives, desires, and preferences. As a consequence, choices made by the same individuals can vary dramatically from one social context to another.

A crucial question for our actor-based approach is whether we can obtain detailed and reliable information about the motives and objectives that underpin the behaviour of individual actors. After all, the underlying intentions motivating individuals' behaviour cannot be directly observed. However, the problem is even more fundamental, given that individuals often act strategically, and therefore have an outright interest in keeping their intentions secret or lying about their motives and inner thoughts. Thus, researchers often need to *interpret* the actions of individuals in order to understand their motives and goals. The researcher should, in a way, try to enter the minds of the actors. As one can imagine, this is an enormously challenging task.

Basically, the researcher can observe two sorts of things: (a) actions and interactions, or, in other words, actual behaviour; and (b) individuals' verbal statements about these actions, their underlying motivations, and their expectations of the resulting effects. One problem, however, is that actual behaviour and people's explanations for their behaviour are often inconsistent. Indeed, more often than not, there is a large divide between what people say and what they do. While, for example, many citizens express strong concerns about the environment or the bio-industry, many of these same citizens still end up taking their car even when travelling short distances or buying non-organic rather than organic eggs. For this reason, some researchers – especially economists – are sceptical of the usefulness of interviews with individual actors and prefer to look at actors' behaviours as their *revealed preferences*.

In contrast, we contend that social scientists can go some way toward identifying the motives of actors. They can exploit clever interview designs as well as carefully set-up experiments that manipulate specific elements of individuals' action contexts in a controlled way. In terms of the latter, for example, in recent decades behavioural economists have helped to uncover individuals' preferences on fundamental matters such as fairness, solidarity, and altruism through stylized experiments in a wide range of social settings. It is also important to note that it is not necessary to be aware of the exact motives and intentions of all actors in every situation. Social scientists study large numbers of people and, as long as the researcher can attain reliable approximations of people's motives and intentions, interesting claims about societal phenomena can be made.

As soon as such approximations of the motives and intentions of individual actors are available, the researcher can imagine themself in the position of individual actors – step into their shoes, as it were – and then try to understand their actions and strategies. Weber advocated this approach about a century ago, when he introduced the concept of *verstehen* (interpreting) as a guideline for social scientists (Weber 1978[1925]). The economist and Nobel Prize winner Thomas Schelling (1984) also champions the idea of stepping into the actor's shoes and speaks about the method of *vicarious problem-solving*. This entails the following steps: (a) put yourself in the position of the actor; (b) assume that they have certain preferences and objectives; (c) consider what you would do yourself in their position; and (d) search for situational motives and constraints that may further influence the behaviour of the actor.

In this chain of reasoning, the researcher does not assume a normative position, judging whether the actor's preferences are right or wrong. Instead, the researcher attempts to discern how the actor's behaviour follows from his set of preferences. The contents of these preferences are treated as a given here. Of course, this is not to say that it is uninteresting or irrelevant to study why people have certain preferences. One may, for example, wonder why some people oppose immigration whereas others do not, why people want to curtail or expand gay rights or why certain individuals prefer to use drugs on a daily basis. Nevertheless, when we want to understand people's behaviour, we have to leave such questions aside and assess how their behaviour (such as voting for a far-right party) is an expression of their actual preferences (for example, the desire to restrict immigration).

Models of human behaviour

At this point it is useful to introduce the concept of *rationality*, which we do not view as a complete description of the behaviour of actors, but as a basis for understanding their choices. The rationality concept boils down to the idea that individuals act in a sensible manner and use their knowledge and available resources for achieving their goals, given the circumstances they are in. In other words, a rational individual behaves in such a way as to optimally satisfy their preferences – whatever these preferences happen to be. Rationality is therefore a property of behaviour, not of preferences. Preferences cannot be rational or irrational; only behaviour can.

We can draw a connection here with two prominent models of human behaviour that have divided the social sciences for a long time. On the one hand, there is the *Homo Economicus* – a selfish actor who bases his behaviour on cold-blooded, cost–benefit calculations – and on the other hand, there is the *Homo Sociologicus* – an altruistic actor who takes into account the interests of others and strives to abide by social norms. Which of these two is a more accurate description of how people behave? We follow the behavioural economists Ernst Fehr and Herbert Gintis (2007) in arguing that both models are wrong or, alternatively, that both models are only partially right. As Fehr and Gintis point out, self-regarding and other-regarding behaviour can co-exist even within the same individual, whereby the specific social context determines which actor type gets activated – or which one dominates the other. What is more, Boudon (1996) has pointed out how both the Homo Economicus and the Homo Sociologicus can be considered to be rational.

Boudon builds in this regard on earlier ideas by Weber (1978[1925]), who distinguishes between two kinds of rationality: *Zweckrationalität* or *instrumental rationality* and *Wertrationalität* or *value-oriented rationality*. According to Boudon, the central question in explaining this distinction is which reasons individuals put forward as a justification of their actions. In the case of instrumental rationality, these reasons will refer to the consequences of their actions. In particular, an actor will engage in certain behaviour if he believes that this brings about consequences that can be regarded as good and desirable: the consequences justify the decision. Someone who does volunteer work in a homeless shelter may, for instance, motivate this behaviour by arguing that it looks good on their CV, and will thus help them get ahead in the labour market. In the case of value-oriented rationality, the actor follows a certain value or norm, regardless of the consequences that their behaviour will have. Here we can think of another volunteer within the same homeless shelter, who motivates their behaviour by arguing that everyone has the right to a roof above one's head and that we have a duty to help those who are struggling in this regard.

Reconciling these two forms of rationality, Boudon (1996) coins the term *cognitivist actor* to refer to an actor who acts as sensibly as possible from the perspective of cognitive reasons that can be offered as justifications for their behaviour. In this framework, actions are rational if a neutral observer is able to say that an actor had good reasons for taking a certain action, whether these reasons pertain to the consequences of the action (i.e., instrumental rationality) or the values that the actor adheres to (i.e., value-oriented rationality). From this perspective, it is clear that both the Homo Economicus and Homo Sociologicus are rational beings – they happen to be driven by different motives but are equally rational in trying to act on these motives.

Importantly, however, there are limits to individuals' rationality. The American Nobel Prize winning economist and political scientist Herbert Simon (1947) puts forward the concept of *bounded rationality*. Simon uses this concept to explain that in real-world situations people are often unable to optimize their behaviour given their preferences. In many situations, people cannot gain access to all of the information that would be needed to determine their optimal behaviour, but even if they could, their minds are bound by cognitive limits when it comes to processing this information. As a result, Simon argues that people often do not end up being *optimizers* but rather *satisficers*, who settle for "good enough". The concept of bounded rationality is especially relevant in the information-rich world we live in nowadays – where people are nearly constantly connected to the internet and the wealth of information it contains. This easy access to information enables many gains and improvements, but at the same time it confronts us with our cognitive limits.

We can draw a link here with the work of the social psychologist Daniel Kahneman, who has spent many decades investigating, through experiments, how people think and make decisions – often together with his colleague Amos Tversky. Kahneman's book *Thinking, Fast and Slow* (2011) provides a summary of his findings. One of his main conclusions is that many of the choices that people make do not conform to the assumptions behind *rational choice theory*. Rather than consistently and purposively pursuing whatever line of action provides the highest utility, people's behaviours are often subject to *cognitive biases*.

For example, Kahneman shows that people tend to exhibit an optimistic bias, giving rise to, among other things, an *illusion of control* (the idea that we have a substantially greater degree of control over our lives than we actually do) and a *planning fallacy* (the common tendency to overestimate the benefits and underestimate the costs of risky projects). Another prominent bias concerns *loss aversion*, whereby people are more averse to losses of a certain amount than they are eager for gains of the same amount, reflecting that people start to attach more value to things once they have them in their possession as well as a general desire to maintain the status quo. Many of these insights are combined into *prospect theory* – a theory Kahneman developed to account for how people make decisions, especially under conditions of uncertainty and risk.

Complex aggregations: How micro-level actions translate into macro-level outcomes

If for now we assume that individual actors usually act rationally given their personal objectives, will this then also translate into socially desirable outcomes at the societal level? The answer is unfortunately in the negative; rational individual choices do not necessarily lead to desirable outcomes at the societal level, just like undesirable societal outcomes cannot necessarily be traced back to irrational or malicious individual actors. As we will explain, the key to this paradox lies in the aggregation process whereby micro-level actions are converted into macro-level outcomes.

Let us first consider the example of living in a highly corrupt society. As Chapter 10 discusses, a high level of corruption is an undesirable societal outcome for many reasons, including its eroding impact on social trust, its undermining influence on the legitimacy of public governance, and its detrimental effects on economic growth. However, can the individual actors engaging in corruption be regarded as irrational? The answer is no. Even though these individual actors may strongly despise the corrupt system they are part of, it may still be rational for them to play along, as refraining from corrupt interactions might, for example, lead to worse access to health care, significant delays in administrative procedures, such as getting a planning permission or a business licence, or a lack of protection by the police. Moreover, as for many public bads, it is impossible for a single individual to make any real change to the level of corruption in society by refraining from corrupt interactions themselves. This would be nothing but a drop in the ocean.

This example demonstrates why undesirable macro-level situations may arise when there is a tension between the individual and societal impacts of micro-level actions. Unless there is collective action or coordination among individual actors, most people will primarily follow their individual interests in such cases, because prioritizing societal interests is costly to them, and each individual in isolation has only a small amount of influence on the overall macro-level outcome. In other words, no matter whether *everyone else* contributes to the underlying public good, or whether *no one else* does so, individual actors have an incentive to just follow their private interests. After all, their contribution to the public good will be negligible from a macro perspective, while still costly to them personally. As a result, very few people will end up putting in the effort necessary to achieve the optimal societal outcome.

The aggregation of individual behaviours can thus lead to unintended and undesirable macro-level outcomes. This phenomenon is known as the *problem of aggregation* and has its origin in the interdependence of individual actors. This interdependence implies that the preferred strategies and choices of each individual actor depend on the choices of all other individual actors. In other words, the behaviour of micro-level actors depends on the macro-level context in which they are embedded (see arrow 1 in Figure 2.1). In terms of the previous example, whether it makes sense to engage in corrupt interactions depends on how many other actors are corrupt. As already seen, there often exists a conflict between the optimal behaviour for an individual actor given the choices of all other individual actors, and what would be the individual's optimal behaviour if attempting to maximize social welfare. Individual actors may even be perfectly aware of this social dilemma, but – without any coordination – it is generally difficult to avoid the unintended and undesirable macro-level outcomes. The *prisoner's dilemma* illustrates some of the dynamics behind this phenomenon.

The prisoner's dilemma

The prisoner's dilemma is a prominent model within *game theory* – a branch of economics that analyses social interactions among rational actors where the outcome for each actor depends on the behaviour of the other actor(s) involved. These circumstances are also referred to as *strategic interdependence*, and under these conditions each actor has an incentive to form expectations about the behaviour of others before deciding on their own behaviour. The prisoner's dilemma provides a concise but powerful illustration of how two actors – each acting perfectly rationally – may attain an outcome that is suboptimal for both of them if they are unable to coordinate their actions.

The model, developed around 1950 by the mathematicians Merrill Flood and Melvin Dresher, became known as the prisoner's dilemma when another mathematician, Albert Tucker, explained it using a story about two prisoners. These prisoners are accused of having committed two crimes together: one major and one minor offence. However, there is only sufficient evidence available to sentence both prisoners for the minor offence. A conviction for the bigger offence is only possible if one, or both, of the suspects make a confession.

During the investigation, the judge locks the suspects in separate cells, so that they cannot communicate with each other, and offers each of them a choice. If both suspects confess to the bigger crime, they will both be sentenced for it, but as a reward for their honesty their sentence will only be five years in prison, as opposed to the ten years prescribed by law. On the other hand, if only one of the suspects confesses to the bigger crime, this person will be rewarded by being released immediately, whereas the other suspect who keeps denying the crime will get the full sentence of ten years. Keep in mind that if neither of the prisoners makes a confession there will be insufficient evidence to convict them for the bigger crime. In this scenario, both will only get convicted for the smaller offence, each getting a sentence of 1 year in prison. This incentive structure is illustrated in Table 2.1. The first number in each cell represents the sentence for Prisoner A and the second number the sentence for Prisoner B. The sentences are expressed in number of years to be spent in prison.

It is important to realize that when the prisoners subsequently take their options into consideration, they cannot communicate with each other. After all, they are locked up in separate cells. They can thus only make assumptions about the behaviour of their fellow suspect. Based on those assumptions, they will then determine what they should do themselves. For instance, if Prisoner A believes that Prisoner B will confess, it is clearly better for Prisoner A to also confess and avoid the full sentence of ten years. However, if Prisoner A believes that Prisoner B will keep his mouth shut, there is still an incentive for Prisoner A to confess, because in that case he can avoid prison altogether. In other words, the *dominant strategy* of Prisoner A is to confess: regardless of what the other suspect does, Prisoner A is always better off confessing.

Due to the symmetric set-up of this game, Prisoner B happens to have the exact same dominant strategy. Hence, following this perfectly rational decision procedure, both prisoners will

Table 2.1 The incentive structure behind the prisoner's dilemma

		Prisoner B	
		Confession	Denial
Prisoner A	Confession	5 ; 5	0 ; 10
	Denial	10 ; 0	1 ; 1

Note: The numbers in each cell reflect the prison sentences (in years) for, respectively, Prisoner A and Prisoner B.

confess and be convicted for five years. This situation is called a *Nash equilibrium* (named after the mathematician and Nobel Prize winner John Nash): none of the actors can improve their situation as long as the other actor does not change their strategy. Nonetheless, a crucial observation is that each of the suspects would have been better off if both of them had refrained from making a confession. In that case they would only have been sentenced to 1 year each. However, because they were unable to coordinate their actions, they had no certainty about the other's behaviour, making it too risky to deny the crime.

Coleman (1990) distinguishes in this regard between what he calls a social equilibrium and a social optimum. The term *social equilibrium* indicates the existence of some kind of equilibrium among interacting individuals, where – once this state is achieved – no individual has an incentive, or is willing to, change their behaviour. The Nash equilibrium described before, where both prisoners get a five-year sentence, is an example. However, as the example also illustrates, not every social equilibrium is also a social optimum. Indeed, the term *social optimum* refers to the situation that would be most desirable from the societal perspective. This situation, in turn, may or may not be a social equilibrium. In the prisoner's dilemma just described, the outcome where both prisoners get a one-year sentence is the social optimum. Yet, unfortunately for the prisoners, this particular social optimum does not constitute a social equilibrium, as each prisoner in the situation of a joint denial has an incentive to still confess in order to get away without any prison sentence at all.

The prisoner's dilemma can also be applied to more complex situations in which many more actors are involved. One example concerns the consumption of organic or fair-trade food products. Many people say that they prefer such products over so-called dirty alternatives, because they are better for the environment, animal welfare, or create better working conditions in the country of production. However, those positive macro consequences are only achieved if a sufficiently large number of people buy organic or fair-trade food – otherwise, the suppliers will likely go bankrupt sooner or later, leaving the entire market to their dirty competitors. Yet, each individual consumer needs to pay a premium for the responsible products regardless of how many others buy them as it is simply more expensive to produce these products.

This creates a similar situation as in the example of the two prisoners. This time the payoffs to each individual can be interpreted as the "utility" that they experience, which relates negatively to their food expenses and positively to the realization of ideals such as sustainability, animal welfare and fair trade. Once more, in the absence of coordination, individuals can only determine what would be their optimal behaviour given the potential actions of everyone else. From a societal point of view, the best outcome would be if everyone only buys organic and fair-trade products. In that case, the environment will be served, animals will have a pleasant life, and no workers will be exploited. Moreover, even though the consumer will still pay a premium for these responsible products, economies of scale in production imply that the premium will be relatively small. However, because the responsible products are still more expensive than their dirty competitors, each individual in this situation has an incentive to switch from the former to the latter. After all, their own behaviour will have little direct effect on the macro-level outcomes, whereas personally they can save a good amount of money by buying the dirty products (notice that this behaviour constitutes a form of free-riding as described in the section "A typology of goods" in Chapter 1). Because this logic would apply to each and every individual, the equilibrium that will eventually arise is one in which nobody – or only a small number of ideological diehards – is willing to pay for organic or fair-trade products.

Just like the previous example, many real-world situations exhibit a certain degree of resemblance to the prisoner's dilemma. The core message of the prisoner's dilemma is that it cannot be taken for granted that individuals – and especially larger groups of individuals – will spontaneously cooperate with each other for the public good, even when it is in their best interest to do so. Although each individual actor may follow a rational strategy, without an opportunity to coordinate their actions, the aggregate outcome that arises could be detrimental for all of them. Rational behaviour can thus bring about undesirable societal outcomes.

As we have emphasized, one of the core reasons why no cooperation emerges between the two actors within the prisoner's dilemma is the fact that they cannot communicate with each other and therefore cannot coordinate their actions. If we imagine that they were somehow able to do this, say through a shared lawyer, they would have a better chance of achieving the outcome in which they both deny the major crime and get away with a minor sentence each. Along these lines, there has been much game theoretic work investigating under what conditions social cooperation is more likely to emerge.

For instance, while the standard prisoner's dilemma is a *simultaneous game* (in which actors have to simultaneously decide on their behaviour), it has been shown that *sequential games* (in which actors decide on their course of action one after another) provide more potential for social cooperation. Among other things, there is often in such cases an opportunity for the second-mover to discipline the first-mover through punishing bad behaviour on the part of the first-mover, while the first-mover has an opportunity to signal his intentions to the second-mover. Factors like trust and credibility play a big role in such interactions. Moreover, there are also *repeated games*, in which the actors play the same game multiple times. This offers the actors the opportunity to gradually learn about the behaviour of the other actor(s), which can in turn facilitate a cooperative outcome. Especially when there is no clear end point or when the game is repeated indefinitely, actors have a strong incentive to realize a cooperative equilibrium.

Free-riding behaviour and collective action

There are a number of sociological theories that assume that people form groups spontaneously, because they have an instinct for herding together, because they are naturally connected through kinship relations, and because individual and group interests often coincide. However, as the prisoner's dilemma powerfully demonstrates, once we take a closer look at the incentives that individuals face at the micro level it is by no means obvious that social cooperation will emerge spontaneously.

The American economist Mancur Olson analyses this problem in his book *The Logic of Collective Action* (1965), in which he discusses the challenges involved in establishing *collective action*. Olson's starting point is the observation that no social cooperation is achieved in many cases where this would, in fact, benefit everyone involved. This observation motivates Olson to present an alternative theory of collective action for cases in which the micro-level incentives of individual actors do not align with the interests of the group as a whole.

His core argument can be summarized as follows: Imagine that there is a group of individuals who are in favour of certain societal changes, such as more investment in infrastructure or education. Every single member of such a group then faces the decision of whether or not to take part in collective action to achieve these changes – one could, for example, think of a protest march to call for attention for these issues. For every individual in isolation it is, however, not rational to participate in such an initiative. After all, while each individual incurs non-negligible costs by participating, such as transport costs to get to the protest march or giving up time that could have been spent in other ways, the relative contribution of each individual to the initiative as a whole is pretty much negligible and thus unlikely to make a real difference – not even the most vigilant observer will notice whether there are 100,000 people at the protest or only 99,999.

Therefore, it is rational for each individual to become a *free rider* and to let other people expend efforts attempting to achieve societal change. In this context, the desired societal change can be viewed as a public good, and because public goods are characterised by *non-excludability* (see the section "A typology of goods" in Chapter 1), the free riders can still reap the benefits of the societal change even if they have not helped in achieving it. For example, when a social movement eventually succeeds in securing more investment in education through protest marches and other pressure tools, all students, and teachers will benefit, regardless of whether they took the trouble to attend a protest march themselves. Since every individual in isolation faces the exact same trade-off, in the end nobody, or only a handful of hard-core activists, may show up at the protest march, while many people who are in principle also in favour of societal change will stay at home. As such, free-riding behaviour undermines social cooperation.

There are indeed many real-world examples where social cooperation is not achieved, even when people have good intentions and agree on what is desirable. Many societal causes, such as the promotion of better public health care and responsible energy usage, receive support among wide circles of the population. Yet, the free-riding option is popular among the very same people. As a result, we see individuals trying to evade taxes and ignoring hosepipe bans during draughts. In both cases, each individual actor might justify their own behaviour by referring to their negligible impact on the overall problem, but when everyone thinks like this, the problem could well persist into eternity.

In general, free-riding behaviour is less likely to occur in small groups in which people know each other and can monitor each other's behaviour. Personal relations can, under these circumstances, facilitate social control and mutual solidarity, making collective action easier to achieve. In larger groups, on the other hand, social control is much weaker, leaving free-riding for the greater part unpunished. Nonetheless, Olson puts forward three potential solutions to this collective action problem in larger groups.

The first concerns the enforcement of cooperation by a higher-level authority. Take the example of taxation. Even though citizens evidently have an interest in the state providing certain public services, they would most likely refuse to pay taxes for this if tax payments were entirely voluntary. For this reason, the state uses its power of compulsion to incentivize tax payments. Likewise, leaders of religious groups often exert pressure on their followers to make sure they participate actively and do not leave. The sociologist Michael Hechter (1987) builds on this point, arguing that in order to maintain group solidarity one needs *monitoring* and *sanctioning*. Monitoring is aimed at preventing undesired behaviour by keeping an eye on group members. It can either occur from above, such as prohibiting relations with outsiders and increasing the costs of exiting the group, or by having members spy on each other. Sanctioning, in turn, concerns the punishment of deviant behaviour once it has taken place.

The second tool that Olson proposes for achieving collective action is *moral persuasion*. For example, social movements usually appeal to the ideological or moral convictions of their members, asking them to do something "for the good cause". One can think, for instance, of protest marches against nuclear weapons, in defence of LGBTQ rights, against globalization, with respect to abortion rights (pro-life or pro-choice), and against gun laws and police violence directed towards ethnic minorities. In all of these cases, individuals will face incentives to free ride and abstain from protest participation, but one may still be able to get them involved by appealing to overriding moral principles. Nevertheless, moral persuasion alone is usually not enough to keep many people committed in the longer run.

The third solution that Olson suggests is to introduce *selective incentives* – that is, incentives that appeal to individuals' self-interest yet simultaneously encourage them to take part in collective action. Selective incentives thus align individual interests with group interests. They are often used by large organizations such as labour unions. These organizations pursue targets that are in the interest of their members such as higher wages and better working circumstances for all, but individuals mainly join these organizations because of the individual benefits they receive as a member such as attractive insurance schemes, legal assistance in case of emergencies. The public goods provided by these organizations thereby turn into a by-product of the private goods that the organizations offer to their members.

Macro-micro-macro explanations using social mechanisms

As discussed earlier, in order to explain societal problems – or, more generally, phenomena at the macro level – we need to turn to individual actors and their interactions. In this process, there is a key role for *social mechanisms*, which are stylized representations of how the behaviour of individual actors is affected by macro-level factors, how individual actors interact with one another at the micro level, and how the behaviours of many individual actors add up to certain macro-level outcomes. In other words, social mechanisms are concise theories that can be used as building blocks for more complex theories. As such, they connect the different nodes in *Coleman's boat*, as indicated in Figure 2.2.

Explanations of macro-level relationships (i.e., the effect of A on D in Figure 2.2) gain credibility if one can link the macro-level phenomena involved through the actions and interactions of micro-level actors (that is, in terms of Figure 2.2, through the effect of A on B, the effect of B on C, and the effect of C on D). To make these links we need social mechanisms. In particular, we distinguish three categories of social mechanisms, each of which relate to an arrow in Figure 2.2: (1) situational; (2) action-forming; and (3) transformation mechanisms (Hedström and Swedberg 1998). Next we will discuss each type of mechanism in greater detail.

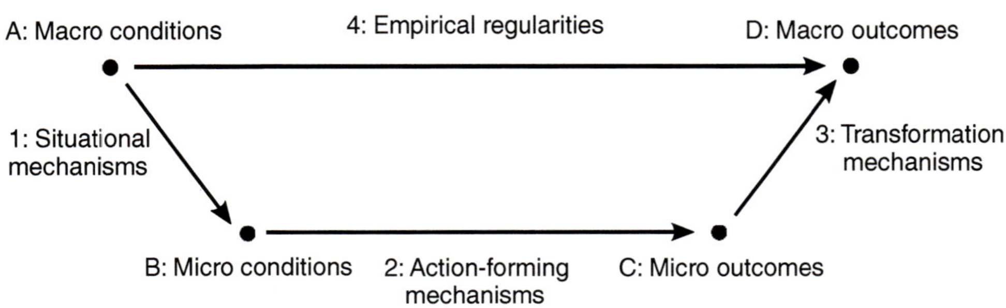

Figure 2.2 Social mechanisms and the macro-micro-macro model of explanation

The macro-to-micro link: Situational mechanisms

Situational mechanisms concern the macro-to-micro link in Coleman's scheme: individual actors are embedded in certain macro-level contexts (e.g., organizations, networks, neighbourhoods, countries) and these contexts influence the behaviour of the individual actors.

There are several sub-groups of situational mechanisms. An important sub-group are so-called *belief-formation mechanisms*, whereby the social context in which individual actors are embedded shapes their beliefs about the consequences of their actions, what is socially deemed acceptable, and the behaviour of other actors. The sociologist Robert Merton introduced one of the best-known examples of such a mechanism: the *self-fulfilling prophecy* (Merton 1968). This mechanism explains how an initially false conception of a situation induces behaviour that eventually makes the false conception come true. Self-fulfilling prophecies are, for instance, very common in financial markets, so we return to them in Chapter 11. One renowned example is the rumour that a bank has insolvency problems such as that it is running low on money, threatening the bank's capacity to repay its debtors. When such a rumour arises, even if it is initially unjustified, some customers will start to withdraw money from their accounts, afraid that they might otherwise lose their money. Other customers, observing this, will get nervous and start to retract money from their accounts too. The eventual result will be a bank run, which makes the initially false rumour that the bank has insolvency problems come true. Similarly, Thomas Schelling once noted: "If people expect a coffee shortage, there will be a coffee shortage" (Schelling 1998:38). In these cases, the rumours about the solvency of the bank or the state of the coffee market are the macro-level contexts that influence the expectations and ultimately also the behaviours of micro-level actors.

There are many more examples of collective behaviour that emerges in this way, such as the buying madness that from time to time takes possession of financial speculators, panic in a crowded theatre when a fire alarm goes off, all kinds of fashion fads, mood reversals in public opinion such as the popularity of a certain politician, and religious conversion waves. According to Coleman (1990) these phenomena share a set of common elements: a large number of individuals at the same time take part in the collective activity; the behaviour of individuals can change all the time; and individuals do not act independently but rather mutually affect each other's behaviour.

By imitating each other's actions, individuals effectively hand over the right of control over their behaviour to others. Individuals may do this because they have more confidence in the judgement of others than in their own. They presume that other people are better informed about risks, threats, opportunities, and trends. When individuals transfer control over their behaviour to others, they may also feel relieved from the moral responsibility for their actions. Suddenly there no longer seem to be boundaries or constraints. The resulting outcomes are often explosive and unpredictable. Phenomena of *herding behaviour, mass hysteria*, or *social contagion* can then be observed.

The collapse of the Communist regime in East Germany in 1989 provides a well-known illustration of such dynamics. While it used to be impossible for citizens to openly criticise the East German regime – for fear of incarceration or worse – this changed when in 1989 protest demonstrations emerged in Berlin and it became clear how many citizens secretly despised the regime. As the number of protesters grew, it became less risky for others to join.

The police and the army were practically powerless against the fast growing numbers of protesters, and thus decided to stay passive. The government was also caught by surprise by the sheer size of the demonstrations. When the protesters subsequently began to tear down the wall between the Eastern and Western parts of the city, the East German state collapsed, and less than a year later the reunification of East and West Germany was a fact.

As this example underlines, the behaviour of other people in the same setting can have a big impact on the behaviour of individuals. If many people are behaving a certain way, it is easy for an individual to jump on the bandwagon. Large numbers can thus influence people's perceptions of the attractiveness of a certain behaviour or their views on whether it is the right thing to do. At the same time, as a result of large numbers and the anonymity they bring, people might feel less exposed to risks (whether such feelings are justified or not).

The micro-to-micro link: Action-forming mechanisms

Action-forming mechanisms relate to the ways in which individuals reach decisions and arrive at actions and interactions. Being rooted in social psychology, these mechanisms show how particular combinations of individual-level preferences, beliefs, and opportunities lead to certain behaviour. In other words, they concern the micro-to-micro link in Figure 2.2.

A classic example of an action-forming mechanism is the theory of *cognitive dissonance*, developed by the social psychologist Leon Festinger (1957). This theory posits that people aim for cognitive consonance – that is, a coherent and consistent set of attitudes, beliefs and behaviours. Cognitive dissonance occurs when a person has various views that clash with one another. Views should in this regard be interpreted very broadly, encompassing, among other things, values, norms, beliefs, attitudes, feelings of identity and belonging, knowledge about the world, and decisions. For example, a rich person may on the one hand feel like they should do something to help the poor, but on the other hand feel reluctant to give up any of their own wealth. Or a male manager might be a strong proponent of gender emancipation in the workplace, yet still prefer working with male peers. According to Festinger, such conflicting views give rise to a sense of discomfort and people will therefore try to reduce such inconsistencies. In particular, Festinger's psychological experiments revealed that a person who experiences such dissonance would abandon one of his conflicting views, thereby resolving the cognitive dissonance.

A closely related mechanism put forward by the economist Timur Kuran (1995) concerns *preference falsification*. Kuran also considers a situation in which there is a conflict between someone's own views and the prevailing views within society. However, aside from simply sticking to one's own views or adopting the dominant views, Kuran distinguishes a third option that consists of maintaining the difference between one's own views and those prevailing within society but keeping one's own views secret. This boils down to saying things that one does not really believe, which is what Kuran means by the term preference falsification. This phenomenon is sometimes also referred to as the *emperor's dilemma*, after Hans-Christian Andersen's tale of an emperor going around naked but being complimented by everyone on his beautiful clothes. Such situations are most common under totalitarian political regimes, where people are forced to accept the doctrines and dogmas of the ruling elites, and fear the consequences of going against these norms. In such systems, individuals have to publicly defend points of view that they may resent in their hearts. As long as this political situation remains stable, the authorities may not notice that the people do not share their views. Yet when the political situation changes, public opinion can change swiftly and resistance against the regime can spread rapidly (see the East German example discussed previously).

The micro-to-macro link: Transformation mechanisms

The third category of social mechanisms concerns the micro-to-macro link in Figure 2.2. These *transformation mechanisms* are needed to explain how behaviours at the micro level, when aggregated, lead to certain outcomes at the macro level. These macro-level outcomes may be intended or unintended, and optimal or suboptimal.

One example with a positive outcome – at least theoretically – is the free market model in neoclassical economics. The institutional structure of the market promotes competition and activates the motive of profit maximization among entrepreneurs. Yet, although the sellers and buyers meeting each other in the marketplace are motivated by pure self-interest, this does not result in anarchy but in market clearance and an equilibrium price, leaving both sellers and buyers satisfied. As Adam Smith argues in his seminal works *The Theory of Moral Sentiments* (1759) and *An Inquiry into the Nature and Causes of the Wealth of Nations* (1776), the interaction of selfish individuals thus leads to a macro-level outcome that is beneficial for all, as if the whole process is administered by an "invisible hand". Among other things, he notes: "Every individual . . . neither intends to promote the public interest, nor knows how much he is promoting it . . . he intends only his own gain, and he is in this . . . led by an invisible hand to promote an end which was no part of his intention". More poetically, he also states: "It is not from the benevolence of the butcher, the brewer, or the baker, that we expect our dinner, but from their regard to their own interest". In other words, there are *positive externalities* to individuals' behaviours: consequences that the individual actors do not take into account when deciding on their actions but that beneficially impact other actors and thereby society as a whole.

Critical mass models such as described by the American economist Thomas Schelling (1978) are another example of transformation mechanisms. While these models have, among other things, been widely applied to explain the success or failure of social movements, Schelling explains these models using the example of the "dying seminar", illustrated in Figure 2.3. This example tells the tale of a weekly seminar where academics discuss their research. Most academics will only attend these meetings if they are sure that many of their colleagues will do so as well, because the seminar will only yield interesting discussions when there are a sufficient number of attendants (when a critical mass is reached). In Figure 2.3, this relationship between expected and actual attendance is depicted by the solid S-shaped curve. The dashed diagonal line, in turn, reflects how people form their expectations regarding the number of people that will attend the seminar: they assume that the number of attendees in a given week will be the same as in the preceding week.

For example, suppose that people expect the seminar to have 40 attendees in a certain week, because that number of individuals attended the week before. With this expectation, potential participants will hesitate about whether or not to attend, since they prefer somewhat larger

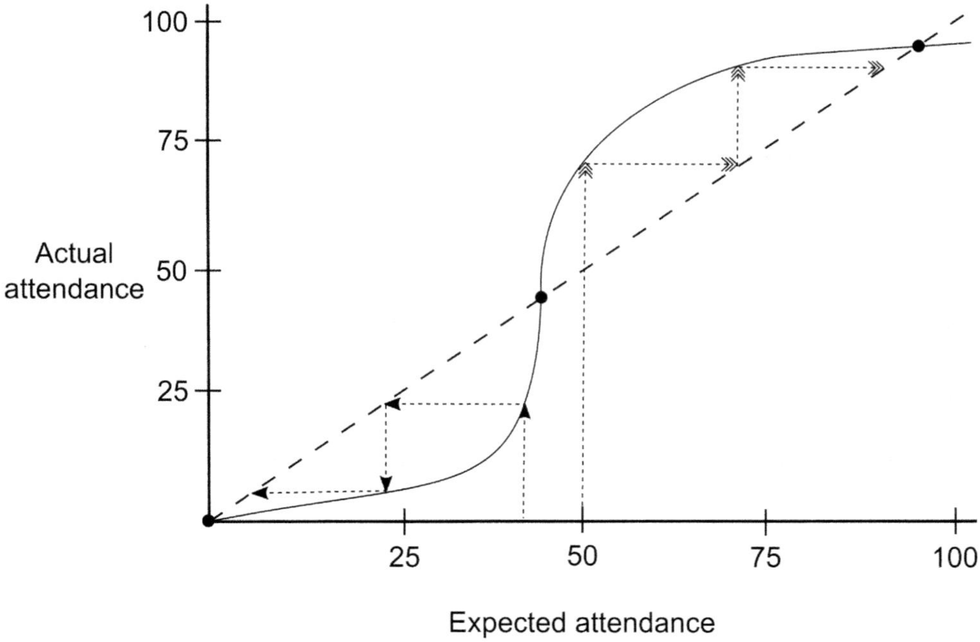

Figure 2.3 Expected and actual attendance at a weekly research seminar

Note: The solid S-shaped curve shows how many people will actually attend the seminar, given the expected number of participants (this curve is based on the aggregation of every individual's *reaction curve*). The dashed diagonal line is an auxiliary tool, depicting situations where the expected attendance equals the actual attendance. The dotted arrows demonstrate what will unfold when one starts off with an expected attendance level of, respectively, 40 and 50 participants.

seminars, and some of them will, in the end, decide to skip the session. As a result, only about 25 people will attend. Most of these people will leave disappointed after the seminar, because they had hoped for a bigger group and the discussions were not hugely interesting. Based on this experience, people expect only around 25 people to return for the next seminar, which means that eventually less than ten people actually show up. The next week there will, as a consequence, be even fewer attendees. The seminar will thus approach a point of extinction. This path of events is illustrated by the dotted arrows on the left-hand side of Figure 2.3.

On the other hand, when the initial expectation is that 50 people will attend the seminar, around 75 people will show up and nobody will be disappointed afterwards. Subsequently, the expected number of participants for the next instalment will be 75, and in the end more than 90 people will join. At these attendance levels, the expectations and the actual attendance rate roughly balance each other. These dynamics are displayed by the dotted arrows on the right-hand side of Figure 2.3.

Hence, in this critical mass model the interaction between expectations and behaviour has two potential outcomes: low expectations decrease the actual attendance rate, eventually causing the seminar to die, while high expectations ensure that the seminar will flourish. Notice that both outcomes constitute a social equilibrium, in the sense that – given these outcomes – nobody has an incentive to change their behaviour. Both equilibria are also stable. That is, if a few people in the extinction equilibrium decide to give the seminar another chance, they will be disappointed again and soon enough the seminar is back at its equilibrium. Similarly, if a few people in the flourishing equilibrium cannot make it in a given week, the rest will still have a good time and, as a result, the seminar can easily re-establish its equilibrium. Therefore, if in a given week a few more people than usual decide to attend the flourishing seminar, the number of people attending in the next few weeks will also shift back to the initial equilibrium, because the few extra people create over-crowding, leaving, for example, insufficient chairs for all participants. Figure 2.3, in fact, also contains a third social equilibrium at an attendance level of 45 individuals. However, this equilibrium is unstable insofar as small deviations from this situation will ultimately lead to one of the other equilibria.

Where public goods are concerned, we can often observe transformation mechanisms that lead the interacting individuals to outcomes that are not just unintended but even perverse. Garrett Hardin's (1968) model of the *tragedy of the commons* provides an example. As seen in the section "A typology of goods" in Chapter 1, Hardin explains his model using the example of a piece of common land, with open access, where farmers let their livestock graze. Every single farmer aims to maximize their profits and therefore has an incentive to keep expanding their herd. However, when every farmer follows this course of action, the overall result will be overgrazing, leaving less grass for each animal. This means that the yield derived from each animal will drop. Nevertheless, for an individual farmer it will still be optimal to continue expanding their herd. After all, every additional animal will increase their revenues, whereas the negative effect of overgrazing is spread over all animals grazing on this land, implying that the individual farmer only carries a fraction of this cost. As a consequence, all farmers have an incentive to continue increasing their herd, ultimately leading to the disappearance of all the grass and the death of their animals. At the heart of this problem is the fact that the farmers' behaviour is characterized by *negative externalities* as they do not fully take into account the detrimental impact of expanding their stock on the other farmers using the land.

The tragedy of this situation is that every single farmer is locked into a competitive system that forces them to expand their business or go bankrupt, even though they are embedded in an environment of limited resources. One farmer deciding to stop expanding would have virtually no effect in avoiding exhaustion of the common land, as their individual impact on the overall problem is negligible. Only when all farmers decide to restrain the growth of their herds can the common land be preserved. However, this is difficult to achieve given the open-access character of the land and the competitive system that all farmers are part of.

The tragedy of the commons demonstrates that individual actors often lack incentives to take public interests into account fully. When their goal is profit maximization in the short run, it can be entirely rational for them to exploit collective resources, even when the community as a whole – including these individual actors – will, in the longer run, experience harm from these exploitative actions. Hardin suggests that one solution to this problem is to give powers to a higher-level institution (e.g., the local council) that can regulate access to the collective resource. This could restrain the competitive pressures that would otherwise lead to the exhaustion of the resource.

Schelling's (1978) model of *tipping points* represents another category of mechanisms linking micro-level behaviours to macro-level outcomes. Schelling uses this model to explain social segregation on the basis of, among other things, sex, ethnicity, language and socio-economic status. He focuses on residential segregation along these dimensions, but the underlying logic is more widely applicable. The way in which the model operates can be illustrated by thinking of a checkers board with two types of stones – black stones and white stones – as well as some empty squares. The stones represent two groups of people, like men and women, different ethnic groups, old people versus young people, or any other dichotomy of clearly recognizable and homogenous groups. These black stones and white stones are initially randomly allocated across the checkers board, with one stone for each square. A few squares remain empty. For the sake of this example we assume that the black stones want at least 50 percent of their neighbours to be black, and that the white stones want at least 25 percent of their neighbours to be white. We additionally assume that every black or white stone for which this requirement is not met will move to another square.

Depending on the initial distribution of stones and the exact preferences of the different types of stones, not much may happen initially if most stones are happy with their location. However, it is unlikely that all stones will be satisfied and a few of them will, therefore, probably move to empty squares. This will, in turn, change the surroundings of other stones, some of whom may now become unhappy with their location and thus move elsewhere. Yet, this will again change the surroundings of other stones, who may now also prefer to move. As this sorting process is iterated, the checkers board gradually becomes divided into homogenous neighbourhoods of either black or white stones. That is, the small number of first-round moves set off a chain reaction that eventually leads to complete segregation. Crucially, diverse neighbourhoods can be maintained as long as the stones are sufficiently tolerant of the other colour. However, as soon as their hostility towards the other colour passes a certain threshold – the tipping point – an unravelling process takes place, with complete segregation as the end result.

Similar processes occur in real life, for example with regard to residential choices, school selection or the leisure clubs that people join. An important element of the tipping point model is that the different groups are fairly homogenous in their preferences for social mixing. This implies, for example, that neighbourhoods may remain quite stable for a long time when there is a gradual inflow of immigrants. However, when the presence of immigrants continues to grow, there will at some stage be a tipping point, at which a substantial portion of natives no longer want to live in that neighbourhood and move away. This will then influence the behaviour of the natives that initially chose to stay, setting off a segregation cascade.

Schelling shows that such aggregate-level processes may unfold even when people are quite sympathetic towards other groups and only have a very mild preference for the company of those similar to themselves. Vehement racism is thus by no means required for stark racial segregation to arise. Also notice that this tipping point model can be regarded as the mirror image of the critical mass model. In the latter, a desirable situation can only be maintained if a certain threshold is met; in the former, a desirable situation is maintained as long as a certain number stays under a threshold. If these conditions no longer hold, the desirable situation will fall apart in both cases.

Authority structures: Principal-agent relations

In this section we dig deeper into how individual actors behave and interact at the micro level, thus shedding further light on what happens between point B and C in Figure 2.2. In general, individual actors have the right of control over their behaviour. This is a fundamental right in democratic societies and as such it is typically entrenched in countries' constitutions, similarly to freedom of speech, property rights, and the right to privacy. Nevertheless, in all democratic societies individuals also transfer some control over their actions to others (the state, their employer). By handing over these rights, the actors make themselves subordinate to those others. In this way, structures of authority are created.

In its simplest form, an authority relation consists of a supervisor and a subordinate. We call this a *principal-agent relation* (Coleman 1990). The *principal* or supervisor (an employer) employs the *agent* or executor (an employee) with the purpose of having him do activities for a certain reward. One could, for example, think of a minister of transport (the principal) and a civil servant overseeing a specific infrastructure project (the agent). At the same time, this civil servant could be the principal within another relation, such as with a private firm supplying materials for this project. In a democratic context, we could also view voters as principals and elected officials as agents who have to execute the will of the voters. As illustrated in Figure 2.4, the principal will generally provide instructions to the agent, accompanied by certain rules and incentives, and the agent will execute the instructed tasks and report back on the execution of these tasks.

Principal-agent relations are surrounded by detailed contracts, extensive legislation, and jurisprudence that establish the rights and duties of both parties in relation to one another. This suggests that principal-agent relations are not always straightforward. Indeed, although principal-agent relations are omnipresent in society, they are also a source of problems and conflicts. The fundamental problem is that agents may not behave in accordance with the principal's wishes. In a nutshell, the principal is for the achievement of her goals dependent on the behaviour of the agent, who is supposed to execute the principal's orders. However, even though the agent has transferred some control over his actions to the principal, he still has his own interests too, which need not coincide with those of the principal. Although the principal can try to monitor

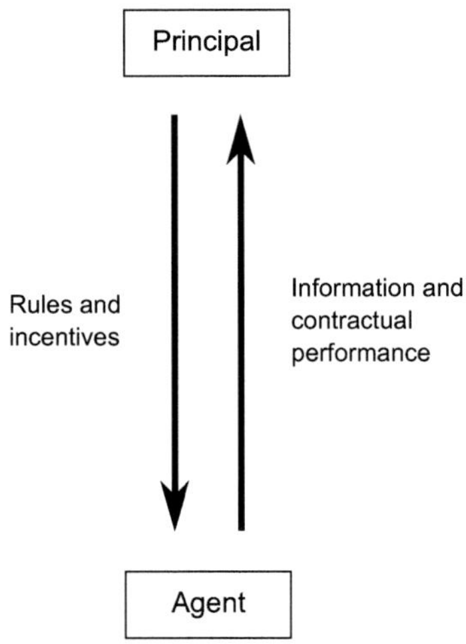

Figure 2.4 The principal-agent model

the actions of the agent, they cannot monitor everything the agent does, especially since principals often have more than one agent under them. In order to make efficient use of their time and money, the principal must therefore entrust some tasks to the agent. At the same time, the agent inevitably possesses more information about the execution of these tasks than the principal. This information advantage gives the agent the chance to behave opportunistically, in ways to promote their own interests rather than the interests of the principal.

Thus, we arrive at the core of the principal-agent problem: the principal can give detailed instructions to the agent for all of the tasks the agent must perform, but it is simply impossible for the principal to fully monitor all aspects of the agent's behaviour. As a result, employees may slack off, steal from their boss, fiddle the books, waste resources, fail to report defects, give preference to particular customers, and so on, without any of this behaviour being detected by the employer.

Telling examples of similar problems can be found among civil servants in Italy. In 2015, seven civil servants in Rome were prosecuted for their involvement in a bribery scandal around road works. The civil servants had accepted large sums of money from construction companies to obtain tenders, but these companies subsequently neglected the work once the order was in, leading to sub-standard roads and an increase in road accidents. In the same year, 200 civil servants in San Remo were prosecuted for not doing their job. Hidden camera footage had showed that these civil servants arrived at work to swipe in at the time clock every morning, but left straight after doing so. Some even arrived in their pyjamas or swimming costumes. The challenge for the principal is to develop instruments for measuring the agent's performance (e.g., a time clock was not sufficient in the example) and for realigning the agent's interests with their own interests (e.g., output-based bonus structures).

The nineteenth century *modern bureaucracy model* – very common since the French Revolution and extensively described by Weber – is an attempt to put restraints on the behaviour of civil servants. This is done via a comprehensive system of rules, prescriptions, and top-down monitoring. However, such a stringent system may also lead to perverse outcomes, by stimulating bureaucrats to concentrate on rigidly applying the rules instead of trying their best to achieve the underlying goals of the organization. For example, when police officers are evaluated based on how many criminal facts they record or how many cases they solve, they have an incentive to direct most of their attention to minor traffic offences and petty crimes such as shoplifting, leaving bigger criminals that are harder to catch undisturbed. Likewise, schoolteachers that are assessed based on the exam results of their pupils have an incentive to start teaching to the test. Strict rules are, furthermore, less effective in contexts involving complex tasks that vary strongly on a case-by-case basis. Under such circumstances the principal has no choice but to leave many issues to the discretion of his agents.

In reality, the principal often does not supervise just a single agent but rather a group of agents who work together in a team. In these situations, it is more difficult for the principal to measure the contribution of each individual team member. This is especially the case when the teams are relatively large. It is then fairly easy for a team member to slack off and become a free rider. This could mean that, as a team grows in size, the contributions of individual team members shrink. Yet, the principal will not have sufficient information to remove or punish the free riders. At the same time, team members who are annoyed by their colleagues' lack of effort are unlikely to incriminate them. After all, unwritten rules tend to proscribe such behaviour – traitors always have a bad reputation. Depending on the work culture and power dynamics within the team, hard-working team members may, however, be able to impose social control on their shirking counterparts. This may be a viable pathway if the majority of team members are hard-working and highly committed to serving the company the best they can. Conversely, when the shirking team members are dominant within the team, the hard-working team members may be more likely to give up and also start putting in less effort.

The collapse of the Barings Bank in 1995 illustrates how the principal-agent problem can result in disaster. The problems originated in the Singapore branch of the bank, where the young stock trader Nick Leeson took immense risks on unauthorized speculative trades. Initially he made large profits on these trades, earning himself big bonuses, but soon enough he started to incur massive losses. Leeson hid these losses in so-called error accounts, and gradually risked more and more of the bank's money as he tried to make up for his losses. Leeson's transactions culminated in a total loss of US$ 1.4 billion. Barings Bank was unable to cover these losses and fell into bankruptcy. In the end, Leeson was sentenced to prison for fraud, but the board of directors of Barings Bank was also criticized for having weak internal auditing and risk management procedures. In other words, they had awarded their employees too much discretion, assuming that the employees would do what was best for the bank. This, however, meant that the employees could no longer be effectively monitored.

The collapse of Barings does not stand on its own. In fact, in 2008 the French bank Société Générale had a similar affair, losing US$ 6.7 billion following unauthorised transactions by the trader Jérôme Kerviel. The similarities between the two cases are striking. Kerviel was sent to prison for his actions, but he still claims that similar practices were widespread across the bank and that his initial profits made his superiors turn a blind eye. In 2016, several judges acknowledged that Kerviel was at least partially right. They greatly reduced the damages that Kerviel had to pay to Société Générale, while the bank was ordered to pay Kerviel compensation for firing him unlawfully. More examples of principal-agent problems and challenges faced by supervisory authorities can be found in Chapter 10 on corruption, in Chapter 11 on problems in financial markets, as well as elsewhere in this book.

Problems due to information asymmetry: Moral hazard and adverse selection

In the preceding section we have discussed how an unequal division of information between actors – more specifically, a principal and an agent – can lead to problems. Indeed, information problems are the source of many societal problems. In this section we look at two types of information problems that are especially common: *moral hazard* and *adverse selection*. Both of these problems are ultimately the result of an asymmetry in the amount or quality of information that different actors have at their disposal. This either gives actors an incentive to behave opportunistically towards each other or makes them refrain from transactions that would be beneficial from a societal point of view.

The principal-agent problem can be seen as a specific case of moral hazard. Moral hazard arises from *ex-post* information asymmetry. This means that *after* a certain agreement has been reached between two actors, one of them (actor A) has an incentive to engage in costly or risky behaviour, knowing that the other actor (actor B) will eventually bear the costs of this behaviour. The opportunity for risk-taking behaviour by actor A originates from the fact that actor B can only partially observe or monitor the actions taken by actor A. In other words, actor A has an information advantage over actor B. Actor A can thus decide to take actions that first and foremost serve their own interests rather than the actions that they had agreed with actor B. It is not difficult to see how the actions of Leeson and Kerviel described in the previous section can be seen as a form of moral hazard.

A classic example of moral hazard is how people may change their behaviour once they have purchased insurance for an object. For example, once someone has acquired insurance against bike theft, they may suddenly be less concerned about where they park their bike, or only lock it up with a cheap lock rather than a safer, but more expensive, one. The bike owner knows that if his bike is stolen, the insurance company will compensate him for this. Therefore, the bike owner faces weaker incentives to prevent his bike being stolen. Meanwhile, the insurance company can only to a limited extent monitor where the bike is parked or how carefully it is locked up. The bike owner can exploit this information asymmetry.

Similar problems occur at a higher scale. One clear example relates to banks, the *too-big-to-fail problem*. That is when certain banks have such a central position in the economy – in terms of how many people have an account with them, how strongly they are connected to other banks, and so on – that their collapse would inevitably lead to a severe economic crisis. Governments would never want this to happen and would, therefore, try their utmost to prevent that struggling banks collapse. They could do this, for example, by lending the bank money at favourable rates or by taking over some of its debt. However, knowing that governments would be willing to take such action to prevent their collapse, banks subsequently have much weaker incentives for prudent behaviour. Instead, they are more likely to engage in riskier behaviour in an attempt to increase their profits. After all, should they get into trouble, the government will come to their rescue anyway. However, this riskier behaviour, in turn, makes it more likely that the banks will indeed get into trouble. At the same time, it is difficult for governments and regulators to monitor the exact behaviour of banks, especially since financial products have grown increasingly complex and banks have become more interdependent. According to various commentators, the too-big-to-fail problem is one of the core causes behind the 2007 global financial crisis, with financial institutions taking on too much risk in the assumption that they would be bailed out should things go wrong.

Adverse selection is the sibling of moral hazard and its origin lies in *ex-ante* information asymmetry. This means that *before* two parties engage in a transaction, they have unequal information about the quality of the good being traded. One of the most famous examples of adverse selection concerns the market for "lemons", as described by the economist and Nobel Prize laureate George Akerlof (1970). In this context, lemons are second-hand cars that turn out to have problems after they have been bought. As Akerlof explains, second-hand car sales always exhibit a certain degree of information asymmetry between the buyer and the seller. The seller usually has more accurate information on the condition the car is really in. For buyers, on the other hand, it is hard to tell apart good and bad cars, particularly if they look equally well maintained on the outside. Because of this uncertainty, buyers are only willing to pay a price that averages the value of a good and a bad car. However, at that price level all sellers of good cars would be making a loss, so they will withdraw from the market. As they do so, the buyers will sooner or later come to realize that there are fewer good cars left in the market. Accordingly, they will lower the price they are willing to pay. Following such dynamics, the market for second-hand cars will in the end unravel. Thus, the owners of good used cars are no longer able to sell their cars and the only cars left in the marketplace will be lemons.

Another area where problems of adverse selection are pervasive is the insurance sector. Think of health insurance. In this case, there is an information asymmetry to the extent that individuals have better insights into their health status than insurance companies do. Since insurance companies have a profit objective but cannot exactly observe the health status of the people they insure, they will set premiums at a rate between what they would charge healthy and unhealthy people if they were able to distinguish the two. Yet, at those premium levels, only unhealthy people will be interested in taking the insurance. The result will be an insurance market in which no healthy person wants to buy insurance. However, with only unhealthy people left in the market, insurance companies would no longer make a profit and would therefore leave the market, leaving everyone uninsured. The same type of unravelling process could occur with regard to the insurance of labour market risks, such as falling unemployed.

One way to attenuate adverse selection problems in insurance markets is for insurers to charge different premiums to different people, based on their risk of getting ill or becoming unemployed. They could, for example, do this based on where people live, which sector they work in, how old they are, whether they smoke, or whether they have any pre-existing medical conditions. All of these factors are related to the probability of getting ill or becoming unemployed and thus help insurers to obtain more precise predictions of individuals' risks of falling victim to these forms of hardship. These better predictions will, in turn, help them determine to whom they should offer insurance. That said, moral objections could be raised against some of these selection criteria. After all, is it fair to deny someone insurance based on their gender, age, or a certain pre-existing medical condition that is beyond their control? For this reason, governments often step in to regulate social insurance schemes. For example, the Patient Protection and Affordable Care Act in the US – also referred to as *Obamacare* – stipulates that health insurers need to accept all applicants and charge the same premiums to everyone, regardless of gender and certain pre-existing conditions.

Individuals can also attempt to reduce the amount of information asymmetry themselves through *signalling* – that is, taking certain actions to signal information to the other party. In the animal world, male peacocks signal their physical prowess and genetic fitness to peahens by their tails (although, strictly speaking, this rather concerns a sign than a signal). As it is physically demanding to grow and carry a long and bright tail, the brightness and length of a peacock's tail is a reliable sign of his health and fitness, which would otherwise be hard to judge for peahens looking for a mate.

The textbook social science example of signalling comes from the economist and Nobel Prize winner Michael Spence (1973) and concerns job-market signalling. The starting point is that employers always face information asymmetry when hiring new employees, in the sense that they cannot really know how smart and skilful a candidate is. Yet, candidates can send signals about this to the employer, for instance by showing their educational qualifications. As long as a certain level of intellect and skill is required to obtain a specific classification, employers can calculate the intelligence and level of skill of the candidate. This holds true regardless of whether the actual knowledge gained from the qualification is useful for the job or not – in the same way as peacocks' tails have no function apart from their signalling value.

Signalling also occurs in many other life domains. For example, in prisons criminals can signal their toughness to each other through displaying their scars. The idea is that someone who has many knife or bullet scars is not to be messed with, since he apparently went through many fights and survived (Gambetta 2009). However, while signalling can reduce information problems, it is not always optimal for society. The reason is that effective signals are by definition costly, but not necessarily of much productive value. As a result, many societal resources can be wasted as individuals pursue certain goals (e.g., educational degrees) for the sole purpose of signalling.

Recommended readings

- Jon Elster (2007) provides a broad introduction to understanding social interactions, relying on numerous examples from a wide variety of disciplines. He pays attention to the motives, beliefs, and emotions that underlie human behaviour and subsequently addresses how these factors, together with the constraints and opportunities offered by specific social contexts, translate into concrete actions. Elster's approach is built around social mechanisms.
- Ernst Fehr and Herbert Gintis (2007) provide further background on the foundations of human behaviour. Based on experimental and anthropological evidence, they demonstrate that we are a hybrid between the Homo Sociologicus and Homo Economicus, and that it depends on the concrete situation which forces are most dominant for our behaviour. Their insights help to better understand issues such as social order and collective action.
- Daniel Kahneman (2011) explains how our behaviour often deviates from what rational choice theory predict. Drawing on many decades of psychological research, he shows that our behaviour is rather subject to systematic cognitive biases, such as loss aversion and anchoring. Kahneman's work is invaluable for better understanding the limits to rational choice as well as one's own behaviour.
- Mancur Olson (1965) discusses the fundamentals behind collective action problems and free riding behaviour. He explains how collective action is generally very difficult to achieve in large groups, even when most members have the same interests. While these dynamics threaten the provision of public goods, Olson also proposes several solutions to overcome collective action problems.
- Garrett Hardin (1968) outlines his concept of the tragedy of the commons, whereby common pool resources will inevitably be exhausted unless a community manages to regulate their exploitation. The tragedy of the commons is a powerful illustration of the tension between individual and collective interests and of negative externalities to individual behaviour. Hardin further illustrates his argument with the example of overpopulation.
- Thomas Schelling (1978) outlines the logic behind critical mass models and his theory of tipping points. He shows how social systems can rapidly and irreversibly shift from one equilibrium to another once a certain threshold is reached. Among other things, he explains how even very weak in-group preferences can lead to extreme levels of segregation when aggregated at the macro level.

Bibliography

Akerlof, George A. 1970. "The Market for 'Lemons': Quality Uncertainty and the Market Mechanism". *Quarterly Journal of Economics* 84:488–500.

Boudon, Raymond. 1986. *Theories of Social Change: A Critical Appraisal.* Cambridge: Polity Press.

Boudon, Raymond. 1996. "The Cognitivist Model: A Generalized 'Rational Choice Model'". *Rationality and Society* 8:123–150.

Coleman, James S. 1990. *Foundations of Social Theory.* Cambridge, MA: The Belknap Press of Harvard University Press.

Elster, Jon. 2007. *Explaining Social Behavior: More Nuts and Bolts for the Social Sciences.* Cambridge: Cambridge University Press.

Fehr, Ernst, and Herbert Gintis. 2007. "Human Motivation and Social Cooperation: Experimental and Analytical Foundations". *Annual Review of Sociology* 33:43–64.

Festinger, Leon. 1957. *A Theory of Cognitive Dissonance.* Stanford, CA: Stanford University Press.

Gambetta, Diego. 2009. *Codes of the Underworld: How Criminals Communicate.* Princeton, NJ: Princeton University Press.

Hardin, Garrett. 1968. "Tragedy of the Commons". *Science* 162:1243–1248.

Hechter, Michael. 1987. *Principles of Group Solidarity.* Berkeley, CA: University of California Press.

Hedström, Peter, and Richard Swedberg. 1998. "Social Mechanisms: An Introductory Essay". Pp. 1–31 in: *Social Mechanisms: An Analytical Approach to Social Theory*, edited by Peter Hedström and Richard Swedberg. Cambridge: Cambridge University Press.

Kahneman, Daniel. 2011. *Thinking, Fast and Slow.* New York, NY: Farrar, Straus and Giroux.

Kuran, Timur. 1995. *Private Truths, Public Lies: The Social Consequences of Preference Falsification.* Cambridge, MA: Harvard University Press.

McClelland, David C. 1961. *The Achieving Society.* Princeton, NJ: Van Nostrand.

Merton, Robert K. 1968. "The Self-Fulfilling Prophecy". Pp. 475–490 in: *Social Theory and Social Structure*, edited by Robert Merton. New York, NY: The Free Press.

Olson, Mancur. 1965. *The Logic of Collective Action.* Cambridge, MA: Harvard University Press.

Raub, Werner, and Thomas Voss. 2017. "Micro-Macro Models in Sociology: Antecedents of Coleman's Diagram". Pp. 11–36 in: *Social Dilemmas, Institutions, and the Evolution of Cooperation*, edited by Ben Jann and Wojtek Przepiorka. Berlin: De Gruyter.

Schelling, Thomas C. 1978. *Micromotives and Macrobehavior.* New York, NY: Norton.

Schelling, Thomas C. 1984. *Choice and Consequence: Perspectives of an Errant Economist.* Cambridge: Cambridge University Press.

Schelling, Thomas C. 1998. "Social Mechanisms and Social Dynamics". Pp. 32–44 in: *Social Mechanisms: An Analytical Approach to Social Theory*, edited by Peter Hedström and Richard Swedberg. Cambridge: Cambridge University Press.

Simon, Herbert A. 1947. *Administrative Behavior: A Study of Decision-making Processes in Administrative Organization.* New York, NY: Macmillan Company.

Smith, Adam. 1759. *The Theory of Moral Sentiments.* http://www.earlymoderntexts.com/assets/pdfs/smith1759.pdf.

Smith, Adam. 1776. *An Inquiry into the Nature and Causes of the Wealth of Nations.* http://www.earlymoderntexts.com/assets/pdfs/smith1776_34.pdf.

Spence, Michael. 1973. "Job Market Signaling". *Quarterly Journal of Economics* 87:355–374.

Weber, Max. 1978[1925]. *Economy and Society: An Outline of Interpretive Sociology* (Wirtschaft und Gesellschaft: Grundriss der Verstehenden Soziologie). Berkeley, CA: University of California Press.

3 The promises and pitfalls of state intervention

Chapter overview

As a common response to societal problems, state intervention merits special attention. We begin this chapter by defining state intervention, and by tracing it over time. We illustrate how the growth of the interventionist state has occurred in parallel with the rise of industrial capitalism, and how the relationship between the market and the state has evolved along the way. We next consider various arguments for state intervention, and their links to beliefs about the engineerability of society. Transnational problems such as environmental pollution and increasing migrant streams are discussed as examples that call for co-ordinated state intervention. We also examine how a well-functioning bureaucracy can be regarded as a public good, which may be undermined by inefficiencies and corruption. Throughout this chapter, we demonstrate that state intervention can provide solutions for societal problems, but sometimes may also generate new problems of its own. By referring to the principal-agent model, and the concept of perverse incentives, we point to some problems that can emerge from too much state intervention.

Varieties of state intervention

Adherents of different political ideologies advocate different amounts of state intervention, and in different areas. *Socialists* typically advocate extensive state intervention in many areas of life, including the labour market, the housing market, and the educational system. They are also in favour of income and wealth redistribution of income. *Conservatives* typically advocate less redistribution of resources, but may support intervention in areas such as trade, in an effort to protect workers in traditional industries. *Liberals* typically advocate the least amount of state intervention, preferring market solutions to central planning. This chapter defines state intervention, and traces the course of increased state intervention over time.

Almost the entire world population now lives under some form of state. The number of individual nation states increased markedly over the course of the twentieth century, having nearly tripled in number since the Second World War. In 2018, the count is at 195 internationally recognized, independent states. These comprise the 193 members of the United Nations plus Palestine and the Holy See, which both have an observer status at the United Nations. Some of these states are governed democratically, others by authoritarian regimes, still others are so weak that they practically lack any power and can thus be considered *failed states*.

The government bureaucracy constitutes the means for state intervention, while the powers to tax, spend and regulate serve as the instruments of state intervention. Many state institutions – especially an efficient state bureaucracy – have certain public good characteristics, and are therefore subject to free-rider problems (see Chapter 2). As a result, in some states, the state apparatus has been plagued by inefficiency and corruption. However, even when state institutions are accountable and meritocratic, there are still limits to how much can be achieved through intervention.

Disparate models of state intervention predominate different parts of the world. In Western industrialized countries, the state typically intervenes comparatively little in the areas of government ownership, monetary intervention, international trade regulation, and private property rights, while it intervenes extensively in the area of spending and taxation. In developing countries, on the other hand, the state typically intervenes extensively in the areas of government ownership, private property rights, monetary intervention, and international trade regulation, yet intervenes comparatively little in the area of spending and taxation. For example, state intervention in the form of currency debasement, expropriation of private property, and protectionism are commonplace in many developing countries. In contrast, sustained high levels of government spending are rare in such countries, mainly because the state is incapable of raising enough tax revenue to support such spending.

Of course, not all state intervention occurs within individual nations. Intergovernmental organizations sometimes exert considerable influence over the populations of nation states. Examples include the Organization for Petroleum Exporting Countries (OPEC), the World Trade Organization (WTO), the United Nations (UN), and the European Union (EU). Some commentators argue that the continuing development of such organizations fatally undermines the nation state, warning that the nation state may not survive to the end of the twenty-first century. Nevertheless, this chapter focuses primarily on intervention within individual nation states.

The rise of industrial capitalism and growing state intervention

The emergence of the *interventionist state* and its evolution is closely intertwined with the rise of industrial capitalism. A simple definition of *capitalism* is given by Zimbalist and Sherman (1984:6–7): "Pure capitalism is defined as a system wherein all of the means of production (physical capital) are privately owned and run by the capitalist class for a profit, while most other people are workers who work for a salary or wage (and who do not own the capital or the product)". Although market-based societies are much older (Van Bavel 2016), industrial capitalism emerged in England at the end of the eighteenth century, at the time of the industrial revolution. Subsequently, it spread over Western Europe and North America during the nineteenth century, and then spread to other parts of the world during the twentieth century.

During pre-capitalism, the technology used for economic production was relatively simple and the producers (farmers and craftsmen), who worked on a small-scale, usually owned the means of production (machines and tools). The industrial revolution brought forth a series of technological innovations that required greater investments of capital. Simultaneously, private markets underwent an enormous expansion: not only were markets for goods and financial products enlarged, but for the first time a large-scale market for wage labour was established. Goods markets underwent a particularly colossal expansion, as new industrial processes (e.g., weaving in cotton mills) paved the wave for new goods (e.g., textiles).

The evolutionary process whereby capitalism developed can be characterized by technological innovations. These innovations brought about new forms of production, but also altered social organization itself, and demanded new areas of state intervention. The invention of steam engines, railroads, and iron steamships were the drivers of the first phase of industrial capitalism. Subsequently, industrial capitalism further developed under the influence of inventions that stemmed from the discovery of how to harness electricity (telegraph, telephone, electrical equipment), the introduction of the gasoline engine, atomic energy. Most recently, innovations in electronic data processing (information technology), biotechnology, and artificial intelligence are the big drivers.

Each of these technological innovations have resulted in massive economic growth. However, even before the industrial revolution there were some specific periods of stark economic growth. For example, the economic historians Roger Fouquet and Stephen Broadberry (2015) show that Gross Domestic Product (GDP) per capita in Holland grew with 70 percent in the sixteenth century, and 50 percent in the second half of the seventeenth century. However, such growth spurts were different in nature than the growth that resulted from the industrial revolution – for example, the former was often strongly influenced by the exploitation of colonies. Typical for the period of industrial revolution, was a steadier, more domestically-driven, and more sustainable process of economic growth, during which societies underwent a radical economic transformation. Among other things, the state became increasingly involved in economic life, and transformed labour relations by constructing systems of social security and public healthcare that eventually evolved into *welfare states* (see Chapter 4).

The interventionist state can be seen as both a product of economic growth and a precondition for its occurrence. Economic growth provided the tax revenues necessary to fund the state apparatus. However, at the same time, the state also created circumstances conducive for economic development by protecting private property, providing legal frameworks for the functioning of markets, and improving education through public schooling. In the industrial world today, the interventionist state has become so intertwined with capitalism, that most discussions about more or less state intervention and about more or less reliance on markets, are discussions about relatively small shifts in policy. Even in the most liberal societies, such as the US, state institutions have become firmly embedded and are widely recognized for the ways in which they can facilitate the proper functioning of markets.

In general, the market is a mechanism for allocating goods on the basis of supply and demand. Producers supply goods, and consumers demand them. The market mechanism is most effective for allocating private goods and club goods; it is less effective for common-pool resources and especially public goods (recall the typology of goods presented in Chapter 1). The price of a good at any particular time and price changes act as a signal to prospective producers and consumers. If prices are rising, the signal to producers is to increase production of the good, and the signal to consumers is to cut back on consumption of the good. If the market functions properly, the interaction of supply and demand eventually results in an equilibrium price being reached, where supply of the good is equal to demand. These dynamics, as already described by Adam Smith in his treatise on *The Wealth of Nations* (1776), are covered extensively in all modern-day economics textbooks.

However, in many instances markets do not quite live up to this idealistic portrayal and are rather subject to *market failures* that hinder their functioning. Therefore, certain state institutions that correct such market failures are often indispensable. At the most basic level, well-functioning markets require the following institutional arrangements:

1 A stable and reliable currency (one not subject to forgery or excessive inflation);
2 A legal and judicial system to facilitate dispute settlement and contract enforcement;
3 A system of transparent and defendable private property;
4 Society-wide recognition of the right to make a profit;
5 A well-functioning and well-protected financial system of lending and borrowing;
6 Oversight by the state as to the quality of products and services, the reliability of measures and weights, and the veracity of product information.

Societies that adopted a version of capitalism with such institutional safeguards have prospered since the industrial revolution. Their experience stands in sharp contrast to the experience of societies that instead adopted a *communist* or *collectivist system* following the industrial revolution. Such systems originated from the observation that during the industrial revolution, those labouring on the means of production – such as workers using machines – no longer had ownership over them. Whereas before the industrial revolution individual artisans had produced and sold their own wares, armies of labourers now worked in factories owned by single wealthy capitalists.

In the mid-nineteenth century, the socialist philosophers Karl Marx and Friedrich Engels criticized this state of affairs, and the private ownership of the means of production by the economic elites in particular. They advocated transferring ownership of the means of production to the people. This was put into practice when the Russian Communist Party took power in Russia in 1917. However, not all the ideas of Marx and Engels were put into practice – for example, the means of production did not end up in the hands of the people, but in the hands of the state – and the collapse of the Soviet Union at the end of the twentieth century heralded the end of the collectivist model.

In terms of our macro-micro-macro perspective, the communist model was arguably based on a misunderstanding of individual action, and of the distinction between intended aims results and actual consequences. The economic demise of the Soviet Union demonstrated, among other things, that at the individual level, people need incentives to be productive. For example, when they collectivized agriculture, the communists did not take into account the incentives faced by individual farmers. Why would a farmer invest in collective production if his own contribution to the collective good is negligible and he can earn more by cultivating crops on a piece of private land? In short, communist institutions gave rise to all sorts of inefficiencies and sub-optimal outcomes.

In capitalist societies, the government apparatus has grown costlier over time as it has assumed a greater number of functions. The growing state has to be paid for through higher tax revenues. As a consequence, the period of increasing state intervention (roughly from the middle of the nineteenth century to the end of the twentieth century) exhibits two parallel trends: increasing government expenditures as a percentage of GDP, and increasing tax revenues as a percentage of GDP. Figure 3.1 displays trends in government expenditures as a percentage of GDP for the period 1870–2011 for Japan, the United States, the United Kingdom, Sweden, France, and Germany. A precipitous rise is visible in all of these countries from around ten percent in the late nineteenth century to between 30 and 60 percent by the end of the twentieth century.

In the more recent past, however, we can observe more notable differences in the trends across these countries. For example, while the United Kingdom has experienced a strong increase in government expenditures between 1995 and 2010, Sweden has witnessed an equally strong decrease over this period. That said, Sweden still has the second-highest level of government expenditures across this subset of countries (after France, whose expenditures did not drop in recent years), and public expenditures in the United Kingdom have also started to drop in the most recent years.

It is notable that, in most Western countries, government expenditures as a percentage of GDP have increased more than tax revenues as a percentage of GDP. This partially reflects that politicians find it politically profitable to increase spending without raising taxes, and making up for the shortfall by borrowing money in domestic and international markets. This has the effect of increasing the stock of public debt, which will have to be paid off by future governments. Most Western governments have thus accumulated sizable public debts, and for many countries the yearly payments of interest on these debts take up a large, and increasing, percentage of total government expenditures. According to the economic sociologist Wolfgang Streeck (2014), these trends have transformed most Western countries from *tax states* to *debt states*, which makes them economically more vulnerable. In addition, this transformation may increase

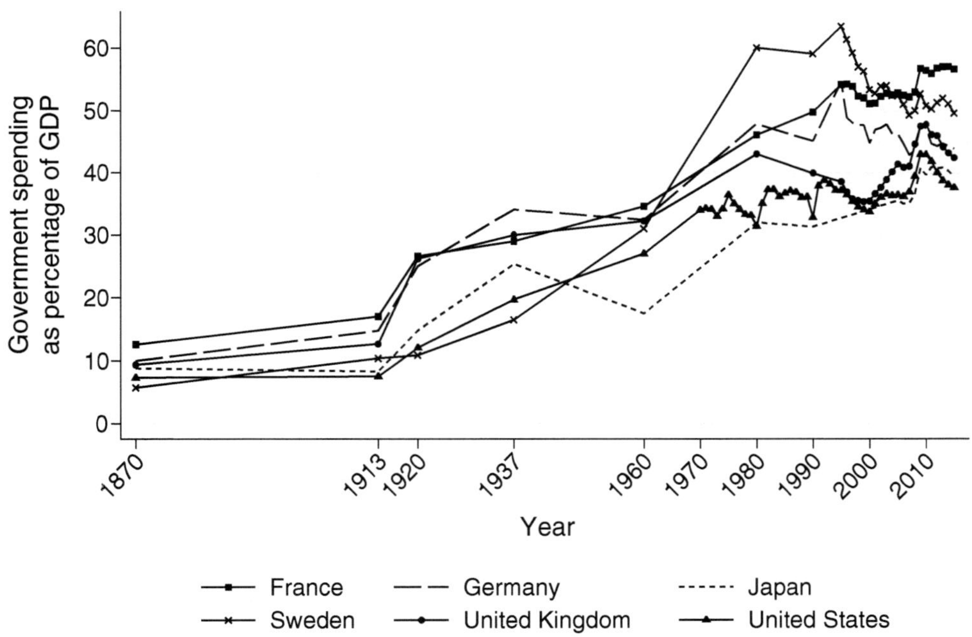

Figure 3.1 Trends in government expenditures as a percentage of GDP

Note: Data until 1996 are from Tanzi and Schuknecht (2000); all data thereafter are from the National Accounts at a Glance section of the OECD Database.

economic inequality, as the economic elites tend to benefit the most from reduced taxation and a growing stock of government bonds.

Also important in the link between state intervention and the market is the *crowding-out effect*. This is an example of a perverse consequence of governmental intervention. The idea is that an increase in government spending leads to a public deficit that is financed by increased borrowing by the government. This increased borrowing will lead to an increase in the interest rate, which also makes it more expensive for private parties to borrow money. As a result, private investments will drop, and economic growth may stagnate. This, in turn, may lead to reduced tax revenues for the government as well as increased expenditures in the form of unemployment benefits and social assistance, and thus a further increasing public deficit, which again requires additional borrowing by the government. As such, a vicious cycle of a worsening public budget and a stagnating economy may arise. That said, the empirical evidence for such crowding-out effects is somewhat inconclusive. For example, for several years we have now seen, despite high governmental borrowing rates, very low interest rates. Increased international capital mobility is part of the solution to this puzzle, with investors from growing economies such as China financing the public deficits of Western countries.

However, there is more criticism with regard to extensive government intervention than just the issue of building up debts and the associated negative consequences. As early as 1792, Wilhelm von Humboldt wrote an essay to define the limits of the effectiveness of the state that are still relevant today. Von Humboldt (1980[1792]:90) argues: "The state should refrain from all positive action for the benefit of citizens' prosperity, and only do what is necessary to keep them safe from each other and outside enemies; to no other end should their freedom be curtailed". His argumentation for this view is: "If everyone relies on the care and assistance of the state for himself he also relies on the state to take care of his fellow citizen, and even more so. This weakens people's willingness to take responsibility and their readiness for mutual help" (Von Humboldt 1980[1792]:75).

Government expansion and the engineerability of society

In line with the growing costs of state intervention described in the previous section, the number of societal areas affected by state intervention has increased considerably over the past centuries. As part of this expansion, several phases can be distinguished. At the end of the eighteenth century, the main government functions were still limited to defence against foreign enemies; police and law enforcement; courts of law; infrastructure; public education; and economic institutions guaranteeing currencies, contracts, and quality of products. One important area in which the state increasingly began to intervene in the nineteenth century was education.

During the twentieth century, the government assumed yet more functions as they started to influence the course of the economy more actively. For example, during the economic crisis of the 1930s (the Great Depression), governments ramped up public spending and undertook large infrastructure projects in order to stimulate the economy and create jobs. After the Second World War, the *welfare state* was introduced in Western industrial countries. The welfare state comprised a comprehensive system of social security provisions for the poor and other vulnerable groups in society. About the same time, there was an increasing emphasis on taking care of health, safety, and environmental issues leading, for example, to the establishment of governmental inspection services.

In an ideal world, the state as a collective actor is the guardian of universal interests. From this perspective, the state will only intervene in society if this serves the universal interest, and state intervention will thus always be a good thing. However, this assumes that there is consensus within the population as to what constitutes the universal interest and how it can best be served. It is more reasonable to assume that groups and individuals within society have different beliefs and values in this regard, for example about the respective desirability of reducing inequality, maximizing freedom, or safeguarding basic needs. Relatedly, they will have different views on the degree to which the outcomes that result from free market interactions are desirable or warranting state intervention. Such differences will be expressed in their political ideology. As a result, precisely which functions are best for the government to undertake is still – and will probably always remain – a matter of dispute among scholars, politicians, commentators, as well as the general public.

Perhaps one of the clearest examples of why at least a certain amount of state intervention is necessary is the failure to build up a well-functioning capitalist system in Russia after the collapse of the Soviet Union. Many people at the time assumed that a well-functioning capitalist system would evolve automatically, steered by the invisible hand of the market, without any need for top-down coordination by the state. However, as we already have established, and irrespective of the political ideology that one may adhere to, markets require certain minimum institutional arrangements in order to function well, including a stable and reliable currency, a legal and judiciary system to facilitate dispute settlement and contract enforcement, and a system of transparent and defendable private property rights. Such institutions are virtually impossible to create without state intervention. This became painfully clear after the collapse of the Soviet Union, when the absence of solid legal, economic and political institutions meant that Russia did not become a well-functioning democratic and capitalist society. Instead, it rather quickly turned into an authoritarian *oligarchy*, with political and economic power concentrated in the hands of a small group of people that took advantage of the unrest after the collapse of the Soviet Union.

The state expansion that took place over the course of the nineteenth and most of the twentieth century was driven by an increasing appetite for government intervention. Specifically, the idea that society could be engineered for the good, and even perfected, gained popularity. This idea had its roots in the Enlightenment, when science and technology began progressing rapidly, and there was a feeling that any human problem could be overcome with sufficient application of reason and evidence. By the end of the nineteenth century, many scientists and intellectuals believed that it was possible to create a completely planned society through the application of scientific principles. One could discern in these beliefs, which were found among sociologists and economists alike, elements of an engineering mind-set: namely that society could be constructed in the same way that an engineer designs a bridge.

By the 1930s and 1940s, the belief in the engineerability of society had gained even greater prominence. It was seemingly confirmed during the Second World War, an enormous exercise in planning and logistics on the part of the allies, which resulted in victory. Such top-down forms of management seemed to be very successful, and – after the war – were applied to other areas of society. This state expansion was also facilitated by strong and consistent economic growth during the 1950s, 1960s and 1970s, which meant governments had plenty of resources on hand.

Since the 1970s, however, the belief in the engineerability of society has been waning. The primary reason being that extensive state intervention appeared to have been unsuccessful in many countries. By the late 1980s, the social security systems of Western welfare states had proved more expensive than anticipated. Stagnating economic growth and rising rates of long-term unemployment in many Western countries came to be seen as a symptom of too much state expansion. Throughout the West, commentators began arguing that the state had grown too large, and had assumed too many functions.

It became popular to allow for a greater role for the market vis-à-vis the state, and the philosophy of *laissez-faire economics*, which contends that citizens will be best off if the state interferes as little as possible in the workings of the market, gained intellectual prominence during the 1980s. The laissez-faire advocates of this era, such as the economist Milton Friedman and politicians Margaret Thatcher and Ronald Reagan, opposed policies such as labour market regulation, generous unemployment benefits and social assistance, government ownership of industry, and high marginal tax rates. Later, in the 2000s, following the Great Recession that emerged after the 2008 financial crisis, many governments were forced to implement further cuts in their spending programmes, in order to keep these programmes affordable and prevent their public debt from skyrocketing.

Challenges to state intervention: New demands and limitations

Although there has been increasing pressure to scale back state intervention since the 1970s and 1980s, there is at the same time a continuous stream of new demands on the state, as society continues to evolve, thereby giving rise to new problems that need to be addressed. For example, there are many transnational societal problems that have gained prominence in recent decades, and call for new forms of state intervention and international coordination. Global warming, as discussed in Chapter 12, represents one example. This problem is impossible to address by individual nation states on their own and requires collaboration between countries. However, such collaboration is difficult to achieve, as each individual country faces free-riding incentives – that is, it is attractive for individual countries to take a back seat and let other countries take measures to reduce greenhouse gas emissions.

Another example is the increasing internationalization of organized crime (see Chapter 9), as is, for example, clearly apparent in the area of drugs trafficking. Control of movements of goods and persons across borders has always been an essential component of the sovereignty of nation states. Legal arrangements such as passports, visas and entry permits are employed by states to manage immigration and import flows into a country. Border controls and entry barriers demarcate the territorial hegemony of the nation state. However, the growing international trade of drugs and its associated problems call for far-reaching cross-country cooperation in terms of border control.

What is more, borders are today not only vulnerable to the smuggling of goods but also to the illegal entry of individuals. The US has traditionally, for example, been subject to illegal immigration from the South, and now intends to build a wall on its border with Mexico, but one may wonder whether this will bring the number of illegal residents in the US down (see Chapter 6). In Europe, Italy is a country that, due to its long coastline, finds it particularly difficult to prevent the inflow of illegal immigrants from North Africa, which has surged since the 2015 European migrant crisis. Many of these immigrants are not even aiming to settle in Italy, but rather elsewhere in Europe, as the Schengen Agreement means that it is relatively easy to move between countries once one has entered one of the countries of the Schengen region.

From this perspective, the Italian coast guard is not just patrolling its own border but rather the border of the European Union. As such, Italy needs and deserves the help of other countries in protecting its coastal borders, yet other countries again face free-riding incentives.

An important threat to a well-functioning state apparatus is *corruption* (see Chapter 10), which endangers a proper and efficient execution of governmental tasks. In this context, the sociologist Max Weber (1978[1925]) outlines what a state bureaucracy should look like. His conception of a *modern bureaucracy* is based on a sharp distinction between public and private interests. More specifically, Weber's modern bureaucracy comprises the following elements:

1. A system of mandates and authorities that are organized according to clear rules;
2. A hierarchy whereby each governmental office is supervized by some higher office, with the bureaucracy as a whole falling under the supervision of the country's political leaders;
3. Written records of administration, and archiving of relevant papers;
4. Specialization across different governmental offices and civil servants that are well-trained for their tasks;
5. Civil servants execute their tasks in a spirit of objectivity and impartiality, free of ideological or other biases, in exchange for a salary;
6. A strict distinction between private and public means: civil servants manage any public money according to clearly defined rules and do not use it for private purposes, which would amount to corruption and warrant penalization.

To make the bureaucracy function properly, it should have a purely instrumental nature – that is, the apparatus of civil servants is just an instrument for achieving the goals of the highest political authority. The apparatus of civil servants should have no independent authority of its own. However, over the course of the twentieth century, it became clear that Weber's bureaucratic model is at odds with how many real-world bureaucracies actually operate. Consider the principle of the strict separation of private and public means under point six in the list above. According to Weber, this principle would prevent any corruption. Nevertheless, although most governments adopt this principle as well as the other principles from the list, corruption within their bureaucracies is still a widespread phenomenon.

There are fundamental limitations to Weber's model. According to the sociologist James Coleman (1990), the fundamental flaw in his theory is Weber mainly reasons from the perspective of the highest political authority and their interests, incentives, and motivations. In doing so, he largely overlooks that every individual employed within the bureaucracy is not just a chess piece that can be moved around in any way by the highest political authority and will always obey this authority, but instead has their own interests, incentives, and motivations, too. In this light, the *principal-agent model* outlined in Chapter 2 offers a more useful tool to understand the interactions between civil servants and their superiors, as it recognizes the divergent incentives faced by actors in different positions. In Chapter 10, we zoom further in on the principal-agent model as a tool to explain corruption.

Aside from the issue of corruption, the state expansion processes in the twentieth century have had the unintended consequence of making government bureaucracies more inefficient and harder to manage. Dramatic increases in the size of the bureaucratic organization have made it far more difficult for officials at higher positions to effectively supervize and manage their subordinates. The distance between managers and civil servants lower down has gradually widened, which has led to a decline in the efficiency with which information is transferred up the hierarchy, and with which commands are transferred down the hierarchy. Furthermore, the number of tasks carried out by the bureaucracy has increased as well, which implies that citizens have to follow a body of rules that is ever-growing in size and complexity. This, in turn, implies that citizens may not always receive optimal treatment by the government, and that the government has to assign additional bureaucratic resources to check whether citizens abide by its wide variety of rules.

The ultimate aim of any bureaucracy is to serve the public, by implementing the instructions of elected politicians. Yet, due to internal organizational dynamics, forms of behaviour may arise that run counter to this ultimate aim. For example, when there is competition between departments, a departmental head can enhance his own status by appointing more people to work for them, even when this does not increase their departmental output. Similarly, department heads may often find it worthwhile to spend their budgets before the end of the year, so as to not have their funding cut, even when this results in wasteful purchases that are not needed.

Another example is what is known as passing the buck, which is where the head at each organizational level hastily tries to find a person lower down to whom they can attribute any poor performance, so as to absolve themself of blame. This process leads to successive iterations of attribution until a level is reached where the blame cannot be passed any further. An internal squabble may then very well ensue. The ultimate effect is goal displacement: individuals directing effort and energy toward absolving themselves of blame rather than on figuring out how to solve the problem at hand. It is important to note, however, that such problems are not unique to government bureaucracies, but in fact occur in many large organizations, including large companies.

Political processes and governments' toolkit

In this chapter we have discussed the history and nature of the interventionist state. The reason for doing so is that the state is of crucial importance for tackling societal problems. We have also mentioned some of the transnational developments that require new ways of addressing problems. For example, the migration crisis affecting the European Union since 2015 presents new challenges, namely how to coordinate migration policy across 28 diverse nation states. It also increases the importance of supra-national institutions such as the EU Parliament, the Council of Ministers and the European Commission.

In much of our discussion so far we have, to some extent, assumed that when there is a societal problem that cannot be solved through private endeavour, the government will inevitably step in to solve it. However, is this a realistic assumption? The most plausible answer is in the negative. As already pointed out, many people and groups in society will have different views on when exactly state intervention is desirable, and democratic governments will have to negotiate and navigate between all these divergent opinions. While this is in itself a costly and time-consuming process, the end result may also simply be a decision to not intervene in society, even if it is clear that there is a problem that cannot be solved by private parties alone.

In addition, politicians and bureaucrats are not pure altruistic actors that only care about how to best serve society, but also have their own interests and incentives, such as a politician's interest in being re-elected. Among other things, this means that politicians sometimes may go against the best interests of society as a whole, if this can enhance their own position; see also the concepts of *short-termism* and the *political business cycle* introduced in Chapter 1. Moreover, they have to take into account organized private interests, such as labour unions, business lobbies, influential private donors, prominent advisory bodies and foreign governments. As a consequence, government policy may often respond more to pressure on the part of large vested interests rather than to voting on the part of individual citizens.

Furthermore, as already alluded to earlier in this chapter, governments do not have access to unlimited resources, and they can spend their money only once. This means that governments only have a limited capacity in terms of their intervention in society societal problems, and always have to trade-off different spending opportunities against each other. Accordingly, there may be cases in which governments do not intervene to address a particular societal problem, even if they ideally would want to, simply because some other problem is generally considered more pressing.

As a final observation, while we have in this chapter discussed state intervention in a fairly abstract sense, there are many different ways in which states can concretely intervene in society. Among the most widely used policy tools are taxes on income, wealth or specific types of consumption; product regulations and production standards; subsidies for specific goods or activities; insurance for certain social and economic risks; financial benefits for particular groups in society; direct government spending on things such as infrastructure; state ownership of companies; bans on specific activities; regulated planning procedures; and information campaigns.

Aside from traditional forms of state intervention, states can also intervene in more subtle ways. This is pointed out by the behavioural economist and Nobel Prize laureate Richard Thaler, and the legal scholar Cass Sunstein (2008). The policy strategy of *nudging* that they propose has become popular among many governments in recent years. For example, under David Cameron the British government established a "behavioural insights team", which became better known as the "nudge unit". In line with Daniel Kahneman's (2011) research on cognitive biases that we referred to in Chapter 2, Thaler and Sunstein contend that people often make poor decisions, even about things they deeply care about, such as pensions and our planet, or spend a lot of thought on. They additionally argue that policymakers can harness insights on cognitive biases to present choices in a different way to people, thus nudging them towards decisions that are more optimal for themselves as well as society.

The key to nudging that is that policymakers only change the "choice architecture", without actually coercing individuals into certain behaviour. As such, it does not directly curtail people's freedom of choice. Nudging is also regarded as a cheap way of intervention in times when governments are forced to cut expenses. That said, nudging does not only have benefits and is not embraced by everyone. For example, from within philosophical circles, nudging has been criticized for covertly trying to manipulate citizens' behaviour, thus at least indirectly meddling with the freedom of choice. Moreover, nudging is accused of being a form of *governmental paternalism*, whereby governments may start to influence citizens' decisions in all kinds of previously unregulated areas of life, in ways so as to make citizens do what the government believes is best for them.

Recommended readings

- Vito Tanzi and Ludger Schuknecht (2000) provide a comprehensive overview of the enormous rise of public spending since 1870. Drawing on many insightful examples from across the industrialized world, they describe the rise of government spending, and also address the links between government spending and economic performance. Finally, they discuss how public spending has come under pressure in recent decades and how various countries have reformed their public sector in response to this.
- In light of the 2008 financial crisis and the Great Recession that followed, Wolfgang Streeck (2014) reflects on the relationships between capitalism, the state and democracy, and how these have changed since the 1970s. Taking a critical view, he describes the increasing tensions between the interests of voters, business and governments, and the transformation from "tax states" to "debt states". He also pays special attention to how the European Union has changed European states.
- While this chapter focuses on state-related issues, the concepts of state and nation are tightly interwoven. From this perspective, Andreas Wimmer (2018) provides a fascinating study in which he attempts to answer the question why some states have succeeded at building an integrated nation, whereas others are characterized by political inequality, contentious politics, or inter-group conflict. Among other things, he shows that the state's capacity to deliver public goods is of vital importance for uniting its citizens.

Bibliography

Coleman, James S. 1990. *Foundations of Social Theory*. Cambridge, MA: Belknap Press of Harvard University Press.

Fouquet, Roger, and Stephen Broadberry. 2015. "Seven Centuries of European Economic Growth and Decline". *Journal of Economic Perspectives* 29:227–244.

Kahneman, Daniel. 2011. *Thinking, Fast and Slow*. New York, NY: Farrar, Straus and Giroux.

Smith, Adam. 1776. *An Inquiry into the Nature and Causes of the Wealth of Nations*. http://www.earlymoderntexts.com/assets/pdfs/smith1776_34.pdf.

Streeck, Wolfgang. 2014. *Buying Time: The Delayed Crisis of Democratic Capitalism*. New York, NY: Verso.

Tanzi, Vito, and Ludger Schuknecht. 2000. *Public Spending in the 20th Century: A Global Perspective*. Cambridge: Cambridge University Press.

Thaler, Richard H., and Cass R. Sunstein. 2008. *Nudge: Improving Decisions about Health, Wealth, and Happiness*. New Haven, CT: Yale University Press.

Van Bavel, Bas. 2016. *The Invisible Hand: How Market Economies Have Emerged and Declined Since AD 500*. Oxford: Oxford University Press.

Von Humboldt, Wilhelm. 1980[1792]. "Ideen zu einem Versuch, die Gränzen der Wirksamkeit des Staats zu Bestimmen". Pp. 56–233 in: *Werke in Fünf Bänden* (Complete Works in Five Volumes), Volume 5, edited by Andreas Flitner and Klaus Giel. Darmstadt: Wissenschaftliche Buchgesellschaft.

Weber, Max. 1978[1925]. *Economy and Society: An Outline of Interpretive Sociology* (Wirtschaft und Gesellschaft: Grundriss der Verstehenden Soziologie). Berkeley, CA: University of California Press.

Wimmer, Andreas. 2018. *Nation Building – Why Some Countries Come Together While Others Fall Apart*. Princeton, NJ: Princeton University Press.

Zimbalist, Andrew, and Howard J. Sherman. 1984. *Comparing Economic Systems: A Political-Economic Approach*. Cambridge, MA: Academic Press.

4 Welfare states: Affordability and perverse incentives

Chapter overview

Welfare state policies are a kind of state intervention designed to help citizens pool social risks and to guarantee a minimum standard of material well-being. In this chapter, we begin by outlining the historical development of welfare states during the twentieth century. Subsequently, we consider how welfare states are viewed by different political ideologies. We proceed to demarcate different types of welfare states, based on the degree to which they guarantee the economic well-being of their citizens. We then discuss how welfare states may create perverse incentives, which lead to undesirable societal outcomes such as benefit fraud and welfare dependence. At the end of the chapter, we turn to the affordability of welfare states. Here we review the complex relationship between government expenditures and economic growth, as well as the drivers of welfare state retrenchment.

Worlds of welfare

The welfare state is an institution of social insurance and redistribution organized by the government. It is designed to ensure the collective welfare of citizens by helping them to pool risks, by cushioning them against economic shocks, and by guaranteeing them a minimum level of material well-being. The degree to which the welfare state focuses on social insurance as opposed to pure redistribution of resources varies across countries.

Three main types of welfare state can be distinguished (Esping-Andersen 1990). First, there is the *liberal welfare state* of the Anglosphere (US, Canada, Australia etc.), which focuses on providing means-tested benefit programmes for the poorest members of society. Second, there is the *corporatist welfare state* of central Europe (Germany, Austria, France etc.), which is centred around social insurance schemes for the working population. Third, there is the *universal welfare state* of the Nordic countries (Sweden, Denmark, Norway etc.), which provides comprehensive social programmes to all citizens, regardless of need.

In the final decades of the twentieth century, a widespread feeling emerged that the welfare state had reached the limits of what it was capable of achieving. During the 1980s and the

1990s, the ideology of *laissez-faire economics*, which asserted that the government should intervene as little as possible in the economy, regained intellectual prominence. This ideology was promoted by economists such as Milton Friedman and was, among others, implemented by the Thatcher government in the UK and the Reagan government of the US.

One important corollary of laissez-faire economics was that welfare policies could have perverse incentives. For example, providing generous unemployment benefits might encourage people to stay unemployed; providing benefits specifically to single mothers might encourage couples to get divorced. Another important corollary of laissez-faire economics was that the welfare state would eventually prove unaffordable, given the large amounts of tax money that were required to pay for it. In Europe, concern over the welfare state's affordability has increased since the financial crisis of 2008, due to the large public debts that many countries accumulated in its immediate aftermath. As Western populations continue to age, thereby further increasing the costs of the welfare state, some commentators have warned that public debt will become unsustainable unless cuts are made to healthcare, pensions, and other social welfare programmes.

The development of the welfare state

The Oxford English Dictionary describes the *welfare state* as "a system whereby the state undertakes to protect the health and well-being of its citizens, especially those in financial or social need, by means of grants, pensions, and other benefits". The welfare state arose in Western countries in the years following the Second World War. However, its foundations, in the form of basic social security programmes, had already been laid down after the Wall Street crash of 1929 (see Chapter 11). The mass unemployment that ensued during the 1930s had led to considerable social disruption in nearly all Western countries. It was widely felt that the markets had failed, and that government intervention was therefore needed to maintain full employment and to achieve consistent economic growth. The success of large-scale economic planning during the Second World War seemed to refute the claim that free markets without any government intervention were necessary for the economy to function properly. In addition, some policymakers feared that if the government did not make efforts to shore up the welfare of the working classes, they might rise up and revolt against the state, as the Bolshevik revolutionaries had done in Communist Russia.

Consequently, so-called mixed economies developed during the 1950s and 1960s, influence amongst others by the work of the British economist John Maynard Keynes. He had argued that the business cycle (the meandering upward trajectory of GDP in which periods of expansion are punctuated by economic recessions) could be dampened by means of counter-cyclical fiscal and monetary policy. During periods of expansion, the government would need to cut spending and slow down the rate of money creation so as to prevent demand from outstripping supply. During periods of contraction, the government would need to increase spending and speed up the rate of money creation so as to prevent supply from outstripping demand. As part of the post-war consensus on how society was best organized, it was agreed that an optimal combination of social equality and economic efficiency could be achieved within the capitalist system. Accordingly, the outright state control of the communist countries and the laissez-faire policies of the nineteenth century were both rejected.

It is useful to view the building of the welfare state within the context of the three political ideologies that we demarcated in Chapter 1: socialism, liberalism, and conservatism. Socialists tend to view the welfare state as something that is needed to help poor, weak, and vulnerable citizens, who would otherwise be exploited by more powerful members of society. The most avid socialists advocate a very large and universal welfare state, which permits individuals to pursue their own goals without having to rely on their families, communities or any market actors. As such, they regard the welfare state as a valuable public good. Indeed, they argue that a state of affairs in which no member of society has to rely on any other is inherently desirable.

Liberals, on the other hand, tend to view the welfare state as something that interferes with people's freedom to make their own choices and spend their own money. In their eyes, the welfare state thus represents a coercive transfer of resources from some individuals to others that undermines fundamental freedoms. They also believe that welfare state policies distort the incentives of the poor, thereby preventing them from rising out of poverty. The most avid liberals advocate cutting down on all welfare programmes. They argue that the workings of free markets are sufficient to raise hard-working individuals out of poverty in the long run.

Conservatives, in turn, tend to view the welfare state as a valuable institution that averts the worst manifestations of societal deprivation, but which should not be allowed to grow unchecked, lest it undermine crucial solidary bonds of family and community. The most avid conservatives advocate basic welfare programmes, but strongly oppose any policies that might lead to family breakdown or weaken the ethic of personal charity that prevails within small communities. In other words, conservatives accept the welfare state as a tool for achieving a society free from abject squalor, but consider it as a threat to family ties, community and social stability.

The various institutional changes that culminated in the establishment of the welfare state during the post-war period were famously chronicled by the sociologist Thomas Marshall in his work *Citizenship and Social Class* (1950). He argued that citizenship in the West had developed in three successive stages. From the eighteenth century onwards, citizens were granted *civil rights*, such as freedom of speech and religion, fair administration of justice, and protection of private property. Then from the nineteenth century onwards, citizens were granted *political rights*, most notably the opportunity to participate in the political process through the ballot, which was extended to increasingly large groups – and eventually all non-institutionalized adults. In the twentieth century, according to Marshall, citizens were finally granted *social* and *economic rights*, such as access to education, healthcare, social security, and housing. Of course, to what extent all individuals within society (including minorities of various kinds) have equal access to all of these rights is still a matter of intense debate.

How different welfare states manage social risks

Since its very inception, the welfare state has been designed to mitigate the most extreme social risks that citizens may face. Risk can in this context be broadly defined as the chance of a negative event occurring. In industrial societies, people face a variety of risks, such as having an accident at work, being made unemployed, suffering from ill-health, having to combine work and childcare, or being stranded in old age without any living relatives. In agrarian societies, these risks were partly mitigated within smaller social groups such as the family. In early industrialized societies, they were partly mitigated via civic society institutions such as worker associations and charity organizations. It was only in the twentieth century – and during the post-war period in particular – that the state itself assumed responsibility for ameliorating social risks.

Observe however that, even today, not all social risks come under the purview of the state. In most Western countries, car insurance, home insurance, life insurance, and many other forms of insurance are all provided by the market. Private insurance works as follows: a category of individuals who are at risk of some sort of negative event is identified; the fraction of those people who will be exposed to the event is estimated through statistical modelling; then the total size of a fund needed to compensate all those who will eventually be exposed to the event is calculated; and, finally, the premium that purchasers of the insurance policy will need to pay is derived. The insurer will set this premium such that they can make a profit on selling the insurance policy. However, not all insurance policies will in practice be profitable for private entrepreneurs, for example because the people they are aimed at cannot afford the premiums that they are required to pay. In such cases, private insurers will not find it profitable to provide insurance. According to the early proponents of the welfare state, such a situation calls for the state to step in.

During the first two decades after the Second World War, Western societies flourished economically, with virtually uninterrupted economic growth. The labour force comprised a large base of unskilled and semi-skilled workers, as well as a smaller elite of technical and administrative personnel. Women's labour force participation was rather low. The family was generally considered to be the building block of society, and economic life was built around this conviction: the husband served as the breadwinner, while his wife took care of the household (the *male breadwinner model*; see Chapter 8). Existing pension systems were affordable, because a typical male would start working at the age of 16 and then work for more than 40 years. Given that life expectancy was much lower than nowadays (for example, in the UK it was 67 in 1950 vis-à-vis 82 in 2018), a working career was followed by, on average, only seven years of retirement. Because birth rates had been low in many Western countries in the 1930s and 1940s, there was a relative shortage of labour, meaning that wages were high. Moreover, governments were facilitating full employment through Keynesian demand management. In practice, this resulted in a low overall risk of unemployment.

However, by the mid-1970s, the economic situation had changed markedly. Many countries now experienced the phenomenon of *stagflation*: high inflation, combined with low growth and high unemployment. There were a number of reasons for this trend break. First, there was the 1973 oil crisis, in which the Organisation of Petroleum Exporting Countries (OPEC) established a production cartel, causing the price of oil to rise fourfold in just a few months. Second, there was the collapse of the Bretton Woods system of monetary management, which had required each Western country to maintain a more-or-less fixed exchange rate with every other currency. Third, as transportation costs diminished and political tensions in the Pacific subsided, manufacturing began to move from the industrialized West to the industrializing East, where wages were lower and regulations less onerous. Fourth, women moved into the labour force in large numbers, which increased the supply of labour relative to demand, thereby bidding down wages.

After the Second Word War, as noted previously, three different types of welfare states developed, each with a different approach to how much responsibility the state carried with respect to protecting its citizens against various risks. In particular, one could distinguish liberal, corporatist, and universal welfare states. The Danish sociologist Gøsta Esping-Andersen (1990) arrived at this classification via his *decommodification index*, which measures the overall degree to which states guarantee the economic well-being of their citizens – as opposed to having them rely on their families, communities, and the market. The index captures quantities such as the duration and level of unemployment benefits, the level of compensation when one becomes ill or disabled, and the generosity of public pensions. Although Esping-Andersen's classification has been subjected to various types of criticism (see also below), his three-pronged schema is still useful. The three welfare state regimes can be described as follows.

Liberal welfare states (sometimes also referred to as Anglo-Saxon welfare states) take a minimalist approach, directing assistance overwhelmingly towards those at the very bottom of society, in particular disabled people and those below a certain income threshold. Society is therefore divided into two parts: first, a majority of citizens who have the means to secure their own welfare through the market; and second, a minority of citizens who do not have the means to do so, and who consequently depend on government support. Welfare programmes in liberal welfare states tend to be means-tested, which implies that only people who meet certain criteria (e.g., earning less than a certain amount per month and having no savings to fall back on) are eligible. The US, the UK, Canada, Australia, and New Zealand are all examples of liberal welfare states. Indeed, this particular system tends to be found in countries where competition is deemed central to a flourishing society, and where a large role is assigned to markets. The overall level of welfare provisions is modest, and – as mentioned previously – heavily dependent on one's income and wealth. In general, the social rights of citizens are comparatively limited, so as to ensure minimal distortion of their market incentives.

In *corporatist welfare states* (sometimes also referred to as Christian-Democratic welfare states), individual professions are considered to be closed membership groups in which members are connected by mutual solidarity and cooperate with one another in order to promote their collective interests. Social security programmes differ from one profession to the next, and are adjusted to the particular risks faced by each profession. Participation in these programmes is mandatory. Compared to people who are working or used to work, those without much work experience are constrained in their access to welfare programmes. As the family is deemed to be an important social unit worthy of preservation, the corporatist welfare state typically provides family allowances. In general, many corporatist welfare states developed from close cooperation between church and state. Italy, France, Belgium, Germany, and Austria are examples.

Universal welfare states (sometimes also referred to as Social-Democratic welfare states) provide comprehensive social programmes to all citizens, regardless of need or employment history. There is minimal means-testing of recipients, and no variation in programme content across different sectors of the population. There is a sense of solidarity not merely between members of a single professional category, or between members of a precarious underclass, but between all members of society. Programmes related to unemployment benefits, pensions, family allowances, and healthcare tend to be generous in nature and have universal application. The overarching aim is to maximize the autonomy and the independence of each citizen, whatever their exact position in society. The universal welfare state is costly in terms of the amount of tax revenue that is required to maintain it, but is comparatively efficient insofar as administration costs are low – given that the same policies tend to apply to everyone.

Denmark, Finland, Norway, Sweden and, to a lesser extent, The Netherlands all are examples of universal welfare states.

A recent analysis by Vincent Navarro (2011) suggests that the division of welfare state regimes as proposed by Esping-Andersen lacks an important distinction – one that became very palpable in the years following the 2008 financial crisis. According to Navarro, the Eurozone countries of Greece, Spain, and Portugal all share a common political history, namely that fascist-like military dictators ruled from the late 1930s or early 1940s until the late 1970s. This authoritarian heritage has contributed to a relatively weak welfare state in each of these countries. At the same time, Greece, Spain and Portugal have the most police officers per 100,000 inhabitants, as a mark of its authoritarian past. As Navarro argues, successive governments in these countries have cut taxes and engaged in wasteful infrastructure spending in cahoots with special interests, which – until the financial crisis – was masked by rapid economic growth. According to Navarro, the economic problems in these countries, and the *Eurozone crisis* they gave rise to, can only be properly understood within the foregoing historical context.

The costs and effectiveness of welfare states

Compared to earlier types of state intervention, welfare state policies involve a lot of government spending. The steep increase in government spending since 1960, as revealed in Figure 3.1, is a clear indication of this. However, government spending on welfare as a percentage of GDP differs noticeably between the three systems. It is highest in the universal system, middling in the corporatist system, and lowest in the liberal system. Especially the difference between liberal and universal welfare state regimes is pronounced.

Compared to liberal welfare states, universal ones provide social security for a greater range of risks and of a more generous nature. This higher spending, in turn, also requires higher taxation. Indeed, in the US – as a textbook example of a liberal welfare state – the overall tax burden is much lower than in the Nordic countries – as textbook examples of universal welfare states. Of course, the exact amount of spending on social programmes is affected by numerous factors. For example, the current state of the economy will matter, as higher levels of unemployment require larger public outlays on unemployment benefits, holding all else equal. There is also, of course, change within countries over time, depending on the political colour of the government. Within any given welfare system, left-wing parties typically spend more tax money on redistribution and social programmes than right-wing parties.

Figure 4.1 displays figures for spending on social programmes in six welfare states between 1980 and 2016. In line with our previous discussion, Figure 4.1 shows that liberal welfare states, such as the UK and the US, tend to have the lowest levels of social spending. Until 1995, Sweden – as the only universal welfare state within this sample – had the highest level of social spending, followed by France and Germany – as two corporatist welfare states. However, due to a big drop in social expenditures in Sweden between 1995 and 2000, Sweden has since been surpassed by France, which now has the highest level of social spending. In the Section "Limits to the welfare state", we zoom in on the Swedish case and explain what caused its decline in social spending after 1995.

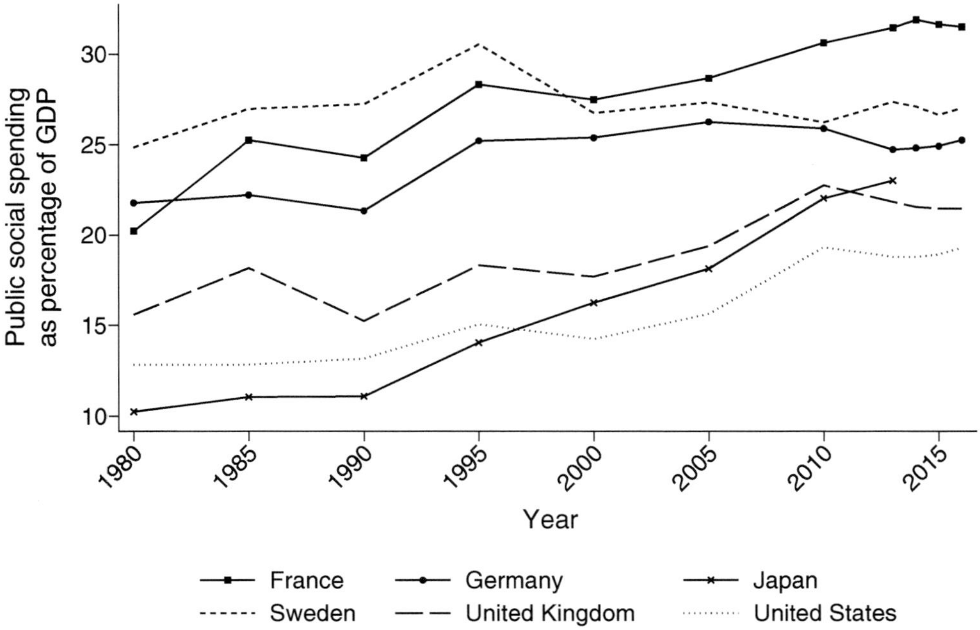

Figure 4.1 Public spending on social programmes in six welfare states, 1980–2016
Note: Data are from the OECD Social Expenditure Database (SOCX).

In terms of trends over time, we can divide Figure 4.1 roughly into three periods. First, most countries experienced a slow and modest increase in social spending from 1980– 2005. Second, following the 2008 financial crisis, some countries (Sweden, Japan, the UK, and the US) experienced more abrupt increases between 2005 and 2010, while in other countries (France and Germany) social expenditures remained relatively flat during this window. Third, from 2010 onwards, public social expenditures have not changed much in most of the countries. However, as already alluded to, the reader should be aware that changes in government spending as a percentage of GDP should not be taken as firmly indicative of policy changes. This is exactly because events like economic recessions can give rise to marked increases in public social spending (e.g., the amount of money spent on unemployment benefits increasing drastically), without any policy changes taking place.

Figure 4.2 next draws a link between levels of public social spending and the percentage of children living below the poverty line in different countries. This figure shows a negative relationship, with the child poverty rate on average being lower in countries with higher levels of social spending. However, the relationship is not particularly strong, with the Republic of Korea, for example, having a low level of social spending combined with a low child poverty rate, while countries such as Spain and Greece combine much higher levels of social spending with also much higher rates of child poverty. Overall, the cross-country correlation coefficient between social spending and child poverty amounts to −0.37.

Whereas this negative number might suggest that social welfare spending has some effect in reducing child poverty, we have to be careful with drawing such conclusions. After all, we are

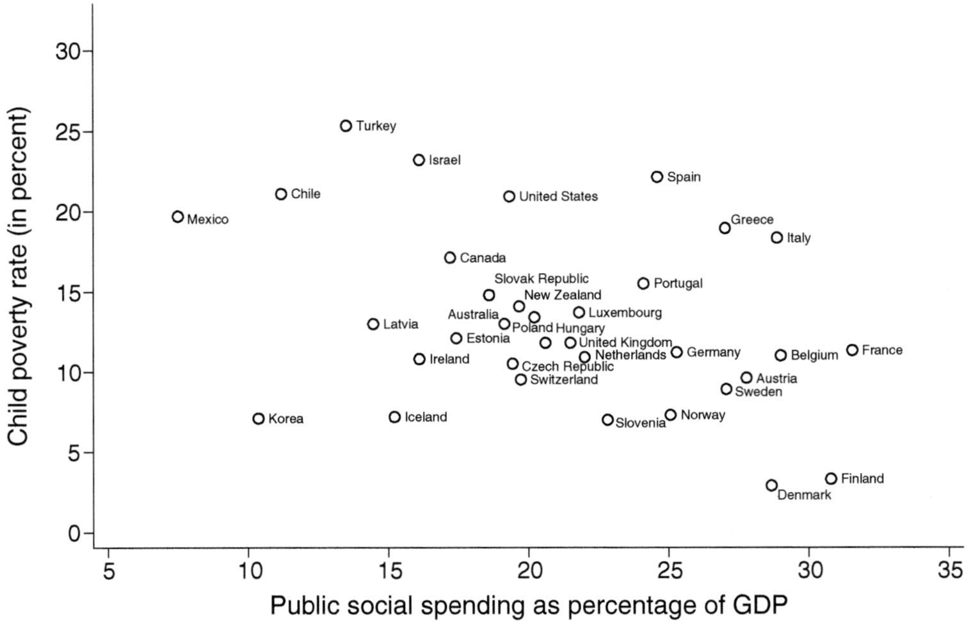

Figure 4.2 The relationship between public social spending and child poverty

Note: Data are from the OECD Social Expenditure Database (SOCX). The public social spending data are for 2016 or the latest available year before that; the child poverty data are for 2017 or the latest available year before that.

merely looking at the relationship between two factors at a single point in time, and there are many other factors that might influence this relationship. As a result, the fact that countries with higher social spending tend to have lower child poverty rates does not necessarily imply that *increases* in social spending will also be associated with *decreases* in child poverty.

In Figure 4.3 we shift our attention to the cross-country relationship between social welfare spending and income inequality as measured by the Gini coefficient. In the section "Measuring inequality: Lorenz curves and Gini coefficients" in Chapter 7, we provide more details on how Gini coefficients are calculated; for now it suffices to know that a higher Gini coefficient corresponds to a higher degree of income inequality. At first glance, Figure 4.3 suggests that countries with higher levels of public social spending have a lower Gini coefficient and thus a more equal distribution of income. In line with this observation, the cross-country correlation coefficient equals −0.58.

However, upon closer inspection, this negative association seems largely driven by the inclusion of Mexico and Chile, as two countries with extremely low levels of public social spending and extremely high levels of income inequality. If we remove these two countries from Figure 4.3, there is no longer a negative relationship between social spending and income inequality, but rather no relationship at all. This suggests that the impact of social spending on income inequality is not as pronounced as one might expect given the clear differences between universal, corporatist, and liberal welfare states, and their underlying political ideologies. Yet, again, it is important to stress that we cannot interpret Figure 4.3 in a causal fashion.

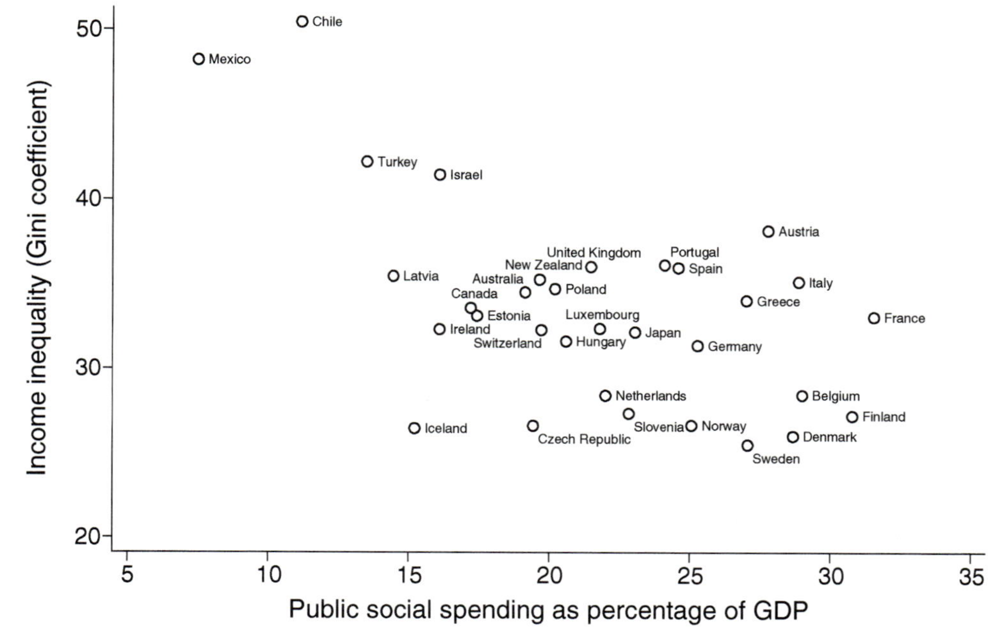

Figure 4.3 The relationship between public social spending and income inequality

Note: Data are from the OECD Social Expenditure Database (SOCX). The public social spending data are for 2016 or the latest available year before that; the income inequality data are for 2016 or the latest available year before that. See Chapter 7 for more details on the calculation of the Gini coefficient.

Welfare states and the problem of perverse incentives

One of the big problems of the welfare state is that its social care arrangements could have perverse consequences, such as abuse of social programmes by those not eligible for them, welfare dependence, and black-market labour. One of the earliest, but also most controversial studies in this regard is the book *Losing Ground* (1984) by the political scientist Charles Murray. He claimed that anti-poverty programmes introduced by Lyndon Johnson's Great Society initiative had had the opposite effect from that which had been intended, namely an increase in the total number of poor people, rather than a decrease. He argued that welfare programmes distort individuals' decision-making by reducing the incentive to find work, and by reducing the incentive to retrain if that is what is needed to find a new job. Murray posited that if an individual has the choice between working for a low wage or taking benefits of equivalent value, then they will rationally opt for the benefits. Insofar as this disincentivizes them from taking entry-level jobs, where they could build up skills and acquire job experience, it may permanently blunt their labour market prospects.

Higher unemployment and poverty are not the only phenomena that Murray attributes to the expansion of the US welfare state during the 1960s. He contends that rising single motherhood, rising teen parenthood, the increasing use of drugs, and the increase in other forms of criminality may all have been exacerbated by the Great Society programmes. For example, some welfare benefits were only made available to single mothers, which – according to Murray – had the effect of making single motherhood relatively more attractive. In the absence of such welfare benefits, women would have had more incentives to obtain a promise of marriage from men before having sex with them; and couples going through a spat would have had more incentives to resolve their difficulties.

Murray's analysis was eagerly cited by conservative and liberal hardliners, who advocated restricting access to welfare programmes or abolishing them altogether. By the late 1990s, policy changes were implemented in the US in an attempt to eliminate some of the perverse incentives embodied in the Great Society programmes. Murray's book was cited as part of the inspiration for these changes. However, Murray's book provoked a fierce debate among social scientists, many of whom contested his conclusions. Indeed, according to many critics, a more plausible explanation for the rise in poverty, unemployment, and single parenthood since the early 1970s is the deindustrialization of American cities, and the consequent loss of decent jobs for low-skilled and semi-skilled workers. Nonetheless, Murray's work is of interest, given that he was one of the first social scientists to draw attention to potential perverse incentives offered by government programmes and their harmful effects at the macro level. Below we discuss several other examples of perverse effects.

Unfit for labour: The Dutch case

In 1995, it turned out that 12.3 percent of the Dutch working-age population was registered as temporarily or permanently ill or disabled (Van de Goor 1997). In fact, the number of people on disability benefits increased from 165,000 in 1968 to nearly one million by 2000. Given that the working-age population in 2000 encompassed less than nine million people, it seems rather implausible that such a large proportion of them were genuinely unfit for labour. Indeed, the Dutch disability register comprised – relatively speaking – three to four times as many people as in comparable European countries at the time. A commission was set up to look into this phenomenon: the Donner Commission. In 2001, it concluded that the precipitous increase in the number of Dutch people on disability benefits was mostly due to the eligibility conditions having been far too lenient. The principal-agent model, which we discussed in Chapter 2, and which we here extend to a *principal-agent-client model*, provides a concise explanation for how this situation arose.

Recall that the original principal-agent model concerns an interaction between a supervisor (principal) and a supervisee (agent). In the principal-agent-client model we add a third party, namely a *client*. In the context of the disability register, the three players are: the responsible politician (the principal), the occupational health physician lower down in the bureaucracy (the agent), and the individual whose fitness for labour is to be assessed (the client).

If the occupational physician (as agent), to begin with, deems the individual to be unfit for labour, this does not have any financial consequences for themself. The effect of their actions on the disability rolls, and therefore on the overall expenditure on disability benefits, will be imperceptible. Another important point is that, because individuals can appeal decisions made by occupational physicians (which can prove time-consuming and expensive), physicians will tend to diagnose individuals as unfit for labour relatively quickly in case of doubt.

For example, if an individual turns up with psychological complaints that are hard to test, the occupational physician may still end up diagnosing them as unable to work. To add to this, occupational physicians were often overburdened, having to judge each case in only five to ten minutes.

As to the responsible politician (as principal), they are generally not in a position to criticize the judgments of the occupational physician. Given the physician's surplus of knowledge vis-à-vis the politician when it comes to medical science, the physician is simply better qualified to determine whether the individual is healthy or not. As such, the specialized nature of the physician's job gives them a high degree of autonomy, and makes their work difficult to monitor for the responsible politician further up the bureaucratic hierarchy.

The individual (as client), in turn, will weigh up the costs and benefits of different actions. In some cases, they may conclude that going on the disability register makes them better off than changing jobs or attempting to access unemployment benefits. As a consequence, a good number of healthy people that could actually work are likely to apply for disability benefits. This is especially the case if the disability benefits are relatively generous, as they were in the Netherlands at the time.

The Donner Commission (2001) concluded that this complete system of non-aligned incentives and limited monitoring opportunities was to blame for the dramatic increase in the number of Dutch citizens on the disability rolls. Indeed, the previously described incentive structures can lead to unsustainably high expenditures on disability benefits if they are not somehow kept in check. In other words: a process of strategic interaction at the micro level can lead to an undesirable outcome at the macro level. The question then is, given the incentives faced by the various actors, how can costs be kept under control? The answer is that the responsible politician – as the principal – has to find a way to make the incentives faced by the occupational physician (agent) and the potential applicant for disability benefits (client) compatible with their own objectives.

There are various ways to achieve this. First, the politician can reduce the generosity of the benefits, reducing the individual's incentive to opt for disability over work. Second, the politician can limit the choice set of the occupational physicians, by putting forth stricter guidelines, and penalizing those physicians who do not follow them. This should reduce the incentives for physicians to accept individuals onto the disability rolls too easily. A third way for the politician to address the rising disability expenditures is via introducing so-called *premium differentiation*. The premium is a fee that an employer has to pay when employees of their company are determined to be unfit for labour. Premium differentiation would imply that the premium rises as more employees are deemed unfit for labour. As such, these premiums provide employers with incentives to find alternative work for people who become unfit for their current job, thus keeping them off the disability rolls. In particular, since many health complaints stem from a lack of job satisfaction, employers have an interest to identify health complaints at an early stage, and – if necessary – to move the relevant employee to a different place of work or alter his working conditions in some other way.

In view of its escalating disability rolls, the Dutch government in the end opted for an approach that combined all of these policy measures. Together, these various policies proved highly effective, substantially reducing the country's disability rolls by the mid-2000s.

Perverse effects of QUANGOs: The performance paradox

Measures to increase government efficiency are nearly always taken with the best intentions in mind. Unfortunately, these measures can have unintended negative consequences. Since the early 1990s, some Western governments have adopted the policy of making certain parts of the bureaucratic apparatus largely independent. Such organizations are called *QUANGOs*, which is short for quasi-autonomous non-governmental organizations.

According to the public policy scholar Sandra Van Thiel (2000), QUANGOs were created with the following four objectives in mind: (1) increased efficiency in the execution of public policy; (2) greater involvement of citizens in the execution of public policy; (3) more technocratic oversight by experts; (4) greater time available for politicians to focus on developing efficacious policies. Examples from the Netherlands that Van Thiel mentions are agencies such as the immigration and naturalization service, the national mail service, and the pension fund for civil servants. A well-known example in the UK is the British Broadcasting Corporation (BBC), although this has been an independent body for many decades.

Despite the honourable objectives, the establishment of QUANGOs has had unintended consequences. Chief among these is the so-called *performance paradox*, which refers to the fact that there is often only a weak correlation between reported performance indicators and actual, objectively-measured performance (Meyer and Gupta 1994). The principal-agent model can once again be invoked to explain this paradox. The heads of the QUANGOs (the agents) must report to a government minister (the principal). Typically, the head of a QUANGO will meet with the minister and will present them with a report summarizing the QUANGO's performance. Often prior to such a meeting, the head will have subordinates take measures to adjust the data in such a way as to give the impression that the QUANGO is performing better than it actually is ("fudging the numbers"). This is especially likely to happen if the government has given the QUANGO very specific performance targets.

A well-known case of the performance paradox arose in the British National Health Service (NHS) in the late 1990s (Van Thiel 2000). At that time the NHS implemented a rule that patients should not be on a waiting list for an operation longer than two years. It was initially concluded, on the basis of reports given to the government, that waiting times had indeed decreased following the introduction of this new rule. However, further inspection revealed that what had actually happened was that patients' dates of registration for operations had been meddled with, having in reality occurred earlier than they were recorded in the books. Such "creative bookkeeping" made it look like total waiting times had decreased, while this was actually not the case. This deception originated from a combination of very rigid performance targets, paired with a lack of effective monitoring.

The performance paradox is not unique to QUANGOs. It can also be observed in non-independent government organizations. Indeed, in recent years, governments have been investing heavily in performance measurement. The call for more data pertaining to performance evaluation has had important unintended consequences. For example, the excessive emphasis on performance criteria, benchmarks and rankings has led essentially all American universities to model themselves on the most prestigious Ivy League institutions – even though this model is not necessarily appropriate for all universities.

Similarly, the common practice among many governments to fund universities in proportion to the number of graduating students can also have perverse consequences. Such funding arrangements increase the pressure on universities to attract as many students as possible and subsequently give them an easy time obtaining their degree. As a result, more and more people will get a university degree, but the quality of these degrees will diminish – a phenomenon known as *degree inflation*. Once again, this shows how difficult it is to develop incentive structures that do not give rise to perverse effects.

Moral hazard and the decreasing influence of regulation

One of the big issues of welfare states concerns the number of situations where *moral hazard* (see Chapter 2) occurs. A prime example concerns the job search behaviour of people that are receiving unemployment benefits. Especially when the unemployment benefits are generous in terms of their payment level and the duration for which they can be received, many unemployed individuals may stop looking for a new job. After all, looking for a job is time-consuming and difficult, and benefit recipients know that the state will effectively bear the costs of their prolonged unemployment. Benefit recipients thus increase their risk of continued unemployment, knowing that the state will carry the burden of this risk.

There are various ways for states to respond to such moral hazard. One way to react is by making benefits less generous. The macro-level result is that the costs of social programmes go down, and the system remains affordable. However, the obvious downside is that citizens who actually need help no longer have access to the benefits they previously enjoyed. Alternatively, states can also react by introducing intrusive regulations and new forms of means-testing in an attempt to limit abuse and overuse of the system. Yet, this too may have unforeseen negative consequences.

Indeed, the expansion of rules leads to what is called *rule densification*, which – paradoxically – may increase rather than decrease the number offences committed. After all, with a plethora of rules, one may not realistically expect citizens to be fully informed about all of them. In addition, more regulation, by its very nature, leads to more offences being committed: there are then simply more rules that can be violated. In addition, as the regulatory thicket grows ever more tangled, the monitoring of compliance requires increasingly draconian forms of state intervention. A rather scary example is the introduction in China of a pervasive system of algorithmic surveillance that constructs detailed profiles of each citizen and calculates individual "citizen scores". In China's surveillance state this score determines, among other things, how quickly an individual gets access to certain public services.

Limits to the welfare state

Over the years, the costs of the welfare state have increased in all countries. This state of affairs often alarms economists, especially when it is combined with a hefty public debt level. One of the concerns is that the larger the share of a country's income that is spent by the state, the smaller the remaining share available for consumption and investment by individuals and firms. Reduced consumption and investment could, in turn, harm longer-term economic growth.

Due to growing welfare spending, the ideology of laissez-faire economics therefore regained traction in many Western countries in the 1980s. To many people, it seemed that the welfare state had reached its limits, and many governments (most notably the Reagan government in the US and the Thatcher government in the UK) began implementing policies such as lowering tax rates, downsizing welfare schemes, and deregulating labour markets (Pierson 1994). This trend continued into the 1990s, with clear evidence of welfare state retrenchment in many Western European countries (Korpi 2003).

An age-old question in economics is that of how high taxes can get, as a percentage of GDP, before economic performance is significantly harmed. In the years after the Second World War, a number of American economists argued that any public spending beyond 25 percent of GDP would seriously damage the economy. However, a number of European countries actually reached higher levels of public spending relatively soon afterwards, without any disaster unfolding. In the 1970s, the economist Milton Friedman suggested that 60 percent of GDP was a critical threshold, above which a country risked not only economic collapse but even the downfall of democracy and freedom. Yet, again, reality showed to be more complex, as several countries crossed this threshold without any (immediate) disaster unfolding.

Figure 4.4 plots average public social spending as a percentage of GDP from 2002 to 2015 against average annual growth in GDP per capita over the same period, for all countries in the OECD for the relevant data are available. As it turns out, there is a moderately strong, negative association between social spending and economic growth: the cross-country correlation coefficient is -0.54. In other words, countries with high levels of social spending (such as Denmark, Finland, and France) generally witnessed lower economic growth than countries with lower levels of social spending (such as Turkey, Estonia, and Ireland).

However, as for the earlier figures in this chapter, it is important to emphasize that such a cross-country comparison does not allow us to conclude that higher levels of social spending *cause* lower economic growth. For example, if we ignore Mexico, Chile, Turkey and Ireland as evident outliers, the remaining countries that experienced the highest growth over this time period (such as Estonia, Slovakia, and Poland) are all former Communist countries. At both the beginning and end of the 2002–2015 period, these countries were considerably poorer than the slower-growing countries of Western Europe (such as Denmark, France, and Belgium). One might have expected these countries to experience more rapid growth, as part of a catching-up process with the rest of Europe. A second caveat is that the relationship in Figure 4.4 may actually represent causality from low economic growth to high social spending. After all, during an economic recession, GDP growth stagnates while public outlays on unemployment benefits and other forms of welfare assistance increase considerably. As such, low growth may be the driver of high social spending, rather than the other way around.

The economists Andreas Bergh and Magnus Henrekson (2011) provide a review of the literature on the relationship between government size, as a percentage of GDP, and economic growth. Their review is limited to studies of rich countries that investigate the association over time, rather than in a cross-section. In line with the cross-sectional pattern in Figure 4.4, Bergh and Henrekson find a relatively consistent negative relationship, such that a ten-percentage point rise in government expenditures is associated with 0.5 to one percentage point fall in annual economic growth.

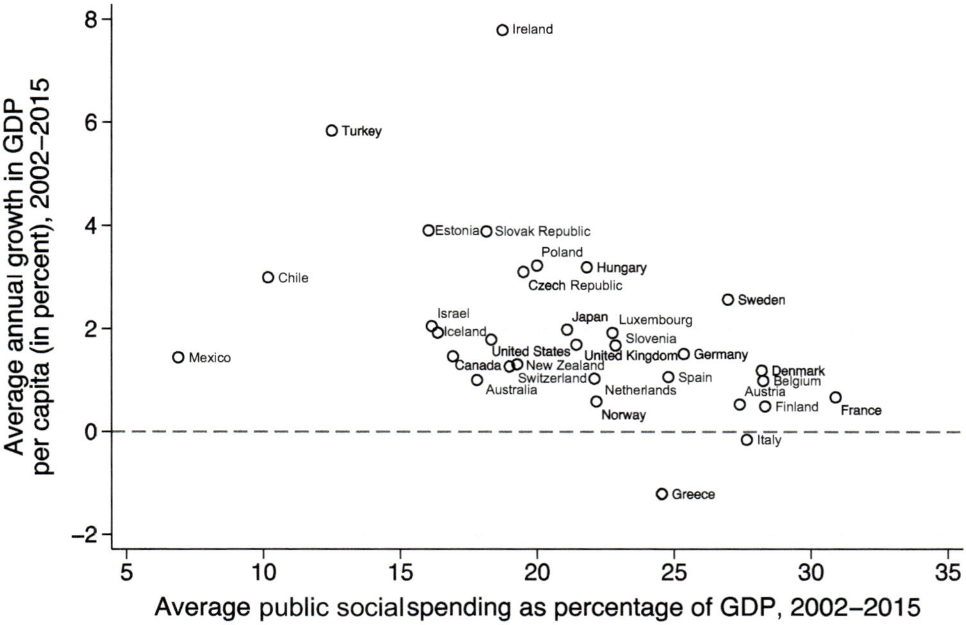

Figure 4.4 The relationship between public social spending and economic growth
Note: Data are from the OECD Social Expenditure Database (SOCX).

Nevertheless, it is important to stress that Bergh and Henrekson look at *all* government spending, instead of only governments' *social* spending. These two entities do not always correlate very strongly; consider the case of the US, as a country with a high level of total government spending, yet a fairly low level of social spending. Furthermore, a team of economists from the International Monetary Fund (IMF) that investigated the relationship between income redistribution and economic growth over time, conclude that only at extreme levels of redistribution is there any evidence of a deleterious impact of redistribution on growth (Ostry, Berg, and Tsangarides 2014). This discussion shows that it is difficult to establish whether there is a limit to public social spending beyond which this spending starts to create more problems than it solves.

The cradle-to-grave system in Sweden

As noted in the section "How different welfare states manage social risks", the Swedish welfare state constitutes a universal system of social insurance and redistribution. The key characteristic of this system is that social programmes are not focussed on particular groups (for example, individuals below a certain income threshold, or individuals employed in a certain industry), but rather on every member of society. Sweden represents a particularly interesting case, because many of its politicians had, for several decades, promulgated the bold claim that the country had discovered a "third way" between capitalism and socialism (Milner 1994). Sweden was widely regarded as a model for social democrats and others on the centre-left throughout Europe. After the collapse of communism, many political leaders in Eastern Europe proclaimed a desire to follow in Sweden's footsteps. However, Sweden has had to change tracks somewhat since the 1990s.

The creation of the Swedish welfare state was mostly the work of the Social Democratic Party, which had ruled the country almost without interruption from 1932–2006. The philosophy of the Social Democratic Party was one of national solidarity, namely that every member of society should be able to live "from the cradle to the grave" in an environment of security and sanctity. In order to realize this goal, the state had consistently intervened in both economic and socio-cultural life.

The Swedish welfare state traditionally encompassed a plethora of different social programmes: day nurseries, free or heavily subsidized education, free or subsidized childcare, social housing, national healthcare, and public pensions for the elderly. In order to finance all of these programmes, high taxes were necessary. Moreover, the government followed highly centralized industrial practices. In cooperation with the labour unions, it tried to influence the direction of industry by providing subsidies, tax advantages, and regulatory benefits to certain large companies. It even encouraged the formation of cartels.

However, by the start of the 1990s, an economic crisis was looming. From 1990–1995, the cumulative economic growth was only 0.4 percent, and growth had even been negative for a few years. Unemployment rose from 1.6 percent in 1990 to 7.7 percent in 1993. At the same time, inflation was high, giving rise to a situation of stagflation. While all of this was happening, total government expenditures increased from 60 percent of GDP in 1989 to 74 percent in 1993. In general, the government had grown very large: one third of all those in employment worked for the government, compared to only one fifth in the EU as a whole. To sustain this large stock of public sector employees, a high level of taxation was required. Another symptom of the welfare state crisis was that leaves of absence from work had grown out of control (14 percent, versus seven percent in the EU as a whole).

Several political parties argued that the government had become too large and intrusive, and that the economy had suffered as a result. The dominant idea was that Sweden's large social sector had become incompatible with a well-functioning economic system. Although the social-democratic government had tried to make the two compatible with one another by increasing the public debt and devaluating the Krona (the national currency), these measures eventually had the opposite effect. In the autumn of 1992, the Swedish central bank announced an emergency situation: the value of the Krona had drastically decreased, and in a vain attempt to defend the currency, the central bank had increased interest rates to 500 percent.

Within three days' time after this alarm, all major political parties agreed on a far-reaching plan of action, including the following elements:

1 Pensions were cut by two percent, and the retirement age of 65 was raised by one year.
2 The generosity of disability benefits was reduced.
3 The system of funding health insurance out of general revenues was abolished and replaced by an insurance system to be jointly managed by employers and employees.
4 Child benefits were frozen and student scholarships were cut.
5 The planned benefit of 24,000 Krona per year to working mothers was postponed.
6 Housing subsidies were reduced.

7 The commitment to spend one percent of GDP on foreign aid was relaxed.
8 Despite all these budget cuts, taxes were not lowered and, in some cases, even increased.

A large part of the Swedish population supported these reforms, which led to a drop in total government expenditures from 74 percent of GDP in 1993 to 50 percent of GDP in 2016. Despite these major retrenchments, polls have consistently shown that the welfare state remains popular in Sweden. It appears that particularly the universal programmes – those for which all citizens are eligible (healthcare, pensions, childcare, child support and unemployment benefits) – remain popular, while means-tested programmes directed towards specific groups of poor people are less popular. The large influx of immigrants in the last couple of years puts further pressure on the popularity of benefit programmes, as many citizens oppose immigrants having full access to these programmes, and thus forces politicians to think about adjustments to the Swedish welfare state.

Future threats to the welfare state

We have so far discussed several problems that put the welfare state under pressure. A very generous welfare state, despite the good intentions on which it is built, is likely to be more susceptible to perverse effects. These perverse effects might eventually undermine the legitimacy of the welfare state. We have also discussed the process of welfare state retrenchment that has taken place in most Western countries since the 1990s, but despite these spending cuts, many countries have continued to struggle with an increasing stock of public debt and, correspondingly, also an increasing interest burden. Given that these debts and the corresponding interest payments will have to be covered by future generations, further welfare state retrenchments may turn out to be inevitable.

Aside from these general issues, we can distinguish at least three other important threats to the welfare state. One of them is the impact of a large influx of immigrants. While many European welfare states have already absorbed a significant number of immigrants over the past few decades, more recently there has been another surge in immigration following the European migrant crisis that started in 2015 (see Chapter 6). In most countries, a large share of the population is opposed to benefits that go to people who have not previously contributed to the costs of the programmes themselves, which is true for many immigrants. This partially explains recent increases in the popularity of right-wing political parties in practically all European countries. Many people particularly oppose newcomers having immediate and full access to public benefits, fearing that this would turn the country into a "welfare magnet". As such, large-scale immigration may cause a drop in overall public support for the welfare state.

Nevertheless, it is important to realize that in many Western countries there is actually a need for immigration. For example, the UK Office for National Statistics has shown that in order to keep Britain's healthcare, its hospitality sector, and its wholesale and retail sector going, net immigration is required. In 2017, a total of 1.5 million immigrants were working in these sectors in the UK. Furthermore, due to demographic trends of population ageing and declining fertility (see Chapter 5), the native workforce is shrinking in many Western countries, requiring a continuous stream of immigration for several years to come. Hence, while immigration is often seen as a threat to the welfare state, it is at the same time badly needed to keep the welfare state running. In this context, the desirability of immigration to some extent depends on the educational training, age and language proficiency of immigrants and what kinds of occupations there is a shortage of in the native workforce.

Another important threat to the welfare state has to do with the affordability of the public pension systems that are embedded into the welfare state. Whereas in poor countries, the elderly are mostly dependent on their children for assistance in their old age, in post-industrial welfare states the elderly receive a state pension, or else they rely on one which they have built up themselves over the course of their working lives.

State pensions are typically *pay-as-you-go programmes*. This is where people of current working age are taxed in order to fund the pensions of the current elderly population. The pay-as-you-go model is therefore not an insurance system, in which people save for their own pensions, but rather one in which there is a continuous transfer from working-age people to the elderly. An interesting feature of this system is that the first generation of elderly people to receive state pensions did not have to fund anybody else's pensions themselves. However, in general the principle of justice is expected to operate over time, because the working people of today are the elderly of the future.

That said, the intergenerational social contract on which pay-as-you-go systems are based is vulnerable in several ways. For one thing, even if someone has paid old-age premiums throughout their working life in order to fund the pensions of the elderly population at the time, there is no guarantee that future workers will do the same for them, as policy changes may occur. Moreover, the fact that generations differ in size can introduce a certain degree of intergenerational inequality. For example, the process of population ageing implies that a shrinking working-age population has to fund the pensions of an increasing elderly population, resulting in rising tax pressure.

An alternative way of financing pensions (a *fully funded system*) is by having people save for their own future pensions during their working lives, by encouraging them to put a certain percentage of their annual salary into a fund, which they will be able to access upon retirement. This alternative system is therefore a true system of insurance. The pension funds are usually managed by private organizations.

As mentioned, pay-as-you-go pensions system are especially susceptible to the influence of population ageing. Most of these systems were designed in the decades after the Second World War, when all European countries had relatively high fertility, strong economic growth and almost full employment. In light of these factors, the expectation at the time was that the pay-as-you-go systems would remain affordable in perpetuity. However, in the last two decades of the twentieth century, it became clear that this expectation was not necessarily justified. Fertility had decreased, life expectancy had increased, unemployment had risen, and economic growth had slowed down. During the latter half of the twentieth century, the number of working-age people (taxpayers) had decreased substantially relative to the number of elderly people (pension recipients). Whereas in most countries there had been three to four working people for each pensioner in the 1950s, this ratio had dropped to only one to two by the year 2000, putting increasing pressure on current and future taxpayers. This especially holds true for countries such as Italy, Germany and Spain, where the pension system is (almost) entirely pay-as-you-go. There are comparatively few savings in these countries' pension funds, which will likely cause serious problems in the future.

Yet, fully funded systems cannot fully escape from the problem of population aging either, although its effect is less dramatic. In the case of population ageing, when it gets time for retirees to sell the assets that they have been investing in throughout their working lives (which is necessary to fund their consumption needs during old age), there will be many people trying to sell such assets at the same time and relatively few people trying to buy these assets. Greater supply combined with lower demand leads to a lower value of these assets. Therefore, the value of retirees' pensions will be lower when the population is ageing than when it is more youthful. A solution would be to increase the retirement age and to decrease the generosity of pensions that retirees actually receive. However, because the elderly constitute a growing share of the electorate and generally have higher turnout rates than those in younger age groups, such policy measures tend to be politically very unpopular. Nonetheless, pension reforms of this kind have already been implemented in countries such as Germany, the UK, and the Netherlands.

A third important future threat to the welfare state is the danger of a new economic or financial crisis. During the 1980s and 1990s, pension funds began investing an increasing amount of their funds in stocks and shares. Starting from the early 1980s onwards, there was an expectation that the stock market would rise continuously. This increasing dependence on the stock market made pension funds more vulnerable, and the expectation of continuously rising stock prices was indeed fairly quickly proven to be wrong, resulting in significant pension cuts. More generally, we discussed the welfare state retrenchments during the 1990s, which were partly a consequence of an economic recession in the early 1990s. More recently, the 2008 financial crisis also provided enormous challenges to the affordability of various welfare states. A telling example is Greece, where public debt rose to unsustainably high levels and large cuts had to be made to healthcare, pensions and other social welfare schemes, throwing a substantial proportion of society into poverty.

Recommended readings

- Gøsta Esping-Anderson's (1990) *The Three Worlds of Welfare Capitalism* has been hugely influential in shaping research and public debates on welfare states, by introducing his typology of universal, corporatist and liberal welfare states. This typology is derived from Esping-Andersen's decommodification index, which describes to what degree individuals have to rely on the state or the market for their material well-being. Aside from introducing this typology, the book gives a rich historical overview of the evolution of welfare states.
- Walter Korpi (2003) provides an early overview of welfare state retrenchment in Europe. He explains how this retrenchment process is the outcome of a complex interplay between voters, welfare state clients, interest groups, political parties and welfare state institutions, set off by the return of mass unemployment and corresponding increases in public budget deficits. He additionally demonstrates how welfare state retrenchment alters the "postwar social contract" on which European welfare states were initially based.
- Peter Starke (2006) also discusses the process of welfare state retrenchment, but from a more specific political science perspective. His central puzzle is why, given the fact that welfare state retrenchment is such an unpopular political endeavour, we have observed it on such a grand scale. In trying to find an answer to this puzzle, Starke reviews the literature on the politics of retrenchment, arguing among other things that the exact political motives and mechanisms driving retrenchment are still little understood.

Bibliography

Bergh, Andreas, and Magnus Henrekson. 2011. "Government Size and Growth: A Survey and Interpretation of the Evidence". *Journal of Economic Surveys* 25:872–897.

Donner Commission. 2001. *Werk Maken van Arbeidsongeschiktheid: Advies van de Adviescommissie Arbeidsongeschiktheid* (Making Work of Disabilities: Advice from the Advice Commission on Disabilities). The Hague: Ministry of Social Affairs and Employment.

Esping-Andersen, Gøsta. 1990. *The Three Worlds of Welfare Capitalism*. Princeton, NJ: Princeton University Press.

Korpi, Walter. 2003. "Welfare-state Regress in Western Europe: Politics, Institutions, Globalization, and Europeanization". *Annual Review of Sociology* 29:589–609.

Marshall, Thomas H. 1950. *Citizenship and Social Class and Other Essays*. Cambridge: Cambridge University Press.

Meyer, Marshall W., and Vipin Gupta. 1994. "The Performance Paradox". *Research in Organizational Behavior* 16:309–369.

Milner, Henry. 1994. *Social Democracy and Rational Choice: The Scandinavian Experience and Beyond*. London: Routledge.

Murray, Charles. 1984. *Losing Ground: American Social Policy 1950–1980*. New York, NY: Basic Books.

Navarro, Vincent. 2011. "Crisis and Class Struggle in the Eurozone: The Cases of Spain, Greece, Ireland, and Portugal". *CounterPunch*, August 19–21. https://www.counterpunch.org/2011/08/19/crisis-and-class-struggle-in-the-eurozone/.

Ostry, Jonathan D., Andrew Berg, and Charalambos G. Tsangarides. 2014. "Redistribution, Inequality, and Growth". *IMF Staff Discussion Note*, 17 February 2014. https://www.imf.org/en/Publications/Staff-Discussion-Notes/Issues/2016/12/31/Redistribution-Inequality-and-Growth-41291.

Pierson, Paul. 1994. *Dismantling the Welfare State – Reagan, Thatcher and the Politics of Retrenchment*. Cambridge: Cambridge University Press.

Starke, Peter. 2006. "The Politics of Welfare State Retrenchment: A Literature Review". *Social Policy and Administration* 40:104–120.

Van de Goor, Anne G. 1997. *Effects of Regulation on Disability Duration*. Amsterdam: Thesis Publishers.

Van Thiel, Sandra. 2000. *Quangocratization: Trends, Causes and Consequences*. Utrecht: ICS Dissertation.

5 Population growth while fertility drops

Chapter overview

The world population has never been as large as it is today and it is likely to increase to almost ten billion in 2050. Over the past century, a decline in mortality rates has caused an acceleration of the growth of the world population. However, in many countries fertility is decreasing, and that decrease is slowing global population growth. In this chapter, we illustrate how, over the course of several decades, changes in fertility and mortality can give rise to a different population structure. We explain how socio-economic changes cause demographic changes, and how demographic changes in turn can have major societal consequences. In doing so, we take micro-level cost-benefit analyses as our starting-point, and examine how these ultimately translate into population-level outcomes. We proceed to discuss an important dichotomy, namely that in most countries in Asia, Africa, and Latin America, fertility has started to decline only in the last few decades, whereas in Northern America, Europe, Japan, South Korea, and Russia, fertility has been below the replacement level for some time. In the former cases, population growth puts considerable pressure on available resources. In the latter, population ageing has started to strain the institutions of the welfare state.

Population growth throughout the centuries

Population problems comprise slow-moving but inevitable transformations of society. That is, changes to mortality (deaths) and fertility (births) are both causes and consequences of a number of complex societal changes, but take a long time to exert a noticeable impact, except when they are particularly pronounced (for example if there is a widespread plague).

In most countries in Asia, Africa, and Latin America fertility has been high until recently, and has started to decline only in the last few decades. Both the high initial level and the recent declining trend can to a large extent be attributed to economic and public health factors. However, due to lagged effects, these regions still have growing populations, which propel global population growth and put pressure on available resources such as the environment (see Chapter 12).

In contrast, countries in Europe, the Anglosphere, and East Asia have already witnessed fertility declines for longer. Population growth in these areas has either halted or is being maintained by high levels of immigration. Similarly to explosive population growth, also this situation of stagnating population growth can give rise to societal problems. For example, the increasing size of the elderly population relative to the working-age population threatens many Western welfare states (see Chapter 4).

Few demographic topics have raised as much discussion in the last few decades as the issue of overpopulation. There is in this regard no doubt that the world population has increased enormously, although the causes and consequences of this growth continue to be hotly debated by pessimists on one side and optimists on the other. Figure 5.1 provides an overview of the history of global population growth. As can be observed, the vast majority of this growth has occurred during the relatively short period of human history since 1850.

At the start of the first industrial revolution, around 1750, world population was in the region of 800 million people, which implies an average population growth rate of almost zero percent per year for the first 50,000 years of human history (starting from the emergence of the current *homo sapiens* with full *behavioural modernity* – which is capable of abstract thinking, elaborate planning, artistic and musical expressions, etc. – out of earlier human-like species). Between 1750 and 1950, however, the world population increased by about 0.7 percent a year on average, so that by the middle of the twentieth century it had reached 2.5 billion. Between 1950 and 2000, the annual rate of population growth rose to two percent, so that by the turn of the century there were more than six billion people on our planet. This number is projected to increase to almost ten billion by 2050, and more than 11 billion by 2100.

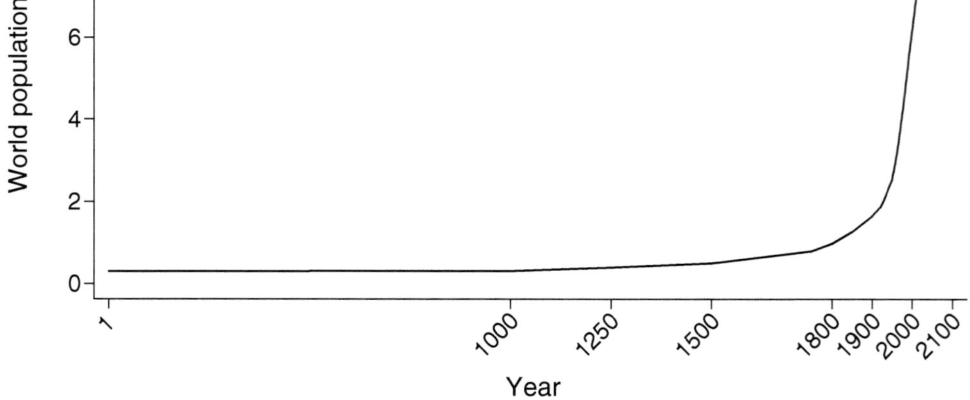

Figure 5.1 The growth of the world population since the year AD 1

Note: Data are from *The World at Six Billion* (UN 1999) and the World Population Prospects (UN 2017). Future projections are based on a medium-fertility scenario.

As already alluded to, there have in the recent past also been significant changes in the geographic distribution of the global population, which are forecasted by the UN (2017) to continue going forward, as shown by Figure 5.2. The most striking pattern in this figure is the stark rise in the share of the global population that lives on the African continent – from about ten percent in 1950 to as much as 40 percent by 2100. Moreover, while in 1950 more than 20 percent of the world population lived in Europe, this share has already more than halved. Asia continues to have the greatest share of the world's population, even though a decline in this share is forecasted during the twenty-first century. According to current projections, more than 80 percent of the world's population will live in either Asia or Africa by 2100.

Coming back to Figure 5.1, which maps the overall growth of the world population, the future trend displayed in this figure is based on a medium-variant scenario for fertility. This scenario is visualized in Figure 5.3, alongside three other scenarios: a low-fertility scenario, a high-fertility scenario, and a constant-fertility scenario. All of these projections are from the latest UN *World Population Prospects* report (UN 2017).

We can see from Figure 5.3 that, if fertility were to remain constant, there would be an explosion of the global population over the next 80 years, from its current level of 7.6 billion (in 2018) to about 26 billion by the year 2100. Such a trajectory would likely lead to large-scale societal problems, such as environmental degradation, famine and conflict over natural resources (see Chapter 12). Moreover, in light of the fact that the growth of the global population will be concentrated in the poorest parts of the world with limited economic opportunities, one could also expect a surge in international migration (see Chapter 6). While this constant-fertility scenario is unlikely to materialize given ongoing trends in fertility, the more plausible

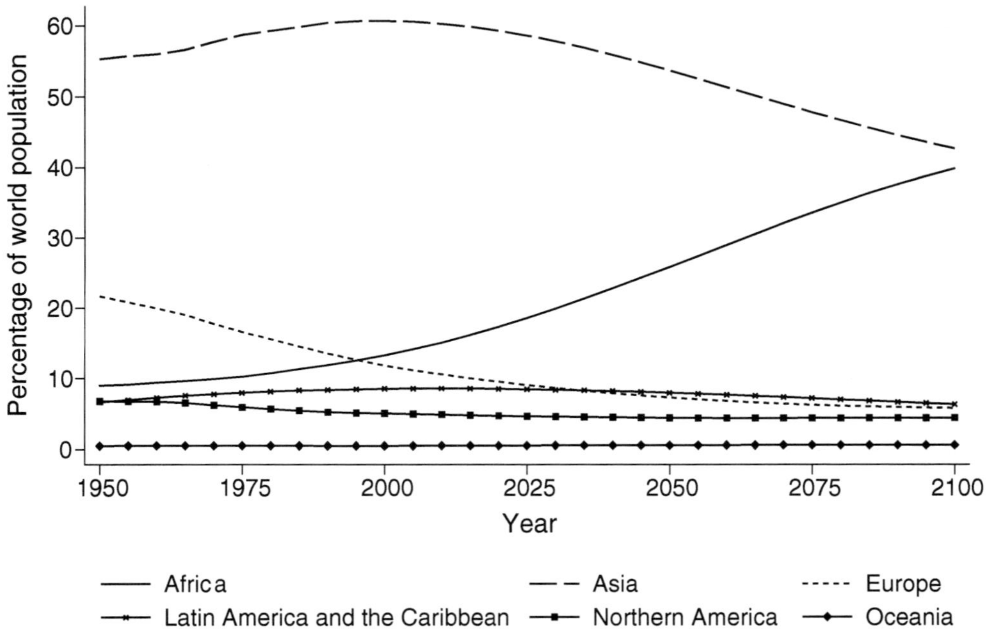

Figure 5.2 The changing geographic distribution of the world population, 1950-2100

Note: Data are from the World Population Prospects (UN 2017). Future projections are based on a medium-fertility scenario.

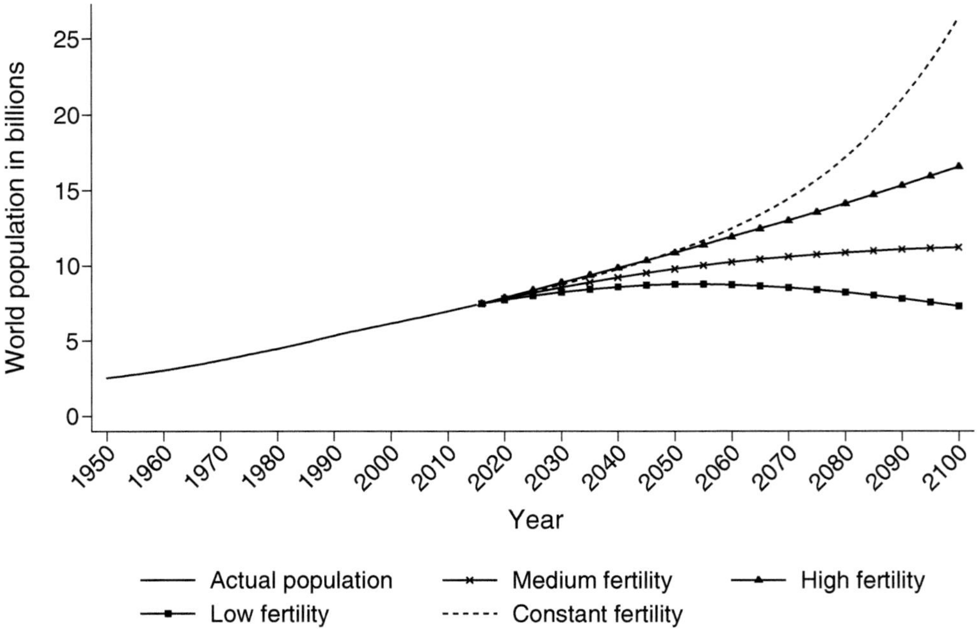

Figure 5.3 The future growth of the world population according to different projections

Note: Data are from the World Population Prospects (UN 2017).

high-fertility scenario would still imply more than a doubling of the global population by the end of this century. And although the medium-fertility scenario expects global population growth to flatten off from about 2050, only the low-fertility scenario projects a world population in 2100 that is no bigger than it is now.

Before the mid-nineteenth century, high mortality rates were characteristic of all human societies. By today's standards, the average age in the population was low and parents generally expected that one or two of their children would die before reaching adulthood. In addition to suffering from periodic famines, as well as violent conflicts, humans often died from infectious diseases such as cholera, dysentery and tuberculosis. During the transition from hunter-gatherer and horticultural modes of subsistence to agricultural ones, around 5,000 to 10,000 years ago, population densities had increased substantially, meaning that diseases could spread easily. In the largest towns and cities, where the microorganisms that cause infectious diseases could multiply in stagnant water sources, outbreaks of disease were particularly common.

Nevertheless, over the course of the nineteenth century, child mortality diminished substantially, and by the mid-twentieth century, mortality rates in industrial countries had decreased to below one percent, while mortality rates in developing countries have continued to decrease since the Second World War. The reduction in overall mortality and child mortality is arguably one of humankind's greatest achievements. The most important contributing factors to the mortality reductions were: the general increase in the level of wealth, the development of public sanitation (sewage systems, clean drinking water), improved personal hygiene (especially hand-washing), mass vaccinations against infectious diseases, and higher-quality nutrition. One particularly important event was the discovery of bacteria and the role that these microorganisms play in the spread of disease. Another important event was Edward

Jenner's discovery of immunity, which led to the development of the smallpox vaccine. Later, Alexander Fleming's discovery of penicillin in the 1930s made it possible to fight infectious diseases quickly and cheaply.

However, despite further improvements in public health and the application of new medical knowledge, many parts of the developing world still suffer from numerous infectious diseases. For example, cholera is still responsible for 20,000 to 140,000 deaths worldwide each year, and in recent years there have been several serious outbreaks of the ebola virus (mainly in West Africa). Furthermore, in the 1980s, a devastating new disease appeared on the world stage, namely HIV/AIDS. This disease soon gave rise to an epidemic, since the start of which more than 60 million people have become infected.

The demographic transition model

For demographers, the comparison of the *fertility rate* and the *mortality rate* provides important information on the future size of the population. In the past, the most prominent measures for both rates were the *crude birth rate* (the number of births per year per thousand people in the population) and the *crude death rate* (the number of deaths per year per thousand people in the population). By subtracting the death rate from the birth rate, one gets the net balance of new people per thousand people already present, which can be transformed into a percentage simply by moving the decimal point.

One very important model in which crude birth and death rates are compared is the *demographic transition model*. This is an interpretation of demographic history, which was developed independently by the American demographer Warren Thompson in 1929 and by the French demographer Adolphe Landry in 1934, and then developed into a more formal theory by the demographer Frank Notestein in 1945. The model, which comprises five stages, is illustrated in Figure 5.4. We summarize each stage below.

Stage 1. In the first stage (pre-industrial society) population growth is close to zero, because both birth and death rates are high. The natural birth rate in a population where birth control is absent lies around 40 births per year per thousand people in the population. The death rate lies typically just above or below that, at a level of between 35 and 45 deaths per year per thousand people in the population, depending on whether there is a war, famine or an outbreak of disease. This stage describes most of human history to date.

Stage 2. During the emergence of industrial societies, the second phase takes off. The quality of nutrition improves and institutions such as public sanitation and mass vaccinations are introduced, substantially reducing the death rate (especially childhood mortality). At the same time, the birth rate remains high, as families have not yet adapted their fertility behaviour to the reduced mortality levels. As a result, the population grows rapidly, with families having many children. Some of the poorest countries in the world are still stuck – and have been so for a long time – in this stage, as a consequence of stagnant overall development.

Stage 3. In the third phase, the death rate decreases further but, more importantly, the birth rate also starts to go down. In Northern Europe, the decline in fertility began in the nineteenth century as a consequence of societal changes such as urbanization, the end of subsistence agriculture, and a reduction in the value of children's work. Since there is, however, still a large difference between the birth and death rates, the population continues to grow, although at a

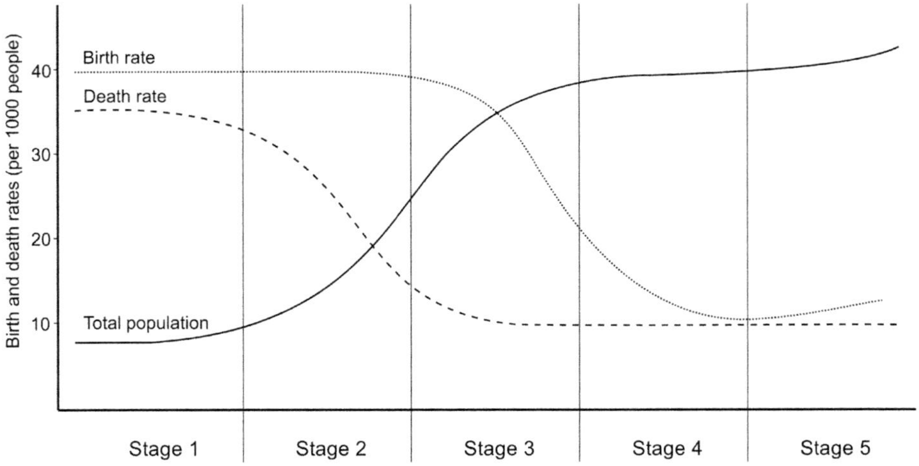

Birth rate	High	High	Falling	Low	Rising again
Death rate	High	Falls rapidly	Falls more slowly	Low	Low
Total population	Stable or slow increase	Very rapid increase	Increase slows down	Falling and then stable	Stable or slow increase

Figure 5.4 The demographic transition model

Note: This chart is an adapted version of a diagram by Roser and Ortiz-Ospina (2018).

decreasing rate. This stage is where many developing countries that have set off on paths of economic growth currently reside. These countries tend to pass through the demographic transition rather quickly, due to fast social and economic change.

Stage 4. In the fourth stage, birth rates decline even further and death rates more or less stabilize. Since the birth rate has now largely caught up with the death rate, the result is that population growth stabilizes at a low level or stops altogether. Most developed countries are currently in this stage, and in some of them (for example, Germany, Italy and Japan) the birth rate has in fact dipped under the death rate, translating into negative population growth. At the same time, there is evidence that some developed countries are moving on to stage 5 already.

Stage 5. In the fifth phase – which is still subject to debate among scholars – the birth rate recovers again somewhat, with women having on average two children each. As a result, societies that were previously subject to population decline will now return to stable population size, or even a slightly positive natural rate of population growth. This stage is currently ongoing in some of the most highly developed countries, with women (especially higher-educated women) tending to be having slightly more children again than they used to have in previous decades. This phenomenon is also known as the *fertility reversal*; see, for example, Esping-Andersen and Billari (2015).

In order to get a more specific idea of the trends in crude birth and death rates across the world, Figure 5.5 shows the average birth and death rates for each continent, from 1950 onwards with projections going up to 2100. The data are from the latest UN *World Population Prospects* report (UN 2017), and the projections assume a medium-fertility scenario.

The distinction in Figure 5.5 between the most and least developed regions is palpable. For the African continent, the declines in the birth and death rates were parallel during the second half of the twentieth century. The two lines have only started to approach one another in the last decade, as the decline of the death rate has started to flatten off. This puts the continent as a whole on the edge between the second and third stage of the demographic transition model. Moreover, its birth rate is forecasted to stay ahead of its death rate up to the year 2100 and beyond. The main reason for Africa's relatively low current death rate compared to the other continents is the young age structure of its population; see also the section "Shifting age distributions". In contrast, Europe's birth and death rates already converged before the end of the twentieth century and are currently at about the same level. The medium-fertility projections for the remainder of the twenty-first century forecast that the death rate in Europe as a whole will be higher than the birth rate. This would imply a negative rate of natural population growth.

While birth rates and death rates play an essential role in the demographic transition model, it should be noted that the crude birth rate and crude death rate are not ideal for comparisons of fertility and mortality across countries. The reason is that countries differ in age structure. For example, if a country happens to have a very elderly population, the age cohorts with the highest rates of fertility (20–40 year olds) will be relatively small, whereas cohorts with the highest rates of mortality (75–95 year olds) will be relatively large. In such a country, the birth rate will appear relatively low – even if all women aged 20–40 have many children – while the death rate will appear relatively high – even if all the elderly grow very old. The crux is that in this country there are simply few people "at risk" of getting children, while there are many people "at risk" of dying.

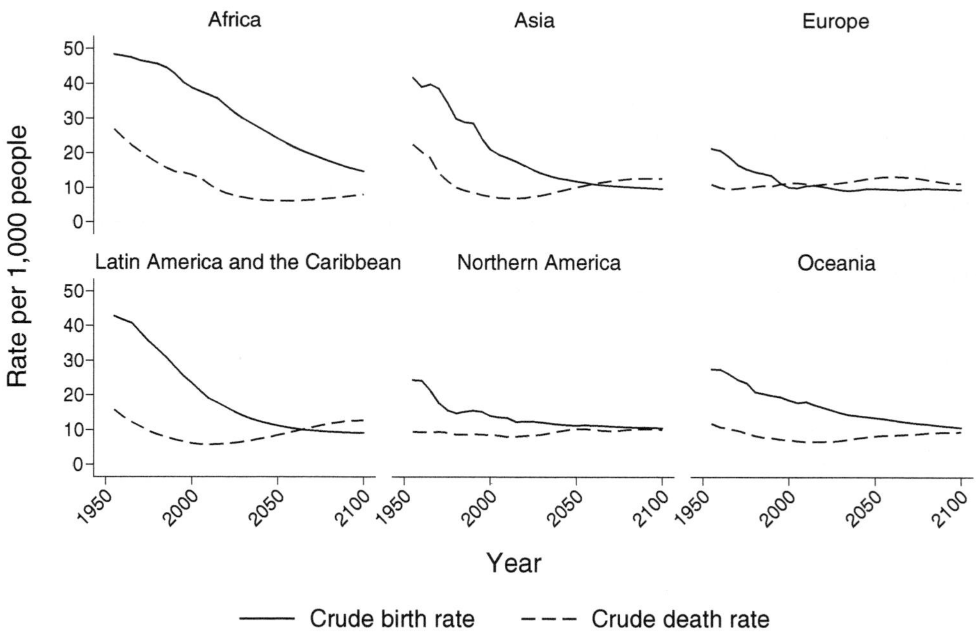

Figure 5.5 Trends in crude birth and death rates by continent, 1950-2100

Note: Data are from the World Population Prospects (UN 2017). Future projections are based on a medium-fertility scenario.

Standardized measures of mortality and fertility are, therefore, generally preferred for purposes of comparisons across countries.

The most common standardized measure of mortality is *life expectancy* – the average age to which an individual would live if they experienced the current age-specific mortality schedule. The most common measure of fertility is the *total fertility rate* (*TFR*) – the average number of children a woman would have in total if she followed the current age-specific fertility schedule. In principle, a TFR of two – two children per woman – would be sufficient to keep the population constant, but because there is always a certain amount of mortality among young people, the *replacement level* of fertility is generally considered to be 2.1. In that case, there is neither an increase nor a decrease in the total population size. Currently, the average TFR across the most developed countries is 1.7, as compared with an average TFR of across the developing world.

Figure 5.6 plots past trends and future projections of the TFR and life expectancy (at birth) by continent, analogous to Figure 5.5 on the crude birth and death rates. One of the things shown in Figure 5.6 is that life expectancy is rising across all continents (with the exception of a brief stagnation in Africa around the year 2000), including those continents for which the death rate is constant or increasing. Furthermore, variation in life expectancy across the continents is subject to convergence. That is, in 1950 there was a gap in life expectancy between Africa and Northern America of nearly 30 years, but by the year 2100 all continents are projected to have a life expectancy of between 80 and 90 years.

As to fertility, Figure 5.6 also shows a convergence process. In 1950, the TFR in Africa was almost seven, compared to a TFR of less than three in Europe, but by the end of the twenty-first century all continents are projected to have a TFR of around two – that is, replacement level.

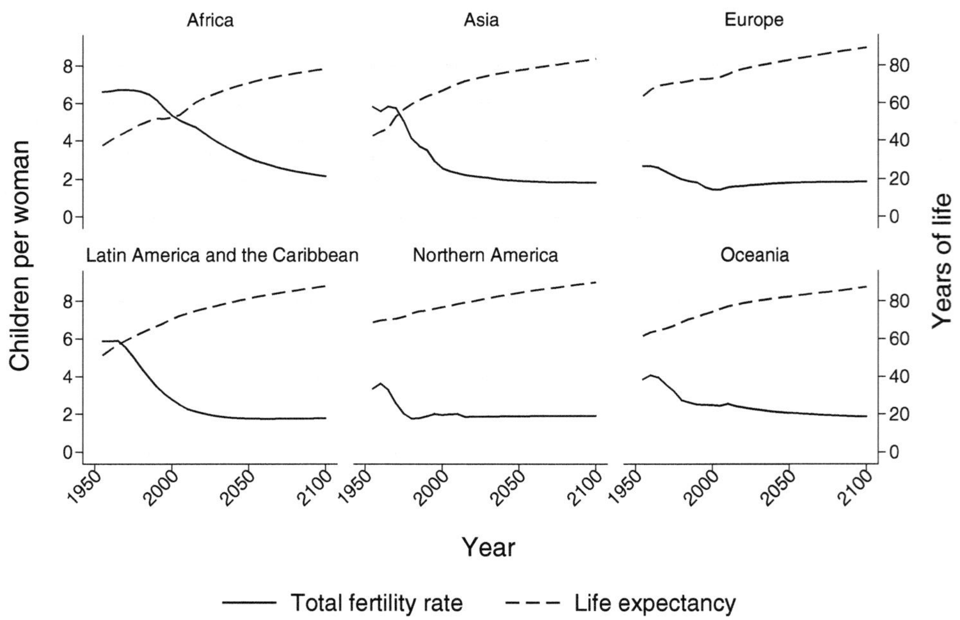

Figure 5.6 Trends in total fertility rate and life expectancy (at birth) by continent, 1950–2100

Note: Data are from the World Population Prospects (UN 2017). Future projections are based on a medium-fertility scenario.

As part of this convergence, we can observe small upticks in Europe's and Northern America's TFR from the minimum levels of fertility they hit in the late-twentieth century. This is consistent with stage five of the demographic transition model. Another thing to note in terms of fertility is that the fertility decline in the developing regions of the world lags behind the fertility decline in the more developed regions.

Explanations of fertility levels

Historically, no human society has been observed to have a TFR higher than eight over a long period. At the present time, in countries with the highest levels of fertility, where there is little availability or willingness to use birth control, the TFR is around seven. For example, the average TFR in Niger over the period 2000– 2015 is 7.4, while for Somalia it is 6.6. By contrast, in countries with the lowest levels of fertility, such as Singapore, South Korea and Taiwan, the TFR over this period equals 1.2, 1.2, and 1.1, respectively.

The determinants of fertility levels can be divided into two categories: those affecting couples' *willingness* to have fewer children, and those affecting couples' *ability* to have fewer children. With respect to couples' willingness to have fewer children, one can point to factors such as rising wealth; declining childhood mortality; rising education, especially for girls; rising female labour force participation; or increased independence on the part of women. Regarding couples' ability to have fewer children, one can point to factors such as: falling costs of birth control, increased practicality and reliability of available contraception methods, and changes in laws governing birth control (for example, prohibitions on abortion).

In traditional societies, couples used methods of birth control such as: a long breastfeeding period (the chance of a woman conceiving is much lower if she happens to be breastfeeding, and in hunter-gatherer populations, breastfeeding periods of two to three years were not uncommon); coitus interruptus (the withdrawal method); the calendar method (which requires precise knowledge of the menstrual cycle on the part of the woman); and abstinence. In modern societies, couples typically have a number of other, more refined methods at their disposal, such as: the contraceptive pill; condoms; vasectomy (the man having his tubes tied); an intrauterine device (the coil); and voluntary sterilization.

During the first few decades after the Second World War, social science research specified few details of the explanatory mechanisms underlying the reductions in fertility that were taking place. Most models of fertility change were couched at the macro level – the previously discussed demographic transition model being the most obvious example. Indeed, sociologists, historians and economists identified the cause of the demographic transition in very general terms as the marked increase in wealth that accompanied the industrial revolution. In Europe, agrarian societies had become industrial societies, and as part of this process cities had increased in size and a middle class had emerged. According to the dominant narrative, economic development was the key explanatory variable causing the fertility rate to decline. All changes, including shifts in family behaviour, were interpreted as elements of a general process of modernization.

However, as argued in Chapter 2, a correlation between two macro-level indicators (i.e., economic development and declining fertility) does not provide much information about what is actually driving the association between these indicators. In order to get a more complete understanding, micro-level mechanisms need to be specified. In other words, one needs to explain why a certain macro-level change causes individual couples to make different decisions concerning what number of children to have.

In this context, both the preferences of couples and the respective costs and benefits of different options carry importance. Indeed, we can assume that couples make fertility decisions in the same way that they would make many other decisions, namely by analysing the costs and benefits of different options, in relation to their own preferences. Costs and benefits should be interpreted broadly here, for example encompassing feelings of missing out if one does not end up having children or the time it takes to look after children. In accordance with our macro-micro-macro model of explanation (see Figure 2.1), the various costs and benefits will be influenced by the macro-level context within which family planning decisions are being made.

Based on simple cost calculations, the prevailing view among demographers in the 1950s and 1960s was that having a large family would be an economical burden. Since children are expensive, it was assumed that a family with many children would be poorer than one with few. This principle was believed that to apply to both societies as a whole and individual families. However, anthropological research by John Caldwell (1982) in Africa, India, Sri Lanka, and Bangladesh contradicted this prevailing view. Caldwell learned through conducting interviews with local community members that having a large family not only involved costs, but also equated to power, influence, and economic success. For example, small families with few allies in their community experienced economic crises much more often. In this light, Caldwell could explain the high fertility levels of many poor families by pointing to their potential gains from transferring income, wealth or other resources between generations. Having a large family was seen as some kind of insurance device.

In this respect, it is important to make a distinction between the following two situations. In agrarian societies, to start with, there is a wealth flow from the children to the parents, or – within the wider group of kin – from the younger to the older generation. Young people work for the benefit of their parents and older family members; their incomes are transferred to the older generation. For example, what is typical is for children and adolescents to help out on the family farm. Under these conditions, it pays a family to have as many children (i.e., income generators) as possible. This is reinforced by the fact that these children usually attain little or no education beyond the primary level, and that other members of the wider kinship network (e.g., grandparents, uncles and aunts, nieces and nephews) are available to help with child-rearing. Both of these factors reduce the costs of having children.

In industrial societies, on the other hand, there is a wealth flow in the opposite direction, namely from the older generation to the younger. In these societies, children represent a net economic cost to their parents. Rather than working to provide for the family income, children are sent to school and then university, for which parents typically have to pay or at least financially contribute. What is more, the nuclear family tends to be fairly isolated from the wider kinship network, meaning that parents cannot rely on their kin to contribute to child-rearing efforts. Hence, a lower fertility rate is the outcome of rational behaviour on the parts of individual families.

Economists have developed an increasingly complex theoretical calculus concerning the costs and benefits of having children (Werding 2014). In the economic model of fertility decision-making, the costs of having children are: (a) direct costs, such as purchasing food, clothes, and paying for a child's primary education; (b) *opportunity costs*: the costs of giving up the time and resources required to raise children, which could otherwise have been directed to some other pursuit; (c) future costs for funding the child's professional education etc.

Obviously, all of these costs depend on the macro-level context. In traditional or agrarian societies, these costs are generally low, among other things because women have fewer (attractive) opportunities for paid labour. In urban-industrial societies, in contrast, such opportunity costs are high, with women facing more attractive labour market opportunities. In such a society, having a lot of children would incur substantial opportunity costs. This gives families an incentive to limit the number of children they have.

The benefits of having children are manifold – for example, children can help out on the family farm or business, contribute to the family income by conducting paid labour, and provide future benefits, such as both financial and emotional support to their parents when they are old. In addition, there may be intrinsic benefits such as the joy of seeing one's children growing up or a sense of purpose, identity and personal fulfilment that one derives from their role as parent, or there may be social benefits, such as a certain level of status associated with a greater number of children.

Once again, these benefits can be assumed to have different weights in different macro-level contexts that societies provide. In general, many of the aforementioned benefits carry a stronger weight in agrarian societies than in urban-industrial societies. Among other things, welfare state institutions in the latter make it less necessary to have children in order to guarantee care in old age. That said, given the increasing size of older cohorts, there is a risk that welfare states will not be able to provide enough care for the elderly within a couple of decades; this might increase again the potential benefits of having children (see Chapter 4).

Not only do the benefits of raising children vary over time, the same is true for the costs. For example, in industrial societies it has become important for children to attain a good education, up to a university level. As a consequence of labour demands engendered by the industrial revolution, the human labour force had to become as highly educated as possible. Parents thus started to consider that spending time and money on their children's education was a worthwhile investment. Consequently, from the mid-nineteenth century to the present, the costs of rearing and educating children have increased considerably.

The US Department of Agriculture has computed estimates of the costs of raising children from birth to age 17 from 1960 onwards. The average costs of providing nutrition, transportation, clothing, healthcare, and education to children has – after adjusting for inflation – grown from US$ 191,723 in 1960 to US$ 234,900 in 2011 (both amounts are in 2011 US$). This increase was mainly due to an increase in childcare and education expenses, from two percent to 18 percent of a family's total budget. If we expand the calculation to raising a child until the age of 21, the costs increase even more, and mainly due to educational costs. The corresponding numbers for European countries give a largely similar picture. For London in particular, the Centre for Economic and Business Research calculated that the cost of raising a child until the age of 21 was a little over 250,000 British Pounds in 2016. The dramatic increase in the costs of child-rearing over the last five decades has almost certainly contributed to the decline in fertility in industrial societies.

It is tempting to explain the fertility decrease in Western Europe during the nineteenth century by technical innovations regarding contraception. However, an influential study edited by the demographers Ansley Coale and Susan Watkins (1986) showed that the availability of a highly convenient means of contraception, such as the condom (invented in 1839 and first produced in 1855), did not play a central role in this decrease. The decrease in fertility was mostly achieved through the use of traditional birth control measures, such as coitus interruptus, abstinence, and abortion. The decline in fertility took place in all segments of the population, despite the fact that the churches and the medical profession initially resisted it.

In the later phases of the fertility decline – during the twentieth century – modern contraceptive methods appear to have played a larger role. In Europe, women started to use the contraceptive pill on a sizeable scale during the 1960s and 1970s. The particularly rapid decline in fertility since the 1970s can be partly attributed to this. The fertility decreases in the developed countries of East Asia can be partly attributed to the use of modern contraceptive methods as well. That said, recent evidence indicates that the effect of oral contraception was complex and pluriform.

The public policy scholars Elizabeth Oltmans Ananat and Daniel Hungerman (2012) show in this regard that, in the short run, the diffusion of the birth control pill across society led to a decline in fertility and fewer children born in poor conditions (i.e., poor health themselves, or into poor households). Yet, in the long run, the diffusion of the pill did *not* affect fertility levels, but did increase the share of children with college-educated mothers, and it decreased the share of children with divorced mothers. Overall, this evidence suggests that the declining fertility level in the short run reflects women postponing rather than foregoing motherhood, and using this postponement to invest more time in obtaining higher education and building a stable relationship.

Population politics

In some cases the government proactively attempts to influence the fertility rate. In order to increase fertility rates in industrial countries, one can think of generous parental benefits, child-related tax credits, and the provision or subsidizing of high-quality childcare. For example, in 2017 Russia announced a policy package worth US$ nine billion to encourage its citizens to have more children. Among other things, this package includes mortgage subsidies for families with children, allowances to support young families, and lump-sum bonuses for every new child. Similarly, the sociologist Ozan Aksoy and demographer Francesco Billari (2018) demonstrate for Turkey that the local strength of the Islamist and pro-natalist (i.e., reproduction-promoting) AK Parti of President Erdogan has a causal effect on local fertility levels, most plausibly channelled through local welfare schemes that encourage and facilitate people to have more children.

By contrast, in the Chinese case, the government has for many decades run a staunchly antinatalist policy attempting to reduce the fertility rate. As background to this remarkable policy, China has experienced explosive population growth for many decades, with the population growing from less than one billion in 1980 to more than 1.4 billion by 2015. China's government, afraid of the negative consequences of overpopulation, aims to stabilize the population at 1.5 to 1.6 billion people by around 2040.

Until recently, Chinese couples were therefore discouraged by the government from having more than one child. This *one-child policy* was introduced in 1979. Officially, couples were merely incentivized to only have a single child, with rewards such as decent housing for the family and good schooling for the child. However, in actual fact, strong pressure was exercised over couples. For example, if a woman happened to become pregnant with a second child, the government would often pressure her into having an abortion.

This far-reaching anti-natalist policy may have had a number of unintended consequences. To begin with, the one-child policy may have brought about a sizable skew in the *sex ratio* (the ratio of males to females in the population). The overall sex ratio at birth in China is around 118 boys for every 100 girls, and in some areas, there are up to 180 boys for every 100 girls. Note that the normal sex ratio at birth is around 106 boys for every 100 girls. The reason why the normal sex ratio is slightly male-skewed is that male mortality is higher, meaning that by the age of peak reproduction at around age 20, the sex ratio is approximately balanced. It has been hypothesized that, due to a combination of the one-child policy and the traditional Chinese preference to have at least one boy, women who became pregnant with a girl often aborted it or killed it soon after birth. One estimate is that hundreds of thousands of girls were killed for this reason in China every year (see Sen 1990).

Another unintended consequence may have been an increase in the number of unregistered persons. This may especially apply in the countryside, where rules are often evaded, and where couples may thus have had a second or third child without registering them. These constitute so-called *hidden children*, who cannot go to school, cannot vote, and are not represented in national insurance programs. As a result, there is currently a floating population of individuals who have left their region of birth and moved to the city to look for work, but who cannot register there. According to estimates, the number of unregistered persons amounts to many tens of millions.

Related to the hidden children phenomenon, a study by the economists Yaojiang Shi and John Kennedy (2016) claims that most of China's so-called *missing girls* were not killed or aborted, but rather not registered until many years after their birth. Shi and Kennedy analysed Chinese census data and found that the sex ratio decreased from around 118 at age zero to the natural level of around 103 by age 20. Most of the drop occurs between the ages of 13 and 16. This finding suggests that parents have been postponing the registration of their daughters until their teenage years, as opposed to aborting them or killing them in infancy. Shi and Kennedy suggest three reasons why parents may have been doing this. First, couples may put off registering their daughter until they have a son. Second, couples who have an out-of-plan (illegal) birth must pay a large fine and may therefore delay registering the birth until they can afford to pay the fine. Third, in many rural areas, children can attend elementary school without a registration certificate, but cannot attend junior high school without one.

If the registration theory of China's missing girls turns out to be false or only responsible for part of the difference, there will be a sizeable and growing number of young men in China who will not be able to find a partner and will therefore not be able to start a family, leading to all kinds of frustrations and psychological problems. Such a surplus of young men can also have a destabilizing effect on society as a whole. This is because young men are the demographic group with the highest propensity towards criminality. Indeed, according to evolutionary psychologists, young men compete with one another for dominance and social status, often through violent means, in an effort to secure mates (Kanazawa and Still 2000). Men's criminality decreases substantially after the mid-20s, and marriage itself appears to have a pacifying effect on male violence and criminality.

Another unintended consequence of the one-child policy is that many people in China no longer have people in their vicinity to whom they can apply the traditional kin terms such as sister, brother, uncle and aunt. This may have undermined extended family and support networks, and ushered in a new sort of family system in China.

Finally, the one-child policy will have the effect of considerably decreasing the number of future births in China, due to the smaller number of women in each cohort entering the child-bearing years. As of 2013, the Chinese Government appears to be cognizant of this potential problem, and has therefore begun lifting some of the sanctions on second children. In 2016, it officially abolished the one-child policy, now allowing families to have two children, so as to avert a demographic crisis where there are not enough young people to support the growing number of elderly people. At current fertility rates, the UN projects a Chinese population of more than 1.44 billion in 2030, 1.42 billion in 2040, 1.36 billion in 2050, 1.21 billion in 2070 and 1.02 billion in 2100. In fact, the one-child policy thus seems to have proven too successful, given that the government's goal was to reduce the population to 1.5 to 1.6 billion by around 2040.

Shifting age distributions

In order to gain insight into the consequences of a low and a high fertility rate for the age distribution, we can look at *population pyramids*. Figure 5.7 shows population pyramids for six countries in 2015 and 2050: China, India, Japan, Nigeria, the UK and the US. In the first three stages of the demographic transition model, population distributions by age tend to have the shape of a pyramid and that is why these distributions are called population pyramids, even though for some countries they no longer resemble pyramids. Indeed, for the countries in Figure 5.7 only the age distribution of Nigeria still has the neat shape of a pyramid.

Nigeria is an example of a fast-growing population in a developing country, with a high TFR. In 2015, the population totalled 181 million people; in 2050, it is projected to total 411 million people. Both the 2015 and 2050 age pyramids exhibit the wide base that is typical for fast-growing developing countries. Such population pyramids are also referred to as *expansive*, corresponding to a young and growing population. The underlying TFR is still well above five children per woman in 2015, and albeit declining, it is expected to still be at around 3.3 in 2050. If this trend continues, Nigeria will have 794 million people by 2100. Such an increase in population size will undoubtedly be accompanied by serious societal problems, such as intense competition over resources and a large stream of emigration to other parts of the world such as Europe (see Chapter 6).

Although not resembling a perfect pyramid, India's population pyramid in 2015 still very much looks like one, with a broad base and getting gradually narrower towards the top. In line with this expansive shape, population growth in India is set to continue for the coming decades. However, as can be seen from its 2050 pyramid, India is on a different development path than Nigeria. This pyramid is more characteristic for a society with little or no population growth, and thus referred to as *stationary*. Indeed, while India's population has almost doubled between 1980 and 2015, from 697 million to 1.31 billion, it is only projected to increase to 1.66 billion by 2015, after which the population size will stabilize and then slowly decline to about 1.51 billion. In line with this trend, the TFR has declined from almost five children per woman in 1980, to 2.4 in 2015, and by 2050 the TFR will be below replacement level at about 1.8.

In contrast with Nigeria and India, the population pyramid for Japan no longer has the shape of a pyramid, but rather one that is characteristic of a shrinking population with a low TFR, with increasingly more elderly vis-à-vis young people. Such population pyramids are also

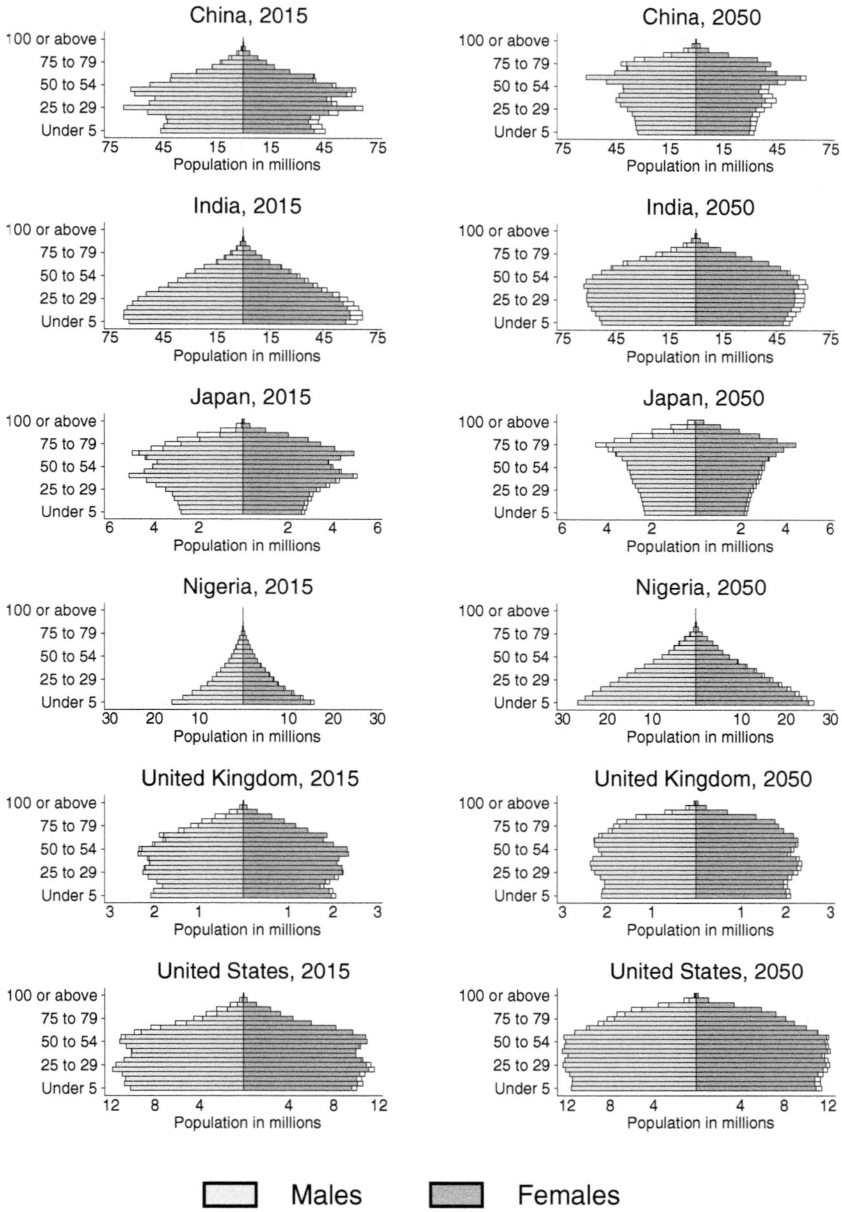

Figure 5.7 The age distribution by gender for a selection of countries in 2015 and 2050

Note: Data are from the World Population Prospects (UN 2017). The projections for 2050 are based on a medium-fertility scenario. Any white sections at the ends of the horizontal bars indicate an excess of the opposite sex in a given age group.

referred to as *constrictive*, corresponding to an elderly and shrinking population. Indeed, the TFR in Japan has been below replacement level since the 1970s, currently standing at about 1.4 children per woman. As a result, the population has already started to decrease compared to its maximum size of 129 million around 2010. The projected population sizes for 2050 and 2100 are 109 million and 85 million, respectively.

The shape of the population pyramids for the UK and US are also characteristic of developed countries with a relatively low level of fertility, but where – unlike for the Japanese case – the situation of slow population growth has not yet turned into negative growth. Their pyramids display similarities to the 2050 pyramid for India and, moreover, do not change much over time. The estimated population growth in the UK is from 65 million in 2015 to 75 million in 2050, and for the US these numbers are 320 million and 390 million, respectively. The TFR for both countries stands at about 1.9 children per woman in 2015, and is projected to still be at that level in 2050. This is slightly below replacement level, indicating that the projected population growth is mainly fuelled by increased life expectancy and net immigration.

Finally, for China we observe population pyramids that are largely consistent with those of Japan, insofar as they depict a shrinking and ageing population over time. As mentioned in the previous section, while China's population is projected to continue growing in the next few years from its current level of 1.40 billion, it will start to shrink from about 2030. In line with this trend, the TFR is currently about 1.6, and although it is expected to recover somewhat in the next few decades, it is projected to stay below replacement level for the remainder of this century.

One of the most interesting things to observe for China, however, is the surplus of men in the population, which is indicated by the little white bars in Figure 5.7. These bars show for every age group how much more men there are than women, or vice versa. This surplus of men seems a consequence of China's one-child policy as well as the cultural preference for boys over girls. Notice that we, in fact, observe similar male surpluses in India, while these surpluses are far more negligible for the other countries displayed.

Rapid population growth and overpopulation

Almost every discussion of the dangers of overpopulation begins with a reference to the British economist and preacher Thomas Malthus (2015[1798]). In his work *An Essay on the Principle of Population*, Malthus was the first to offer a quantitative analysis of population problems. Malthus compared the growth rate of the population to the growth rate of food production, and he observed that while food production grows according to an arithmetical series (1, 2, 3, 4, etc.), population increases according to a geometrical series (1, 2, 4, 8, etc.). This led him to conclude that any increase in economic production would only ever lead to a temporary rise in living standards, since it would soon lead to an expansion of the population, and a corresponding fall in the amount of food production per capita. This would, in turn, lead to a plethora of societal problems. Hence, according to Malthus, large increases in population were soon checked by disease, famine and war.

Early critics argued that Malthus's predictions were disconfirmed over the course of the nineteenth century, due to various technological innovations that made food production grow much faster than predicted by Malthus. Because food production increased immensely, both population and food production per capita could rise. Nevertheless, the debate over whether Malthus would eventually be proved right has never really stopped. In the second half of the twentieth century, the discussion was expanded beyond food production to encompass issues such as the limits to economic growth and environmental degradation.

The rise of the environmental movement in the 1960s rekindled interest in the ideas of Malthus, particularly the notion that an increasing global population and the accompanying increase in consumption would inexorably lead to human misery. Supporters of Malthus's body of thought, therefore, advocate putting brakes on the process of population growth, which would ideally lead to a stabilization or even a decrease of the global population. The critics of Malthus and his present-day supporters maintain, however, that population growth can continue without restraints. Their conviction is that human inventiveness will always generate new technological fixes to any problems stemming from overpopulation. The concept of *sustainable development* represents something of a compromise between the neo-Malthusians and their opponents, by in principle allowing for any amount of economic and population growth, as long as it leaves intact the opportunities of future generations. In Chapter 12 we return to these issues.

At the start of the twenty-first century, there are still many areas of the world where population growth is very high. As a consequence, the world as a whole also exhibits a high level of population growth. In this context, the UN projects that nearly all of the population growth until 2050 will occur in Sub-Saharan Africa – a region that is already characterized by low standards of living, limited state capacity, and political instability (UN 2017). By 2050, seven of the world's most populated countries will be in Africa. These are troubling developments in view of the societal problems that overpopulation can give rise to.

However, no matter how undesirable these population trends on the African continent may seem, it will be extremely difficult to slow them down or even revert them. After all, the seeds for these trends have already taken root, as most African countries have huge cohorts of young people that have just or are about to reach childbearing age – see Nigeria's population pyramid in Figure 5.7. Furthermore, one should realize that, in the end, people do not primarily make their decisions about how many children to have based on policies or prescriptions imposed from above, but rather on the basis of a wide range of micro-level motives and circumstances, as we discussed in the section "Explanations of fertility levels".

The exponential curve and doubling time

The American physicist Albert Bartlett (1994) was one of the foremost advocates of Malthusianism during the latter half of the twentieth century, giving constant warnings about the dangers of high population growth. His best-known contention was that, "The greatest shortcoming of the human race is our inability to understand the exponential function". The *exponential function* is a mathematical expression that describes the behaviour of something that increases by a fixed percentage per unit of time.

According to Bartlett, population growth to a large extent follows an exponential pattern, whereby an increase in the number of children born today means that in a few decades there will be more people of childbearing age than there are now, which then translates into an even larger number of children born, who will later give birth to again an even bigger number of children, and so on. This exponential growth process is subject to substantial multiplier effects, leading to accelerated increases of the global population, not unlike the value of an investment that grows by compound interest. When presented graphically, exponential growth is depicted as an upward-sloping curve that gets increasingly steep over time. This is illustrated in Figure 5.3 with the global population growth under a constant-fertility scenario.

Bartlett formulated several laws relating to population problems. One of Bartlett's laws states that the response time of populations to changes in fertility is equal to the average length of a human life – namely around 70 years. This explains why one still observes fast population growth in a number of Asian countries, despite the fact that fertility has decreased. This lagged response is also referred to as *population momentum*. Another law posits that the size of the global population that can be sustained (the earth's *carrying capacity*) and the sustainable average standard of living of the global population are negatively related. That is, the higher the standard of living that one aspires, the more urgent it is to slow global population growth. Still another of Bartlett's laws contends that the benefits of population growth accrue to relatively few individuals, while the costs of population growth are spread across all members of society.

As already alluded to, the assumption that the rate of population growth is constant is of central importance to Bartlett's predictions. In that case, even a small positive growth rate of only a few percent or a fraction of a percent per year means that the overall population size will fairly soon spiral out of control. This is illustrated by the concept of *doubling time*, which is defined as the number of years it takes for a population to double in size. The following formula that approximates the doubling time of a population gives some insight into the effect that a certain growth rate has on future population size: $T = 70 / r$. Suppose now that a certain country has 100 million inhabitants in 2015, and that the annual growth rate is two percent per year. Using the aforementioned formula, one calculates that in 35 years' time, around 2050, the population will be in the region of 200 million.

All of this said, in light of the evidence presented earlier in this chapter on fertility trends, it is difficult to maintain the assumption of a constant population growth rate over time. As such, it is unlikely that the global population will be subject to an "exponential explosion" in the coming century. For this reason, the medium-fertility projection of the UN plotted in Figure 5.3 entails much slower growth than the constant-fertility scenario. However, despite these caveats, Bartlett's laws contain many interesting and sometimes counterintuitive insights that are worth keeping in mind when thinking about population trends.

Population ageing

Just when global population was reaching new heights around the turn of the century, a new problem came to the fore in the industrialized countries of the West: due to the substantial fall in fertility during the preceding few decades, combined with the continuous rise in life expectancy, populations began to age. The population pyramid of Japan in Figure 5.7 illustrates the consequences: an increase in the share of elderly people in society (population ageing). Even though the retirement age is also being increased in many countries, the group that demographers classify as elderly dependents is expected to increase substantially.

The increase in the elderly population is attributable to two factors. First, there is a decrease in the fertility rate. As we showed in Figure 5.6, the TFR in European countries and in Northern America decreased substantially during the latter half of the twentieth century. Currently, all European countries have fertility rates below the replacement level (UN 2017). Fertility is particularly low in Hungary, Poland, Moldova, Slovakia, Bosnia-Herzegovina, Croatia, Greece, Italy, Malta, Portugal, Spain, and Germany, which all have a TFR of less than 1.5 and are expected to experience declines in population in the range of 15 percent or more by 2050 (UN 2017). Second, there is an ongoing increase in life expectancy, as also showed in Figure 5.6, which will continue in all Western industrialized countries, with the exception of the US.

The extent to which population ageing is a problem can be captured by the *old-age dependency ratio*. This is equal to the number of elderly dependents (all people older than 64) divided by the working-age population (all people aged 15–64), usually expressed as a percentage. According to the World Bank, the old-age dependency ratio in the world as a whole has increased from 8.6 in 1960 to 12.6 in 2015. During the last few decades of the twentieth century, this percentage was around 20 to 25 in most European countries and Japan. At the start of the twenty-first century, it began to increase and in light of the low current fertility rates, it will only continue to grow. This expectation applies under the assumption that immigration from countries such as Nigeria will not increase, or only by a limited extent. The overall expectation is that several societal problems are likely to arise as a consequence of population ageing and the increasing old-age dependency ratio.

One of the potential consequences of the shrinking working-age population within Europe is that it will lead to economic stagnation. Another consequence, as discussed in Chapter 4, concerns the sustainability of pension systems. The ageing of the population implies that there will be relatively fewer working people to support the pensions of the elderly. As a consequence, it is possible that tensions between younger and older generations will increase in the future, since younger people may be reluctant to give up a large part of their income to support the pensions of an increasing number of elderly people, especially knowing that their own future pension entitlements may be less generous. Some commentators argue in this regard that the "class struggle" that traditionally used to divide politics will be replaced by a "generational struggle". The emergence in some countries of parties specifically targeted at young people or the elderly illustrates this shift.

One particularly acute problem is the replacement of the *baby boom generation* by the generation that succeeded it. The baby boomers comprise those born in the decades immediately following the Second World War (roughly between 1945 and 1975), when fertility rates were particularly high. In the US, the TFR peaked around 1957, after which there was a dramatic decrease until the mid-1970s. The same occurred in Europe, although the TFR peaked slightly later, around 1964. The baby boomers began receiving their pensions in around 2010. Due to the size of this group, pension outlays as a percentage of GDP will increase as they move through the older age categories of the population pyramid. Similarly, a huge increase of medical costs is likely to occur as well, since it is the elderly that need the most health care.

One potential solution to these various challenges would be to adopt more liberal immigration policies, which would release some pressure off the shoulders of the native working-age population. However, such policy changes are unlikely to offer a full-scale solution. In order to compensate for the population decrease brought about by low fertility, the numbers of immigrants that would have to be admitted yearly would likely exceed the absorptive capacity of the receiving countries. This is especially true in light of growing hostility to immigrants in many Western countries (see Chapter 6).

In terms of other solutions, an increase in the fertility rate would be possible to engineer, at least in principle, by incentivizing young couples to have more children. As mentioned in the section "Explanations of fertility levels", several countries have indeed introduced financial incentives for families to have additional children. However, in the same way as it is difficult to reduce fertility in a context of explosive population growth, a large and sustained increase in the fertility rate is unlikely to be achievable without fundamentally altering current social structures, as couples' fertility decisions are influenced by a complex interplay of factors (such as women's level of education and labour force participation, the availability of childcare facilities, the costs of raising children, not to mention cultural norms), each of which cannot be changed easily.

That said, Gøsta Esping-Andersen and Francesco Billari (2015) argue that fertility rates in industrialized countries will recover somewhat as norms of gender egalitarianism spread through society, marking countries' entry to the fifth stage of the demographic transition model. The idea is that, as women become more highly educated, they will demand a greater involvement of their partners in childrearing and household activities. This, in turn, will help women to combine having children with participating in the labour market, thus effectively reducing the costs of having children. As such, it becomes easier for couples to attain their desired number of children, which for most people still equals 2. In line with this narrative, the fertility rates in the US, the UK and several Nordic countries have recovered in recent years, although they have not yet returned to the replacement level. See Chapter 8 for a more comprehensive discussion of the theoretical underpinnings of this fertility reversal.

Recommended readings

- Max Roser and Esteban Ortiz-Ospina (2018) provide an accessible and incredibly rich overview of all kinds of data regarding global population growth, summarized in illuminating charts. The data include information on historical trends (starting from 10,000 BC), the changing geographic distribution of the world population and projections on what the future has to bring. Roser and Ortiz-Ospina also delve into the drivers of global population change, including changes in fertility levels.
- While the demographic transition is often discussed as being caused by social change, David Reher (2011) zooms in on the societal changes that have occurred in response to the demographic transition. He shows that during its different phases the demographic transition provides a different mix of positive and negative effects, or opportunities and challenges. Reher assesses both the experiences of demographic forerunners as well as countries that are still going through the demographic transition, and also discusses policy implications.
- John Bongaarts and Christophe Guilmoto (2015) provide a state-of-the-art analysis of the trends in the number of "missing women" around the world, looking back over the past 40 years and ahead to 2050. Among other things, they show that there has been a recent rise in the number of missing women in many countries. In accounting for these trends, Bongaarts and Guilmoto explore the role of post-birth sex discrimination, as well as the role of pre-birth sex selection, which has become increasingly relevant due to availability of new technologies.

Bibliography

Aksoy, Ozan, and Francesco C. Billari. 2018. "Political Islam, Marriage, and Fertility: Evidence from a Natural Experiment". *American Journal of Sociology* 123:1296–1340.

Bartlett, Albert A. 1994. "Reflections on Sustainability, Population Growth, and the Environment". *Population and Environment* 16:5–35.

Bongaarts, John, and Christophe Z. Guilmoto. 2015. "How Many More Missing Women? Excess Female Mortality and Prenatal Sex Selection, 1970–2050". *Population and Development Review* 41:241–269.

Caldwell, John C. 1982. *Theory of Fertility Decline*. London: Academic Press.

Coale, Ansley J., and Susan C. Watkins (eds.). 1986. *The Decline of Fertility in Europe: The Revised Proceedings of a Conference on the Princeton European Fertility Project*. Princeton, NJ: Princeton University Press.

Esping-Andersen, Gøsta, and Francesco C. Billari. 2015. "Re-theorizing Family Demographics". *Population and Development Review* 41:1–31.

Kanazawa, Satoshi, and Mary C. Still. 2000. "Why Men Commit Crimes (and Why They Desist)". *Sociological Theory* 1:434–447.

Malthus, Thomas R. 2015[1798]. *An Essay on the Principle of Population and Other Writings*, (ed.) Robert Mayhew. London: Penguin Classics.

Oltmans Ananat, Elizabeth, and Daniel M. Hungerman. 2012. "The Power of the Pill for the Next Generation: Oral Contraception's Effects on Fertility, Abortion, and Maternal and Child Characteristics". *Review of Economics and Statistics* 94:37–51.

Reher, David S. 2011. "Economic and Social Implications of the Demographic Transition". *Population and Development Review* 37:11–33.

Roser, Max, and Esteban Ortiz-Ospina. 2018. "World Population Growth". https://ourworldindata.org/world-population-growth.

Sen, Amartya. 1990. "More than 100 Million Women are Missing". *New York Review of Books*, 20 December 1990, pp. 61–66.

Shi, Yaojiang, and John J. Kennedy. 2016. "Delayed Registration and Identifying the 'Missing Girls' in China". *The China Quarterly* 228:1018–1038.

UN. 1999. *The World at Six Billion*. New York, NY: United Nations.

UN. 2017. *World Population Prospects: The 2017 Revision*. New York, NY: United Nations.

Werding, Martin. 2014. "Children Are Costly, but Raising Them May Pay: The Economic Approach to Fertility". *Demographic Research* 30:253–276.

6 Migration and the multicultural society

Chapter overview

In 2015, more than a million migrants crossed into Europe. This European migrant crisis has intensified concerns about how to deal with large-scale migration. In this chapter, we focus on the arrival of non-Western migrants into Europe and Northern America during the twentieth and twenty-first centuries. We provide explanations for these migration flows, and evaluate policy reactions in the host countries. Since the 1970s, the US, Canada, and many European countries have adopted a policy of multiculturalism, whereby migrants have been encouraged to preserve their own culture rather than to embrace the culture of the host society. Yet, there is an ongoing debate about the merits of multiculturalism. The US has been confronted with considerable immigration from Central America, while European countries have been confronted with rapidly growing populations of Muslim immigrants. In both cases, social tensions have been rising, and structural poverty among immigrants is substantial. We point to segregation as an important obstacle to successful integration, and explain the process of segregation by means of our macro-micro-macro framework. Finally, we link criticism of multiculturalism to the increasing popularity of far-right and anti-immigration parties.

The rising salience of migration

At the peak of the European migrant crisis in 2015, more than a million migrants from North Africa and the Middle East crossed into Europe. These migrants comprised several different sorts of people: labourers, asylum seekers and refugees, and those merely hoping to be reunited with their families. In this chapter, we focus on the arrival of non-Western migrants into Europe and Northern America during the twentieth and twenty-first centuries. Of the groups who have arrived and settled in the West, Muslims have been a particularly important source of social tensions, as evidenced by growing anti-Muslim sentiment and the growing electoral success of prominent anti-Muslim political parties, such as Marine Le Pen's National Front (since June 2018 called National Rally) in France and Geert Wilders' Party for Freedom in the Netherlands.

In many countries, non-Western migrant groups face major challenges. Among other things, they are over-represented in unemployment statistics (Heath, Rothon, and Kilpi 2008). To a large extent, this can be attributed to their lower levels of educational attainment and language proficiency. However, while immigrants' levels of education have risen markedly since the 1990s, especially among second-generation immigrants, the aforementioned employment gaps have barely diminished. Within migrant communities, there is consequently widespread indignation about systematic disadvantages in the labour market and perceived discrimination on the part of employers. Furthermore, non-Western immigrants face additional challenges in many other domains of society. For example, compared to members of the native population, they are relatively more frequently suspects of crime but also relatively more frequently victims of crime, and they often live in segregated or deprived neighbourhoods, with limited social ties to native residents (e.g., Huijnk and Andriessen 2016).

Since roughly the 1970s onwards, both the US and many European countries have adopted a policy of *multiculturalism*, whereby migrants have been encouraged to preserve their own culture, rather than to embrace the culture of the host society. This policy was motivated by a belief that acknowledgement and respect for cultural differences between natives and newcomers would foster integration. In both the US and Europe, doubts about the veracity of this belief have become increasingly common, which has fomented anti-immigrant sentiment and contributed to the rise of anti-immigrant parties. Due to high rates of structural poverty within some migrant groups, as well as continuing social tensions between migrants and natives, dissatisfaction with the policy of multiculturalism has been increasing.

After the financial crisis of 2008 and the resulting economic recession, immigration and multiculturalism have overtaken the economy as the most salient political fault lines in the Western world. In France, the anti-immigration National Front party reached the second round of the 2017 general election, and garnered 34 percent of the vote. In Austria, the anti-immigration Freedom Party of Austria garnered 46 percent of the vote in the 2016 presidential election, and joined the governing coalition following the 2017 parliamentary election. In Germany, the anti-immigration Alternative for Germany, which received 5 percent of the vote in the 2013 election, won 12.6 percent of the vote at the 2017 election. In the Netherlands, the anti-immigration Party for Freedom increased its share of the vote between 2012 and 2017 elections from ten percent to 13 percent. In Sweden, the anti-immigration Sweden Democrats, which received 13 percent of the vote in the 2014 election, saw their vote share rise to 18 percent in the 2018 election. And, of course, concern over immigration played a key role in the UK's vote to leave the European Union in 2016, as well as the 2016 election of Donald Trump as President in the US.

When dissatisfaction about immigration started to increase in the early 1990s, and there was a corresponding uptick in the number of xenophobic incidents, several European countries implemented stricter migration controls. Between 1992 and 2000, the rate of immigration from countries outside the EU therefore decreased. In France and Germany, for example, the requirements for asylum seekers to be accepted were made more stringent, which led to a temporary decrease in the number of asylum seekers admitted to those countries. At the same time, the integration of the children of migrants was encouraged, for example via laws granting them citizenship in their countries of residence. Italy and Spain granted a legal amnesty to hundreds of thousands of foreigners who were resident illegally in those countries. The trend toward reduced levels of migration in Europe was reversed dramatically in 2014, when tens of thousands of migrants (including many refugees) began entering the continent from the Middle East and North Africa. Levels of migration into the US have remained consistently high for the last few decades.

Explaining international migration

The total migrant stock in the world has increased substantially over time, from around 75 million in 1960 to about 100 million at the beginning of the 1980s. Since then, the growth of the global migrant stock accelerated, reaching a level of more than 240 million in 2015. One of the big factors driving this recent growth has been the high fertility rate in Africa (see Chapter 5) combined with the meagre economic perspectives on that continent. As an illustration of the growth of the global migrant stock, Figure 6.1 plots the share of migrants in the total population by continent since 1960.

While there is no notable change in the migrant share in Africa, Asia, and Latin America – with this share being consistently low over the whole period – since the 1980s there has been a marked rise in the share of migrants in the populations of Europe, Northern America, and Oceania. In Europe, the migrant share rose from below four percent in 1985 to around 11 percent by 2015. In Northern America, this share nearly doubled from about eight percent in 1980 to almost 16 percent in 2015. Also in Oceania, which always used to have a much higher base level, there has been a clear surge, especially since 2000.

With respect to explaining international migration, the sociologists Douglas Massey and Nancy Denton (1993) make a distinction between explanations of the *initiation* of migration and of the *continuation* of migration. For explaining the initiation of migration, early neoclassical

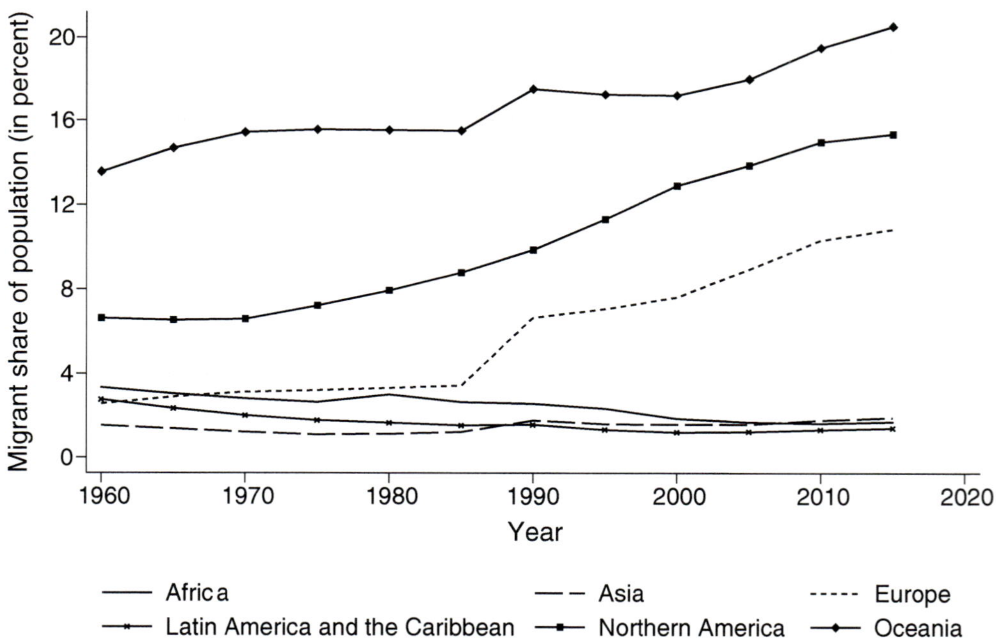

Figure 6.1 The share of migrants in the total population by continent, 1960–2015

Note: Data are from the UN Population Division.

economic models of international migration emphasize wage differentials between countries. These models are based on the assumption that self-interested individuals will attempt to maximize their incomes and are in principle willing to migrate to achieve this goal. In line with this argument, the strong wage differentials between the rich industrialized countries of Western Europe and Northern America on the one hand, and the poor countries of Africa, Latin America, and South West Asia on the other, from the 1960s onwards, have provided powerful incentives for people from poorer countries to migrate in search of work and greater economic prosperity.

In response to the neoclassical economic models, Oded Stark and David Bloom (1985) introduced the *new economics of labour migration* (NELM). This approach conceptualizes migration not as a decision taken by a single individual to maximize their own income, but rather as a way for risk-averse families or households to diversify their sources of income in the face of uncertainty. In particular, families in developing countries generally face high levels of uncertainty regarding their income flows, due to political instability, economic turbulence, social conflict, and a relatively strong reliance on agriculture.

In order to deal with this uncertainty and reduce the risk of falling into greater poverty, families adopt informal strategies to, for example, spread the risk of unemployment. This can be done by employing particular family members in one business and other family members in another business. A similar, but more far-reaching, strategy is to have one or more family members migrate to work in another country. The family members who have migrated can then send part of their income back to their relatives in their home country.

For several African countries such remittances form a substantial part of the national income. According to the economist Edward Taylor (1999), this money also positively influences economic development in the home country. Indeed, these payments are often invested in productive activities, such as the acquisition of more land, cattle and tools, or education for younger family members. More generally, remittances seem to have a multiplier effect in the migrant-sending countries, as the extra cash inflow leads to more spending, which in turn results in more production and thereby also increased employment and domestic income. However, the strength of such multiplier effects varies greatly between countries. Moreover, a problem for the migrant-sending countries is that it is often their most talented, well-trained and resourceful citizens who emigrate. This *brain drain* may undermine the opportunities for domestic growth and development in the migrant-sending country.

As mentioned before, the continuation of migration requires different, although related explanations. One central phenomenon concerns *chain migration*. This term refers to the tendency that when a few migrants from a certain country of origin have established a foothold within a certain host country, the magnitude of the migratory flow between these two countries will increase over time. The pioneers incur the fixed costs of setting up a new community. They then send information back to friends, relatives and associates in their home countries, encouraging others to follow suit. When the next wave of migrants arrives, they typically move into the community set up by the pioneers. This is especially true when the decision to migrate takes place at the level of the family rather than the individual.

Networks of relatives, friends, and associates bind the country of origin to the country of destination through several mechanisms. First, they function as conduits for information about the country of destination, including about the availability of jobs. Second, they may influence decisions about which members of the community, or which members of the family, will migrate, and where they will settle themselves in the destination country. Third, they offer assistance to migrants who arrive in the destination country in the form of housing, money, information, and emotional support. Insofar as this is the case, they facilitate the integration of migrants into existing communities and into the host country. As the sociologist Douglas Massey (1988) notes, social networks amplify migration flows by lowering the costs of migration for people who are considering moving.

Is there an optimal level of immigration?

The prominent development economist Paul Collier (2013) contends in his book *Exodus: How Migration is Changing our World* that social scientists have often been too preoccupied with the question whether immigration is good or bad. Collier compares this question with the question of whether eating is good or bad, arguing that it is far more interesting to ask the question how much eating or immigration is optimal. Yet, the question of how much immigration is optimal is difficult to answer, because, among other things, the costs and benefits of immigration are unequally distributed across society. That is, some people may benefit from immigration, whereas others may be harmed by it.

Collier argues that the two main groups who benefit from immigration are landlords and large employers in labour-intensive industries. Both of these groups will experience an increase in profits, because there is more demand for housing and because immigration will put a downward pressure on wages (all else being equal). Drawing on Mancur Olson's theory of collective action (see Chapter 2), Collier subsequently argues that these groups – being relatively small and well organized – are very successful at pressuring governments to adopt policies that facilitate immigration. In doing so, they often join forces with human rights advocates, who view immigration as a way to help people from poorer countries.

According to Collier, the costs of immigration are mainly felt by individuals living in already deprived areas, who experience competition from immigrants for scarce jobs, houses, schools and government services. Yet, these indigenous disadvantaged are large in number and politically disorganized, and therefore often unable to exert influence on government policy. However, this is not always the case, as illustrated by the 2016 Brexit referendum in the UK, which many citizens took as an opportunity to speak out against the inflow of immigrants.

Collier believes that the answer to the question of how much immigration is optimal very much depends on how rapidly immigrants merge with the indigenous society. If this is a relatively fast process, Collier believes that more immigrants can be absorbed, whereas a slow process of integration more easily gives rise to inter-group conflict and economic costs, reducing the absorptive capacity of the host society.

With regard to the social consequences of immigration, Collier expects that moderate migration will lead to overall social benefits, while rapid migration may reduce levels of trust and cooperation, thus threatening to undermine the social fabric that keeps together society. As far as the economic consequences of immigration are concerned, how much immigration is optimal depends very much on the situation of the receiving country. If a country is, for example, confronted with an ageing population and the problems that come with that (see Chapters 4 and 5), immigration could be beneficial for society, increasing the workforce and helping to keep pension and healthcare systems affordable. Other examples concern the shortage of skilled IT workers in Germany in the 1990s and of nurses in Britain in the 1970s. Immigration of workers with those skills in both cases had a beneficial economic impact.

In the end, there is no single straightforward answer to the question how much immigration is optimal. Instead, the answer very much depends on how different factors are politically weighed against each other in a country. For example, during the 2016 Brexit referendum a substantial proportion of the British population expressed a willingness to give up part of their wealth as long as Britain would regain total control over its inflow of immigrants. Finally, moral issues may be at stake as well, such as if the immigrants in question are refugees rather than economic migrants, which is typical for the large inflow of immigrants into Europe since 2015. In this context, the UN 1951 Refugees Convention guarantees the basic rights of refugees, which arguably override the question of how much immigration is optimal.

Immigration control policies

Governments of societies receiving migrants have to find a balance between the interests of the migrants and those left behind in their home country versus the interests of the indigenous population. However, whatever this balance may look like exactly, some control on the entry of immigrants is likely to be required. Yet, exerting effective immigration control is notoriously complex. Despite the fact that barriers to illegal entry have been erected in many countries over the past few decades, considerable numbers of illegal migrants continue to slip through the net.

An additional problem for the EU in particular is that very few resources have been invested in the control of its external borders, especially the southern borders of Greece, Spain and Italy. Due to the ease of cross-border movement within the EU, these southern borders do not merely function as national borders, but rather as entry barriers to the EU as a whole. From this perspective, all EU member states should work together to patrol and protect these borders, yet – as reality shows – member states face strong free-riding incentives to take a back seat and leave these issues for the southern member states to sort out.

As the European migrant crisis unfolded, many EU member states began implementing their own border controls, in some cases in violation of the EU's Schengen agreement. However, no matter how strict the border controls, individuals attempting to enter a country illegally are often highly resourceful. The methods used are endless, but some of the most used are that these illegal immigrants pass through border checkpoints with forged papers; they enter a country on a tourist visa and then disappear into the population or they leave asylum centres and then lie low to prevent repatriation.

As the stock of illegal migrants living in Western countries has increased, governments have sought to restrict their access to public goods, such as education, healthcare, social benefits and the labour market. By introducing measures to prevent migrants from accessing jobs and public services, governments aim to incentivize "self-deportations" whereby illegal immigrants voluntarily leave the country. Indeed, this was the plan that the Republican presidential candidate Mitt Romney proposed in 2012 to deal with the large illegal immigrant population in the US.

The problem, however, is that such regulations have to be executed by actors within the civic and market spheres (such as schools, hospitals, letting agencies and businesses), which have not traditionally possessed such powers. Schools would be legally obliged to reject individuals who could not show valid passports or residency permits. Doctors would be forced to deny medical care to such individuals. Similarly, letting agencies and companies would also be put in charge of tasks that used to fall under the realm of the state. A reasonable objection to these regulations is that civic and market organizations should not be burdened with tasks that actually come under the purview of central government.

A striking example of an immigration control policy that backfired is the US border enforcement that tried to reduce the inflow of Latino immigration from the south. The undocumented population in the US grew to 12 million in 2008. According to Douglas Massey, Karen Pren and Jorge Durand (2016), the threat of Latino immigration, partly propounded by politicians who could benefit from exploiting this threat, gave rise to a moral panic that ultimately led to border enforcement in a rather military fashion. The militarization of the border was not only disproportionate to the size of the undocumented inflow, but had actually no real effect on the likelihood of gaining entry in the course of a series of attempts.

The unintended consequences, however, were manifold. More migrants went to hostile territories to cross the border and increasingly had to rely on paid smugglers, which increased the costs and risks of undocumented crossings. This context made immigrants who previously had been following a pattern of *circular migration* (e.g., moving into and out of the US on a seasonal basis while maintaining their home country as their primary base) less willing to return home, since they knew it would be difficult to subsequently get back into the US. As a consequence, in 2010 hardly any undocumented migrants returned to their home countries, in contrast to previous years when the border control was looser. This once again shows that policies often have unintended effects.

This example notwithstanding, it is not the case that policies designed to reduce illegal immigrant streams are necessarily always doomed to fail, as Stephen Castles (2004) shows. Several countries have in fact had a large measure of success in controlling immigration. Both South Korea and Japan, two industrialized countries with productive economies and high standards of living, have had very low rates of immigration for decades. As of 2016, the foreign-born population is only 2.9 percent in South Korea and only 1.9 percent in Japan. By contrast, the foreign-born population in the US, for example, is 14.3 percent, in the UK 13.2 percent, in Canada 21.9 percent, and in Australia 27.7 percent. Note that these figures understate the total differences in immigration rates over the last few decades, given that the English-speaking countries have many second and third generation immigrants as well (i.e., individuals born in the receiving country to parents who immigrated or their children), whereas South Korea and Japan have almost none. The latter, in combination with a low fertility rate, results in an ageing and ultimately shrinking population (see Chapter 5 for a discussion of the Japanese case).

The puzzle of economic development and increasing emigration

A policy measure to control immigration that is often discussed in Europe is to facilitate economic development in poorer countries in order to reduce incentives for young people from those countries to emigrate. The reasoning is that if one can make a decent living in one's home country, one is less likely to emigrate. As the Gallup World Poll indicates, it is indeed the case that in the richest countries people are less likely to emigrate than in the poorest nations. However, as the economist Michael Clemens has shown convincingly (2014), the relationship between economic development and emigration is not linear. What is more, Clemens argues that an increase in the economic performance of a very poor nation will more likely lead to an increase than to a decrease of emigration. To understand why this is the case, we need to once more descend to the micro level of individuals behaving in a certain macro-level context.

Figure 6.2 illustrates with a macro-micro-macro model why rich countries can expect an increase in the supply of immigrants from poor countries in case of increasing economic development in those poor countries. Let us take, for example, migration streams between Africa and Europe. The reasoning is as follows: assume that there is a ten percent increase of GDP in a poor African nation (point A in Figure 6.2). As a consequence, the middle classes will get slightly richer. However, despite becoming slightly richer, they are still likely to make much more money in their potential destination country and, importantly, they have more resources to invest in a better education and in a more successful emigration in general (point B in Figure 6.2). Hence, in such a context, individuals belonging to the middle class are more likely to emigrate than before the economic growth took place (point C in Figure 6.2). At the macro level, this ultimately leads to a bigger supply of emigrants to Europe (point D in Figure 6.2). Furthermore, what we have learned from the demographic transition model in Chapter 5 is that more wealth leads to lower child mortality in relative poor nations, but fertility will not decline. This situation may lead to even more emigration, due to an increase in the population size of the poor country and the increased pressure for domestic resources this brings about. Of course, if in the long run the economic growth in the home country becomes very substantial, leading to prosperous prospects of its citizens, the incentives to emigrate will ultimately decline.

As this example underlines, successful policy making on migration is rather complex. Even more so if one realizes that cooperation between African and European countries might be essential in order to reduce the brain drain from African countries and the large inflow of immigrants into European countries. This cooperation is especially problematic when authoritarian regimes are concerned. European leaders are usually reluctant to cooperate with such regimes, and for good reasons, but this makes it harder to exert a bigger control over immigrant flows.

Immigrants' integration into the host society

The level and speed of integration in the receiving country is relevant for the support for immigration among the indigenous population. When it comes to immigrants' integration, a key issue

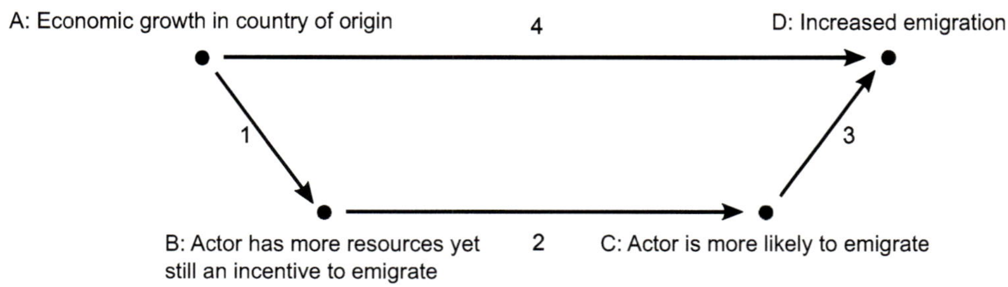

Figure 6.2 How economic development in a poor country can stimulate emigration

concerns citizenship of the host country, which will in all kinds of ways help immigrants to fully and unrestrictedly take part in the host society. The rules for acquiring citizenship differ from one country to another, and of course change over time, as new laws are adopted. Partly as a result of this, naturalization rates (whereby people acquire citizenship of the host country) vary substantially across European countries as well as within countries over time; see Figure 6.3.

In practice, most countries have legislation that combine the principles of *jus sanguinis* (the right of blood) and *jus soli* (the right of soil). Jus sanguinis grants citizenship to those who descend from members of the original nation state. It is based on an ethnic/cultural conception of the nation, namely the idea that people are connected by extended kinship, and have a common culture rooted in the country's history. Jus soli grants citizenship to those born in the territory of the nation state. This could also be children born to parents who are themselves not citizens of their country of residence because they were born elsewhere.

A third principle that has become increasingly popular over time is *jus domicili* (the right of residence), which grants citizenship on the basis of long-term residence in a country. According to this principle, foreign residents can typically make an application for citizenship once they have lived in the country for a sufficient number of years. In addition to these three traditional citizenship criteria, some countries also grant citizenship to foreign nationals who have made significant economic investments in that country, or who are simply willing to pay a large amount of money to the government in order to obtain citizenship.

There are fierce discussions within many Western countries on who should be granted citizenship. One of the questions is whether naturalization should come with the whole package of

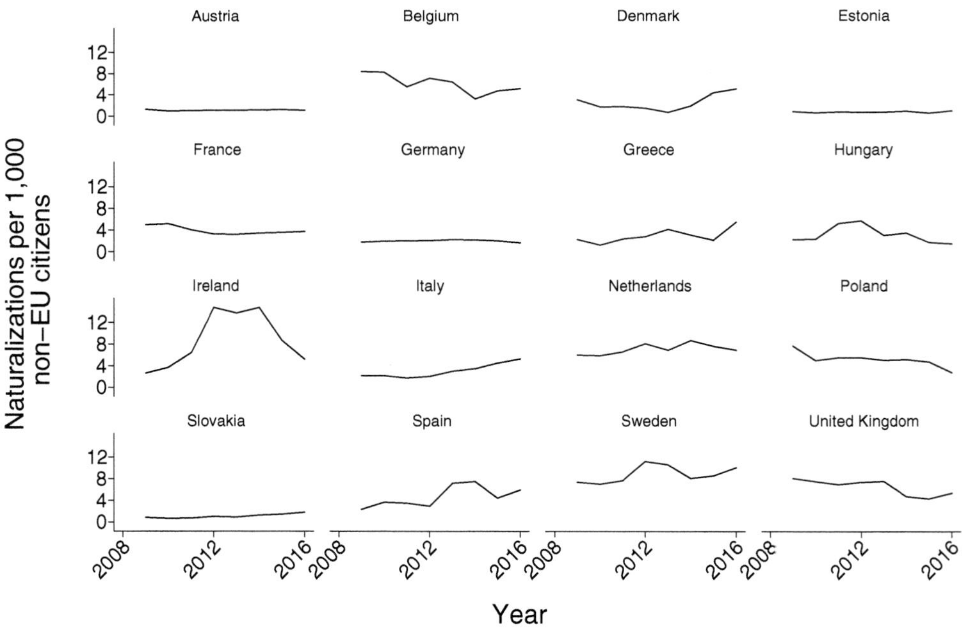

Figure 6.3 Trends in naturalization rates across a selection of European countries

Note: Data are from Eurostat. The denominator of the naturalization rate is the number of residents (in thousands) in a country that do not yet have EU citizenship prior to naturalization.

rights attached to the welfare state. If the number of immigrants is very large, there is usually less willingness to supply the whole package, as this might threaten the continued affordability of the welfare state. Another question that often comes up, given desirability of rapid assimilation of newcomers to the national community, is what measures should be taken to stimulate immigrants to learn the language and to practice national traditions. For example, should this also imply that they should foreswear the culture of their country of origin?

For a long time, governments in Western countries have assumed that migrants would automatically integrate as they spend more time in the host country. In the last decades of the twentieth century, however, it has become clear that the process of social-cultural, as well as structural, integration does not happen that easily. Many migrants keep operating predominantly in their own socio-cultural environment (e.g., mainly having friends from their own ethnic group, joining clubs and associations with mostly members of their own group, and marrying people from the same country of origin) and there are clear processes of segregation in housing, work and school. In most countries immigrants also have a socio-economically disadvantaged position compared to the native population, lagging behind in terms of educational attainment, employment rates and earnings. What is more, it is not uncommon for immigrant groups to be overrepresented in crime and delinquency statistics, whereas they tend to be underrepresented in the political arena.

One factor that sometimes holds back immigrants' integration into the host society is that they are also still closely tied to their country of origin and influenced through such transnational ties. For instance, wealthy elites in Saudi Arabia give financial support to mosques and other Islamic organizations in Europe and the US to expand their global influence. Similarly, political leaders in countries such as Morocco and Turkey regularly make attempts to influence the behaviour of Moroccan and Turkish minorities in European countries. In recent years, Turkish president Erdogan has, for example, been shown to have a long arm – among other things attempting to influence what Turks living outside Turkey should vote for during elections in their host country. In many cases, such foreign influences work against the process of integration by encouraging migrants to retain the values and allegiances from their home country, which may be in conflict with the values and identity of their host country.

Assimilation versus multiculturalism

In terms of how host societies approach the integration of immigrants, we can distinguish two dominant schools of thought, one favouring assimilation and the other advocating multiculturalism. *Assimilation* refers to the process whereby immigrants become gradually more resembling of the native majority, adopting their norms and values, behaving in the same way, and mixing with natives in the workplace, schools and neighbourhoods. By the time immigrants are completely assimilated, they have become indistinguishable from the native majority. Proponents of assimilation usually claim that only by fully adjusting to the culture of the host country, can immigrants successfully participate in society and peacefully co-exist with the native majority. This line of reasoning tends to be popular among political conservatives.

Multiculturalism, on the other hand, can be seen as an expression of a liberal political ideology. In a multicultural society, groups do not have to sacrifice their cultural or ethnic identity. Proponents of multiculturalism believe that it is very well possible for different social groups to peacefully co-exist while staying loyal to their cultural origins. They also state that it should be possible to have more than one official national language and that, consequently, immigrant children should be allowed to receive education in the language of their own ethnic group. Furthermore, many multiculturalists believe that cultural diversity should not just be tolerated but even cherished or stimulated, as it will in the end make for a more flourishing society. To attain such diversity, they also see a role for *affirmative action* under certain circumstances, whereby places in sports teams, government departments or public universities are reserved for members of minority groups (Kymlicka and Bashir 2008).

The assimilation school was most prominent for most of the eighteenth and nineteenth centuries. During this period, nation states of Western Europe attempted to limit the ethnic, religious and linguistic diversity within their populations, with the aim of fostering a sense of nationhood as a homogenous, unified entity. Since the 1970s, however, multiculturalism has been the primary philosophy guiding immigration and integration policies in most Western countries (Kymlicka 2012). With that said, since the start of the twenty-first century, multiculturalism has come increasingly under attack, being blamed for the lack of integration among certain immigrant groups.

Yet, despite such criticisms, multiculturalism continues to enjoy many advocates. The Canadian political philosopher Will Kymlicka (2012), for example, argues that in most Western countries multicultural policies have had a positive impact on political participation and social capital. He furthermore shows that, since the turn of the century, social policy has in fact become more multicultural in a number of European countries (viz. Belgium, Finland, Greece, Ireland, Norway, Portugal, Spain and Sweden), although there has been a big turn away from multiculturalism in the Netherlands and, to a lesser extent, Denmark and Italy. It is important to note, however, that since the publication of Kymlicka's report, several other European countries (including Austria, Belgium, France, Germany, Hungary, Sweden, Switzerland and the UK) have also grown more sceptical of multiculturalism. Overall, Kymlicka concludes that multiculturalism seems to work best when immigrants come from many different countries of origin, rather than overwhelmingly from a single country. In the latter case, there seems a greater risk of ethnic conflict.

Multiculturalism in the United States

The US is a country with a mixed ethnic community where various cultural traditions co-exist. Chinatown in San Francisco is an example of an ethnic enclave with its own culture. Another example are the Hispanic communities where the majority speaks Spanish. An important cause for this ethnic diversity is that in 1965, the US congress passed the Immigration and Nationality Act, which abolished the system of national quotas that had been established in 1924. This opened the door for non-Western immigrants and this liberal immigration policy has resulted in a large influx of migrants, mostly from Central America and South-East Asia. At the same time, the US also adopted a policy of multiculturalism, which has given rise to quotas in certain parts of society (universities are probably the most well-known example) that seek to achieve ethnic and religious diversity. Both the high rates of immigration and the policy of multiculturalism have come in for criticism, and have led to political tensions. These concern fundamental and potentially unresolvable dilemmas of the multi-ethnic society.

The 1965 Immigration and Nationality Act established rights to family reunification, and eliminated the special importance attached to prospective immigrants' level of education. All these elements of the law had the effect of reducing the amount of immigration from Western Europe, and increasing the amount of immigration from Central America and South-East Asia. From 1965 onwards, large numbers of migrants entered the country: about half a million each year during the 1970s, up to about one million each year during the 1990s. Many of the immigrants that have entered the US since the 1965 immigration act was passed have done so illegally. As a consequence, there are currently around 11 million people living in the US who do not have official residency permits, although some claim the number is as high as 22.8 million (Fazel-Zarandi, Kaplan, and Feinstein 2018).

The Pew Research Center reports that in 2015, 6.6 million immigrants living in the US are from Mexican origin. This is 27 percent of all US immigrants, although more Asians than Hispanic immigrants have arrived each year since 2010. Most of the Hispanic immigrants have a low level of education. Low-skilled Mexican immigration has had the effect of driving down wages for unskilled labour, which has negatively affected the wealth of unskilled native workers. The Pew report also concludes that Mexican families were much more likely to live below the poverty line and to use social welfare programs than native white families. These conclusions have been reinforced by the economist George Borjas's (2016) recent book, *We Wanted Workers*.

The large influx of migrants from Latin America and Asia has engendered a fierce debate about the American nation and the fundamental values in American society. In many people's view, traditional American *WASP* (White Anglo-Saxon Protestant) culture is being undermined by the arrival of large numbers of people from different cultural backgrounds. For example, whereas American public schools were traditionally mandated to teach pupils in English, many now teach exclusively in Spanish, to the dismay of many White Americans. Donald Trump's Presidential victory in 2016 can be seen as another indicator of the increasing societal dissatisfaction with multiculturalism and its emphasis on cherishing diversity and differences. Conversely, according to the proponents of these new multiculturalist policies, the previously dominant Anglo-Saxon culture should be pushed aside in favour of a culture that embraces diversity and differences.

Interestingly, the concept of diversity was introduced into American politics in 1978 by Justice Lewis Powell, an Associate Justice, when the Supreme Court gave its verdict on *Regents of the University of California versus Bakke*. The University of California had been pursuing a policy of affirmative action by admitting students to the faculty of medicine partly according to race, rather than wholly according to academic merit. Their objective had been to increase the number of students from minority groups graduating from college. A white student named Allan Bakke had been rejected, despite the fact that he had better qualifications than some of the minority applicants who were admitted. Bakke sued the university, based on the proposition that whites should be no less protected from race-based discrimination than non-whites.

California's highest court ruled in favour of Bakke, but the university appealed to the Supreme Court. This court also ruled in favour of Bakke by a narrow majority. As a consequence, the medical faculty of California was forced to admit Bakke. However, the court's ruling stipulated that, although specific racial quotas were prohibited, colleges were allowed to use race as one factor in the admissions decision. In his decisive judgement, Justice Powell rejected quota systems for certain racial groups on the grounds that these were tantamount to racism, yet he simultaneously extolled the importance of diversity within society, and argued that institutions such as colleges could serve to lift black Americans out of their disadvantaged positions. Related discussions still continue. A recent example relates to the decision of the University of Texas to reject the application of the white Abigail Fisher due to affirmative action. Fisher appealed this decision, but in two cases that ended up at the Supreme Court (in 2013 and 2016) the judges both times decided to uphold the affirmative action and reject Fisher's complaints.

Muslims in Europe

Over the last few decades, a large number of migrants from predominantly Muslim countries have settled in Western Europe. The presence of these migrants in Europe can be seen as an unintended consequence of decisions that were made almost half a century ago. During the post-war period, European governments admitted large numbers of guest workers from Turkey, Morocco, Algeria, Tunisia, and Pakistan. No one expected at the time that more than a trivial number of these guest workers would stay longer than the duration of their labour contracts. However, eventually, they began bringing their wives and children over from their countries of origin, by means of family reunification policies. There is now a large second and third generation of Muslim immigrants, who were born in the European countries that their (grand)parents migrated to. This explains why it has become more common to speak of ethnic minorities rather than immigrants.

For a long time, many Europeans embraced an inclusive and diverse society, but the growth of the Muslim population and contentious norms and practices among many Muslims provides challenges to the multicultural ideal. Currently, mainstream politicians, including German Chancellor Angela Merkel, publicly criticize multiculturalism and speak of the dangers involved. This is also influenced by findings that religious fundamentalism among Muslim immigrants and their offspring is not a marginal phenomenon. For example, based on interviews with Muslims across six European countries the sociologist Ruud Koopmans (2015:51) concludes, "Up to three quarters of Muslim respondents affirmed that Muslims should return to their roots of the faith, that there is only one interpretation of the Quran that is binding for all believers, and that religious rules are more important than secular laws".

According to the Pew Research Center (2017), there are about 25.8 million Muslims living in the EU as of 2016. Since Muslim numbers are increasing due to both continued immigration and above-replacement fertility, Islam is now the second most widely practiced religion in Europe after Christianity. Muslims comprised 3.8 percent of the European population in 2010, 4.9 percent in 2016, and – if trends continue – will comprise 11.2 percent by 2050. Table 6.1 gives an overview of the percentage of Muslims in different European countries.

It is interesting to consider whether a process of religious secularization has taken place within the Muslim community in Europe. There seem to be good reasons why this might be the case; after all, Muslim immigrants generally end up in societies that are less religious than their country of origin, so processes of assimilation may push them to lower levels of religiosity. On the other hand, it has also been argued that especially Muslim immigrants in secular societies may feel more motivated to stick to their religious identity. So, what do we see? The answer is that the evidence is somewhat mixed.

Table 6.1 The percentage of Muslims in different European countries in 2016

Country	Percentage of Muslims in the population	Country	Percentage of Muslims in the population
Poland	0.0	Slovenia	3.8
Slovakia	0.1	Italy	4.8
Lithuania	0.1	Denmark	5.4
Czech Republic	0.2	Norway	5.7
Estonia	0.2	Greece	5.7
Latvia	0.2	Germany	6.1
Portugal	0.4	Switzerland	6.1
Hungary	0.4	United Kingdom	6.3
Romania	0.4	Austria	6.9
Ireland	1.4	Netherlands	7.1
Croatia	1.6	Belgium	7.6
Malta	2.6	Sweden	8.1
Spain	2.6	France	8.8
Finland	2.7	Bulgaria	11.1
Luxembourg	3.2	Cyprus	25.4

Note: Data are from the Pew Research Center (2017).

A study of young people in the Netherlands by Han Entzinger, Claudia van Lotringen and Karen Phalet (2000) found that, while the vast majority of Turkish and Moroccan youth consider themselves to be religious, very few are fully practising adherents to the Islamic faith. However, a more recent Dutch study (Huijnk 2018) reveals hardly any differences in mosque attendance between adolescents and young adults (ages 15 to 24) of Turkish and Moroccan origin versus their counterparts aged 45 and above. This study suggests that religiosity among young Muslims has increased compared to the 1990s and early-2000s. In line with this evidence, another recent study of younger cohorts of Turkish and Moroccan descent also documents markedly higher opposition to homosexuality, divorce and pre-marital sex among Dutch Moroccans and Dutch Turks than among Dutch natives (Kalmijn and Kraaykamp 2018; see also Koopmans 2015).

The rise of the extreme right

In the last two decades immigration, multiculturalism and inter-ethnic relations have become highly salient political fault lines in the Western world, as indicated by the increase of political parties centred around anti-immigration, anti-minority, and anti-multiculturalist views. The rise of such extreme-right parties is generally viewed as a sign of increased hostility to immigrants. In this context, a recent poll carried out by the British think tank Chatham House (see Goodwin, Cutts, and Raines 2017) reveals an alarming level of opposition to Muslim immigration. Citizens in ten European countries were asked to say whether they agreed with the statement, "All further immigration from mainly Muslim countries be stopped". Of the respondents, 55 percent answered agree, whereas only 20 percent answered disagree. The highest percentage of agreement was found in Poland, where more than 70 percent of respondents agreed. The lowest percentage of agreement was found in Spain, were only 41 percent of respondents agreed.

The sociologist Marcel Lubbers (2001) analysed far-right voting behaviour in a range of countries in order to see how it related to local living circumstances. He found that the presence of minorities in people's local area was related to support for far-right parties, but that local unemployment rates had no effect. Unemployment did play a role at the individual level (i.e., unemployed people were more likely to vote for far-right parties), yet there was no evidence that unemployment plays a role at the contextual level. More recent studies have supported Lubbers' findings and suggest that perceived *cultural* threats are a much stronger predictor of support for the radical right than perceived *economic* threats (Lucassen and Lubbers 2011; De Rooij, Goodwin, and Pickup 2018). In terms of such cultural threats, one can think of Muslim women wearing traditional headscarves at school and work or the refusal of Muslim parents to allow their daughters to participate in school activities where parts of the body are visible, such as sports and swimming classes.

Incidents of terrorism related to Islamists have also played a role in the recent rise in voting for the extreme-right. Since the turn of the century, such incidents have taken place in many countries, killing many innocent people in the name of Allah. While it is clear that these attacks are committed by a very small group of people that is not representative of the Muslim population as a whole, it does play an important role in increasing hostility towards Muslim minorities.

At the same time, there is also evidence that an increasing number of young, second-generation Muslims living in the West are becoming more radicalized in their beliefs. The driving forces behind this trend include ethnic segregation in large cities, leading to the formation of Muslim ghettos; feelings of social exclusion, leading to the desire for a sense of identity; insufficient jobs and discrimination on the labour market, leading to low rates of labour participation. The fact that radicalization is partly driven by feelings of social exclusion, which may flare up if there is more hostility among the indigenous population, which in turn may intensify when there is more radicalization among Muslims, can give rise to a vicious circle of escalating ethnic conflict.

Prejudice and ethnic conflict

An important underlying question to the rise of the extreme right as well as debates on multiculturalism is under which conditions ethnic conflicts are most likely to arise and under which conditions peaceful and cooperative inter-ethnic relations can be developed. There are various competing theories on this matter.

The *contact hypothesis* posited by the psychologist Gordon Allport (1954) states that direct contact between people from different groups leads to less prejudice, greater tolerance, and better inter-group relations. According to this hypothesis, negative sentiments toward out-group members are the result of mutual isolation, and should disappear when there is more interaction between groups. In general, there is quite a lot evidence for this prediction. It is for instance a common finding that support for right-wing nationalist parties is lower in areas where there are more immigrants or ethnic minorities, even when correcting for the fact that immigrants and ethnic minorities themselves are less likely to support such parties. However, natives living near foreigners sometimes still make a distinction between the good foreigners living down the street and the bad foreigners who are undermining the nation's culture or taking jobs away from native workers.

The *competition hypothesis*, in turn, states that competition for jobs and housing spurs antipathy towards out-group members. In public opinion surveys, individuals often cite lack of jobs and high rents as reasons why they object to further immigration. However, some people argue that immigrants do not compete with natives for jobs, because they do jobs that natives will not do, especially unskilled work such as fruit-picking, cleaning and shelf-stacking. A counter-argument is that, although migrants may indeed be concentrated within certain professions, their presence in the labour market still has the effect of bidding down wages insofar as it increases overall labour supply. When workers are plentiful, an employer does not have to raise wages as much in order to attract workers to his company, since he will always be able to find one or two workers willing to work at the prevailing wage.

A third theory on inter-group relations concerns the so-called *invasion-succession model* and was originally formulated by sociologists from the University of Chicago during the 1920s. The starting point of this theory is that there is competition for valued resources, such as housing. This competition causes an irreversible transition from an equilibrium stage dominated by the incumbent group (natives) to a new equilibrium dominated by the incoming group (immigrants). According to the invasion-succession model, relations between natives and immigrants are characterized by several distinct phases: namely penetration, invasion, and take-over. During the penetration phase, a small number of immigrants, mostly young men, move into a neighbourhood. The reaction of the native population is welcoming and good-natured; the incumbents make an effort to integrate the newcomers. During the invasion phase, the immigrants are reunited with their family members, which leads to rapid growth in the immigrant population. During the take-over phase, a new generation of non-native youth emerges, which further increases the non-native share of the population, as immigrant groups often have higher fertility rates than natives. At this stage, native and non-natives start to adopt more hostile positions to one another.

Cultural persistence and social capital within migrant groups

One dimension along which the assimilation of migrants into their host societies can be assessed is to study the persistence of the culture from their country of origin. That is, do migrants in various ways more closely reflect the culture of their host society or their country of origin? As it turns out, cultural origins can have very persistent effects in many life domains. The economists Raquel Fernandez and Alessandra Fogli (2009) found that among second-generation immigrants living in the US, individuals originating from countries with high rates of fertility (e.g., Nigeria) tended to have more children, whereas those originating from countries with low rates of fertility (e.g., Japan) tended to have fewer children. The key issue to observe here is that we are talking about second-generation immigrants, so people who are born and bred in the US, but who are apparently still influenced by cultural norms from the country where their parents were born.

Likewise, other studies have documented cultural persistence of, among other things, labour force participation, generalized trust, the strength of family ties, preferences for redistribution, attitudes towards women, and educational attainment (e.g., Alesina and Giuliano 2010; Dinesen 2013; Luttmer and Singhal 2011). Since many of these studies are able to exploit variation across second-generation immigrants, they provide fairly strong evidence that migrants bring their cultural beliefs and practices with them when they migrate, and then pass these beliefs and practices on to subsequent generations. The stronger the association between migrants' characteristics and the average characteristics in their countries of origin, the higher the degree of persistence. Strong associations imply that migrants tend to be weakly assimilated into their host societies; weak associations imply that migrants tend to be strongly assimilated into their host societies.

Another method that has been used to examine cultural persistence is to collect data on the distribution of migrants in different host countries, and then look to see whether certain macro-level outcomes in those host countries are associated with the presence of migrants from particular countries of origin. For example, several German economists (Dimant, Krieger and Redlin 2014) gathered data on the presence of migrants in different OECD countries over time and found that countries that had admitted more migrants from states with high levels of corruption went on to experience higher levels of corruption themselves. The authors interpret this finding as evidence that when people cross borders also corrupt practices might migrate. Along the same lines, the sociologist Noah Carl (2017) found that allegations of electoral fraud tend to be more common in areas of the UK with large Pakistani and Bangladeshi communities, which he attributes to norms of nepotism and in-group favouritism that are common in Pakistani and Bangladeshi culture, partially stemming from the practice of cousin marriage (see Chapter 10).

Of course, we need to bear in mind that both of these studies concern relationships at the macro level. As argued throughout this book, explanations of such macro-level relationships require the specification of explanatory mechanisms on the behaviour of individual actors at the micro-level. Hence, it remains to be seen whether these macro-level relationships turn out to be causal or spurious relationships. In this regard, it is also worth stressing that topics such as corruption and fraud are always subject to measurement issues, as we further discuss in Chapter 9 on crime and Chapter 10 on corruption.

One of the reasons why migrants' behaviour often still reflects the culture of their country of origin – even many years or several generations later – is that migrants from the same country of origin often gather together in their host society. Indeed, migrant groups tend to be characterized by strong bonds of mutual solidarity and high levels of social trust towards one another. In other words, there is a great degree of *social capital* within migrant communities: close relationships between people, which emerge after repeated transactions and which provide social benefits, such as resources, information, and emotional support (see also our discussion of social capital as a public good in Chapter 1). This social capital can be traced back to migrants' common geographical and cultural origins.

There is also a strong degree of clustering in where migrants live within their host country. Sometimes the concentration of a specific ethnic group within a neighbourhood is so large that we can speak of an *ethnic enclave*, where people from one particular ethnic group live completely segregated from the native majority as well as other ethnic minorities. This is especially apparent in many big American cities, which have entire neighbourhoods that are predominantly occupied by Chinese migrants (*Chinatowns*), Russian Jews, or people with Italian ancestors, but the same phenomenon can be found in European cities.

There is a debate as to whether ethnic enclaves are conducive toward the integration of migrants or rather a barrier. Sociologists Alejandro Portes and Julia Sensenbrenner (1993) argue that ethnic enclaves are beneficial. The high levels of social capital within ethnic enclaves, for example, means that new migrants can receive a great amount of support and advice geared to their specific situation from those who have already settled down there earlier. This can help them, among other things, in finding work and better housing. Portes and Sensenbrenner cite the relative success of Cuban migrants living in Miami as an example.

On the other hand, others view the enclave as a trap. According to this theory, ethnic enclaves are no stepping-stone to migrants' wider integration into society but rather a factor that slows down this process, by making new migrants disproportionately focused on the culture and language of their country of origin. Moreover, there is evidence that employers within ethnic enclaves sometimes exploit their employees, taking advantage of the high levels of social capital within these communities and the strong dependency of newly arrived immigrants.

The effect of ethnic and cultural diversity on social solidarity

One of the long-standing claims in the literature on immigrant integration and inter-ethnic relations is that ethnic and cultural diversity erodes social solidarity. According to this line of argument, people tend to identify more strongly and feel greater solidarity with those who share their own characteristics when it comes to matters such as race, religion, ethnicity, language, social values. As a result, there will be more ethnic or cultural conflict and people's overall solidarity levels will likely decline when the number of people from other ethnic or cultural backgrounds in society increases.

In a well-known paper, the political scientist Robert Putnam (2007) goes one step further. He presents what he calls the *hunkering-down hypothesis*. According to this theory, diversity does not primarily trigger greater in-group versus out-group conflicts, but most of all feelings of anomie and social isolation. That is, Putnam argues that diversity tends to unsettle people in general, rather than only making them more hostile towards other ethnic groups. The result is that people living in diverse settings will pull in like a turtle, becoming less trusting, less sociable, and less solidary with everyone – including people from their own ethnic group.

The first main channel through which ethnic and cultural diversity may erode social solidarity is by undermining people's trust in their fellow citizens. Social scientists typically measure trust using the so-called *generalized trust* question, "Generally speaking, would you say that most people can be trusted or that you can't be too careful dealing with people?" Generalized trust can be distinguished from particularized trust, which refers to trust in family members, close friends and others with whom one interacts regularly. The social psychologists Peter Dinesen and Kim Sønderskov (2018) recently reviewed the literature on diversity and trust. Their review covered all the studies that had analysed whether the average diversity in an area relates to the level of trust reported by citizens in that area. They discovered that most studies have found negative effects, but that the magnitude of this effect varies substantially depending on the context.

However, one important methodological issue with these studies, as identified by the sociologists Maria Abascal and Delia Baldassarri (2015), is that diversity is typically confounded by the presence of ethnic minorities, who nearly always report lower trust than the majority. In other words, areas that have high ethnic diversity are, by definition, areas where there are many ethnic minorities. One wants to distinguish the purely compositional effect of ethnic minorities' lower trust from the effect of diversity on trust itself. The way to do this, as Abascal and Baldassarri note, is to examine the effect of diversity on trust for each ethnic group separately. When they did this in a US dataset, they found that the fraction of non-whites in an area reduced trust among whites, but the fraction of whites in an area did not affect trust among non-whites.

The second main channel through which ethnic and cultural diversity may erode social solidarity is by undermining people's support for the welfare state. Support for the welfare state is typically measured with survey items asking respondents to say how far they agree that the government should redistribute income from the rich to the poor. An early study in this area was carried out by the economist Erzo Luttmer (2001). He analysed data from the US, and found that whites were less supportive of redistribution when there were more black welfare recipients in their local area, while blacks were less supportive when there were more white welfare recipients in their local area. He also showed that, within the US, levels of redistribution are higher in more racially homogeneous states. In another influential study, Alberto Alesina, Edward Glaeser and Bruce Sacerdote (2001) reported that social spending as a percentage of GDP has a strong negative association with the level of racial heterogeneity across countries.

Building on this work, the economists Woojin Lee and John Roemer (2007) have showed that racism plays a big role in explaining the smaller welfare state in the United States versus many European countries (see also Chapter 4). They show that racism first of all depresses support for redistribution directly, as some voters oppose any welfare schemes that make payments or transfers to people they view as undeserving (i.e., racial minorities). On top of this, even people who are themselves in favour of redistribution, often end up voting for anti-redistributive political parties (in the case of the US this is the Republican party) because their redistribution concerns are overridden by their racial views, which are more closely represented by anti-redistributive parties. Lee and Roemer estimate that through these two mechanisms, racism reduces the income tax rate (and thereby income redistribution) in the US by 11 to 18 percentage points.

Social segregation as an unintended consequence

Segregation is the process or state in which people cluster together in physical or social space with others with similar characteristics as themselves, resulting in social groups becoming increasingly separated from one another. Segregation can occur along many social dimensions, including race, ethnicity, gender, age, religion, education, and occupation. Moreover, it can occur in many different settings, for example with respect to the neighbourhoods in which people live, the clubs or associations they decide to join, their schools or workplaces, but also friendship networks and marriage or sexual relationships.

The significance of segregation is that it constrains people's social worlds, having profound implications for the information people receive, the attitudes and relationships they form, and the interactions they experience. Recall, for example, the contact hypothesis discussed in the section "Immigrants' integration into the host society". In an influential review study of segregation in social networks, the sociologists Miller McPherson, Lynn Smith-Lovin and James Cook (2001) conclude that ethnic and racial segregation is generally stronger than segregation along any other social dimension, and pretty much regardless of which social setting (e.g., friendship networks, neighbourhoods, schools or work environments) is considered.

Generally speaking, segregation arises via one or more of three main processes. The first process occurs when a group of organized individuals conspire to exclude another group of people from a certain activity. Here the segregation arises from intentional behaviour on the part of the organized individuals. Prominent examples of such processes can be found in South Africa under Apartheid, or some areas of the US in the 1950s and before, where non-white individuals were denied service in restaurants, had to sit at the back of buses, and so on.

The second process occurs when individuals in different groups end up being separated from one another due to differential resource constraints. For example, in most countries, ethnic minorities tend to have lower incomes than the native majority. Hence, the native majority tends to be overrepresented in rich neighbourhoods, with the opposite being true for ethnic minorities in the poor neighbourhoods. For similar reasons, ethnic minorities also tend to be poorly represented in private vis-à-vis public schools and expensive elite sports such as yachting, rowing, and horse riding. Here segregation is not primarily the result of intentional but rather resource-constrained behaviour.

Thirdly, and perhaps most interestingly, segregation can also arise in situations where segregation is not actively pursued as an outcome and where resource constraints do not play a major role. Indeed, segregation can occur when there are only minor differences in preferences across social groups, which are subsequently amplified through social interaction. We can draw a connection here with the *tipping points* mechanism that was famously discussed by the economist Thomas Schelling (1978) (see Chapter 2). Whereas we explained the mechanisms earlier by referring to a checkers board with black and white stones, we could now, for example, think of different neighbourhoods with native majority and ethnic minority residents.

The reasoning starts from a situation where these two types of residents are randomly distributed across all available neighbourhoods. We furthermore assume that people from the native majority have a mild preference of living near a good portion of other members of the native majority, whereas ethnic minority members have a mild preference for living near a good portion of other ethnic minority members. These preferences may reflect that people can more easily identify with people similar to themselves and find it easier to predict their behaviour; importantly, these preferences do not need to be driven by actual inter-group hostility. Given these starting assumptions, what do we expect to happen?

Starting with the situation of residents randomly distributed across neighbourhoods, most residents will probably be quite happy with their surroundings. Many will have a mix of native majority and ethnic minority residents as their neighbours, and since people do not have any strong hostility or antipathy against out-group members, most people will be perfectly fine with their mixed neighbourhood. However, for some people this may not be the case. Imagine, for example, a native majority member who prefers that at least 70 percent of their neighbours also belong to the native majority, whereas they happened to end up in a neighbourhood where this is only 65 percent. Therefore, these people will decide to move to another neighbourhood that better meets their residential preferences. However, as a result of this, the native majority percentage in the original neighbourhood will drop to only 60 percent, meaning that now also those native majority members who prefer at least 65 percent of their neighbours to be natives are left unsatisfied. Hence, these people will now also move elsewhere, causing a further drop in the percentage of native residents and inducing yet another bunch of them to move away.

It will be clear where this is going: as these dynamics continue, the eventual result will be a situation of full segregation of ethnic groups, even though people only have mild preferences for their own ethnic in-group. The crucial factor in this reasoning is that any move by a single resident influences the ethnic composition of both the neighbourhood they move to and the neighbourhood they move away from, thereby inducing others to move too. This is a clear example of how micro-level actions can have macro-level spillovers and multiplier effects due to the fact that one actor's optimal behaviour depends on the behaviour of other actors.

Needless to say, the example described above relies on several assumptions and matters get more complicated in real life, when there are, for example, more than just two social groups, when people face constraints in where they can move (due to a limited housing supply or their own means), or when some people may in fact be diversity-seeking. Yet, there are several studies that have found support for the tipping points mechanism and the predictions that can be derived from it for residential segregation.

In the US, for example, there is ample evidence for a phenomenon known as *white flight*: when a few black families move into in a white neighbourhood, this typically has the effect of spurring white families to pick up and leave. In qualitative interviews, these families who leave give their motivation for doing so as that they expected the whole neighbourhood to become black in a relatively short time, and that they therefore left in anticipation of that outcome (Clark 1991). In a large-scale quantitative analysis of the census tracts across the US over the period 1970–2000, the economists David Card, Alexandre Mas and Jesse Rothstein (2008) also find strong evidence that white population flows exhibiting tipping-like behaviour in most American cities. These tipping points seem to range from about 5 to 20 percent of non-white residents in the neighbourhood, with higher tipping points in cities where whites have more tolerant racial attitudes.

Recommended readings

- Paul Collier (2013) offers a comprehensive, multidisciplinary overview of the pros and cons of encouraging or restricting immigration. Presenting numerous data and a variety of case studies, Collier considers this topic from the perspectives of immigrants themselves, their countries of origin, and the host societies that receive them. He demonstrates how economic, social and political arguments are tightly interwoven and that there are no easy answers as far as migration policies are concerned.
- The study *Why Border Enforcement Backfired* by Douglas Massey, Karen Pren and Jorge Durand (2016) provides a fascinating analysis on the impact of stricter border enforcement along the US-Mexican border on the behaviour of illegal immigrants. They show that the militarization of this border – which they argue was a reflection of a moral panic rather than an objective analysis of the situation – backfired by transforming a *circular* flow of illegal immigrants into a vast population of *settled* immigrants.
- Observing that public debates are dominated by those who portray immigration as an existential threat to host societies and those who argue that immigration is a good thing that deserves our unconditional support, George Borjas (2016) seeks to insert some more nuance into these debates. Among other things, he draws attention to the winners and losers created by immigration, and to the fact that immigrants are more than just workers, even if work was the original reason for them coming.

- Will Kymlicka (2012) is a passionate proponent of multiculturalism. In this report, he tracks the experience of a variety of countries with multiculturalist policies since the 1980s. Aside from pointing out the positive contributions of such policies to society, he also discusses problems that have been encountered, as well as ways to tackle these problems. His conclusion is that it is too early to declare the "death of multiculturalism", and that – if properly facilitated – multiculturalism is a low-risk option that generally works well.

Bibliography

Abascal, Maria, and Delia Baldassarri. 2015. "Love Thy Neighbour? Ethnoracial Diversity and Trust Reexamined". *American Journal of Sociology* 121:722–782.

Alesina, Alberto, and Paola Giuliano. 2010. "The Power of the Family". *Journal of Economic Growth* 15:93–125.

Alesina, Alberto, Edward Glaeser, and Bruce Sacerdote. 2001. "Why Doesn't the United States Have a European-Style Welfare State?" *Brookings Papers on Economic Activity* 2:1–69.

Allport, Gordon W. 1954. *The Nature of Prejudice*. Cambridge, MA: Perseus Books.

Borjas, George. 2016. *We Wanted Workers: Unravelling the Immigration Narrative*. New York, NY: Norton.

Card, David, Alexandre Mas, and Jesse Rothstein. 2008. "Tipping and the Dynamics of Segregation". *Quarterly Journal of Economics* 123:177–218.

Carl, Noah. 2017. "Ethnicity and Electoral Fraud in Britain". *Electoral Studies* 50:128–136.

Castles, Stephen. 2004. "Why Migration Policies Fail". *Ethnic and Racial Studies* 27:205–227.

Clark, William A.V. 1991. "Residential Preferences and Neighborhood Racial Segregation: A Test of the Schelling Segregation Model". *Demography* 28:1–19.

Clemens, Michael. 2014. "Does Development Reduce Migration?" Pp. 152–185 in: *International Handbook on Migration and Economic Development*, edited by Robert E.B. Lucas. Cheltenham: Edward Elgar.

Collier, Paul. 2013. *Exodus: Immigration and Multiculturalism in the 21st Century*. London: Penguin Books.

De Rooij, Eline A., Matthew J. Goodwin, and Mark Pickup. 2018. "A Research Note: The Differential Impact of Threats on Ethnic Prejudice Toward Three Minority Groups in Britain". *Political Science Research and Methods* 6:837–845.

Dimant, Eugen, Tim Krieger, and Margarete Redlin. 2014. "A Crook is a Crook. . . But is He Still a Crook Abroad? On the Effect of Immigration on Destination-Country Corruption". *German Economic Review* 16: 464–489.

Dinesen, Peter T. 2013. "Where You Come From or Where You Live? Examining the Cultural and Institutional Explanation of Generalized Trust Using Migration as a Natural Experiment". *European Sociological Review* 29:114–128.

Dinesen, Peter T., and Kim M. Sønderskov. 2018. "Ethnic Diversity and Social Trust: A Critical Review of the Literature and Suggestions for a Research Agenda". Pp. 175–204 in: *The Oxford Handbook on Social and Political Trust*, edited by Eric M. Uslaner. Oxford: Oxford University Press.

Entzinger, Han, Claudia Van Lotringen, and Karen Phalet. 2000. *Islam in de Multiculturele Samenleving: Opvattingen van Jongeren in Rotterdam* (Islam in the Multicultural Society: Views of Rotterdam Youth). Utrecht: European Research Centre on Migration and Ethnic Relations.

Fazel-Zarandi, Mohammed M., Jonathan Feinstein, and Edward H. Kaplan. 2018. "The Number of Undocumented Immigrants in the United States: Estimates Based on Demographic Modeling with Data from 1990 to 2016". *PloS one* 13: e0201193.

Fernandez, Raquel, and Alessandra Fogli. 2009. "Culture: An Empirical Investigation of Beliefs, Work, and Fertility". *American Economic Journal: Macroeconomics* 1:146–177.

Goodwin, Matthew, David Cutts, and Thomas Raines. 2017. "What Do Europeans Think About Muslim Immigration?" *Chatham House*, 7 February 2017. https://www.chathamhouse.org/expert/comment/what-do-europeans-think-about-muslim-immigration.

Heath, Anthony F., Catherine Rothon, and Elina Kilpi. 2008. "The Second Generation in Western Europe: Education, Unemployment, and Occupational Attainment". *Annual Review of Sociology* 34:211–235.

Huijnk, Willem. 2018. *De Religieuze Beleving van Moslims in Nederland* (The Religious Experience of Muslims in the Netherlands). The Hague: SCP.

Huijnk, Willem, and Iris Andriessen (eds.). 2016. *Integratie in Zicht? De Integratie van Migranten in Nederland op Acht Terreinen Nader Bekeken* (Integration in Sight? The Integration of Migrants in the Netherlands in Eight Domains More Closely Examined). The Hague: The Netherlands Institute for Social Research.

Kalmijn, Matthijs, and Gerbert Kraaykamp. 2018. "Determinants of Cultural Assimilation in the Second Generation: A Longitudinal Analysis of Values about Marriage and Sexuality among Moroccan and Turkish Migrants". *Journal of Ethnic and Migration Studies* 44:697–717.

Koopmans, Ruud. 2015. "Religious Fundamentalism and Hostility Against Out-Groups: A Comparison of Muslim and Christians in Western Europe". *Journal of Ethnic and Migration Studies* 41:33–57.

Kymlicka, Will. 2012. *Multiculturalism: Success, Failure, and the Future.* Washington, DC: Migration Policy Institute.

Kymlicka, Will, and Bashir Bashir (eds.). 2008. *The Politics of Reconciliation in Multicultural Societies.* Oxford: Oxford University Press.

Lee, Woojin, and John E. Roemer. 2007. "Racism and Redistribution in the United States: A Solution to the Problem of American Exceptionalism". *Journal of Public Economics* 90:1027–1052.

Lubbers, Marcel. 2001. *Exclusionistic Electorates: Extreme Right-Wing Voting in Western Europe.* Nijmegen: ICS Dissertation.

Lucassen, Geertje, and Marcel Lubbers. 2011. "Who Fears What? Explaining Far-Right-Wing Preference in Europe by Distinguishing Perceived Cultural and Economic Ethnic Threats". *Comparative Political Studies* 45:547–574.

Luttmer, Erzo. 2001. "Group Loyalty and the Taste for Redistribution". *Journal of Political Economy* 109:500–528.

Luttmer, Erzo F.P., and Monica Singhal. 2011. "Culture, Context, and the Taste for Redistribution". *American Economic Journal: Economic Policy* 3:157–179.

Massey, Douglas S. 1988. "Economic Development and International Migration in Comparative Perspective". *Population and Development Review* 1:383–414.

Massey, Douglas S., and Nancy A. Denton. 1993. *American Apartheid: Segregation and the Making of the Underclass.* Cambridge, MA: Harvard University Press.

Massey, Douglas S., Karen A. Pren, and Jorge Durand. 2016. "Why Border Enforcement Backfired". *American Journal of Sociology* 121:1557–1600.

McPherson, Miller, Lynn Smith-Lovin, and James M. Cook. 2001. "Birds of a Feather: Homophily in Social Networks". *Annual Review of Sociology* 25:415–444.

Pew Research Center. 2017. *Europe's Growing Muslim Population. Muslims Are Projected to Increase as a Share of Europe's Population – Even With No Future Migration.* Washington, DC: Pew Research Center.

Portes, Alejandro, and Julia Sensenbrenner. 1993. "Embeddedness and Immigration: Notes on the Social Determinants of Economic Action". *American Journal of Sociology* 98:1320–1350.

Putnam, Robert D. 2007. "E Pluribus Unum: Diversity and Community in the Twenty-First Century: The 2006 Johan Skytte Prize Lecture". *Scandinavian Political Studies* 30:137–174.

Schelling, Thomas C. 1978. *Micromotives and Macrobehavior.* New York, NY: Norton.

Stark, Oded, and David Bloom. 1985. "The New Economics of Labor Migration". *American Economic Review* 75:173–178.

Taylor, Edward J. 1999. "The New Economics of Labor migration and the Role of Remittances in the Migration Process". *International Migration* 37:63–88.

7 Economic inequality

Chapter overview

We begin this chapter with a brief discussion of why economic inequality is problematic, followed by a review of inequality trends around the world. Whereas income inequality has increased *within* most countries since the 1970s, global income inequality has remained stable during most of the twentieth century and has started to decline in the last few decades. This latter trend is driven by reductions in the inequality *between* countries, and global poverty has dropped accordingly. However, extreme poverty remains persistent in many parts of the world, and we discuss several theories to explain why this is the case. In addition, we examine what is happening in terms of income and wealth at the other end of the distribution, to the so-called "top one percent". Next, we consider the relationships between inequality, national income, and economic growth. We demonstrate that it is in this regard important to distinguish between comparisons of different countries at a single point in time versus comparisons within countries over time. We also address the impact of inequality on the well-being of individuals and society more generally, concentrating on the influence of inequality on health as well as intergenerational social mobility.

Economic inequality as a problem

To what extent one regards a certain level of inequality as problematic and cause for state intervention will depend on which of the three political ideologies discussed in Chapter 1 one adheres to: socialism, liberalism, or conservatism. In general, liberals will be most tolerant of economic inequality and socialists the least. The former firmly believe in the value of the market as allocator of resources and distributor of wealth, while the latter often regard market outcomes as unsatisfactory. They therefore call on the state to step in and redistribute resources in order to achieve a more equal distribution. Conservatives will usually side with the liberals on economic issues, yet may deviate from this if it helps to maintain order and stability within society, since the latter are their ultimate priorities.

Nonetheless, whatever one's ideological stance on this issue, from a pragmatic point of view, high levels of economic inequality will generally provide cause for concern. If economic resources are too much concentrated in the hands of only a few, this may harm longer-term economic growth and prosperity. Metaphorically speaking, inequality may not only pertain to how the pie is distributed, but also to how much pie there is to distribute in the first place. Needless to say, lower growth and economic prosperity, in turn, have spillover effects for a wide range of other societal issues; for example by threatening the welfare state, stimulating crime, and making people less willing to invest in the environment.

Aside from its potential impact on economic growth and prosperity, there is also evidence that economic inequality can lead to worse health outcomes, reduced social mobility, and greater inequality in the political sphere. Moreover, an unequal distribution of resources can erode the social fabric that keeps together society, increasing tensions between social groups and undermining norms of trust, reciprocity and solidarity that are key to cooperation, collective action and the production of public goods. Among other things, a negative association between inequality and public goods provision has been found in contexts as diverse as spending on public education across American cities (Alesina et al. 1999), infrastructure maintenance within irrigation communities in India (Bardhan 2000), and behavioural experiments within laboratory settings (Tavoni et al. 2011). In addition, as history has shown over and over again, the risks of social conflict, revolutions and civil wars are much greater when there is a higher degree of inequality.

Importantly, even if economic inequality as such does not *cause* reduced growth, prosperity and societal well-being, the mere existence of economic inequality is still troublesome. After all, a great degree of inequality implies that some members of society lag behind others significantly in terms of their income and wealth. This will, in turn, have implications for outcomes such as health, happiness, and life satisfaction. Indeed, evidence indicates that the positive relationship between income and these outcomes holds both across countries as well as between citizens within countries. There is no satiation point beyond which income is no longer relevant for well-being; at any single point in time, richer people will generally be healthier and happier (Stevenson and Wolfers 2013).

In recent years, public interest in inequality has surged following the publication of *Capital in the Twenty-First Century* by French economist Thomas Piketty (2014). In this book, Piketty raises the alarm about current trends in inequality and where we may be heading. Relying on high-quality data analysis, he shows that in recent decades both income and wealth inequality have risen in most Western societies, to a large extent driven by the now-famous "top one percent": that is, the very richest subset of society. Crucially, Piketty argues that when the rate of return on capital is greater than the rate of economic growth – which is for most Western countries a fairly accurate description of the recent past as well as foreseeable future – wealth and prosperity will over time become increasingly concentrated in the hands of a relatively small group of wealthy individuals. According to Piketty, this would, in turn, lead to economic instability, societal discontent and a weakening of democracy.

In order to avoid this unfolding of events, Piketty contends that it is essential for governments to step in, more specifically via a global wealth tax that limits the power of inheritance as well as other tax reforms to realize greater redistribution. This underlines how economic inequality and its associated societal problems are fundamentally connected to politics. One of the key issues here is that wealthy elites also tend to have a big influence on politics (be it through lobbying, political donations or more subtle channels), which they utilize to resist reforms that may threaten their elite position. As such, highly unequal societies often end up stuck in a stalemate from where it is very complicated to achieve real change.

The economists Daron Acemoglu and James Robinson further elaborate on this topic in their book *Why Nations Fail* (2012). They address how economic inequality and prosperity can be traced back to political institutions that go back for centuries. One of their leading examples concerns the city of Nogales, on the border between Mexico and the United States, separated by nothing more than a fence. The northern part is prosperous and comfortable to live in; the inhabitants are healthy, well-educated, highly committed to democratic values, and feel safe. The southern part of Nogales is a different story altogether; average incomes are three times lower, infant mortality and crime levels are higher, high school completion rates lower, and life expectancy lags behind. Also, economic inequality on the south side of the fence is much more pronounced. As Acemoglu and Robinson explain, northern and southern Nogales have these different fates despite sharing the same geography, climate, ethnic origins, disease environment, and many other factors. Yet, there is one factor that decisively distinguishes them, namely that the northern part is located in the United States and the southern part in Mexico.

In other words, the two parts of Nogales are embedded in different institutional contexts – institutional contexts that can either be conducive to economic prosperity or be structured so as to extract resources from the many by the few, thus undermining overall levels of prosperity and increasing inequality. Acemoglu and Robinson show how the origins of such institutional differences and the resulting economic divergence may lie far in the past, to subsequently lock areas into path-dependent, self-reinforcing development trajectories that continue to this day. It is these linkages between economic outcomes on the one hand and political institutions and decision-making on the other that we should constantly keep in the back of our minds when considering trends and variation in economic inequality.

Measuring inequality: Lorenz curves and Gini coefficients

Before presenting information on trends and cross-country variation in economic inequality, it is worthwhile to first spend a few words on how inequality is measured. By far the most common way to summarize and display inequality is via Lorenz curves and Gini coefficients, which are closely related to one another. Both tools are named after their developers, the American economist Max Lorenz and the Italian statistician Corrado Gini, who came up with these concepts in the early twentieth century. While both tools are most often applied with respect to income distributions, they can, in principle, be applied to all kinds of other distributions too.

If we take the example of income inequality within a country, the *Lorenz curve* can be explained as follows. One would start by ordering all citizens of that country by their income, for instance lining them up in a long queue with the person with the lowest income at one end and the person with the highest income at the other end. The next step would be to calculate the total income earned in this country by all citizens. Subsequently, one can calculate what fraction of the total national income is earned by the person with the lowest income. Then one can proceed by calculating which fraction of the total national income is earned by the two people with the lowest incomes (including now also the person with the second-lowest income in the country), followed by the fraction earned by the three people with the lowest, followed by the four people with the lowest incomes and so forth.

The outcomes of all these calculations can next be plotted in a figure where the horizontal axis represents the cumulative share of the population from lowest to highest incomes and where the vertical axis represents the cumulative share of the total national income. If one then connects all these points, one gets a curve similar to the solid curve in Figure 7.1. This curve essentially plots how much of the total national income is earned by the poorest X percent of the country's population. If income is distributed completely equally across all citizens, the curve will be a straight diagonal line: e.g., the poorest ten percent of the population earn ten percent of the national income, the poorest 50 percent earn 50 percent of the national income, the poorest 90 percent earn 90 percent of the national income. The larger the degree of curvature of the Lorenze curve, the more unequal the income distribution: e.g., the poorest ten percent of the population earn 0.0001 percent of the national income, the poorest 50 percent earn one percent of the national income, the poorest 90 percent earn three percent of the national income (leaving 97 percent of the national income for the richest ten percent). As such, the Lorenz curve provides a convenient way of eyeballing how much inequality there is within a group, a society, or across a selection of countries.

The *Gini coefficient* or *Gini index*, in turn, provides a quantitative measure of inequality. It ranges from zero to one, where zero corresponds to a situation of complete equality

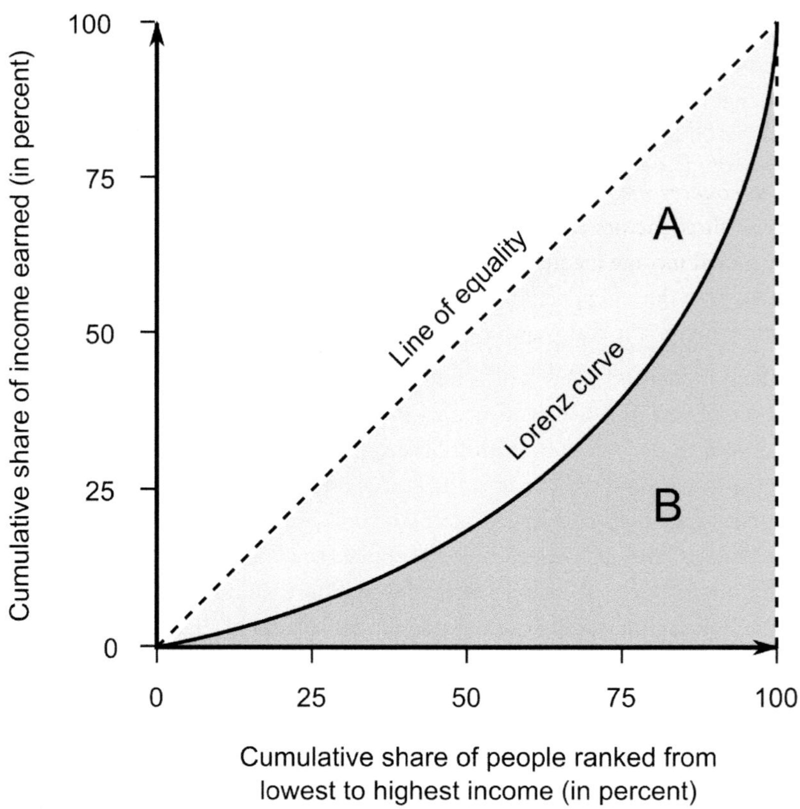

Figure 7.1 The Lorenz curve and the Gini coefficient

(sticking to the example of the income distribution within a country, this would mean that every citizen earns the same income) and one corresponds to a situation of complete inequality (one citizens earns all of the income and everyone else earns nothing). In between zero and one, higher values correspond to a greater degree of inequality. Therefore, the Gini coefficient can broadly be interpreted as the percentage of national income that needs to be redistributed in order to achieve a perfectly equal distribution.

The Gini coefficient bears a direct relationship to the Lorenz curve. That is, it can be calculated by dividing the size of area A (i.e., the area between the diagonal line of equality and the Lorenz curve) by the sum of areas A plus B; see Figure 7.1. In equation form: $Gini = A / (A + B)$. When there is a greater degree of inequality, the Lorenz curve will be located further away from the diagonal line of equality, thus making area A and thereby the numerator of the above formula bigger, resulting in a higher Gini coefficient.

It should be noted that it is not possible to rank all possible income distributions in terms of their degree of inequality by purely looking at Lorenz curves or Gini coefficients. It is, for example, possible that two Lorenz curves intersect somewhere in the middle, leaving it indeterminate which distribution is more or less unequal. Similarly, different income distributions can result in the same Gini coefficient, again making it impossible to decide which distribution is most unequal. Notwithstanding these limitations, both measures are incredibly useful for gaining quick insights into inequality and thus we regularly come back to them throughout this chapter.

Income inequality trends across the world

Global income inequality captures the total degree of inequality in incomes between all citizens of the world. It can be decomposed into three components: a) the income distribution within each country (*within-country inequality*); b) the distribution of average incomes across countries (*between-country inequality*); and c) the population size of different countries. Changes in any of these three factors can cause changes in global income inequality. Figure 7.2 summarizes how global income inequality has evolved since the early nineteenth century. The data from before 1950 in the top panel of Figure 7.2 largely reflect indirect estimates, derived from either the ratio between the real wage of unskilled labour and GDP per capita or the variance in height across individuals (given that height as a proxy for physical well-being is closely related to income levels). The bottom panel of Figure 7.2 zooms in on the more recent past, using more reliable data based on household panel surveys.

Trends in global income inequality: A long-term view

As the top panel of Figure 7.2 shows, global income inequality has risen substantially since the beginning of the nineteenth century until about the middle of the twentieth century. As the two dashed lines demonstrate, this increase was mainly driven by a rise in between-country inequality. Over this period, most Western countries went through a process of industrialization, experiencing high rates of economic growth as a result, while other continents (especially Asia and Africa) lagged behind. Therefore, while at the beginning of the nineteenth century global income inequality mainly reflected income inequality within countries, in the twentieth century it started to reflect first and foremost income inequality between countries.

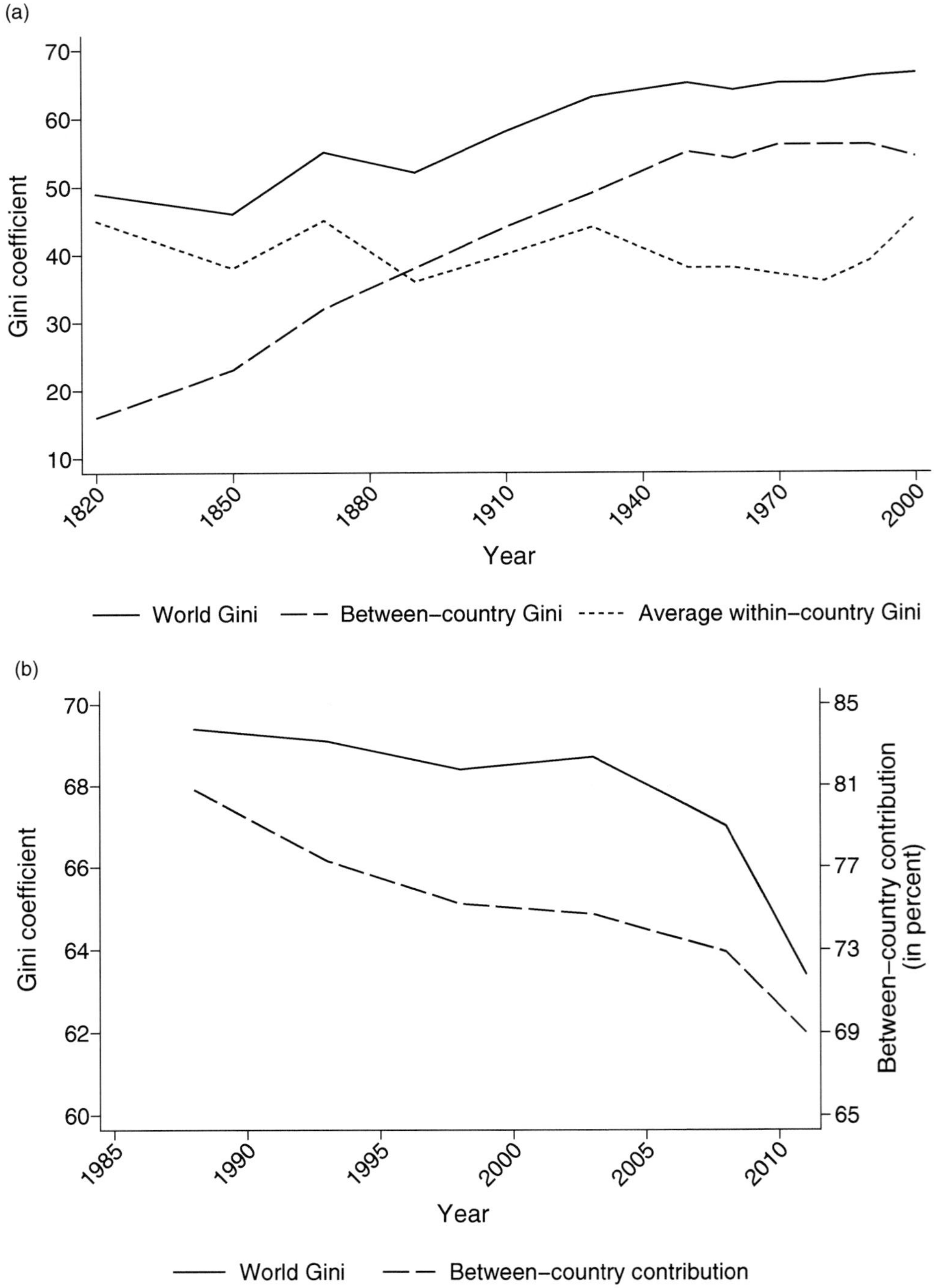

Figure 7.2 Global income inequality over the past two centuries: (a) 1820-2000 (b) 1988-2011

Note: The top panel shows gross income inequality at the household level. Pre-1950 estimates are based on the ratio between the real wage of unskilled labour and GDP per capita as well as the variance in height across individual within countries. The data are from the Clio Infra project and Moatsos et al. (2014). The bottom panel shows net income inequality at the individual level. All estimates are based on household surveys that cover about 90 percent of the world population; see Lakner and Milanovic (2016) for more information.

In light of this reversal, the Serbian economist Branko Milanovic (2016a) states that we nowadays live in a "post-Marxian world". That is, in which country you are born is more important for your income prospects than in which social class you are born within that country. Milanovic notes that around 1870 within-country inequality (i.e., the class component) explained more than two thirds of global inequality, while nowadays more than two thirds of global inequality is explained by between-country inequality (i.e., the location component). Indeed, around 1800 the incomes in the richest regions of the world were only about three times as high as those in the poorest regions, yet by 1913 this ratio had increased to 6:1 between the USA and Africa and by 2010 this ratio had further risen to 15:1 (data from the Maddison Project). As a result, there are now very strong incentives for people from poorer countries to try to migrate to richer countries (see also Chapter 6). Because even those people who are considered poor within the United States or the European Union have incomes that are many times greater than the incomes of poor people in deprived countries, and often also greater than the incomes of the middle classes in deprived countries.

Trends in global income inequality: Lessons from the recent past

Nevertheless, as is also clear from the top panel of Figure 7.2, global income inequality has levelled off since the middle of the twentieth century, as between-country inequality stopped rising. What is more, as the bottom panel of Figure 7.2 indicates, there has even been a decline in global income inequality in recent years. The World Gini for 2011 roughly equals 64, compared to more than 69 in 1988 and still about 67 in 2008. The magnitude of the drop in these last few years suggests that the Great Recession of 2008 (see also Chapter 11) has in fact had an equalizing impact on the global income distribution.

However, these positive developments should not leave any doubt that today the overall level of inequality across the world remains very high. This is illustrated by Table 7.1, depicting each continent's share in the global population, its share in world income, and its average income per capita. To ensure that we can compare these average incomes across countries, they have been converted into US$ at the 2016 exchange rate and corrected for so-called purchasing power parity, to reflect that how much one can buy with US$1 differs from country to country. Table 7.1 shows, for instance, that the share in global income of Europe and North America far exceeds their share in the global population, whereas the reverse is true for Africa and Asia. Importantly, these differences would be even starker if we consider specific subsets of the different continents. For example, Sub-Saharan Africa amounts to 13 percent of the world population yet only three percent of global income, and India represents as much as 18 percent of the world population but only seven percent of global income. Despite recent reductions in global income inequality, these areas are still characterized by incredible poverty.

The crucial force behind the initial stabilization and recent decline of global income inequality (see the bottom panel of Figure 7.2) is the fast economic growth in several Asian countries that are relatively poor yet very populous, especially China and India – together representing almost 40 percent of the world population. In these countries average incomes have been on the rise in recent decades, even though the levels of inequality and poverty within both countries remain high. As a result of this economic growth in these highly populous countries, the global income distribution has shifted away from a bimodal distribution with two peaks (i.e., most people in the world have either a very high or a very low income) to a more even distribution with the emergence of a *global middle class*. Alongside these trends, there has in recent decades been a significant decrease in the number of people in the world living in extreme poverty. And, importantly, this decrease has taken place while the overall world population has grown, meaning that the share of the world population experiencing extreme poverty has decreased even more. See Figure 7.3.

Table 7.1 The distribution of global income in 2016

Continent	Percentage of global population	Percentage of global income	Income per capita (2016 € PPP)
Europe	12%	20%	27,100
North America	5%	17%	50,700
Latin America	8%	8%	15,400
Africa	12%	5%	6,600
Asia	62%	49%	12,700
Oceania	1%	1%	31,700

Note: Data are from the World Inequality Database (WID.world). Income levels per capita have been adjusted for purchasing power parity (PPP).

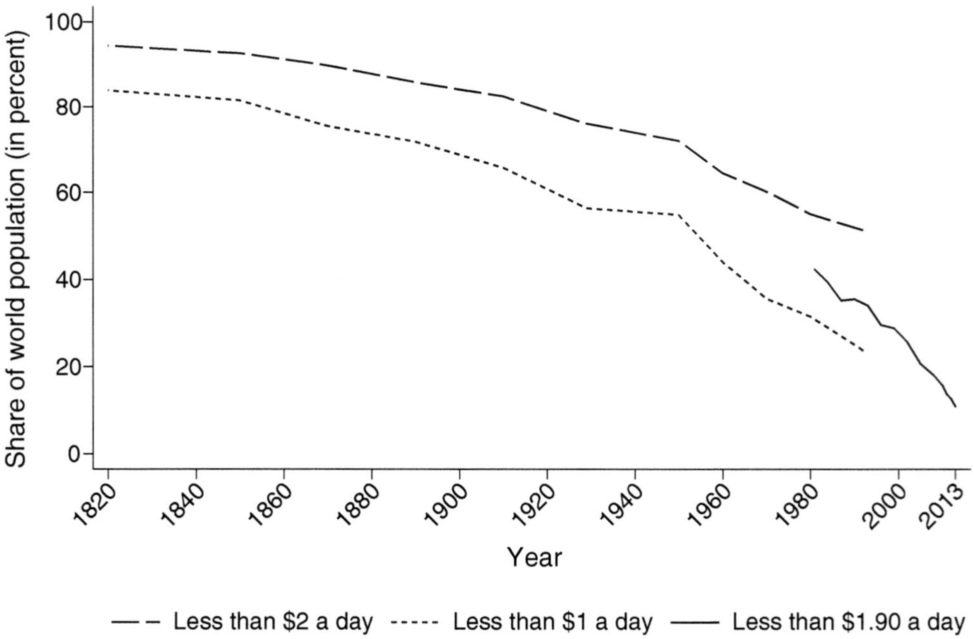

Figure 7.3 Share of the world population living in extreme poverty

Note: Data for the US$1 and US$2 thresholds are from Bourguignon and Morrisson (2002) and measured in 1985 US$, adjusted for purchasing power parity (PPP). Data for the $1.90 threshold are from the World Bank's PovCalNet database and measured in 2011 US$, adjusted for purchasing power parity (PPP).

Inequality trends within countries

As Figure 7.2 illustrates, the fast economic growth in Asia has meant that in recent decades within-country has again gained importance vis-à-vis between-country inequality. While between-country inequality has shrunk over the past few decades, over the same period most countries have experienced stable or even increasing inequality within their borders. This is illustrated for a selection of countries in Figure 7.4, which is derived from Milanovic's *All The Ginis (ALG)* dataset. All of these Ginis concern after-tax incomes, so they already take into account any redistributive policies. This, for example, helps to explain the low Gini in Sweden, where there is a lot of income redistribution (see Chapter 4). Where possible, we show the trend in income inequality across individuals, yet for some countries (e.g., the United States) we have to rely on measure of inequality across households, as there is no high-quality data available on inequality across individuals.

Figure 7.4 shows that income inequality within most countries is rather stable over time and that the differences between countries are generally bigger than within countries. This stability can certainly be observed for most Western countries, although in recent decades there has been a gentle, but steady, increase in inequality in most of these countries. This is in Figure 7.4 most apparent for the United Kingdom and, especially, the United States.

For China we see a much stronger increase in inequality since the country increasingly opened up for trade. As noted earlier, this increased openness and the embrace of capitalism has resulted in fast economic growth, but at the same time inequality has also grown, indicating that the revenues of this growth are unequally distributed across the population.

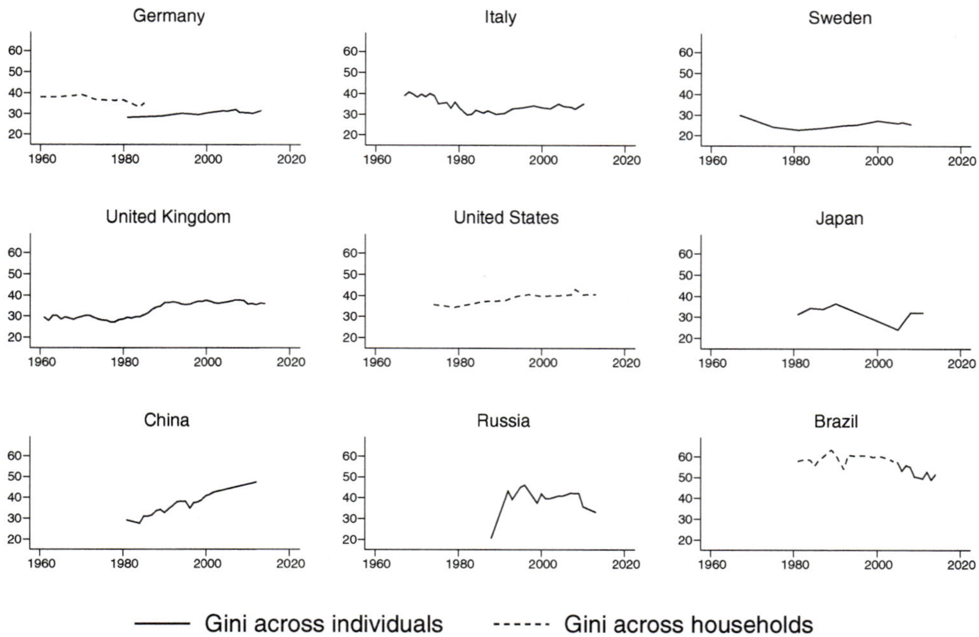

Figure 7.4 Income inequality trends within a selection of countries

Note: Solid lines correspond to income inequality between individuals. Dashed lines correspond to inequality between households. Data are from the All the Gini's (ALG) dataset compiled by Branko Milanovic (version: October 2016); see also Milanovic (2016b).

For Russia we see a massive spike in inequality in the early 1990s following the collapse of the Communist regime. In these years a great amount of property that had previously been owned by the state was privatized. Many of these privatizations took place by giving each citizen a certain share in a previously state-owned company. However, many citizens – being so used to communism – did not know what to do with these shares and sold them for virtually nothing to the few people who were interested in them. The latter subsequently became billionaires, who within a matter of a few years turned Russia from a communist state to an oligarchy.

For Brazil, finally, we observe that income inequality has in fact been decreasing in recent years, but from an extremely high starting point, with Gini coefficients of around 60. Indeed, today Brazil is still one of the countries with the highest degree of economic inequality, alongside several other Latin Americans that are also near the top of this ranking. Acemoglu and Robinson (2012) show how these high levels of inequality can be traced back to extractive institutions that were imposed on these societies by their colonizers several centuries ago. At the same time, these high inequality levels obstruct political and economic reforms to this very day.

As Milanovic and Roemer (2016) discuss, these within-country trends in inequality are very important for people's perceptions of inequality. Indeed, people are very nationally focused in their perceptions of inequality trends. This probably reflects that our world is politically organized into countries and that most decisions about economic and social policies are made at the country level. As a result, the attention of citizens, as well as politicians and the media, is mainly directed to national trends in inequality. This means that many people these days have the feeling that inequality is rising, even though global income inequality is clearly diminishing.

The winners and losers from globalization

An often-heard claim is that *globalization* – that is, increased trade, interaction and integration between people, companies and government across the world, under the influence of improvements in communication and transportation technologies – has increased global inequality. The idea is that rich countries disproportionately benefit from globalization at the expense of poor countries. Notwithstanding that there are certainly perverse dimensions to globalization (e.g., Western multinationals relying on child labour in Asian factories or exploiting poor farmers in Latin America) and that some of the poorest areas of the world are stuck in low or even no-growth equilibria, the claim that globalization has increased global inequality is not supported by the evidence presented in this section. What we see instead is a complex picture in which certain groups in certain countries have gained considerably from globalization, whereas other groups have gained to a much smaller degree or not at all.

Figure 7.5 illustrates these overall patterns, plotting the changes in income over the period 1980–2016 (adjusted for changes in the prices of goods and services) at different points in the global income distribution, where lower percentiles refer to poorer people and higher percentiles to richer people. Due to its shape, this figure is colloquially also referred to as the *elephant curve*, with a long, stretched-out trunk.

As Figure 7.5 demonstrates, the vast majority of people in the world have experienced a rise in real incomes over the last few decades. This signifies that when we are speaking of the losers from globalization, we are speaking about losers in a relative sense, because very few people have experienced an actual drop in income.

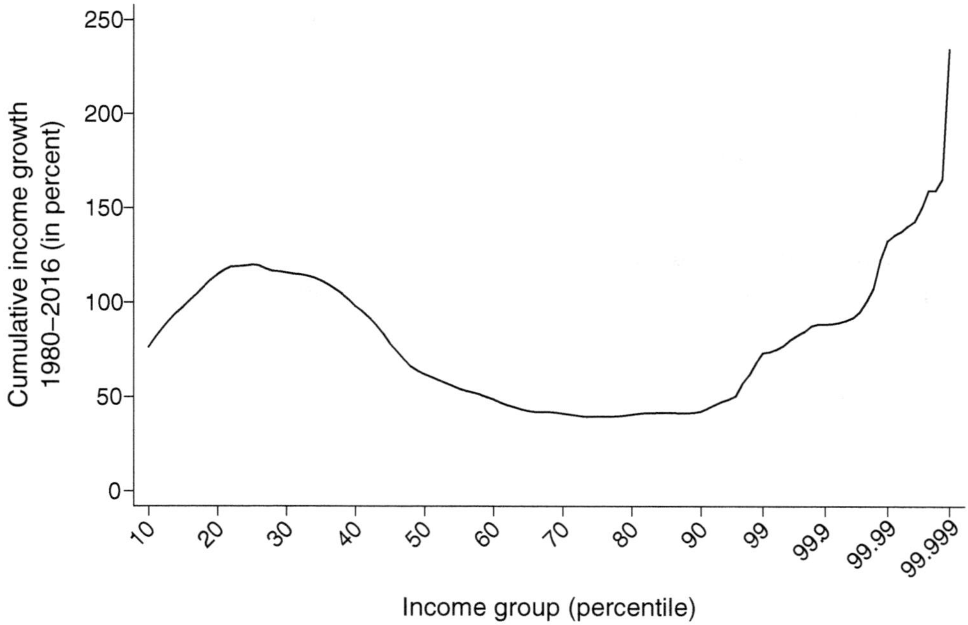

Figure 7.5 Changes in incomes across the global income distribution, 1980-2016

Note: Data are from the World Inequality Database (WID.world); see also Alvaredo et al. (2018). The percentiles along the horizontal axis indicate where people are situated in the global income distribution (e.g., being at the 70th percentile indicates that one is richer than the poorest 70 percent of the world population, but poorer than the richest 30 percent of the world population.

We furthermore observe two groups that have experienced especially large income gains. The first group is located between the 20th and 40th percentile of the global income distribution. This is where, among others, most members of the elites and upper-middle classes in China and India are located. At this point in the global income distribution, incomes have more than doubled over the 1980–2016 period, which accounts for the emergence of a global middle class.

The second group of winners is found at the very top of the global income distribution, covering the richest people within the richest countries: the global *top one percent*. Note, however, that this global top one percent is a much less exclusive club than the top one percent of any given Western country. It comprises more than 60 million people in total and includes, for example, 12 percent of all Americans, with a cut-off annual income of about US$ 50,000 after tax. The top one percent within Western countries, in turn, are often part of the global top 0.1, 0.01 or 0.001 percent. As Figure 7.5 shows, starting from the global top one percent, the further we move towards the top of the global income distribution, the larger the income growth experienced. Another thing to keep in mind here are the base income levels against which the growth rates in Figure 7.5 are measured. For example, a growth rate of 100 percent from an already very high income level is, in absolute terms, much greater than a growth rate of 100 percent from a more modest starting point. This implies, for example, that between 1980 and 2016, the global top one percent has captured 27 percent of the total growth in the world, while the bottom 50 percent has captured only 12 percent of that total growth (Alvaredo et al. 2018).

It is interesting to observe that aside from these two biggest winners from globalization, the bottom decile of the global income distribution has also experienced significant increases in income. The notable exceptions to this rule are the very poorest in the world, but on average people in the bottom decile of the global income distribution have experienced income rises of around 75 percent between 1980 and 2016. These gains have played a big role in the reduction of extreme poverty shown in Figure 7.3 and go against the notion that already rich countries have benefitted from globalization at the expense of poor countries.

The smallest income gains have occurred between the 60th and 90th percentile of the global income distribution. This is where we find the biggest losers from globalization, other than the bottom few percent of the global income distribution. This section of the global income distribution covers the lower classes of the rich countries as well as many citizens of former communist and Latin American countries. The lower classes in the rich countries have especially suffered from a diminished demand for their labour as a consequence of automatization, increased imports and the outsourcing of their jobs to poorer countries. Such losses, as well as the fear of further hardship, are claimed to have played a key role in the recent electoral success of anti-establishment parties and politicians in various Western countries.

The top one percent in Western countries

Many Western countries have, to a greater or lesser extent, experienced rising income inequality in recent decades and are home to some of the biggest winners and the biggest losers from globalization. Indeed, it seems that the large gains among the very rich within Western countries, in particular, play a key role in explaining the overall inequality trends within these countries. More generally, what is happening near the top of the income distribution has come under increasing scrutiny in recent years, among academics, politicians, media as well as the general public. In 2011, the *Occupy Wall Street* movement emerged in the United States protesting the extreme wealth of the top one percent (portrayed as the "filthy rich"), using the slogan "we are the 99 percent". This movement quickly spread to many other Western, African and Asian countries.

Studying what is happening near the top of the income distribution is a tricky business. One reason is that studies of inequality are traditionally based on individual or household surveys in which a certain, usually small, portion of the population is asked about their income. However, the problem with such surveys is that they are often too small to get a reliable picture of what is happening near the top end of the income distribution. Even though a large portion of total income is concentrated near this top, it is in the hands of a relatively small number of individuals, who are often underrepresented in standard surveys. Moreover, even if these very rich people take part in these surveys, they may be less willing to give information about their income.

In recent years, however, economists such as Anthony Atkinson and Thomas Piketty and their colleagues have made major advances by looking at data on tax returns instead of relying on surveys. Although difficult to handle, these data have the advantage that everyone is represented in the data and with their true income, as citizens are legally obliged to fill out their tax returns, and to do so honestly. Using such data, these economists were, for example, able to show that for the United States the share of total national income earned by the top one percent more than doubled from nine percent in 1976 to 20 percent in 2011 (Alvaredo et al. 2013).

Figure 7.6 shows how the income share of the top one percent has developed over the past century in three countries: the United States, France and Sweden. For all of these countries the first half of the twentieth century is characterized by, on average, a drop of this income share, indicating that income became more evenly distributed across society. However, shortly after the Second World War this drop largely stalled, although in France and Sweden a further, more gentle, decline occurred in the 1970s, as their welfare states were created.

From about 1980, the income share of the top one percent has increased dramatically in the United States. One can also see a few major drops over this period (marking the bursting of the "internet bubble" and the financial crisis of 2008), but the income share of the top one percent exhibits a remarkably quick recovery on both occasions. For Sweden we can observe a similar increase in the top income share since the 1980s – though much gentler and from a much lower base level. In contrast, France witnesses only a very marginal increase in the income share of the top one percent over this period.

As the economists Facundo Alvaredo, Anthony Atkinson, Thomas Piketty and Emmanuel Saez (2013) argue, the fact that these three countries with similar technological developments have gone through markedly different patterns of income inequality at the very top suggests that institutional and policy differences across the three countries play an important role in explaining these trends. Among other things, they point to decreases in the top income tax rates, which have occurred in most Western countries, but for example on a much greater scale in the United States than in France.

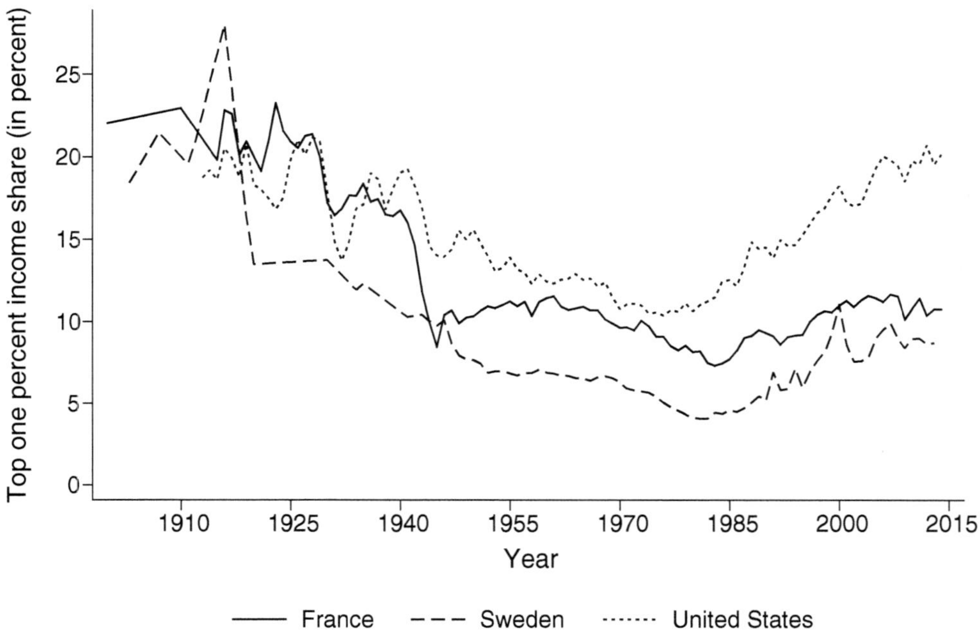

Figure 7.6 Income shares of the top one percent over time in a selection of countries

Note: Data are from the World Inequality Database (WID.world); see also Alvaredo et al. (2013). For France, Sweden and the US from 1962 onwards, the lines depict the top one percent share in pre-tax national income; the line for the US up to 1962 depicts the top one percent share in pre-tax factor income.

When we are talking about the top one percent, it is not only about income differences and certainly not only about income from labour. Wealth and capital income also feature prominently in these debates. The data challenges in this regard are even bigger, among other things because wealth can take many forms (e.g., savings, home ownership, shareholdings) and be stored in different countries. However, it is clear that there has been a large rise in wealth inequality in the United States as well as several European countries. Total wealth is increasingly concentrated in the hands of the very rich. This, in turn, has implications for income inequality. For example, in Europe inheritance income (i.e., income from wealth) has in recent decades become a bigger portion of overall income. Moreover, in the United States the top one percent, in terms of labour incomes, and the top one percent, in terms of capital incomes, increasingly coincide over time. All of this suggests that wealth and capital income taxation will become more central policy tools for curbing economic inequality, as covered in the section "Economic inequality as a problem".

Explanations of underdevelopment and poverty

In the section "Income inequality trends across the world" we noted that the share of the world population living in extreme poverty has dropped significantly (see Figure 7.3) and that many people in the bottom third of the global income distribution have experienced substantial income rises in recent decades (see Figure 7.5). Nevertheless, the very poorest of the world have sadly only shared in these positive developments to a limited degree, and many of them are still stuck in a desperate situation. Over the years, many theories have been proposed for this lack of development.

The need for a big push

Shortly after the Second World War, when people started to think more about international development, it was recognized that most developing countries suffer from a myriad of problems, many of which reinforce one another: for example low savings, a lack of investment, high population growth, tough climatic conditions, weak infrastructure, widespread diseases, a corrupt political system, and a lack of education. In the 1950s, the Swedish economist Gunnar Myrdal developed his theory of *cumulative causation*, which described how each of these problems gives rise to other problems, which in turn intensify the original problems, leading to a vicious circle of poverty. As a result, most of the poorest countries are stuck in "bad equilibria" from which it is hard to escape.

We can illuminate this situation with a *critical mass model*, as depicted in Figure 7.7 (see also our discussion of these models in Chapter 2). This figure is about investments in a country, which can be broadly construed as any type of effort that could help the country get ahead. The figure shows how the investments of one particular actor or group depends on what they expect the total investment level to be. Being totally aware that there are many obstacles to getting the country on a proper development track, the actors are unwilling to invest much if they expect the overall investment level to be low. After all, in that case their own investment will probably end up being a wasted effort. With all actors involved reasoning along these lines, the overall investment level will indeed turn out to be too low to set off a real development.

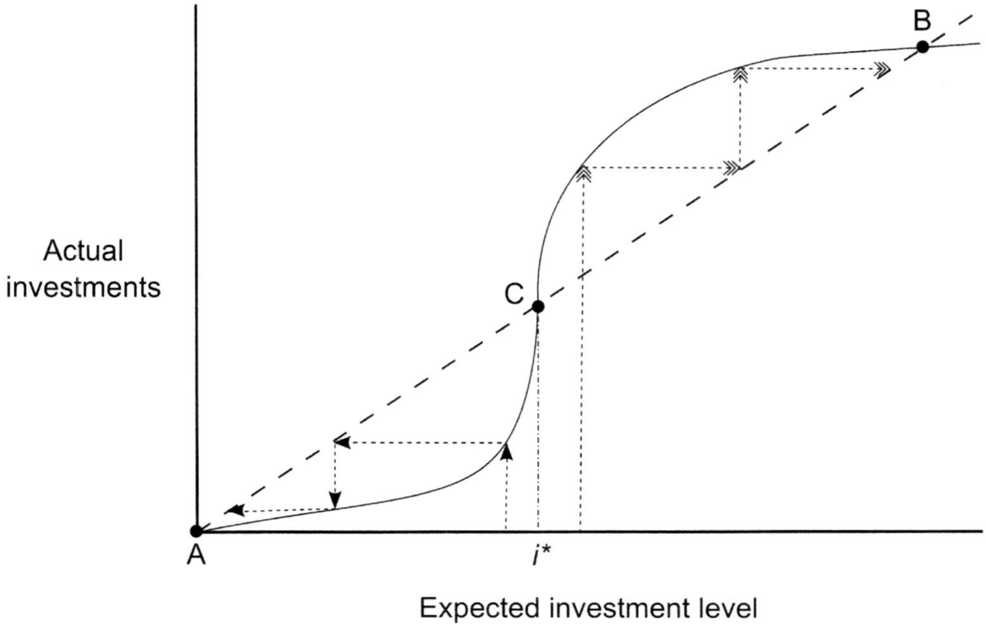

Figure 7.7 Expected investments, actual investments, and multiple development equilibria

This will reinforce actors' pessimistic expectations and the country will, in the long run, remain stuck in a low-investment low-growth equilibrium (point A in Figure 7.7).

As one may recognize, however, there is also a more optimal potential equilibrium with a self-sustaining high investment level (point B in Figure 7.7). Yet, this equilibrium can only be reached if people expect that the overall investment will be higher than a specific threshold, marked by i^* in the figure. At that level of investment, there will be enough momentum to start addressing the problems the country is suffering from, turning the vicious circle of poverty into a virtuous circle of development. This kind of reasoning brought development economists to the conclusion that what developing countries need is a so-called *big push*: a concerted intervention in multiple areas at once, with the goal of kick-starting social and economic development.

Opinions on what such a big push should exactly look like have shifted over time. Initially, the idea was that large amounts of aid from developed countries could do this job. However, over time people came back from this, observing that the development aid created a strong dependency relationship by aid-receiving countries on donor countries rather than setting off an independent, self-sustaining growth trajectory. Moreover, many of the donated funds were not spent in the way they were meant to be, but rather used to strengthen the position of autocratic regimes.

In the 1980s, therefore, government intervention fell out of favour and market mechanisms became more popular and "less state, more market" became the new mantra. This development recipe was also known as the *Washington Consensus* and entailed reductions in government spending, a dismantling of trade and foreign investment barriers, all kinds of market deregulations and the privatization of state-owned companies. Over time, however, this big push did not turn out to be a silver bullet. Many developing countries were simply not strong enough to compete on global markets, specialized into industries that were not conducive to broader development, and many had to turn to the World Bank and the International Monetary Fund (IMF) for loans and financial injections. In addition, political structures remained weak, corrupt, and highly resistant to change.

The importance of institutions

The lack of success of the aforementioned approaches to development has contributed to a new understanding of the ultimate causes of underdevelopment. This new understanding is centred around the role of *institutions*. Following the American economist and Nobel Prize laureate Douglas North (1991), this term should be interpreted broadly, as referring to the "rules of the game" in a society, including both formal rules such as constitutions and laws but also informal constraints such as codes of conduct, behavioural norms and conventions. Defined as such, institutions comprise everything related to the organization of society. The increased focus on institutions is motivated by the observation that it is hard to realize economic development as long as governments are inefficient, unaccountable, and corrupt. Therefore, international organizations such as the World Bank and the IMF nowadays promote "good governance" as a key ingredient for development as well as a condition for receiving loans and aid. They emphasize local capacity-building in terms of ensuring the rule of law, improving the efficiency, transparency, and accountability of the public sector, and tackling corruption.

Unfortunately, however, promoting good institutions is anything but a straightforward task. As noted in the section "Economic inequality as a problem", institutions tend to be particularly sticky and often become closely intertwined with culture as time goes by. Indeed, the economists Daron Acemoglu and James Robinson (2012) show that many differences in economic development today can be linked to institutional differences that have their origins many centuries ago. A particularly powerful illustration is offered in two studies by Acemoglu and Robinson together with Simon Johnson (2001, 2002). One of their starting points is that among all countries that have been colonized by European powers during the past 500 years, those that were relatively rich around 1500 are now relatively poor and vice versa. In other words, a reversal of fortune has occurred and, as Acemoglu and his colleagues demonstrate, this reversal very much relates to historical events shaping countries' current political and economic institutions.

We can illustrate this using a couple of macro-micro-macro schemes, depicted in Figures 7.8 and 7.9. The initial macro-level conditions of interest concern the environments faced by the European powers in their new colonies. Several factors matter in this regard, including the settler mortality rate, the indigenous population density, and the pre-existing level of prosperity in the colony; see Figure 7.8. Together, these factors determine how difficult it is for European colonizers to settle themselves in the area as well as the opportunities for extracting resources from the colony. In particular, settling is easier when settler mortality rates are low and the area is sparsely populated upon the colonizers' arrival. On the other hand, when settler mortality is high, and when there is already a lot of wealth in the area, settling becomes harder yet the potential for resource extraction increases.

By determining the settling climate and extraction opportunities faced by the colonizers, the initial macro-level conditions thus influence whether the colonizers adopt a settlement strategy or merely a resource-extraction strategy. These strategies will, in turn, influence the institutions that the European powers impose on their colonies. If they decide to settle in the colony, *inclusive institutions* securing private property rights for a broad cross section of society are more

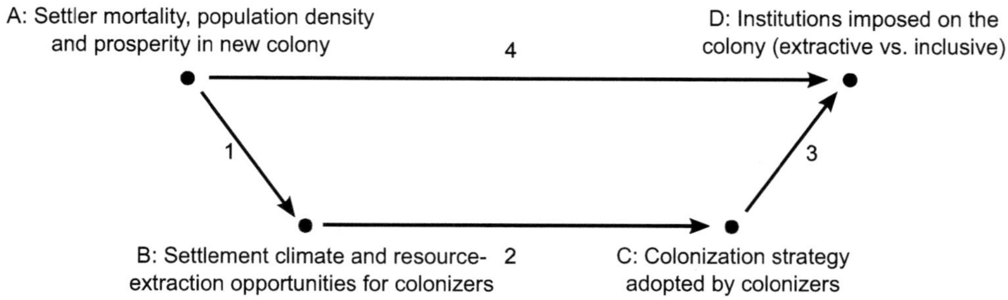

Figure 7.8 The impact of colonization circumstances on the development of institutions

likely to emerge. On the other hand, if they only want to extract resources from the colony, *extractive institutions* are more likely to emerge, which concentrate power in the hands of a small elite and create a high risk of expropriation for the majority of the population.

These institutions subsequently have a profound impact on the development potential of the colonized nations, stretching far beyond the actual period of colonization, given how strongly ingrained in society and resilient to change institutions can be. This is illustrated in Figure 7.9. Here we start from the type of institutions that were imposed by the European colonizers, that is, extractive institutions or inclusive institutions securing private property rights. These in turn shape the investment climate faced by potential investors. In the case of extractive institutions, the investment climate is poor, as there is a high risk of any investments (or investment gains) being expropriated by the small, corrupt elite. In contrast, the investment climate looks much brighter if private property rights are respected. The investment climate subsequently determines how many people are willing to invest when, for example, a new technology becomes available. Finally, because for a technology to properly catch on and set off economic growth investment from a broad section of society is required, success is more likely to be achieved in places with inclusive institutions. Indeed, Acemoglu and his colleagues find that former colonies with a solid system of property rights were able to take advantage of the opportunity to industrialize, while their counterparts with weak institutions failed to do so.

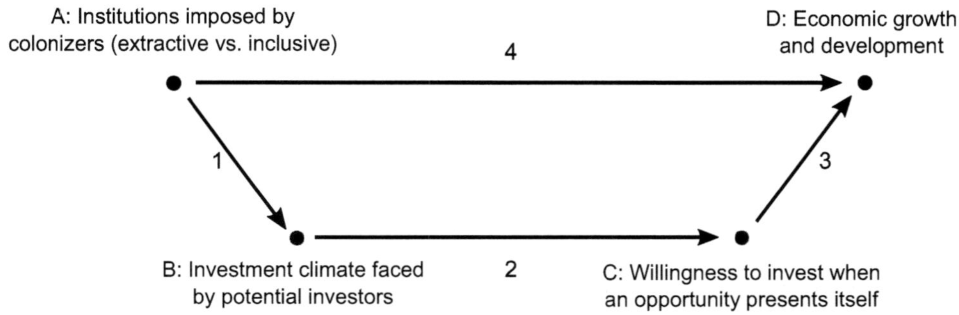

Figure 7.9 The impact of institutions on economic growth and development

The link between inequality, development, growth, and well-being

Having discussed both trends in inequality as well as some explanations of economic development, we now consider how within-country inequality is linked to economic growth and development as well as societal well-being more generally. Are richer countries more equal, how will inequality evolve as countries develop, what is the influence of inequality on economic growth, how does inequality affect public health and social mobility?

Economic development and inequality

Traditional thinking on the relationship between economic development and inequality has been heavily shaped by the American economist Simon Kuznets (1955), who came up with a hypothesis that later become known as the *Kuznets curve.* Looking at trends in income inequality in the United States, United Kingdom and Germany throughout the twentieth century and supplementing these with speculations on earlier trends, Kuznets hypothesizes that the relationship between economic development and inequality looks like an inverted U-shape.

The underlying logic is that in the early stages of development, it is the elites within society that benefit most. During the beginnings of the industrialization, for example, the elites made great returns on their investments, whereas a large influx of people from the countryside into the cities kept wages low. However, as the industrialization came into full swing, more and more people started to share in its fruits, as the supply of labour could no longer keep up with the increasing demand for labour, resulting in rising wages. Consequently, the initially rising trend in inequality started to flatten off. When later on democratization processes took place (e.g., everyone got the right to vote) and eventually also welfare states were built, inequality started to drop, completing the inverted U-shape. Part of this trend is visible for the US in Figure 7.6.

In cross-national comparisons, one can also find support for this hypothesis; see Figure 7.10, which plots the relationship between national income and within-country inequality for 147 countries across the world. While there is admittedly a great degree of variation in terms of inequality among poorer countries, most of the developed countries with national incomes of more than US$ 40,000 per capita have relatively low rates of inequality – the prime exception being the US. Overall, Figure 7.10 thus depicts a negative relationship between economic development and within-country inequality. This suggests that inequality may indeed drop when countries become more developed, but that many developing countries are still stuck in earlier stages of development with higher accompanying rates of inequality.

However, a few points of caution are in order regarding this interpretation of Figure 7.10. First, this figure compares different countries at a single point in time. Therefore, this evidence does not strictly warrant any interpretations in terms of what would happen to a given country as it develops over time. For such interpretations we really need to follow countries over time. Second, we should bear in mind a point that applies to many graphs in this book as well as much social scientific evidence in general, namely that correlation does not imply causation. That is, even though Figure 7.10 shows that there is, overall, a negative relationship between economic development and inequality, this does not imply that higher levels of development *cause* lower levels of inequality. Causality may just as well run the other way around – see the next subsection – or a third factor

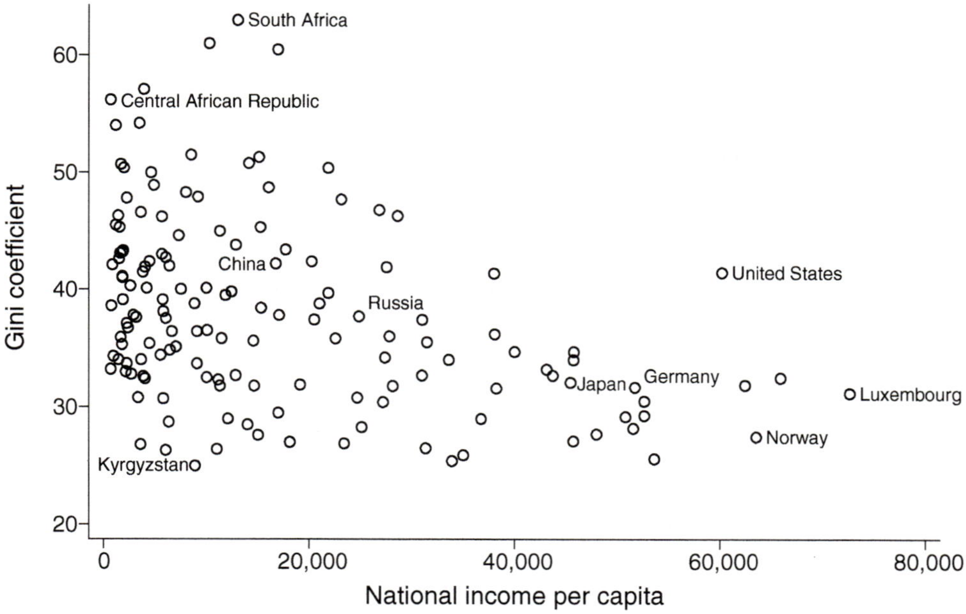

Figure 7.10 The cross-country relationship between economic development and inequality

Note: Data are from the World Bank's World Development Indicators for the year 2017. The levels of income per capita are measured in US$ and have been adjusted for purchasing power parity (PPP).

may be driving the association (just like the strong correlation between ice cream consumption and the frequency of forest fires does not imply that those eating or selling ice cream are to blame for these disasters; hot temperatures are more likely to play a role).

In the later stages of the twentieth century, the Kuznets curve gradually fell out of favour. The main reason for this was the Kuznets curve was unable to account for the fact that inequality had started to rise again in many Western countries, despite the economic growth they were experiencing (see Figures 7.4 and 7.6). While these trends contradicted the inverted U-shaped pattern originally predicted by Kuznets, several scholars have in recent years argued that we should not throw Kuznets's ideas in the bin altogether. For instance, Milanovic (2016a) has suggested that the more recent upswing in inequality in many Western countries could be seen as the beginning of a second Kuznets curve. He introduces in this context the idea of *Kuznets waves* or *Kuznets cycles* to describe recurrent trends of waxing and waning inequality. He furthermore shows how inequality and national income trends in the US over the period 1774–2013, and in England over the period 1688–2010, support the existence of such waves.

The influence of inequality on economic growth

As already hinted at, it is worthwhile to not only consider how economic growth influences inequality but also how inequality influences economic growth. Overall, the evidence on this is remarkably inconclusive: some studies find that inequality undermines growth, others find that it stimulates growth, still others find no effect at all, and finally there are studies that sketch a complex picture whereby inequality affects growth under certain circumstances yet not under others. The evidence that has been most influential on this topic is provided by the American economist Robert Barro (2000, 2008) and – just to emphasize the mixed findings in this literature – some of Barro's more recent findings contradict his earlier ones.

Analysing about 70 countries from the 1960s onwards, Barro (2008) finds that, on average, higher levels of inequality are linked to lower rates of economic growth. Yet, he also shows that the strength of this relationship depends on a country's level of economic development. That is, in poorer countries the negative effect of inequality on growth is by far the strongest, while it seems that for the most developed countries inequality does not matter or even slightly stimulates economic growth. This differentiation may reflect how inequality is embedded within societies. In poor countries high degrees of inequality often go hand in hand with dictatorial regimes, corruption, exploitation of the majority and rent-seeking by the elite, and civil wars. In rich countries, in contrast, inequality may rather be a matter of democratic deliberation and choice, with, for example, the Swedish electorate exhibiting a stronger preference for equality than the American electorate.

It is interesting to discuss a few more studies that have attempted to illuminate the impact of inequality on growth. Firstly, Abhijit Banerjee and Esther Duflo (2003) shift the focus to the impact of *changes* in inequality on economic growth, finding an inverted U-shaped relationship. In other words, changes in inequality – whatever their direction – are associated with lower growth in the next period. This is an intriguing finding, suggesting that the most viable pathway to growth may entail a situation of stable inequality, although Banerjee and Duflo hasten to warn that one should be careful in giving a causal interpretation to this finding.

Secondly, Gustavo Marrero and Juan Rodríguez (2013) argue that some of the mixed findings in this literature may reflect that income inequality is a composite measure of inequality of *opportunity* as well as inequality of *effort*. Attempting to disentangle the influence of both types of inequality using American data, they show that inequality of opportunity reduces growth, while inequality of effort promotes growth. These findings may reflect that inequality of opportunity implies an underutilization of talents present within a society, while inequality of effort could signify the presence of people with a particularly entrepreneurial and hard-working spirit.

Although inequality is not necessarily bad for economic growth and may reflect the outcome of a democratic process, it is important to note that even in the most developed countries (where the impact of inequality seems most benign) current trends in inequality are perceived with a sense of alarm. For example, the renowned economist and Nobel laureate Joseph Stiglitz (2012) has repeatedly warned about the detrimental impacts of America's rising level of inequality on both the economy and society at large. In his view, inequality in the US has reached such a high level that the working and middle class no longer have a real voice within society, with politics being dominated by large corporations heavily engaged in unproductive, rent-seeking behaviour at the expense of the general public. Through lobbying efforts, these elites have managed to achieve corporate subsidies, tax cuts and other favourable policy measures that spur inequality and put a bomb under longer-run growth and prosperity. To place Stiglitz's warnings in a historical perspective, the economic historian Bas van Bavel (2016) has noted, based on an investigation of the emergence and decline of market economies since AD 500, that rapid rises in inequality during times of prosperity invariably lead to economic turmoil sooner or later.

The influence of inequality on societal well-being

The influence of income on well-being is well-established; see, for instance, Stevenson and Wolfers (2013). If we take subjective well-being measures such as happiness or life satisfaction as the benchmark, there is a robust positive relationship between income and well-being both across countries (i.e., people in rich countries tend to be happier than people in poor countries) as well as across citizens within the same country. For certain well-being outcomes, however, the relationship is subject to decreasing returns (i.e., the difference in well-being between a very rich and slightly less rich person is smaller than between a very poor and slightly less poor person). Moreover, the over-time relationship between income and subjective well-being tends to be flat: as countries or individuals get richer, happiness and life satisfaction do not rise. This finding is known as the *Easterlin paradox*, named after the economist Richard Easterlin (1974), and is often explained by the tendency that people's standards and reference points shift upwards as they get used to higher incomes – a process referred to as *preference drift* or the *hedonic treadmill.*

As noted in the section "Economic inequality as a problem", the fact that income has an influence on well-being both across countries as well as across citizens within the same country is already enough reason to be worried about economic inequality. Moreover, the fact that the income-well-being relationship may be subject to decreasing returns suggests that income redistribution could enhance a society's overall level of well-being. Nevertheless, does economic inequality in and of itself also have any impact on societal well-being? It is this question that we turn to next.

A highly influential book on this topic is *The Spirit Level* (2009) by the social epidemiologists Richard Wilkinson and Kate Pickett. This book makes an impassioned case for how many societal ills are not primarily the product of how wealthy societies are, but of how equal or unequal they are. As the subtitle of their book, *Why Equality is Better for Everyone*, implies, Wilkinson and Pickett argue that economic inequality lies at the heart of a range of societal problems. While the list of societal outcomes they look at is long – encompassing among other things community life, obesity, educational performance, teenage births, violence, and imprisonment – the outcome with which they originally started is health. In this respect, Wilkinson and Pickett (2009:44) summarize the core of their theoretical argument as follows: "If inequalities are bigger, so that some people seem to count for almost everything and others for practically nothing, where each one of us is placed becomes more important. Greater inequality is likely to be accompanied by increased status competition and increased status anxiety." They go on to argue that status anxiety is a big source of stress in modern societies and that this stress, in turn, is harmful to health and longevity.

In terms of empirical evidence, Wilkinson and Picket present graphs showing that in more unequal countries more people suffer from mental health problems, drug use is higher, life expectancy is lower, and infant mortality is higher (which can be taken as an indicator of maternal health). However, at this point it is useful to take a step back and ask whether this evidence really proves the claim that inequality undermines health. In particular, these country-level associations between inequality and various health indicators may simply reflect that in more unequal societies there are more poor people and that poor people are especially likely to suffer health problems. As such, these country-level associations do not necessarily imply that inequality undermines health and may rather reflect that poverty threatens health.

This possibility is illustrated in Figure 7.11, where we plot a hypothetical relationship between income and health. This relationship is depicted as a curve, reflecting that income improvements likely have a stronger impact on health among the poor rather than among the rich. Along this curve we have indicated two hypothetical countries with the same average income $\bar{y}$ yet a different degree of income inequality. In Country A half the population has income y_{A1} and the other half y_{A2}; in Country B half the population has income y_{B1} and the other half y_{B2}. Furthermore, we can see that the more equal Country A scores higher in terms of average health than Country B. However, the crux is that this finding simply reflects the particular shape of the income-health relationship and not that inequality *causes* poorer health outcomes.

In short, by solely looking at country-level data to make inferences about how individuals are affected by inequality, Wilkinson and Picket commit a so-called *ecological fallacy*. This observation closely relates to our plea in this book for a macro-micro-macro approach to explain societal problems. Indeed, if one wishes to explain societal phenomena, one needs to descend to the micro-level at which individual actors operate, or else one runs the risk of arriving at false conclusions regarding the micro-level patterns underlying any macro-level relationship. Of course, all of this is not to say that Wilkinson and Picket's theoretical argument is flawed and it may indeed still be the case that inequality does harm health. The only thing we are arguing is that more solid evidence for this claim is needed, showing how individuals are affected by inequality and demonstrating, for example, that rich individuals also suffer when they are embedded in a more unequal environment. However, to the best of our knowledge, the jury is still out on that.

Another relationship that has received a great amount of attention in recent years is the relationship between economic inequality and intergenerational social mobility. *Intergenerational*

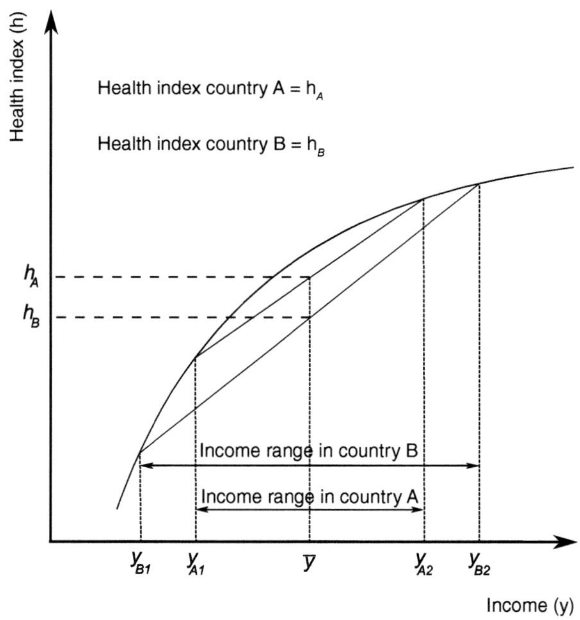

Figure 7.11 Hypothetical relationships between income, income inequality, and health
Note: This figure is adapted from a figure presented by Gravelle (1998).

social mobility can be defined as the degree to which the socio-economic position that children attain reflects the socio-economic position of their parents and a certain degree of social mobility is generally regarded as a valuable feature of a society.

In this context, one may argue that economic inequality does not need to be a bad thing as long as there is sufficient mobility. That is, as long as children from any background face the same opportunities to make it to the top, the main impact of inequality may be that it incentivizes children to put in effort to make the most of their talents. Based on a similar reasoning, Americans' firm belief in the *American Dream* (the idea that anyone can move up the socio-economic ladder) helps to explain why they are generally willing to tolerate more income inequality than citizens of most other rich countries. However, to what extent do high degrees of economic inequality and intergenerational mobility actually go together in real life?

One of the people who has investigated this question intensively is the Canadian economist Miles Corak (2013), who has shown that countries with higher economic inequality tend to have lower intergenerational mobility. This relationship is illustrated in Figure 7.12 and commonly referred to as the *Great Gatsby Curve*, after F. Scott's Fitzgerald's famous novel. While we should once again be careful in interpreting this macro-level relationship causally, it gives the impression that higher economic inequality may skew children's opportunities in the favour of children from better-off backgrounds, resulting in lower intergenerational mobility. In other words, it seems that in more unequal societies it matters more who your parents are. This is a

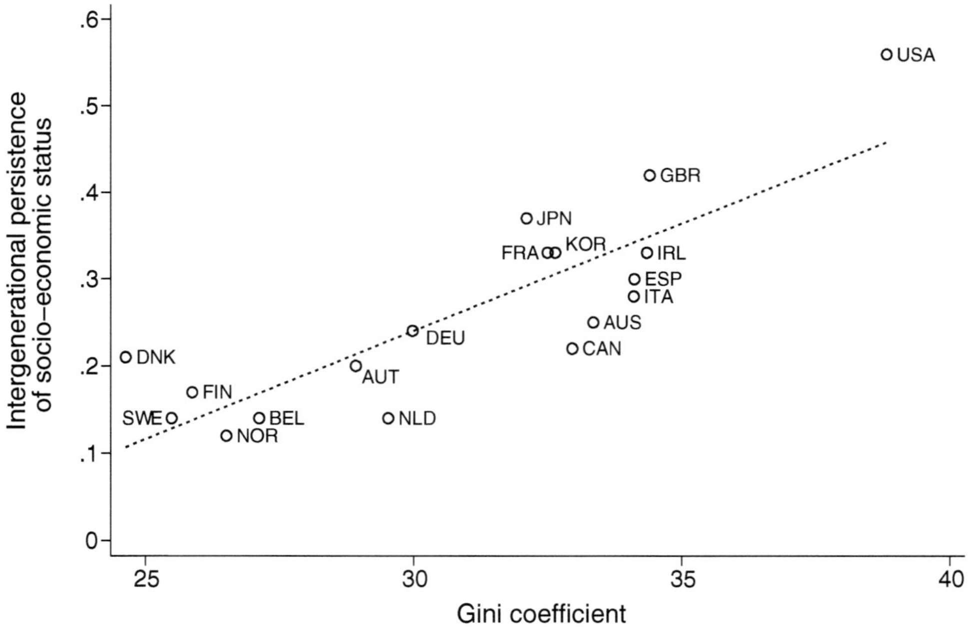

Figure 7.12 The Great Gatsby Curve

Note: The income inequality estimates are from the Luxembourg Income Study (LIS). The estimates for the intergenerational persistence of socio-economic status are from Jerrim and Macmillan (2015) and illustrate how strongly people's labour market earnings reflect their parents' level of education – higher scores indicate stronger persistence of socio-economic status and thus weaker intergenerational social mobility.

troubling observation, as it suggests that in highly unequal societies (compared to more equal societies) children from disadvantaged backgrounds do not only lag further behind children born to well-off parents but also face fewer opportunities to improve their lot. Economic inequality thus tends to be more persistent in more unequal societies. Inequality seems to have, as it were, a paralyzing impact on socio-economic differences within society, probably implying an underutilization of the talents that are present within society.

How could we explain the Great Gatsby Curve as a macro-level regularity that results from the behaviours and interactions of micro-level actors? One potential explanation is illustrated in a macro-micro-macro scheme in Figure 7.13. First, in more unequal societies there is a wider gap between better-off and worse-off parents in terms of their opportunities to foster their children's education and career, as the resources needed for this are more unequally distributed. As Corak notes, among other things, parents' socio-economic status influences a child's health and aptitudes in early years, as well as the quality of neighbourhoods and schools, all of which drive success in primary school, which subsequently feeds into success in secondary and tertiary education. Moreover, the greater financial resources and safety nets provided by better-off parents mean that their children can take more "risky" decisions in their educational career, and these kids usually also have better access to social connections that can influence admission into prestigious schools as well as the jobs they can get. Importantly, however, better-off parents also face greater incentives to invest in their children's education in more unequal societies, as the payoffs to education tend to be greater in those societies. Hence, as a result of both incentives and opportunities, the differential in parental investments in their children between better-off and worse-off parents will be greater in more unequal societies. These differential investments, in turn, will lead to a lower degree of intergenerational socio-economic mobility.

In principle, governments have the opportunity to weaken the linkage between economic inequality and intergenerational mobility, for example by implementing policies aimed at increasing educational attainment among children from disadvantaged backgrounds. However, it cannot be taken for granted that governments will necessarily adopt such policies. In this respect, Corak notes that in the US government programmes do not benefit disadvantaged children but rather the already advantaged, thereby exacerbating rather than blunting the degree to which socio-economic inequalities are passed on across generations. Among other things, the US spends much more on tertiary vis-à-vis primary education, from which children from

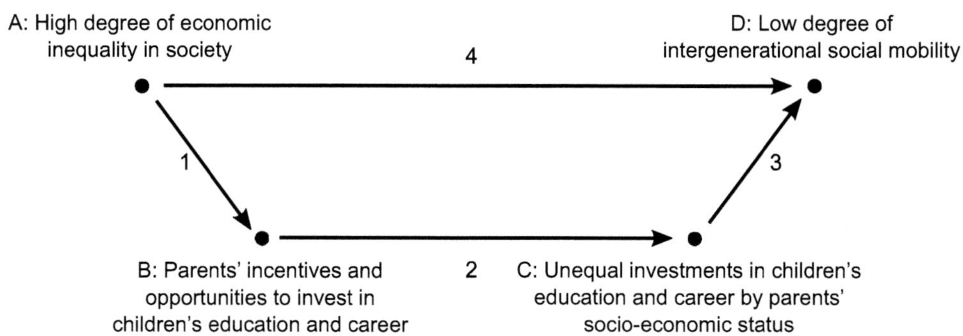

Figure 7.13 Macro-micro-macro scheme to explain the Great Gatsby Curve

advantaged backgrounds (being overrepresented in tertiary education) stand to gain more than their disadvantaged counterparts. This policy focus might possibly reflect the political implications of economic inequality, shifting the balance of power in such a way that better-off parents have a bigger say in which policies are adopted.

In the end, the question to which degree governments should aim to offset inequalities in opportunities really comes down to a value judgment. There is no simple right or wrong answer to this question, but the answer very much depends on one's moral convictions. As such, socialists, liberals, and conservatives are likely to come up with different answers. One example of someone who opposes the current state of affairs in most Western societies is the American philosopher Michael Sandel (2012). In his book *What Money Can't Buy* he argues that in recent decades a process of *marketization* or *commodification* has taken place. By this he means that there has been an increase in the number of things that are treated as products that can be bought and sold. Two of his examples concern education and political influence. According to Sandel, the fact that education and political influence are nowadays much more "for sale" than they used to be implies that income and wealth inequality have become much more consequential. He calls for a serious moral debate on whether this is a desirable development.

Recommended readings

- Thomas Piketty's (2014) *Capital in the Twenty-First Century* is a recent classic with a major influence on public debates around inequality. Being focused on Western countries and relying on an impressive *tour de force* in terms of data collection, Piketty describes trends in inequality and wealth concentration going back to the eighteenth century. He also provides explanations for these trends, outlines the challenges that they pose to societies, and proposes a policy agenda to alleviate the harmful consequences of rising inequality.
- Branko Milanovic is one of the leading experts when it comes to trends in global income inequality. His most recent book (2016a) provides a comprehensive summary of trends in inequality across the world and the benign and malign forces by which they are driven. Furthermore, Milanovic connects these trends to topical issues related to migration, politics and economic justice. A brief and accessible write-up of some of his main findings is provided in Milanovic (2013).
- Daron Acemoglu and James Robinson (2012) present a powerful theory on the longstanding question why some countries are rich and other countries poor. Key to their argument is the role of institutions for economic development. They show that institutions, once established, are hard to change and can influence countries' development trajectory over many centuries. In making these arguments, Acemoglu and Robinson rely on numerous intriguing historical examples from around the world.
- Miles Corak (2013) presents an accessible introduction to the evidence and debates surrounding the Great Gatsby Curve (on the relationship between income inequality and intergenerational mobility). Aside from presenting some underlying data, Corak discusses several mechanisms that may explain the Great Gatsby Curve. He also demonstrates how the inequality-mobility relationship is shaped by public policy and how policy-related questions in this domain cannot be separated from philosophical debates.

Bibliography

Acemoglu, Daron, Simon Johnson, and James A. Robinson. 2001. "The Colonial Origins of Comparative Development: An Empirical Investigation". *American Economic Review* 91:1369–1401.

Acemoglu, Daron, Simon Johnson, and James A. Robinson. 2002. "Reversal of Fortune: Geography and Institutions in the Making of the Modern World Income Distribution". *Quarterly Journal of Economics* 117:1231–1294.

Acemoglu, Daron, and James A. Robinson. 2012. *Why Nations Fail – The Origins of Power, Prosperity and Poverty*. New York: Crown Publishers.

Alesina, Alberto, Reza Baqir, and William Easterly. 1999. "Public Goods and Ethnic Divisions". *Quarterly Journal of Economics* 114:1243–1284.

Alvaredo, Facundo, Anthony B. Atkinson, Thomas Piketty, and Emmanuel Saez. 2013. "The Top 1 Percent in International and Historical Perspective". *Journal of Economic Perspectives* 27:3–20.

Alvaredo, Facundo, Lucas Chancel, Thomas Piketty, Emmanuel Saez, and Gabriel Zucman. 2018. "The Elephant Curve of Global Inequality and Growth". *American Economic Association: Papers and Proceedings* 108:103–108.

Banerjee, Abhijit V., and Esther Duflo. 2003. "Inequality and Growth: What Can the Data Say?". *Journal of Economic Growth* 8:267–299.

Bardhan, Pranab. 2000. "Irrigation and Cooperation: An Empirical Analysis of 48 Irrigation Communities in South India". *Economic Development and Cultural Change* 48:847–865.

Barro, Robert J. 2000. "Inequality and Growth in a Panel of Countries". *Journal of Economic Growth* 5:5–32.

Barro, Robert J. 2008. "Inequality and Growth Revisited". *ABD Working Paper Series on Regional Economic Integration*, no.11. https://www.adb.org/sites/default/files/publication/28468/wp11-inequality-growth-revisited.pdf.

Bourguignon, François, and Christian Morrisson. 2002. "Inequality among World Citizens: 1820–1992". *American Economic Review* 92:727–744.

Corak, Miles. 2013. "Income Inequality, Equality of Opportunity, and Intergenerational Mobility". *Journal of Economic Perspectives* 27:79–102.

Easterlin, Richard A. 1974. "Does Economic Growth Improve the Human Lot? Some Empirical Evidence". Pp. 89–125 in: *Nations and Households in Economic Growth: Essays in Honor of Moses Abramovitz*, edited by Paul A. David and Melvin W. Reder. New York, NY: Academic Press.

Gravelle, Hugh. 1998. "How Much of the Relation between Population Mortality and Unequal Distribution of Income is a Statistical Artefact?". *British Medical Journal* 16:382–385.

Jerrim, John, and Lindsey Macmillan. 2015. "Income Inequality, Intergenerational Mobility, and the Great Gatsby Curve: Is Education the Key?". *Social Forces* 94:505–533.

Kuznets, Simon. "Economic Growth and Income Inequality". 1955. *American Economic Review* 45:1–28.

Lakner, Christoph, and Branko Milanovic. 2016. "Global Income Distribution: From the Fall of the Berlin Wall to the Great Recession". *World Bank Economic Review* 30:203–232.

Marrero, Gustavo A., and Juan G. Rodríguez. 2013. "Inequality of Opportunity and Growth". *Journal of Development Economics* 104:107–122.

Milanovic, Branko. 2013. "Global Income Inequality in Numbers: In History and Now". *Global Policy* 4:198–208.

Milanovic, Branko. 2016a. *Global Inequality – A New Approach for the Age of Globalization*. Cambridge, MA: Harvard University Press.

Milanovic, Branko. 2016b. *Description of 'All the Ginis' Dataset* (version October 2016). https://www.gc.cuny.edu/CUNY_GC/media/CUNY-Graduate-Center/PDF/Centers/LIS/Milanovic/Description-of-the-dataset_16.pdf.

Milanovic, Branko, and John E. Roemer. 2016. "Interaction of Global and National Income Inequalities". *Journal of Globalization and Development* 7:109–115.

Moatsos, Michail, Jörg Baten, Peter Foldvari, Bas van Leeuwen, and Jan Luiten van Zanden. 2014. "Income Inequality since 1820". Pp. 199–215 in: *How Was Life? Global Well-being since 1820*, edited by Jan van Luiten Zanden, Jörg Baten, Marco Mira d'Ercole, Auke Rijpma, Conal Smith and Marcel Timmer. Paris: OECD Publishing.

North, Douglas C. 1991. "Institutions". *Journal of Economic Perspectives* 5:97–112.

Piketty, Thomas. 2014. *Capital in the Twenty-First Century*. Cambridge, MA: Harvard University Press.

Sandel, Michael. 2012. *What Money Can't Buy: The Moral Limits of Markets*. London: Penguin Books.

Stevenson, Betsey, and Justin Wolfers. 2013. "Subjective Well-Being and Income: Is There Any Evidence of Satiation?". *American Economic Review: Papers & Proceedings* 103:598–604.

Stiglitz, Joseph E. 2012. *The Price of Inequality: How Today's Divided Society Endangers Our Future*. London: Allen Lane.

Tavoni, Alessandro, Astrid Dannenberg, Giorgos Kallis, and Andreas Löschel. 2011. "Inequality, Communication, and the Avoidance of Disastrous Climate Change in a Public Goods Game". *Proceedings of the National Academy of Sciences* 108:11825–11829.

Van Bavel, Bas. 2016. *The Invisible Hand? How Market Economies Have Emerged and Declined Since AD 500*. Oxford: Oxford University Press.

Wilkinson, Richard G., and Kate Pickett. 2009. *The Spirit Level: Why Equality is Better for Everyone*. London: Penguin Books.

8 Gender inequalities

Chapter overview

Many areas of society are characterized by gender inequality, in some cases partly driven by discrimination against women. This applies to practically every country across the globe and it implies, among other things, that a large stock of human capital is left underutilized. We start this chapter with a historical sketch of gender inequality and go on to describe and explain the process of gender emancipation, highlighting the three waves of emancipation that took place during the twentieth century. Next, we examine international variation in gender inequality, followed by a discussion of gender discrimination and its role in explaining gender pay gaps. We subsequently address several major trends in female labour force participation and women's educational attainment. Finally, we shift our attention to the influence of women's rising labour market participation and educational attainment on gender-related issues within the private sphere, namely marriage patterns, fertility decisions, and domestic divisions of labour. Our overall conclusion is that, while gender inequality has certainly diminished in many life domains, the gender revolution is still far from being finished.

Discrimination and gender inequality as a problem

Discrimination on the basis of age, gender, sexual preference, race, skin colour or ethnic background is widely denounced in most societies. This sentiment is also reflected in Article 2 of the United Nations' Universal Declaration of Human Rights, which states, "Everyone is entitled to all the rights and freedoms set forth in this declaration, without distinction of any kind, such as race, colour, sex, language, religion, political or other opinion, national or social origin, property, birth or other status". In 1979, the United Nations General Assembly additionally adopted a convention seeking to eliminate all forms of discrimination against women. This underlines that the absence of discrimination is generally regarded as a public good, even though there are also still states that impose rules prohibiting women from entering certain occupations or from engaging in certain activities, such as driving or being out by themselves. For example, in Saudi Arabia the ban on women driving was only lifted in 2017.

Discrimination is undesirable from the point of view of both the individual and society as a whole. An individual who is discriminated against will obviously be hurt and limited in their life chances, however discrimination also hurts society insofar as it undermines generally accepted societal values of equality and results in a sub-optimal allocation of human capital. Women held back by discrimination are, after all, severely restricted in the contribution they can make to society, implying a lot of unfulfilled potential.

Pursuing equal labour market chances for all groups – men and women, members of different races, members of different religions – is one of the most important goals in the fight against discrimination. In 2012, the European Parliament held a survey in honour of International Women's Day that interviewed 25 thousand respondents across the European Union. As many as 58 percent of all women and 46 percent of all men believed that unequal opportunities were an important problem in their country. Unequal rewards were considered to be even more injurious: 76 percent of all women and 62 percent of all men believed that this was an important problem in their country. The fact that, to this day, the UN Commission on the Status of Women keeps emphasizing that women's rights are human rights also shows that discrimination against women is still an important problem in many countries.

Gender inequality and emancipation in historical perspective

Almost all societies in history have had a certain patriarchal orientation. For example, in ancient Greece – often considered the cradle of democracy – women were subservient to men. The subservient position of women in ancient Greek society meant that a man had as much control over his wife as he did over his children. Women in ancient Greece were not entitled to vote and could not leave their house without the permission of their husband. Fast forwarding a few centuries, the position of women in ancient Roman society was substantially better. They were respected and considered as social equals to their husbands. Nonetheless, Roman women were still not granted all of the same rights as men.

Although this description of ancient Greek and Roman society may give the impression of a secular trend over time towards women's emancipation, such an impression would be incorrect. Indeed, when Christianity spread across Europe in the first centuries AD, the social rights of women were curtailed once again. In Europe, Christian influence led not only to the belief that women were a source of sin and sexual immorality, but also that they were inferior to men. These beliefs came to be reflected in the legal canon. English law stipulated, for example, that a man could make decisions relating to his wife's possessions.

If we again fast forward through time, we arrive at the industrialization during the nineteenth century, which brought many changes to society, foremost an immense increase in the wealth available to ordinary members of the population. One might expect that such a large increase in wealth would have afforded women greater possibilities of developing themselves and pursuing their own goals, independent of their husbands or male relatives. However, this is not what happened initially, as the work of the American anthropologist Wanda Minge-Kalman (1978) illustrates. Specifically, she argues that the industrial revolution was in fact precisely what led women to the confined boundaries of the home, doing all household tasks – most notably child rearing.

Minge-Kalman begins by noting that the industrial revolution shifted the production of food and other small-scale goods from families to large businesses. As a consequence of this shift and the newfound wealth within society, a separate market developed for an entirely new form of "family production", namely the raising and educating of children. Indeed, during the first phase of industrialization, it was not yet necessary for workers to have advanced schooling in order to perform their tasks well. Among these workers were also young children and teenagers, as child labour was common until legislation prohibiting child labour was introduced after 1850. At that point – roughly the starting point of the second phase of industrialization – demand for skilled workers also began to increase. This meant children had to be exempted from factory labour, so they could go to school. Parents thus began investing in their children's education, as a way to produce skilled workers. This represented a shift from children being a source of income to children – at least in the short run – being a net cost. Here lies also the essence of Minge-Kalman's argument. It was not so much that the household had ceased to be a unit of production, but rather that the household had started producing different goods, namely skilled workers instead of food and small-scale goods for sale. In this reorganization process, women were assigned the task of rearing the children.

Things started to change again just after the First World War, when more and more women began working outside the house. In the US, women became very prominent in the new class of office workers. Of particular importance were the changes in voting laws that occurred around 1920 in many Western countries. While limited voting rights were already given to women in Scandinavia and certain other parts of the world in the late nineteenth century, full voting rights for women were realized in most countries in the interwar era. For example, Germany introduced universal suffrage in 1918, the Netherlands in 1919, the US in 1920, and Great Britain went through this process in two steps, in 1918 and 1928. On the other hand, in France it took until 1944 before women were granted the right to vote. Overall, the early decades of the twentieth century are known as the period of *first-wave feminism*.

The first wave of emancipation

In the early decades of the twentieth century, women not only gained the rights to vote and to run for political office, but also many other opportunities opened up that were previously unavailable to them. With the introduction of the 1919 Sex Disqualification Act, women in England, for example, gained the right to work in all sorts of professions, although they remained barred from working in mining. Women's rights expanded so rapidly during this period because the emancipation process became irreversible once the number of women in the labour force had increased beyond a certain level. This can be thought of as a *critical mass model*: once a certain number of women had become both economically and politically active, the momentum became such that women were not going to give up these acquirements again.

To explain the increase in women's labour force participation, we must descend to the individual level. Women began moving into the labour force primarily because there was no longer an equally strong economic need for families to have a large number of children. In addition, sterilization of food also meant that women were no longer forced to breastfeed for extended periods following the birth of a child. As a result, we can observe a U-shaped pattern of women's labour force participation over the last two centuries (Richards 1974) – female labour force participation was high before the industrial revolution, declined during the industrial revolution and increased again from the twentieth century onwards.

Another factor that played an important role in the rise of female labour force participation was the Second World War. During the war, there was a shortage of male workers because so many men had been drafted into the army. Additionally, because production of machines, tanks, aircraft, weapons and ammunition had to be ramped up for the war effort, the demand for workers was even larger than usual. Partly through the efforts of government propaganda, which roused people's sense of patriotism as well as their personal self-interest, nineteen million women were drawn into the American labour force by 1944.

However, at the end of the Second World War, the situation changed. Demand for factory labour fell as demand for the machines of war and munitions decreased, and the return of armed servicemen created a glut of labour. Many women could, or simply had to, return to the family home. The economist Claudia Goldin (1991) shows that, of all women who entered the labour force during the war, about half had left the labour force again by 1950. Yet, although the direct impacts of the Second World War on women's employment may have been short-lived, Goldin also presents evidence suggesting that the war left a lasting mark on the attitudes of young women, who had acquired a taste for freedom and independence. Moreover, the war may have altered prevailing norms regarding the behaviour of women in general and their capacity as workers in particular.

All in all, the Second World War marked a clear turning point in terms of women's labour market participation, even though many women ceased paid labour immediately after the war. This turning point is illustrated for the US in Figure 8.1. During the 60 years between 1870 and

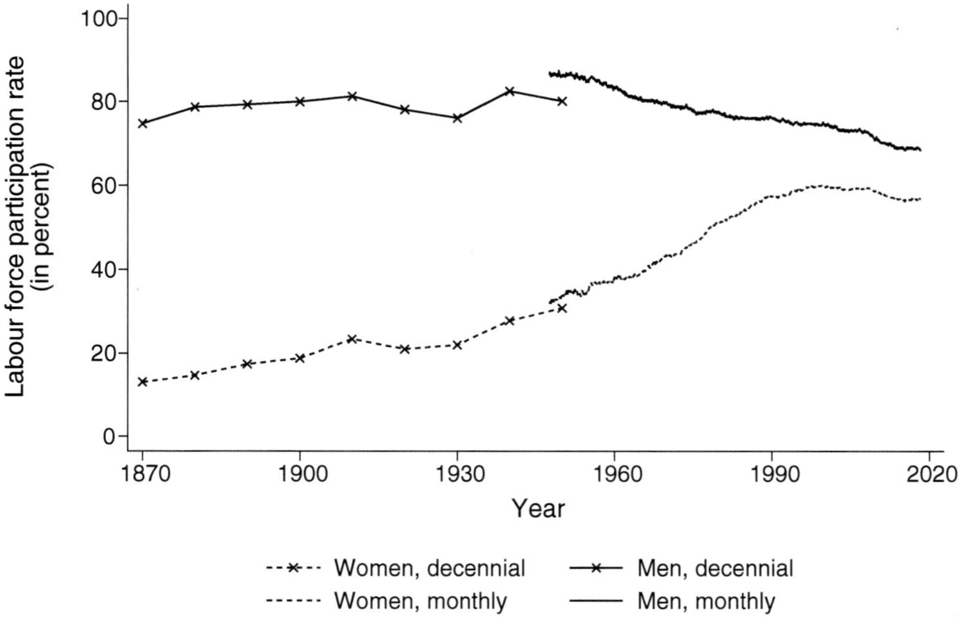

Figure 8.1 Trends in male and female labour force participation in the United States

Note: The decennial data are from the US Census Bureau (1975), and measure the number of people that participate in the labour force (being employed or looking for a job) as compared with the total population aged 14 or over. The monthly data – which are also seasonally-adjusted – are from the Current Population Survey administered by the Bureau of Labor Statistics (BLS), and measure the number of people that participate in the labour force (being employed or looking for a job) as compared with the total population aged 16 or over.

1930, the fraction of American women in the labour force gradually increased from 13 percent to 22 percent. However, in the 20 years from 1930 to 1950, this fraction jumped from 22 percent to 32 percent. It is otherwise noteworthy that, since the early 1990s, women's labour force participation seems to have stabilized at around 60 percent, although there has been a drop in the most recent years.

The second wave of emancipation

Second-wave feminism is usually considered to have gotten underway during the mid-1960s in the US and about five years later in Western Europe. Many prominent feminist groups, associations, and magazines were founded during this period. The second-wave feminists were primarily women of high education who abjured conservative values and argued that women were entitled to more freedoms in the areas of sexuality, marriage, and family. For example, they demanded the right to have an abortion and the right to a no-fault divorce (a divorce for which no evidence of wrongdoing by one of the parties is required). They also decried the stereotypical portrayal of women as only suitable for certain kinds of work, such as teaching, nursing, and secretarial jobs. This was a very valid concern, because even though women's labour force participation had substantially increased since the first wave of emancipation, there were still marked differences between men and women in the type of occupations they fulfilled.

Instead of simply demanding greater opportunities for women, the second-wave feminists sought to equalize the roles of men and women in society. Politicians were expected to respond with measures designed to increase women's representation in areas where they were still underrepresented, such as in mathematical and technical education and occupations, as well as in senior management. At the same time, women were still underrepresented in politics itself. Nonetheless, many governments responded to the feminists' demands and implemented policy programmes or set up working groups to stimulate further gender emancipation. Whether or not it is due to governmental encouragement, women have subsequently become better represented in certain high-status positions within society. The strong increase of female hospital specialists in most Western countries compared to the 1970s can, for example, be regarded as evidence of successful emancipation.

Post-feminism and the third wave of emancipation

During the 1980s, the influence of the second-wave feminists substantially declined, as economic concerns overtook those of gender equality in public debates. In many Western countries, a conservative backlash against feminism got underway. Some commentators even began questioning the relevance of the feminist movement on the grounds that men and women were now treated equally before the law and that the goals of the movement had thus been largely achieved (notice that this constitutes a misrepresentation of at least the second wave of the feminist movement). This point of view, namely that feminism is no longer required, is sometimes termed *post-feminism*. Post-feminists often point to the alleged negative consequences for society of dismantling traditional gender roles.

The feminist scholarship and activism that has developed after the 1990s has been labelled *third-wave feminism*. Third-wave feminism began as a response to the perceived failures of the second wave and to the conservative backlash that followed it. A defining element of this third wave is that it focuses on broadening the feminist agenda beyond highly educated white women. In particular, third-wave feminists seek to include women of diverse sexual, ethnic, and class backgrounds within the movement. Moreover, they pay ample attention to issues of *intersectionality* – that is, how being a woman interacts with other characteristics (such as one's sexuality, ethnicity and class) to produce different kinds of disadvantage. The #MeToo movement that emerged spontaneously at the end of 2017 indicates that sexual harassment, exploitation, and mistreatment of women is still all too common across all spheres of society. From this viewpoint, it seems troublesome that some people argue that feminism is no longer needed.

Gender as a source of inequality

Social class is a long-standing tool for conceptualizing social inequality within society. Members of the elite or middle class generally have higher education, greater income, and more privileges than members of the working class. The social class to which people belong is thus assumed to have a large influence on their life chances – these being defined as the possibilities people have to reach what they deem worthy to pursue (Weber 1978[1925]). However, some social scientists argue that gender has in recent years become a more important dimension of social inequality than social class. They contend that the effect of social class on a wide range of behaviours and attitudes has been decreasing (Inglehart 1990). For example, during the period 1960–2005 the chance of someone from the working class voting for a left-wing political party – once a near certainty – has decreased considerably in many Western societies (Evans and De Graaf 2013). In comparison, gender has become a more powerful predictor of all kinds of behaviours and attitudes over this period.

Internationally, inequalities related to gender have attracted increased attention thanks to the *Gender Development Index* (GDI) created by the UN in 1995. This index is based upon its well-known sibling the *Human Development Index* (HDI), which itself provides a summary measure of a country's development level based on its life expectancy, how it scores on education (a combination of the mean years of schooling for adults and the expected years of schooling for children), and its national income. The HDI can be calculated separately for men and women and the GDI is subsequently computed as the HDI for females divided by the HDI for males. A score of one on the GDI thus indicates perfect gender equality, whereas a score lower than one means that women are relatively worse off than men, and more so the closer the GDI is to zero. In the words of the UN, the GDI shows how much women are lagging behind their male counterparts with respect to health, schooling and income.

In 2010, the UN supplemented the GDI with the *Gender Inequality Index* (GII), in order to address some of the conceptual limitations of the GDI. For example, the GDI had been criticized for not fully capturing the disadvantages that women face in society and for allowing a very good performance on one dimension to compensate for a very poor performance on another dimension. The idea behind the GII is that it measures a country's overall loss in terms of human development due to gender disparities. As such, the GII effectively answers the question how much more developed a country could have been if women faced the same living conditions as men. In terms of its calculation, the GII is a composite index based on three aspects of human development: reproductive health (measured by maternal mortality and adolescent birth rates), empowerment (measured by the proportion of women in parliament as well as the proportions of men and women with at least some secondary education), and economic status (measured by the labour force participation rates of men and women). Importantly, income in no way enters the calculation of the GII, allowing poor countries to still obtain a good score on the GII. A low GII score indicates low inequality between men and women and vice versa.

In Table 8.1 we report the ten highest and lowest ranked countries in terms of the Gender Development Index and the Gender Inequality Index for 2015. With respect to the lowest-ranking countries, the two indices yield a fairly consistent picture, with Côte d'Ivoire, Mali, Chad, Yemen, Niger and Afghanistan ranking very low on both the GDI and GII. Most of these countries have in common that they are poor and located in Sub-Saharan Africa. In addition, a few of these countries represent Islamic countries in the Middle East or Asia, where women are often discriminated against.

Regarding the highest-ranking countries, the GDI and GII sketch a contrasting picture. The best-scoring countries in terms of the GDI comprise many (formerly) communist or socialist countries. All of the countries in the top ten in fact have a GDI score above one, indicating that women do slightly better than men on the dimensions underlying the GDI. This reflects, among

Table 8.1 Country rankings for the Gender Development Index and Gender Inequality Index in 2015

GDI ranking	Country	GDI score	GII ranking	Country	GII score
1	Lithuania	1.032	1	Switzerland	0.040
1	Estonia	1.032	2	Denmark	0.041
3	Venezuela	1.028	3	Netherlands	0.044
4	Mongolia	1.026	4	Sweden	0.048
5	Latvia	1.025	5	Iceland	0.051
6	Belarus	1.021	6	Norway	0.053
7	Uruguay	1.017	6	Slovenia	0.053
8	Russia	1.016	8	Finland	0.056
9	Moldova	1.010	9	Germany	0.066
9	Vietnam	1.010	10	South Korea	0.067
(...)			(...)		
151	Côte d'Ivoire	0.814	159	Sierra Leone	0.650
152	Iraq	0.804	160	CAR	0.656
153	Mali	0.786	161	Tonga	0.659
154	Guinea	0.784	162	DR Congo	0.663
155	CAR	0.776	163	Afghanistan	0.667
156	Chad	0.765	164	Côte d'Ivoire	0.672
157	Pakistan	0.742	165	Mali	0.689
158	Yemen	0.737	166	Chad	0.695
159	Niger	0.732	166	Niger	0.695
160	Afghanistan	0.609	168	Yemen	0.767

Note: Data are from the 2016 UN Human Development Report (UN 2016).

other things, that boys and girls face rather similar basic educational opportunities in formerly communist countries, but also that male life expectancy dropped significantly in many of these countries following the collapse of communism. Yet, interestingly, none of the countries from the GDI top ten reappear in the GII top 10. This suggests that although those countries are gender equal when it comes to basal dimensions such as life expectancy and mean years of schooling, they lag behind in terms of gender equality when it comes to political representation, labour market opportunities, or more refined health indicators. Once we look at the latter dimensions of human development, Western European countries dominate the top 10.

One of the dimensions of human development that has witnessed the strongest gender emancipation in recent decades concerns education. While in all Western countries men traditionally have a higher level of educational attainment than women, in nearly all of these countries women have overtaken men in this respect in the most recent cohorts. In other words, as discussed in greater detail in the section "Trends in female labour force participation and educational attainment", there has been a reversal of the gender gap in terms of educational attainment. This is a very important trend, because a high level of education entails not just greater opportunities in the labour market, but usually also more knowledge, more independent-mindedness, and more outspokenness. Since highly educated women have richer professional credentials, they are able to live more independently than less-educated women. Education can therefore be seen as one of the core driving forces behind the emancipation of women.

Despite these advances in terms of educational attainment, it is important to note that in almost all countries women earn less than men on average. A prime example is the Netherlands. As we will discuss later, a large number of women in the Netherlands prefer to work part-time and this accounts for most of the income difference with their male counterparts, who predominantly work full-time. This discrepancy is partly driven by the fact that both partners do not have to work full-time for the family to enjoy a reasonable standard of living. That said, the fact that it is mainly women who opt for part-time careers is still a cause for concern and may signify that traditional gender norms, whereby women are depicted as responsible for housework and childrearing, are still an influential force. What is more, if we only look at Dutch women who work full-time, they often still lag behind their male counterparts in terms of pay and career progression, even if they fulfil the same job for the same employer. So, although the Netherlands scores relatively well on the Gender Inequality Index, there is still some way to go on the road towards the full emancipation.

The extent to which a disparity between the labour market opportunities of men and women is considered a problem varies from one society to another. Indeed, the same set of facts can be perceived in different ways. As discussed in Chapter 1, the importance of a given societal problem partially depends on how many people view the situation as a problem, and in many cases there will be different opinions in this regard. For example, in the Dutch situation described previously, there may be debate as to whether women's shorter work hours represent a problem. Some people may believe this to be the case, viewing this situation as women being pushed towards more traditional gender roles, while others may disagree, perceiving women's shorter work hours rather as a luxury choice that allows women to achieve a desired work-life balance. The latter group may additionally point to the fact that also among men part-time work is nowadays more common than it used to be – according to Statistics Netherlands, the proportion of men working part-time has risen from 12 percent in 2001 to 17 percent in 2017.

It can be hard to establish for any particular case whether people perceive the same facts differently or whether they have simply adapted their behaviour to different normative or legal circumstances. Overall, there are many different views on gender equality around the world. On the one hand, in many Western countries the dominant perspective is that inequality between men and women is unjust, whereas, for example, in many conservative Islamic societies gender inequality is considered as just. From the perspective of *cultural relativism* one ought to respect other cultures and refrain from judging them on the basis of one's own values. However, it is often difficult to determine what the preferences actually are in a particular society. In most Islamic societies, for example, where there is no separation between church and state, usually only men are permitted to express opinions. Women may be reluctant to express their own opinions under such circumstances, even when asked. Being unaware of the norms that prevail in other societies where women enjoy much greater freedom might possibly also colour the opinions of women living in conservative Muslim societies.

Discrimination in the labour market

One of the most widely postulated explanations for the disadvantaged social position of women is that they are discriminated against in the labour market and in other life domains. The essence of this *discrimination hypothesis* is that women and men are treated differently in society, leading to worse outcomes for women, even if they have the same talents and qualifications as men.

The gender pay gap and the glass ceiling

Data from the Office for National Statistics (2018) in the UK show that as of 2017 the *gender pay gap* is 9.1 percent. This means that the median hourly earnings of women are 9.1 percent lower than the median hourly earnings of men. While the gap is decreasing over time (in 2011 it was still 10.5 percent), it is still substantial and potential evidence of gender discrimination in the labour market. However, before drawing this conclusion, we first have to consider various alternative explanations, as these statistics do not take into account any personal characteristics that may determine a person's pay (e.g., age, education), nor are these pay gaps calculated for men and women who do the same job and according to the same working pattern (e.g., part-time versus full-time). Both sets of factors could explain why the gender pay gap does not necessarily imply any discrimination.

Human capital theory (Becker 1964) states that earnings are dependent, at least in part, on individuals' productive capacity. Three key variables in determining this capacity are work experience, level of education, and the number of hours worked. One can set up a simple model in which income is assumed to be a function of these three variables. Each variable makes a certain contribution to earnings and this contribution is denoted by b_i. These relationships are summarized in the following equation:

$$\textit{Estimated earnings} = b_0 + b_1 * \textit{work experience} + b_2 * \textit{education} + b_3 * \textit{work hours}$$

In this equation, the parameter b_0 denotes the baseline earnings level, independent of work experience, education and work hours. Next, the parameter b_1 denotes the extra earnings that each additional unit of work experience generates. The parameters b_2 and b_3, in turn, denote the earnings increases for each additional unit of educational attainment and each additional hour of work, respectively. By estimating the earnings of men and women separately, one can test whether there is evidence of discrimination. If there is no discrimination, the baseline earnings level, as well as the estimated effects of experience, education, and work hours (i.e., the *b* parameters) should – all else being equal – be the same for men and women. In this context, the UK Office for National Statistics (2018) found, among other things, that men who had worked in the same job for more than 20 years earned 60 percent more than men who had been in their job for less than a year. By contrast, for women this difference amounted to only 48 percent. This implies that the parameter b_1 in the previous equation is smaller for women than for men.

However, does this necessarily mean that women are discriminated against in the labour market? The answer is that this would be a premature conclusion. Recall in this regard that we stressed the condition "all else being equal" (which is often referred to in Latin as *ceteris paribus*). Only if women and men have completely identical personal characteristics and are embedded in completely identical job environments can we take the statistics about the payoffs to work experience as hard evidence of discrimination. If we do not correct for all of these other factors, the possibility remains that men's higher payoffs to work experience reflect something else than outright discrimination. For example, this finding might reflect that men tend to have occupations or work in sectors of the economy where work experience matters more.

Indeed, while we noted that the "raw" difference between men and women in the payoffs to more than 20 versus less than one year of job tenure is 12 percentage points in the UK (i.e., 60 percent minus 48 percent), this difference drops to three percentage points (i.e., 21 percent minus 18 percent) once occupation, business sector, and several other factors are corrected for. Although this difference is much smaller than before, we now have relatively more certainty that this difference represents actual discrimination. In general, the more determinants of earnings are accounted for, the more certainty we can have that discrimination is taking place. However, one should always remain cautious about interpreting any residual gender difference in pay as evidence of discrimination, as one could nearly always think of other potential pay determinants that are not yet corrected for. Bearing in mind this caveat, the reported gender gap in median hourly earnings in the UK can be explained for about 36 percent by factors such as occupation, job tenure, full-time versus part-time status, age and business sector, with occupation having by far the most explanatory power. Importantly, this leaves 64 percent of the gender pay gap unexplained, and thus leaves a lot of room for potential gender discrimination.

To monitor gender pay gaps more closely the British Government has introduced regulations requiring employers with 250 employees or more to publish data on their gender pay gaps from April 2017 onwards. Following these regulations, published data on gender pay differences have regularly stirred up public debate. For example, the gender pay differences of BBC's employees, and especially several of their top-earning employees, became big news in early 2018 when Carrie Gracie, while referring to the Equality Act 2010, resigned from her post as BBC China editor. She accused the BBC of maintaining a culture of gender inequality in pay. In response, the BBC eventually apologized to Gracie and offered her back pay, while several leading male presenters at the BBC volunteered to take a pay cut.

As already suggested by the previously quoted statistics, women are under-represented in the most well remunerated professions, especially at the highest levels. In this context, it is often asserted that women face a *glass ceiling*. According to this metaphor, women are able to move up the corporate or bureaucratic hierarchy, but then remain stuck at intermediate positions, while their male colleagues continue to be promoted to higher levels. The central question here is why do women not reach the highest positions? One possibility is of course discrimination. As suggested by the term glass ceiling, discrimination can occur in subtle and covert manners. In this regard, people often also refer to *old boys networks*, implying that males who went to the same school or university preferentially hire one another, at the expense of women and other outsiders. Moreover, women may be discriminated against as an unintended consequence of the way in which work is organized. For example, most prestigious jobs require working full-time, while women often have a preference for part-time work arrangements, especially when they have children and childcare provisions are weak.

In recent years, however, women appear to have made substantial progress in climbing up the occupational ladder. According to The European Working Conditions Survey, the proportion of employees who report having a female supervisor increased from 24 percent in 2000 to 33 percent in 2015. Of course, this statistic implies that two-thirds of all employees still have a male supervisor. Interestingly, the same survey also revealed a certain degree of gender segregation in the workplace. Namely, while about 50 percent of all female employees have a female supervisor, only about 15 percent of all male employees have a female supervisor. This may possibly reflect that in certain sectors, like heavy industry and transportation, there are scarcely any women, whereas in other sectors, such as primary education and social care, there is a scarcity of men. This scarcity, in turn, may reflect that men and women differ in their educational choices and the careers they specialize in, but may also signify discrimination in hiring practices.

For instance, an *audit study*, in which pairs of carefully matched applications based on hypothetical applicants were made for advertized job vacancies in England, found substantial discrimination against men with regard to typical "female occupations" (i.e., secretarial) and substantial discrimination against women with regard to typical "male occupations" (i.e., engineering) (Riach and Rich 2006). That is, women applying for "male occupations" were significantly less likely to be invited for an interview than their male counterparts, and vice versa. Crucially, the CVs of each pair of hypothetical applicants in this study were exactly the same in every way except for the gender of the candidate. Note that it is much more difficult to apply the same research method to actual job interviews, as this would require matching prospective candidates not only on basic CV characteristics, but on all characteristics that employers might – consciously or unconsciously – take into account when hiring employees, including things such as attractiveness, accent, and charisma.

Statistical discrimination as an explanatory mechanism

The next question one must ask is whether disparate treatments of men and women by employers stem from outright gender preferences or perceived differences in suitability between men and women. According to the notion of *statistical discrimination*, it may be rational for employers to discriminate against groups whose members have lower average suitability for the job in question. This mechanism may, for example, also apply with respect to certain ethnic groups. What is crucial in this context is that employers only have limited information about the suitability of each individual applicant and thus have to make a decision under uncertainty. For this reason, the employer may consider additional information that can help them select the most suitable candidate. For example, the employer may have general information on the average job performance, absenteeism, and ambition of men and women, based on what he observes within his current workforce. Insofar as employers only have incomplete information about the job-relevant characteristics of each individual job candidate, they may rationally apply such general statistical regularities to individual candidates.

It is well-known in this context that women tend to have a stronger preference for part-time work, go on maternity leave when a child is born, and are more likely than men to stay at home with an ill child. Based on such information, it may be rational for employers to be more cautious about selecting female applicants, especially for management positions, where the risk of long-term absence is an important consideration. Therefore, employers may end up discriminating against women given incomplete information, even if the employer is not prejudiced. In many countries such discrimination would still be illegal, yet there is often much scope for employers to come up with alternative motivations for their decisions.

The work preferences of men and women

In general, differences in the labour market outcomes of men and women may also reflect differences in the work preferences of men and women. Studies show, for example, that women attach less importance, compared to men, to having a professional career, having a high salary, and having a job in which one exercises power (Gino, Wilmuth, and Brooks 2015). Women also tend to express a greater preference for working as part of a team, rather than as an individual, and for working with people, rather than with objects, electronic devices or computers. Aside from the possibility that these gender-related differences in preferences result from people independently and deliberately weighing the costs and benefits associated with different types of work, there are two other influential theories that are often used to explain these differences. According to the first, they stem from socialization processes during early childhood and adolescence. According to the second, they are innate and reflect differential selection pressures experienced by men and women during our evolutionary history.

Let us begin with the *socialization theory*. The idea here is that, from an early age onwards, either explicitly or implicitly, women are taught to play female roles while men are taught to play male roles. For example, women learn that they are responsible for child rearing and supposed to provide emotional support to others, while men learn that they are responsible for protecting their family and supposed to fill leadership and technical roles. Men and women are also taught that certain activities and pursuits are inappropriate for them. For example, girls learn that they should not engage in boisterous rough-and-tumble play, while boys learn that they should not show weakness nor be too interested in dolls. Needless to say, these examples concern rather stereotypical gender roles and by no means are all parents assumed to act in accordance with these principles, yet on average across society there certainly seem to be tendencies into the directions described.

Under these influences, women may end up attaching less importance to a professional career. After all, during their childhood, women learn that it is mainly the role of men to earn money and support their family. In this light, women have less reason to invest in human capital at early stages in their life. This can explain why women may attach less importance to a professional career even before they enter the labour market. Moreover, among married couples with children, the woman may, based on her socialization, feel a stronger responsibility to sacrifice paid work for child rearing activities. This might explain why women are less likely to return to work after their maternity leave or, when they do, they do so only on a part-time basis. Of course, in this particular context the availability of child care facilities will also be relevant. In Sweden, for example, where childcare is free, the difference in male and female labour force participation is very small.

The second theory attributes any differentials in the work preferences of men and women to *innate preferences* formed through human evolution. If we go back all the way to the savannahs of Africa approximately 250,000 years ago, humans lived in bands of several hundred people and practiced a hunter-gatherer mode of subsistence. These bands were characterized by a sexual division of labour with respect to food production (Baron-Cohen 2004). Much of the time women were pregnant or breast-feeding, so they were relatively less mobile than their male counterparts. Consequently, they contributed calories to the band's food stores by foraging for fruits, nuts and berries. By contrast, men were not only more mobile, but were also physically stronger, having descended from those who prevailed in intra-sexual contests over females. Consequently, they contributed calories to the band's food stores by hunting large mammals. In addition, bands were characterized by a mating system in which some men mated with more than one woman, but in which all women mated with at least one man. As a consequence, the men who achieved the highest social status within the band – by prevailing in intra-sexual contests and demonstrating their prowess in hunting – left the most children. Altogether, the selection pressures of child rearing, hunting and intra-sexual competition may have left a mark on the evolution of men's and women's preferences in such a way as to make men relatively more strongly committed to paid work outside the home.

Trends in female labour force participation and educational attainment

To what degree has women's labour force participation increased over time and how much variation is there in this respect across countries? Table 8.2 reveals that in all OECD countries there was a clear rise in female labour force participation between 1970 and 2017. However, there is a lot of variation in terms of the steepness of this trend. For example, in Spain and the Netherlands the female labour force participation rate more than doubled from around 30 percent in 1980 to 70 percent or more in 2017, while in Sweden and Finland this rate was already close to, or over, 70 percent in 1980, to only rise a few more percentage points over the next 37 years. Also, in terms of the current levels of female labour force participation, there is a great deal of cross-country variation, from a minimum of 38 percent in Turkey to a maximum of 86 percent in Iceland.

The particularly steep rise of female labour force participation in the Netherlands is worth remarking upon. Indeed, while its 1980 level was still low by international standards, the Netherlands is now among the countries with the highest percentage of working women. Nonetheless, the vast majority of Dutch women only work part-time, namely 74 percent, compared to 27 percent among Dutch men. This implies that the Dutch female employment rate in "full-time equivalents" is only 44.6 percent in 2017. This is the fourth-lowest rate within the

OECD (after Turkey, Italy and Greece) and much lower than the female labour participation rate of 75.2 percent in Table 8.2. Although these two figures may seem contradictory, Dutch women's high rate of part-time work could be a rational response to, on the one hand, a desire to increase family income and develop oneself and, on the other hand, a strong social norm of women taking care of childrearing and housework. Figure 8.2 provides a more comprehensive explanation for the patterns of female labour force participation in the Netherlands, which can also be applied to explain female labour force participation elsewhere.

Table 8.2 Trends in female labour force participation across the OECD, 1980-2017

Country	1980	1990	2000	2010	2017
Australia	47.9	57.4	61.4	66.2	72.3
Austria			59.4	66.4	71.8
Belgium		40.8	51.9	56.5	63.2
Canada	52.6	62.8	65.6	68.8	75.0
Chile			35.1	46.7	57.1
Czech Republic			56.9	56.3	68.7
Denmark		70.6	72.1	71.1	76.1
Estonia		71.9	57.0	60.5	75.0
Finland	66.1	71.5	64.5	66.9	74.9
France		50.9	54.8	59.7	67.9
Germany	49.6	52.2	58.1	66.1	74.0
Greece		37.5	41.3	48.1	60.3
Hungary			49.6	50.6	64.2
Iceland			81.0	77.0	85.7
Ireland		36.6	53.7	56.0	66.4
Israel		41.5	50.9	56.9	68.7
Italy	33.4	36.2	39.6	46.8	55.9
Japan	51.4	55.8	56.7	60.1	69.4
Korea	44.6	49.0	50.0	52.6	59.0
Latvia			62.1	70.8	74.3
Luxembourg		41.4	50.0	57.2	66.2
Mexico			39.6	43.8	46.7
Netherlands	34.2	47.5	62.7	69.4	75.2
New Zealand		58.6	63.2	66.7	76.2
Norway	60.8	67.2	74.0	73.3	75.3
Poland			48.9	52.6	62.6
Portugal	45.8	53.9	60.5	61.1	71.6
Slovak Republic			51.5	52.3	65.9
Slovenia				62.6	71.2
Spain	28.5	31.8	42.0	53.0	69.9
Sweden	73.3	81.0	72.2	69.7	80.6
Switzerland			69.4	72.5	79.3
Turkey		32.9	26.2	26.2	37.6
United Kingdom		62.8	65.6	65.3	73.6
United States	55.4	64.0	67.8	62.4	67.9

Note: Data are from the OECD Labour Force Statistics.

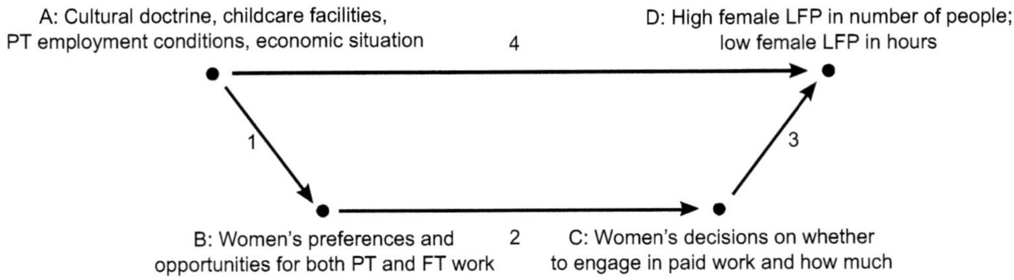

Figure 8.2 Explaining female labour force participation in the Netherlands

Note: PT and FT stand for part-time and full-time, respectively. LFP stands for labour force participation.

At the macro-level we distinguish four main forces (see also Yerkes and Visser 2006). First, there is the prevailing cultural doctrine. In this regard, the Netherlands has historically – and partially religiously inspired – adhered to fairly traditional gender role norms. Until the end of 1950s, for example, it was common for women in the public sector to be fired when they married. Even though substantial emancipation trends have taken place since then, certain elements of these traditional gender role norms remain intact. The fact that housework is still highly gendered can be viewed as an expression of this.

Second, childcare facilities play a role. Until the 1990s such facilities hardly existed in the Netherlands, and despite a strong growth in their supply in recent years, there is currently still a shortage of supply, with far fewer childcare spots than there is demand for and consequently long waiting lists. What is more, unlike in some other countries where childcare is publicly provided, in the Netherlands it is entirely up to the private sector, translating into higher attendance fees.

Third, the employment conditions associated with part-time work matter. In the Netherlands, part-time work is linked to a stronger labour market position than in many other countries, partially reflecting that Dutch trade unions had already started campaigning for the "normalization" of part-time work in the 1980s. They were highly successful and, as a result, Dutch part-time workers are covered by the exact same rights and entitlements as full-time workers. Therefore, part-time work does not constitute "marginal" or "precarious" labour, but can be found in all sectors and occupations, including at the managerial level.

The last macro-level driver concerns the economic situation in the Netherlands, and especially the ratio between wage levels and the cost of living. This ratio determines the degree to which both partners within a couple need to work (and how many hours) to make ends meet. This is also partially dependent on how part-time work is remunerated as well as the career perspectives it offers – see the previous point. In terms of this dimension, there is in the Netherlands, compared to other societies, less necessity for both partners to work full-time.

In summary, these four forces shape Dutch women's preferences as well as opportunities for both part-time and full-time work. Cultural factors imply that women tend to be positively predisposed to part-time work as a way to participate in the labour market while also being able to fulfil other roles such as childrearing. The latter is also more of a necessity given that childcare spots are in short supply, making it difficult for many couples to both work full-time. At the same time, the favourable conditions associated with part-time work – including opportunities for career progression – and the fact that many couples can afford it further increase the attractiveness of the part-time option.

As a consequence, many Dutch women choose to participate in the labour force, but only on a part-time basis. Indeed, there is evidence that part-time work among women in the Netherlands predominantly represents a "choice" on the part of the women: they tend to have high levels of job satisfaction and no desire to change their working hours, with low levels of involuntary part-time work (Booth and Van Ours 2013). At the macro level, the aggregation of women's labour market decisions can account for the combination of a high female labour force participation rate "in number of people" and a low female labour force participation rate "in hours".

Moving our attention back to the trends in Table 8.2, one key contributor in most countries to the increase in women's labour force participation is the enormous rise in the number of women attaining a high level of education. Indeed, while both men and women are nowadays much more educated than they used to be half a century ago, women have gradually started to close in on men in terms of educational attainment, and in many countries women have even surpassed men in this regard. More specifically, as shown in Table 8.3, in 2016 the percentage of 25–34 year olds with a tertiary education is higher for women than for men in all but two of the 36 OECD countries (with only Turkey and Mexico having a male advantage of, respectively, 0.3 and 0.2 percentage points). In 23 OECD countries the gap is ten percentage points or more to women's advantage, with many countries having a female advantage of around 20 percentage points – Latvia tops this ranking with a female advantage of 24.5 percentage points. In contrast, we can see that for those countries for which historical data is available, the gaps were still much smaller, or were to men's advantage, in 1991. Based on current educational enrolments, these gaps are expected to widen further in women's favour in the next few years.

The increasing education levels of women signify how their human capital investments have grown over time under the influence of shifting gender norms and greater educational opportunities. As a result, it is now more attractive for women to enter the labour market, as they have access to more prestigious occupations and career trajectories. Indeed, given their educational investments, the opportunity costs of not participating in the labour market (in terms of factors such as foregone earnings) have risen for women. A bigger puzzle is why – given that women outdo men when it comes to tertiary education in nearly every OECD country – women in most countries still tend to have lower labour force participation rates, and on average end up in lower-paying, lower-status jobs than men. This puzzle can partially be explained by the fact that for older cohorts women's lead over men in terms of educational attainment was non-existent or at least smaller than it is now (see Table 8.3), but we can observe similar labour market differentials when we restrict our attention to younger cohorts.

Furthermore, it is worth pointing out that there is still a high degree of segregation in terms of the fields of study of men and women. This is also illustrated in Table 8.3. In particular, the table includes the percentage among all tertiary-educated men and women aged 25 to 34 year old who have a degree in any of the so-called *STEM fields*: science, technology, engineering, and mathematics. Without a single exception, STEM degrees are rarer among women than among men across the whole of the OECD, and by more than just a little. The gender gap is greatest in Finland (at more than 41 percentage points) and smallest though still very large in the US (at 18 percentage points). The significance of these gaps lies in the fact that STEM degrees are in high demand among employers and this will become only truer going forward. As such, STEM degrees provide access to particularly good pay and career perspectives, certainly compared to many fields in which women are overrepresented such as the humanities and social sciences. Therefore, men and women's selection into different fields of study may also play a role in explaining pay differentials among working men and women.

Table 8.3 Gender gaps in tertiary education across the OECD

Country	25-34-year olds with a tertiary degree (%)				STEM among tertiary-educated 25-34-year olds (%)		
	Women in 2016	Men in 2016	Gender gap in 2016	Gender gap in 1991	Women in 2016	Men in 2016	Gender gap in 2016
Australia	54.6	43.9	10.7	17.1			
Austria	43.2	36.2	7.1		13.5	54.4	–40.8
Belgium	50.8	37.8	13.0	3.6	9.7	38.2	–28.4
Canada	69.6	51.5	18.2	3.0			
Chile	31.4	28.3	3.1		7.9	40.1	–32.3
Czechia	39.0	26.5	12.5		14.2	48.3	–34.0
Denmark	53.2	38.9	14.3	3.3	14.0	33.9	–19.9
Estonia	50.9	31.9	19.0		15.0	48.8	–33.8
Finland	49.5	33.2	16.3		14.0	55.1	–41.1
France	48.6	39.3	9.3	2.4	13.0	45.0	–32.0
Germany	31.5	29.6	1.9	–3.3	14.5	49.3	–34.7
Greece	48.2	34.0	14.2	–0.1	16.3	41.7	–25.5
Hungary	36.6	24.4	12.2		9.9	43.0	–33.1
Iceland	52.3	34.8	17.5		13.1	38.2	–25.1
Ireland	57.7	45.8	11.8	–0.6			
Israel	56.6	38.2	18.4				
Italy	31.7	19.6	12.2	–0.3	16.0	36.4	–20.4
Japan	62.2	58.1	4.0				
Korea	74.8	65.6	9.1				
Latvia	54.6	30.1	24.5		11.3	39.1	–27.9
Lithuania	66.1	44.2	21.9		12.8	50.8	–38.0
Luxembourg	54.4	48.6	5.9				
Mexico	21.7	21.9	–0.2		15.8	39.9	–24.1
Netherlands	50.2	40.3	9.9	–0.7	7.0	30.3	–23.3
New Zealand	46.6	40.1	6.5				
Norway	57.3	40.3	17.0	2.2	10.3	39.1	–28.8
Poland	53.6	33.9	19.7		13.5	40.8	–27.3
Portugal	42.9	26.9	16.0		14.1	34.8	–20.7
Slovakia	41.4	25.7	15.7		14.1	40.5	–26.4
Slovenia	54.9	31.9	23.0		12.5	44.6	–32.1
Spain	47.0	35.0	12.0	2.9	13.3	50.0	–36.7
Sweden	55.4	39.5	15.9	1.6	16.9	46.1	–29.2
Switzerland	48.9	48.8	0.2	–15.3	15.1	43.9	–28.8
Turkey	30.3	30.6	–0.3	–2.8			
United Kingdom	53.4	50.6	2.8				
United States	51.5	43.5	8.1	0.3	16.0	34.0	–18.0

Note: Data are from the OECD Education at a Glance database.

Women's changing roles and trends in the private sphere

While the previous section discussed several trends towards greater participation of women in the market sphere, those trends have also altered the dynamics between men and women in the private sphere. Our starting point here is that one's material and social resources, such as income, wealth, status and social connections, have a large influence on a person's life chances and behaviour. A simple example is that someone with a high level of education is more likely to find a prestigious, well-paid job than someone with a low level of education. However, a person's life chances depend not just on their own resources, but also on the resources of relevant others, such as their parents or – what we focus on below – their partner. Here we venture into the private sphere.

If within heterosexual couples the resources of the man are more important for the prospects and outcomes of the couple than the resources of the woman, we speak of *male dominance*. Figure 8.3 illustrates this idea. In the case of male dominance, the man's resources determine not just his own life chances and behaviour (arrow 1), but also the life chances and behaviour of his partner (arrow 2). In turn, the influence of the woman's resources on her own life chances and behaviour as well as those of her partner will be relatively weaker (arrows 3 and 4). If there is strong male dominance, the woman's own resources will even be less important for her life chances and behaviour than the resources of her partner (arrow 2 is thicker than arrow 4). This applies to within-couple dynamics throughout most of our history, partially reflecting that men used to have more resources than their female partners.

Trends in marriage patterns

However, as a result of the increasing trends in women's educational attainment and labour force participation, described in the previous section, the dynamics of mutual influence within couples have changed over time. In terms of education, for example, it is no longer the case that men are usually higher educated than their partners. In fact, *educational hypergamy* (husbands having more education than their wives) has been decreasing, whereas *educational homogamy*

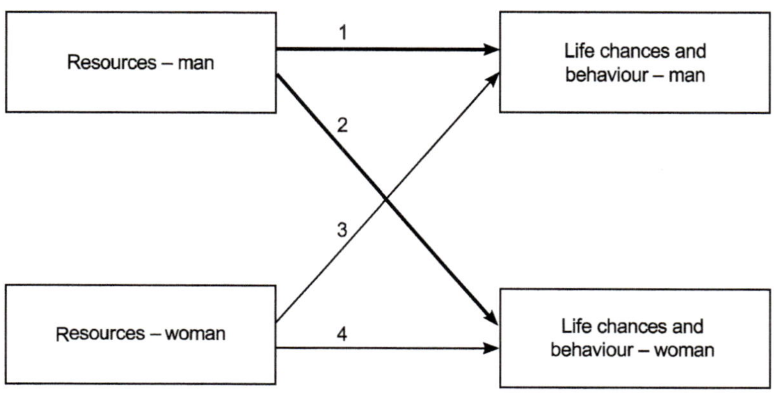

Figure 8.3 An illustration of male dominance within heterosexual couples

(husbands and wives having the same education) and especially *educational hypogamy* (wives having more education than their husbands) have been increasing.

The demographer Albert Esteve and several colleagues (2016) show that these trends are occurring across many countries in the world, largely mirroring the trends in the gender gap in educational attainment described in the previous section. Moreover, the rise in female labour force participation means that a larger share of women can now command a position of economic independence within their relationship. Indeed, Esteve and his colleagues show that women who have a higher level of education than their male partners are more likely to be the highest earner within the household. Since such hypogamous couples have become more common, this implies a shift away from the traditional *male breadwinner model*. While this shift is especially apparent among couples without children, a shift in the same direction, albeit somewhat weaker, can be observed for couples with children.

The economist Gary Becker (1973; 1974) predicted that increases in women's education, employment and earnings, and thereby their economic independence, may erode the institution of marriage. Becker based this prediction on his *exchange theory of marriage*, which assumes that men generally have a comparative advantage in market work whereas women are relatively better in housework, implying that the gains to marriage are greatest when a man with high earnings marries a woman with low earnings. Applying this logic, what a woman stands to gain from marriage will decrease once they become more economically independent. As a result, economically independent women may postpone marriage or not marry at all, and if they do marry divorce becomes a less costly option. However, do we indeed see a decline in marriage rates and an increase in divorce rates?

The concise answer is no. Esteve and his colleagues (2016:619) note in this respect that "marriage patterns adapt to changing demographic realities" and that they do so rather quickly. Instead of an increasing likelihood of non-marriage among highly educated women, for example, the dominant trend is an increase in the likelihood that women "marry down". Moreover, whereas marriages in which the woman is higher educated or out-earns the man were more likely to result in divorce prior to the 1980s (when such couples still represented a rarity), this is not true for marriages formed since the 1990s (Schwartz and Han 2014; Schwartz and Gonalons-Pons 2016). Therefore, while it is true that marriage rates have been on the decline in many OECD countries, this does not seem driven by women's increasing economic independence. And while divorce rates have been rising in most OECD countries up to the mid-1990s, since then most countries have in fact witnessed a decline in their divorce rate. This decline might reflect that with fewer people getting married in total, those couples that do still decide to tie the knot are the ones that are relatively more strongly committed to one another.

Trends in fertility patterns

There are various theories on how women's increasing educational attainment, labour force participation and earnings power might affect fertility patterns. Once again, one of the more influential theories comes from Gary Becker (1976), who argues that as women are increasingly educated to a higher level and actively pursue labour market careers, the opportunity costs of motherhood will rise. That is, women have to give up more to have children and therefore have an incentive to bear fewer children and to only transition into motherhood at a later age. In this context, studies have also shown that there is a *motherhood wage penalty*, implying that postponing motherhood may have additional labour market payoffs.

Most twentieth century evidence lines up well with these predictions: macro-level fertility levels declined over this period, and at the micro level fertility decline and postponement were especially evident among the more highly educated. However, as Esteve and his colleagues (2016) note, there is no direct evidence that women who "marry down" differ in their fertility behaviour from women married to men with the same or more education. In addition, Esping-Andersen and Francesco Billari (2015) show that in recent decades macro-level fertility rates have stopped declining, and in many countries have even somewhat recovered, despite the increases in women's labour force participation and educational attainment reported in Tables 8.2 and 8.3. Moreover, if we compare different countries today, those with higher female employment levels tend to be the ones with higher fertility rates. Also at the individual level there no longer seems to be a clear negative link between educational attainment and fertility, but rather a U-shaped relationship, with the most highly-educated women having more (or at least no less) children than women who are closer to the middle in terms of their educational attainment.

What should we make of these reversals in macro-level fertility and the micro-level education-fertility gradient? Esping-Andersen and Billari explain these trends by referring to changes in gender-egalitarian norms in a context of multiple equilibria and *critical mass dynamics* (see our discussion of these concepts in Chapter 2). We explain their argument using Figure 8.4, which shows how the society-level fertility rate changes with the spread of

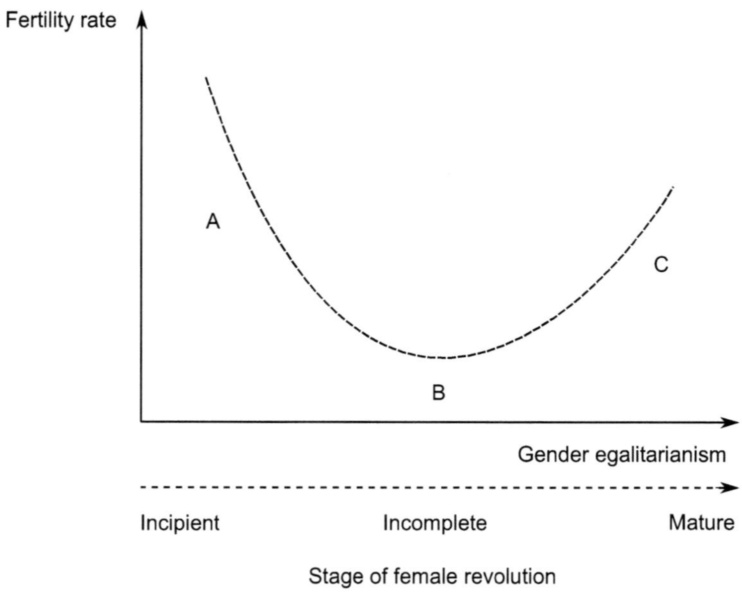

Figure 8.4 Fertility rate and gender egalitarianism as the "female revolution" unfolds

Note: This chart is an adapted version of Figure 1 in Esping-Andersen and Billari (2015:9).

gender-egalitarian norms as the "female revolution" unfolds. In this figure, there are three equilibria: A, B and C.

Before the female revolution takes place, societies are in equilibrium A, which corresponds to a traditional male breadwinner – female housewife arrangement. This situation constitutes an equilibrium to the extent that women, in anticipation of their future role, primarily invest in homemaker skills, thus generating a *self-fulfilling prophecy* whereby it will always be optimal for women to specialize in housework and for men to specialize in paid work.

However, when women start to gain more education, this equilibrium can eventually no longer be maintained and society will gradually move to equilibrium B. More women are doing paid work at this point and gender norms have become more egalitarian. At this point, fertility will be lower than before, since women's childrearing capacity is reduced due to having paid jobs while also still doing the bulk of the housework. Crucial here is that gender norms have only partially adjusted to the new situation of women participating in the labour market. As such, equilibrium B is unstable and reflects a state of "normative confusion". This is, among other things, illustrated by the fact that many women in this situation have unfulfilled desires for children – ideally, they would like to have more children than they are actually having.

Nevertheless, according to Esping-Andersen and Billari equilibrium B is not the end point. Rather, as education levels keep rising (especially also among women), gender-egalitarian norms will continue to spread, with a leading role for more highly educated women, who "demand" such norms from their prospective partners and whose partners (being on average more highly educated themselves) are more susceptible to such demands. At some point, when a certain critical mass is reached, the diffusion of gender-egalitarian norms will accelerate. This allows society to leave the suboptimal equilibrium B and move towards the stable and more harmonious equilibrium C. At that point, gender norms have fully adjusted to women's new role in society, with men, for example, having increased their share in housework. At this point, fertility levels will again more closely reflect people's desires for children. According to Esping-Andersen and Billari, the recent trends in macro-level fertility as well as the micro-level education-fertility gradient may reflect that societies are on their way from equilibrium B to C.

Trends in the division of domestic labour

In our discussion we highlighted the potentially crucial influence of a more gender-equal division of housework for ultimately achieving a more harmonious, efficient and fairer equilibrium with respect to men and women's role in society. However, evidence indicates that social norms regarding housework tend to be very sticky and hard to change. A very influential American study by the sociologist Suzanne Bianchi and several colleagues (2000) addresses this topic using so-called *time diary data*, for which people are asked to keep a diary of all their activities during one or more days. They showed that, while in 1965 women spent six times as many hours on housework vis-à-vis men (i.e., 30 versus five hours), this had dropped to a ratio of two by 1985 (i.e., 20 versus ten hours), indicating a trend towards gender equality. Critically, however, they also showed that subsequently, in 1995, the ratio was still about two (i.e., 18 versus ten hours). In other words, although female labour force participation had continued to grow over this period, not much had happened to the gender division of domestic tasks, leaving women with a "double shift" or "dual burden". The sociologist Arlie Hochschild (1989) famously referred to this situation as the "stalled revolution".

This observation obviously invites the question of whether we have made progress since then. The answer is a complex one. First, it is useful to stress that studying this topic is not straightforward, because time diary data requires a lot of effort (on the part of both researchers and respondents) to collect, while ordinary survey questions about housework have been shown to grossly overestimate the amount of housework people do. With that being said, there are several signs warranting optimism. In particular, several recent time diary studies do indeed suggest that men nowadays spend more time on housework and childrearing (Raley, Bianchi, and Wang 2012; Sullivan 2011). While mothers still spend more time with their children than fathers, the gap is now smaller than it used to be. Moreover, there is evidence that fathers contribute more time when their partners spend more time in the labour market or represent a greater share of household earnings, thus clearly responding to women's labour force participation. In addition, while it was first mainly higher-educated men who made these adjustments, recent findings suggest that now men from lower socioeconomic groups are also making similar adjustments.

Nevertheless, despite these positive developments, it is still too early to call the gender revolution completed. Not only do women, in general, still spend more time on domestic tasks than men, a recent study focused on young couples also reveals that although there is initially no gender gap in housework within these couples, a gap emerges once people have children, with women still shouldering the majority of childcare activities (Yavorsky, Kamp Dush and Schoppe 2015). Women tend to increase their overall work hours – paid work and housework combined – by two hours once children appear on the scene, compared with a 40 minutes increase for men. This evidence is particularly telling given that it concerns young couples, who are generally most progressive when it comes to gender-egalitarian norms. Therefore, gender gaps in housework may have narrowed, but there is most certainly still a good way to go before there is a state of complete equality and fairness in this respect.

Recommended readings

- Gary Becker's influential work *A Treatise on the Family* (1982) offers an original and powerful application of economic theory to various family-related issues and the gender inequalities they bring about. He uses basic economic assumptions, such as that people aim to optimize their behaviour given a set of stable preferences, to derive predictions on marriage formation and dissolution, what people look for in their partners, how many children they want and when they decide to have them, and how they divide their time between paid work, childrearing and other domestic activities.
- Tanja van der Lippe and Liset van Dijk (2002) provide a broad overview of several important issues related to women's participation in the labour market, including their participation rate, the number of hours worked, gender segregation, and the gender gap in earnings. They demonstrate that both macro-level factors (e.g., welfare state regime and family policies) and micro-level factors (e.g., parental status and childcare arrangements), as well as their interactions, are key to understanding women's employment.

- Gøsta Esping-Anderson and Francesco Billari (2015) propose an illuminating theory that connects ongoing macro-level and micro-level trends in fertility with trends in male and female labour market participation, educational attainment, and involvement in childrearing. They show how changes in gender norms are both a driver and a consequence of these various trends, giving rise to feedback loops and social contagion dynamics. They also hypothesize under which circumstances gender egalitarian norms spread more quickly.
- Albert Esteve and his colleagues (2016) discuss the most recent insights on the distribution of education within married couples. In particular, they focus on the shift from a situation in which husbands used to be higher educated than their wives to a situation in which wives are often higher educated than their husbands. They examine cross-country variation in this trend as well as its implications for labour market outcomes, divorce rates, fertility decisions and gender egalitarian attitudes.

Bibliography

Baron-Cohen, Simon. 2004. *The Essential Difference: Forget Mars and Venus and Discover the Truth About the Opposite Sex*. London: Penguin.

Becker, Gary S. 1964. *Human Capital: A Theoretical and Empirical Analysis, with Special Reference to Education*. New York, NY: Columbia University Press.

Becker, Gary S. 1973. "A Theory of Marriage: Part I". *Journal of Political Economy* 81:813–846

Becker, Gary S. 1974. "A Theory of Marriage: Part II". *Journal of Political Economy* 82:S11–S26.

Becker, Gary S. 1976. *The Economic Approach to Human Behavior*. Chicago, IL: University of Chicago Press.

Becker, Gary S. 1982. *A Treatise on the Family*. Cambridge, MA: Harvard University Press.

Bianchi, Suzanne M., Melissa A. Milkie, Liane C. Sayer, and John P. Robinson. 2000. "Is Anyone Doing the Housework? Trends in the Gender Division of Household Labor". *Social Forces* 79: 191–228

Booth Alison L., and Jan van Ours. 2013. "Part-time Jobs: What Women Want?". *Journal of Population Economics* 26: 261–283.

Esping-Andersen, Gøsta, and Francesco C. Billari. 2015. "Re-theorizing Family Demographics". *Population and Development Review* 41:1–31.

Esteve, Albert, Christine R. Schwartz, Jan Van Bavel, Iñaki Permanyer, Martin Klesment, and Joan García-Román. 2016. "The End of Hypergamy: Global Trends and Implications". *Population and Development Review* 42: 615–625.

Evans, Geoffrey, and Nan Dirk de Graaf (eds.). 2013. *Political Choice Matters: Explaining the Strength of Class and Religious Cleavages in Cross-national Perspective*. Oxford: Oxford University Press.

Gino, Francesca, Caroline A. Wilmuth, and Alison W. Brooks. 2015. "Compared to Men, Women View Professional Advancement as Equally Attainable, But Less Desirable". *Proceedings of the National Academy of Sciences* 112:12354–12359.

Goldin, Claudia D. 1991. "The Role of World War II in the Rise of Women's Employment". *American Economic Review* 81:741–756.

Hochschild, Arlie R. 1989. *The Second Shift*. New York, NY: Penguin Books.

Inglehart, Ronald. 1990. *Culture Shift in Advanced Industrial Society*. Princeton, NJ: Princeton University Press.

Minge-Kalman, Wanda. 1978. "The Industrial Revolution and the European Family: The Institutionalization of 'Childhood' as a Market for Family Labor". *Comparative Studies in Society and History* 20:454–468.

Office for National Statistics. 2018. *Understanding the Gender Pay Gap in the UK*. London: ONS Statistical Release, 17 January 2018. https://www.ons.gov.uk/employmentandlabourmarket/peopleinwork/earningsandworkinghours/articles/understandingthegenderpaygapintheuk/2018-01-17.

Raley, Sara, Suzanne M. Bianchi, and Wendy Wang. 2012. "When Do Fathers Care? Mothers' Economic Contribution and Fathers' Involvement in Child Care". *American Journal of Sociology* 117:1422–1459.

Riach, Peter A., and Judith Rich. 2006. "An Experimental Investigation of Sexual Discrimination in Hiring in the English Labor Market". *The B.E. Journal of Economic Analysis & Policy* 5(2), Article 1.
Richards, Eric. 1974. "Women in the British Economy Since About 1700: An Interpretation". *History* 59:337–357.
Schwartz Christine R., and Pilar Gonalons-Pons. 2016. "Trends in Relative Earnings and Marital Dissolution". *The Russell Sage Foundation Journal of the Social Sciences* 2:218–236.
Schwartz, Christine R., and Hongyun Han. 2014. "The Reversal of the Gender Gap in Education and Trends in Marital Dissolution". *American Sociological Review* 79:605–629.
Sullivan, Oriel. 2011. "An End to Gender Display Through the Performance of Housework? A Review and Reassessment of the Quantitative Literature Using Insights From the Qualitative Literature". *Journal of Family Theory & Review* 3:1–13.
UN. 2016. *Human Development Report 2016 – Human Development for Everyone*. New York, NY: United Nations.
US Census Bureau. 1975. *Historical Statistics of the United States, Colonial Times to 1970*. Washington, DC: US Government Printing Office.
Van der Lippe, Tanja, and Liset van Dijk. 2002. "Comparative Research on Women's Employment". *Annual Review of Sociology* 28:221–241.
Weber, Max. 1978[1925]. *Economy and Society: An Outline of Interpretive Sociology* (Wirtschaft und Gesellschaft: Grundriss der Verstehenden Soziologie). Berkeley, CA: University of California Press.
Yavorsky, Jill E., Claire M. Kamp Dush, and Sarah J. Schoppe. 2015. "The Production of Inequality: The Gender Division of Labor across the Transition to Parenthood". *Journal of Marriage and the Family* 77:662–679.
Yerkes, Mara, and Jelle Visser. 2006. "Women's Preferences or Delineated Policies? The Development of Part-Time Work in the Netherlands, Germany and the United Kingdom". Pp. 235–262 in: *Decent Working Time – New Trends, New Issues*, edited by Jean-Yves Boulin, Michel Lallement, Jon C. Messenger, and François Michon. Geneva: International Labour Office.

9 Crime

Chapter overview

This chapter provides a broad introduction to the societal problem of crime. After first addressing the pros and cons of different sources of crime statistics, we proceed with a discussion of international variation in crime levels as well as trends over time in the incidence of different types of crimes. Among other things, we point to the decline in crime levels that has been taking place in many Western countries since the 1990s, and we consider this trend in greater detail for the case of the US. Subsequently, we provide an overview of a selection of theories that aim to explain criminal behaviour. As part of this review, we examine the influence of economic prosperity and inequality on crime. We also speak to the question of what actions can be taken by governments to reduce criminality, drawing a connection with different criminological theories. As a case study, we consider the legalization of drugs as a potential solution to drug criminality. We then zoom in on organized crime as a branch of crime that operates in its own distinct way. Finally, we discuss the recent rise of cybercrime and the challenges it raises.

Pinning down crime

Crime encompasses actions as diverse as murder, robbery, burglary, assault, drunk driving, trade in narcotics, smuggling and trafficking, fraud, distribution of child pornography, and tax evasion. What all these actions have in common is that they violate generally shared norms in society, as well as particular clauses within the law. As such, crime has a major disruptive impact on society, especially when it occurs on a large scale, undermining important public goods such as public safety, law and order, and social trust.

In this chapter, we draw a rough distinction between common types of crime (theft, burglary, vandalism, violence, and other stand-alone criminal acts) and organized crime (the organized production, distribution and sale of illegal goods and services such as drugs and human trafficking by criminal enterprises). We do not focus on so-called white-collar crime (financially motivated, nonviolent crime committed by business professionals or government officials), since this is closely linked to corruption, which we discuss extensively in the next chapter.

Very broadly defined, crime comprises activities that involve breaking the law. However, while this may sound like a clear-cut definition it is, in practice, not always evident what counts as crime. One reason for this is that there are plenty of actions that may violate reigning social norms or be regarded as morally abject by a large portion of the population, but that are not (yet) proscribed by law. Consider legislation related to marital rape in the US. Historically, American law did not say anything about marital rape. However, over the course of the twentieth century, an increasing number of people came to regard marital rape as immoral and unacceptable. In line with this trend, marital rape was first proscribed as a crime in the state of South Dakota in 1975, yet it took until 1993 before the last state, North Carolina, finally outlawed marital rape.

Another example that illustrates the difficulties in drawing a line between criminal and non-criminal activities relates to tax avoidance, whereby citizens come up with inventive ways to minimize their payable tax. At the end of 2016, a major data leak – the so-called *Panama Papers*: 11.5 million leaked documents revealing how financial institutions facilitate corrupt transactions – revealed that many athletes, politicians and business people had engaged in large-scale tax avoidance. Although these activities are, strictly speaking, not illegal, and thus do not necessarily count as "crimes" according to the broad definition presented earlier, they clearly go against the spirit of the law, can be considered immoral, and are costly to society.

As a simple illustration of the scale of criminality, consider the percentage of people living in large cities whose house was broken into at least once in the last five years. The International Crime Victims Survey shows that in Latin American and African countries, between 30 and 60 percent of all households experienced at least one break-in over such a period. What is more, even in supposedly safe European countries, such as France, Switzerland, Denmark, the UK, Netherlands, and Belgium, between ten and 20 percent of all households experienced at least one break-in. Importantly, the fact that these figures concern break-ins during a period of only five years implies that over their lifetime many more people must fall victim to this crime. This demonstrates that crime directly affects large swathes of society, not to mention its broader impacts on safety perceptions and social trust. Crime may undermine feelings of safety and give rise to distrust even among people who are themselves no direct victims of any crime.

Given the undesirable effects of crime on society, states have for long sought to curtail crime. Indeed, ensuring the safety and security of citizens ranks among the very oldest functions of the state. There are a number of institutions by which the state maintains law and order, including its legislative apparatus, its judiciary, its police, and, in exceptional circumstances, its military. When there is a close overlap between social norms and the law, most citizens will tend to be law-abiding, meaning that it will be relatively easy for the state to maintain law and order. On the other hand, when citizens must really be forced into compliance with the law, maintaining law and order becomes a much more costly affair.

Crime statistics and trends

If one wants to obtain insights into spatial variation and temporal trends in the incidence of different types of crimes, there are many data sources that one can turn to, each with their own strengths and weaknesses. Next, we list several of the sources that are most commonly relied upon for this purpose.

First, there are police statistics, which comprise all criminal acts that have been reported to the police. While this may seem a very natural and authoritative way to keep track of crime levels, police statistics are subject to several weaknesses. One key disadvantage is that unreported crimes simply do not appear in police statistics, which may lead to an underestimation of the overall level of crime. Especially for many petty crimes, such as pocket-picking, people often do not bother going to the police. However, also for graver crimes, such as rape, victims may often not contact the police, for example due to feelings of shame and self-blame. Another disadvantage of police statistics is that the record-keeping of crimes is often not consistent across regions and over time, which complicates any comparison.

Another important source of data are victim surveys, such as the International Crime Victims Survey mentioned previously. This survey started in 1989, with the twin aims of filling gaps in the crime statistics recorded by police, and attaining an internationally comparable set of crime rates. In each participating country, a standardized survey is administered, which gathers information about respondents' experiences with crime, crime prevention, and feelings of insecurity. Various countries also have national victim surveys. A key advantage of victim surveys is that they are more easily comparable across countries, as compared with police statistics. Another important advantage is that they also include crimes that have not been reported to the police, and can thus be used to estimate the percentage of victimizations that are unknown to the police. The main downsides of victim surveys are that they often have low reliability, as respondents are not forced by law to tell the truth; that respondents must provide information about events in the past, leading to potential recall errors; and that the survey response rates may be quite low in some countries, casting doubt on the representativeness and coverage of the data. Another limitation of victim surveys is that they are typically administered to individual citizens and, therefore, give no indication of the victimization of companies and government agencies (relating to crimes such as shoplifting, commercial robbery, cybercrime, or fraud).

Aside from asking respondents about their victimization experiences, one can also ask specific groups in society (such as juvenile offenders) or representative samples of the population about their own transgressions of the law. While such self-reports may be interesting to analyse in certain specific settings, they are generally not considered the most useful source of information about crime levels, as they are subject to the same shortcomings as victim surveys as well as some additional limitations. Arguably the most important disadvantage is that self-reports can only shed light on common, relatively innocent forms of criminality, although even in those cases respondents may be unlikely to report any crimes they committed.

Finally, there are many institutions that record information about specific types of crime. Examples include insurance agencies, surveillance authorities, environmental inspections, tax authorities, hospitals and medical agencies, and NGOs in specific fields such as human trafficking. While many of these sources circumvent some of the problems of victim surveys and self-reports, they still have issues of their own relating to coverage and comparability. Moreover, the data collected by many of these institutions are not publicly available.

One area of crime for which reliable data are particularly difficult to obtain is organized crime. In this context, it is well-known that many mafia groups – be it in Italy, the US, Russia, China, or elsewhere – extort individuals or businesses to pay for protection against a threat that the gangsters themselves create. The combination of the severity of these threats and the fact that the charged protection fees are still somewhat affordable means that many victims prefer to pay these fees instead of going to the police or coming forward in any other way. As a result, it is difficult to garner any data at all on organized crime, let alone reliable data.

International variation and trends in crime levels

The United Nations Office on Drugs and Crime (UNODC) provides for a large and diverse sample of countries the annual number of homicides per 100,000 people. Note that homicide comprises manslaughter (nonintentional killings) as well as murder (intentional killings). These figures are mostly compiled from medical sources, providing them with a relatively high degree of reliability and making them well-suited for international comparisons. Statistics for the period 2010–2013 reveal that homicide rates are especially high in many Latin American countries, with rates of 75 in Honduras, 64 in El Salvador and 62 in Venezuela (all per 100,000 people). Homicide rates lower than one per 100,000 people are mainly found in Western European countries as well as countries such Singapore, Japan, Kuwait, and South Korea. In the US – commonly known as one of the most violent countries in the Western world – the homicide rate is significantly higher, at about four to five homicides per 100,000 people. In Russia, in turn, the homicide rate lies in the region of ten per 100,000 people.

What can we, in turn, say about trends in homicides? Figure 9.1 displays these trends for several countries or regions, for which there are data available since 1955. In Europe as well as Japan and South Korea, homicide rates have been consistently low over this whole period,

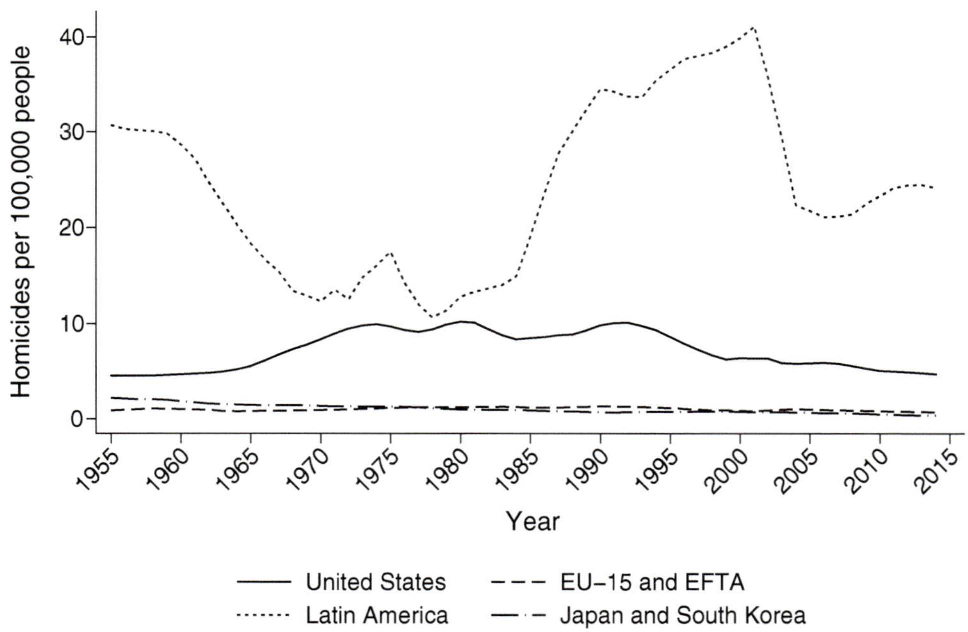

Figure 9.1 Homicide rates across different world regions, 1950-2015

Note: Data are from the WHO Mortality Database, the UNODC Homicide Database, and the World Bank Population Database. The EU-15 and EFTA comprise the first 15 member states of the EU (Austria, Belgium, Denmark, Finland, France, Germany, Greece, Ireland, Italy, Luxembourg, Netherlands, Portugal, Spain, Sweden, and the UK) supplemented with the four countries belonging to the European Free Trade Association (Iceland, Liechtenstein, Norway, and Switzerland). Latin America is represented by the following 24 countries: Argentina, Bolivia, Brazil, Chile, Colombia, Costa Rica, Cuba, Dominican Republic, Ecuador, El Salvador, French Guiana, Guadeloupe, Guatemala, Haiti, Honduras, Martinique, Mexico, Nicaragua, Panama, Paraguay, Peru, Puerto Rico, Uruguay, and Venezuela.

although with some minor fluctuations. Since about the 1990s both regions have experienced a modest decline in their average homicide rate. In the United States, the homicide rate has been substantially higher over the past 60 years. While the US homicide rate was about five per 100,000 people in the 1950s, this number rose to about ten in the 1970s, and stayed at that level until the early-1990s. However, since the 1990s a steady decline in the homicide rate has been taking place, so that around 2010 the homicide rate had halved again to its 1950s level of about five per 100,000 people. In Latin America, we observe both the highest homicide rates as well as the largest fluctuations in these rates. In particular, the Latin American homicide rate was very high in the 1950s, then experienced a major decline through the 1960s, followed by a drastic increase in the 1980s and 1990s, with the early-2000s subsequently witnessing a huge drop in homicides. Since then, the Latin American rate has remained fairly stable at a level of about 20 to 25 homicides per 100,000 people. This is much lower than the peak value of over 40 around the turn of the century, but still much higher than in any of the other areas plotted in Figure 9.1.

As Figure 9.1 demonstrates, many regions of the world have experienced a decline in homicides since about the 1990s or the start of the twentieth century. A similar drop can be observed for several other types of crimes, such as property crimes. Notwithstanding that some specific types of crimes (e.g., cybercrime) have actually witnessed an increase over this period, there thus seems to have been an international drop in crime.

Crime-related trends in the United States

The US is an interesting country to zoom in on when it comes to crime statistics. Not only does the US stand out with respect to the availability of data on crime, it is also widely reputed to have a significant crime problem. In line with this portrayal, Figure 9.1 already showed that the US has a substantially higher homicide rate in comparison to other developed countries. However, what can we say about crime levels and trends in the US when we look beyond homicides?

Let us first consider property crime, which covers violations of other people's property rights, and ranges from low-level offenses such as shoplifting or vandalism to high-level felonies including armed robbery and arson. The dashed line in Figure 9.2 depicts the number of victims of property crime per 100,000 people in the US over the period 1960–2014. This line shows that, between 1960 and 1980, the rate of property crime increased substantially, from less than 2,000 to more than 5,000 crimes per 100,000 people. This high rate of property crimes was maintained until the early 1990s, when it began a swift and steady decrease. As of 2014, the property crime rate in the US stands at about 2,500 crimes per 100,000 people.

The solid line in Figure 9.2 shows the trend in the rate of violent crimes in the US. This trend is remarkable similar to the trend in the property crime rate, although it peaked somewhat later – in the early-1990s. Moreover, the initial rise was even more spectacular: the violent crime rate more than quadrupled from less than 200 crimes per 100,000 people in 1960 to about 750 crimes per 100,000 people in the early-1990s. Nevertheless, since then the rate of violent crimes has halved. Overall, the US can thus be said to have experienced a general drop in crime since the 1990s. Property crime is now back to a level last seen in the mid-1960s and violent crime is back to the same level as around 1970.

As in many countries, however, crime in the US is much more common within some social classes and ethnic groups than others. The differences in crime statistics for the black population

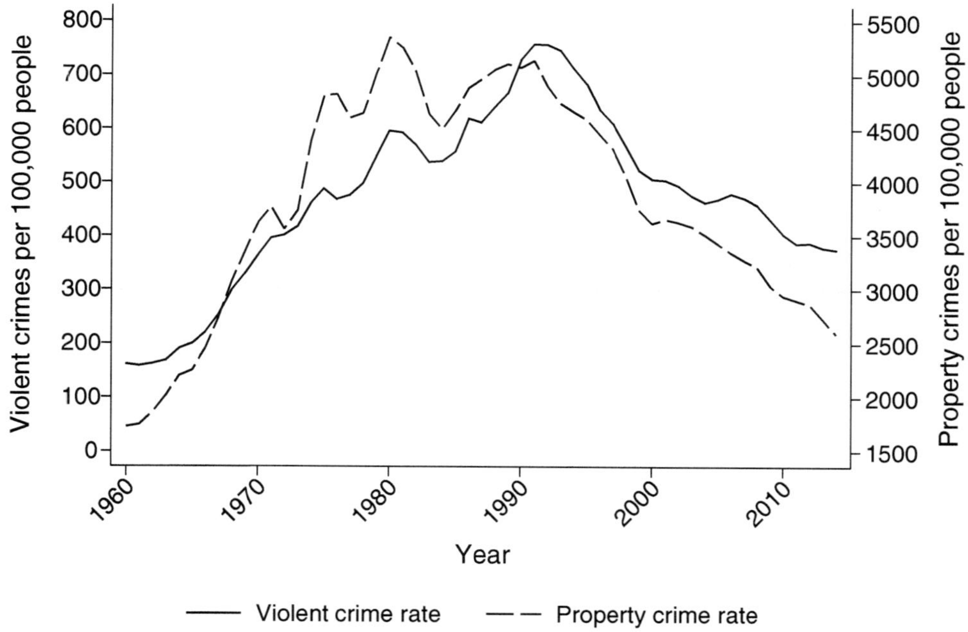

Figure 9.2 Trends in violent crime and property crime in the United States, 1960-2014
Note: Data are from the FBI Uniform Crime Reporting Statistics.

and the non-black population are particularly stark. For example, in 1960 black men were five times as likely as whites to be incarcerated and this ratio rose to 6.4 by 2010 (Pew Research Center 2013). Indeed, black Americans comprise about half of the US prison population. While we should here, of course, point out that there is not a one-to-one relationship between crime rates and incarceration rates (for example, there may be ethnic differences in conviction rates for certain crimes), the homicide rate is also about six times higher among blacks than among non-blacks. In addition, the Hispanic population in the US also exhibits elevated crime rates, although to a lesser extent than the black population.

While the section "Explanations of criminal behaviour" discusses several general explanations for crime, let us for the moment consider two popular explanations for the downward trend in crime in the US since the early-1990s. The first explanation is very specific to the US and centres around the enormous increase that has taken place in the number of people in prison. By locking up more and more people, and for longer and longer durations, the number of potential criminal offenders on the streets has fallen substantially. Several commentators have argued that this increase in the size of the American prison population is one of the main contributors to the drop in crime over the last few decades (e.g., Massing 1998).

The increase in the size of the incarcerated population in the US has indeed been enormous. Between 1960 and 2010, the number of incarcerated Americans rose from around 400,000 to over 2.3 million. The costs of this mass incarceration have become exorbitant – around US$ 80 billion as of 2013. Figure 9.3 decomposes the incarceration trends between 1980 and 2016, distinguishing between the share of the total US population that is in prison, in jail, on parole, or on probation. Prisons are designed for long-term detention and jails for short-term detention, while parole and probation are two alternatives to incarceration. Probation occurs prior to and

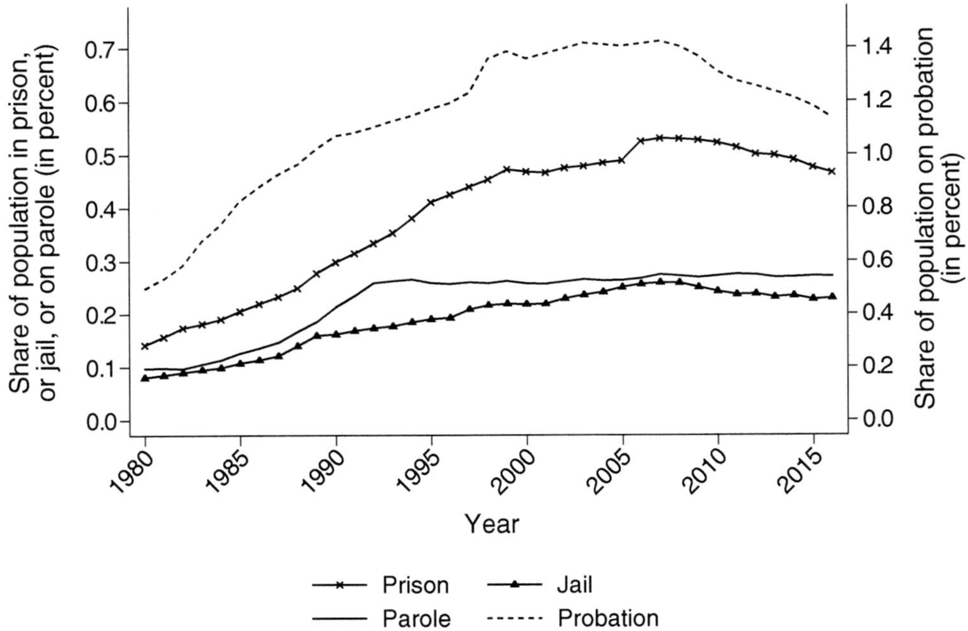

Figure 9.3 Share of the US population that is in prison or jail, or on parole or probation, 1980-2016
Note: Data are from the Correctional Populations database of the US Bureau of Justice Statistics.

often instead of spending time in jail or prison: instead of being sent straight to jail or prison, a criminal is given the chance to improve their life. Parole, in turn, concerns an early release from prison or jail. For both probation and parole, the convicted criminal needs to comply with certain conditions or else they will be sent (back) to prison or jail.

Figure 9.3 illustrates that between 1980 and the early-2000s there has been a significant rise in the share of the US population in prison, in jail, on parole, and on probation. For example, in 1980 only slightly more than 0.2 percent of the population was in jail or prison, yet by 2005 this had risen to about 0.75 percent of the population. Over the same period, also the share of the population on parole or probation had increased dramatically. As a result, the size and cost of the US incarceration system had become unsustainable according to many people. This for example, caused the then Attorney General, Eric Holder, to state that the maxim should no longer be "tough on crime", but rather "smart on crime". Seemingly in line with such a policy shift, there has been a modest decline in the share of the US population in prison or jail since the late-2000s.

All of this said, there is little empirical evidence that increased incarceration has been a key driver of the drop in crime in the US since the early-1990s. In particular, the socio-legal scholars Oliver Roeder, Lauren-Brooke Eisen, and Julia Bowling (2015) argue that the effectiveness of increased incarceration for controlling crime levels has been declining already since before 1980 and is nowadays negligible. They find that increased incarceration accounted for only about six percent of the reduction in property crime in the 1990s and for less than one percent of the reduction in property crime since the turn of the century. Moreover, according to their analysis, increased incarceration had no effect at all on the decline in violent crimes since the early-1990s. As another piece of evidence, Figures 9.2 and 9.3 show that in recent years crime rates have been falling while incarceration rates have also been dropping.

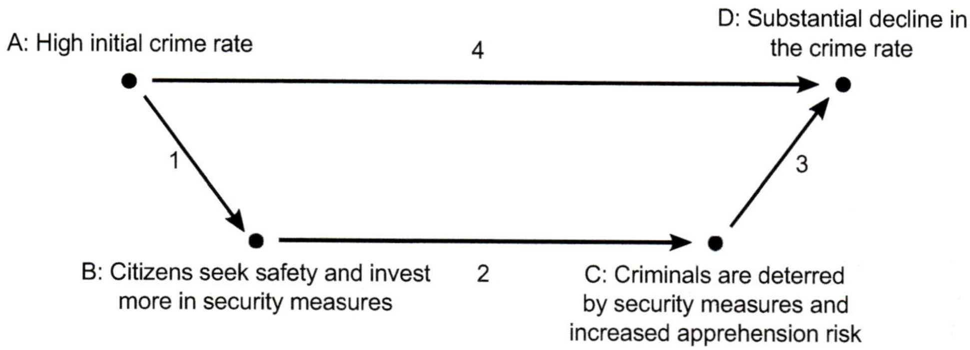

Figure 9.4 Illustration of the security hypothesis for the crime decline

Another prominent explanation for the drop in crime is the so-called *security hypothesis*, which proposes that criminals have been deterred by a variety of improvements in terms of security and crime prevention that have been implemented on a large scale. Based on all available empirical evidence, the security hypothesis seems a much more powerful explanation than the increased incarceration hypothesis. Indeed, after reviewing as many as 15 commonly used explanations for the crime decline, the criminologist Graham Farrell (2013) concludes that only the security hypothesis can explain all of the observed facts.

To better understand the security hypothesis, we can employ a macro-micro-macro scheme to consider how the increase in safety measures came about and how this precisely contributed to the drop in crime – see Figure 9.4. The scheme starts with the high crime rates of the 1980s and early-1990s. Under such circumstances, individual citizens realize that they face a high risk of falling victim to crime. Consequently, they will start to look for ways to reduce these victimization risks. Among other things, they will probably find it profitable to invest in safety measures (such as putting extra locks on one's home and avoiding dangerous neighbourhoods at night), and in doing so, they may be helped or advised by the police or other public authorities. The implementation of such prevention measures on a large scale subsequently means that it becomes more difficult for prospective criminals to commit crimes without being apprehended. As a consequence, prospective criminals – who make their own cost-benefit analyses – are more likely to refrain from committing criminal activities, translating into a substantial decline in crime at the macro level.

Explanations of criminal behaviour

Different forms of criminality require different explanations. For example, explanations of property crime differ from those of violent crime, which in turn differ from those of organized crime. We focus in this section on a selection of explanations of property crime, looking in particular at what sorts of people commit property crimes, and what sorts of circumstances lead them to do so. Most fundamentally, property crime occurs when likely offenders and suitable targets come together in time and space. For explaining crime, it is therefore interesting to both pay attention to factors that may affect the likelihood of becoming an offender, as well as to preventive actions that may influence people's risk of falling victim to property crime.

The first category of explanations for property crime stress socioeconomic disadvantages faced by criminal offenders. The general idea is that when someone is unable to provide for basic needs through legal means, this person is likely to take up illegal means in order to survive (Bonger 1916[1905]). A common variant of this idea is the hypothesis that poverty breeds crime. The flip side of this hypothesis is that criminality should decrease as societies become richer.

The empirical evidence for this claim is somewhat mixed. For example, the fact that crime levels spiked in the US during the economic boom in the 1980s, while they remained fairly constant during the economic depression in the 1930s, seems to contradict the portrayal of poverty as a key determinant of crime levels. However, as the sociologist William Julius Wilson (1987) showed, the booming economy of the 1980s did indeed make many people much richer, but at the same time there was also a surge in inner city poverty due to a loss of manufacturing jobs. As a result, socioeconomic disadvantages became more strongly concentrated within a certain subsection of society, and this may well have played a role in the rise in crime during this period. Additional evidence for the claim that poverty breeds crime comes from cross-country analyses, which demonstrate that crime levels tend to be higher in countries with a lower GDP per capita (Van Wilsem 2003).

A related explanation of crime stresses that socioeconomic inequality not only implies socioeconomic disadvantages for the less well-off, but may also provoke feelings of resentment, envy and indignation among this group, which in turn may lead them to engage in crime. Such sentiments may be compounded by information about what kinds of luxurious goods are available to buy, as well as advertising tricks designed to convince consumers that possessing luxury goods will increase their social status. This hypothesis can be traced back to *relative deprivation theory*. This theory, developed by the sociologist Robert Merton (1938) and also known as *strain theory*, posits that what matters most is not one's absolute level of prosperity, but rather one's relative level of prosperity compared to other members of society.

In particular, Merton states that individuals may experience strain when they see other people achieving success and making a lot of money, while remaining poor themselves. In response, the poor individuals may start to consider breaking the law in order to gain access to that world of wealth. In line with this theory, the criminologist Jan Van Dijk (1991) postulated that an increase in economic prosperity will only reduce crime if it is accompanied by a decrease in economic inequality. Conversely, if the rich experience bigger economic improvements than the poor, crime levels may still increase. In support of this narrative, there is a positive correlation between a country's level of inequality and its level of crime (Van Wilsem 2003), although the warning that correlation does not imply causation applies here once again.

Another potential explanation for a positive relationship between economic prosperity and crime lies in the well-known saying that the opportunity makes the thief (Cohen and Felson 1979). The idea is that it becomes easier to steal a certain product when there is a large supply of that product. For example, if there were only a few bikes in a city, there would presumably be few bike thefts, whereas an abundance of bikes would likely translate in a much larger number of bike thefts. Consistent with this hypothesis, Van Dijk (1991) found that countries with higher rates of bike usage also tend to have higher rates of bike thefts. Indeed, he found the highest rates of bike theft in China and the Netherlands, two countries known for their cycling culture.

Another important theory is Travis Hirschi's (1969) *social bonding theory*, which is sometimes also called *social control theory*. The driving assumption of this sociological theory is that people act in order to maintain social bonds with each other and with society. Such bonds may involve personal relationships with parents, friends, partners, or children, but also broader commitments to society, such as investments in social status, education or jobs, and involvement in sports clubs, religious groups and other civic organizations. Hirschi's key prediction is that when the quality of social bonds is better, and the number of such bonds is greater, people will be less likely to commit crime.

As the sociologist Robert Agnew (1992) pointed out, social bonding theory can help to explain why detainees often exhibit high rates of recidivism. More specifically, detainees often lose their bonds with family, friends, and work colleagues during their stay in prison, and this loss of social connections lowers their inhibition to commit crime in the future. Social bonding theory might also explain why crime rates are sometimes higher within immigrant communities. Although members of immigrant communities often have large kinship networks from which they can draw social bonds, they tend to have relatively fewer commitments to their country of residence, as compared with native residents.

So far, we have mainly discussed theories that focus on the perpetrators of crime. However, as mentioned earlier, we should also pay attention to the behaviour of potential victims of crime. One example of a theory that takes into account these behaviours is *routine activity theory* (Cornish and Clarke 1986). The key idea is that an individual's chance of falling victim to crime increases with the number of opportunities they create, consciously or otherwise, to become such a victim. For example, dual-earner households are more likely to fall victim to burglary than single-earner households where the other partner is at home during most of the day. Similarly, going on holiday for an extended period also increases the risk of burglary, while visiting busy touristic venues may increase the risk of falling victim to pickpocketing.

How to reduce crime

The government has several means at its disposal for fighting crime. Most prominently, they can engage in direct or indirect prevention efforts or rely on deterrence through punishment. In terms of prevention, one frequently advocated line of action is to increase the number of police officers on the streets. This would lead to more formal control, which one might assume would lower the crime rate insofar as it reduces the opportunities available to potential offenders. However, no matter how obvious this sounds, in reality more police on the streets does not always result in lower crime rates. One reason is that the increased police presence may lead to more criminals being caught, which might translate into an increase in the crime statistics of the police, depending on whether all of these crimes would previously have been reported to the police or not. In addition, there may be another type of dynamic at play, which we can best illustrate with another macro-micro-macro scheme – see Figure 9.5.

The macro-level starting-point of Figure 9.5 is an increase in the number of police officers on the street. One of the immediate effects of this increased police presence may be that citizens in concrete micro-level situations feel safer. While this is in and of itself obviously a welcome development, these higher perceived safety levels might make citizens more nonchalant when it comes to the preventive measures they take themselves, such as paying attention to their handbag or locking their windows when leaving their house. As a result, the net impact of the increased police presence on offenders' opportunity structure may in fact be close to zero,

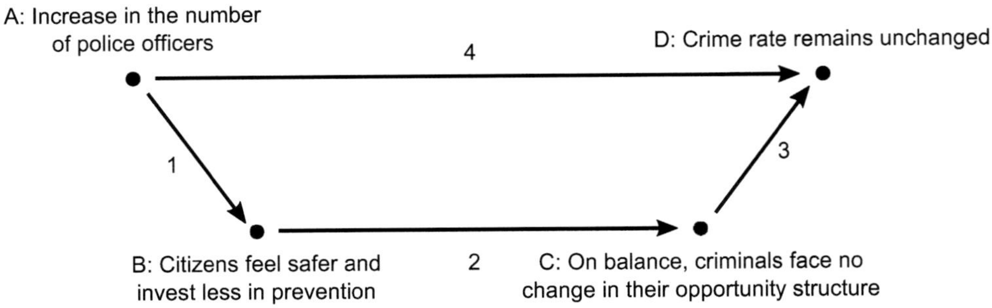

Figure 9.5 Illustration of why an increased police presence may not reduce crime

with the crime-reducing effect of the increased police presence and the crime-enhancing effect of individual actors' weakened precautions cancelling out against each other. Accordingly, the overall macro-level outcome may be that the total crime level remains unchanged. Importantly, however, this does not necessarily indicate that the increased police presence is useless for reducing crime, but rather that there are offsetting dynamics going on at the micro level.

In addition to prevention efforts such as increasing the stock of police officers or encouraging private parties to take more preventive measures of their own, governments may also try to reduce crime through punishing offenders. While such punishment, of course, only comes after a certain criminal act has taken place, the idea is that criminal punishment may have a deterrent effect on future crimes. Indeed, punishment of criminals can set an example that will make citizens think twice before committing a crime, just like parents or teachers can discipline children's behaviour through imposing sanctions.

The deterrent effect of (a threat of) punishment primarily depends on two factors: first, the probability that an offender will be caught and eventually convicted, and second, the severity of the punishment in case of a conviction. In terms of the probability of being caught, many countries have witnessed a decrease over time in the crime clearance rate – that is, the percentage of all crimes that are being solved. Figure 9.6 illustrates this trend with respect to the homicide clearance rate in the US, which has declined from about 90 percent in 1965 to less than 60 percent in 2016. It is worthwhile to note in this context that the clearance percentages for many other types of crimes (such as bike theft, shoplifting, burglary) are even lower. Of course, caution is needed when interpreting this trend, as numerous factors may play a role, from the savviness of criminals to the resources devoted to the police force, but for example also trends in the detection and reporting of crimes – if nowadays a higher proportion of all crimes get reported, that alone might explain the observed drop in clearance rates.

Many criminologists believe that the probability of being caught and convicted is more important for deterrence than the actual severity of punishment. After all, one can establish a draconian punishment for a particular crime, but if the probability of being caught is close to zero, the criminal's expected costs of committing the crime will still not be very high. Moreover, research shows that the rate of recidivism exhibited by punished offenders is only very weakly related to the severity of punishment, at least after a certain point. As mentioned in the previous section, this pattern can possibly be explained by Hirschi's social bonding theory. Finally, as

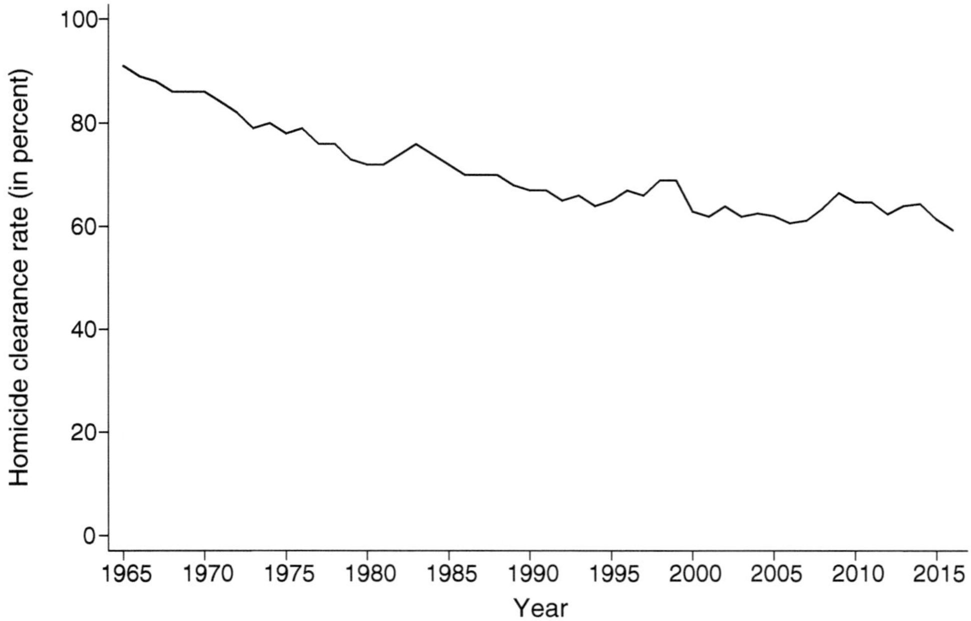

Figure 9.6 Trend in the homicide clearance rate in the United States, 1965-2016

Note: Data are from the annual FBI Crime in the United States reports, as collected by the Murder Accountability Project.

part of this discussion it is also worth keeping in mind that certain severe punishments (take the example of a lifelong prison sentence) can turn out very expensive to the government, and might in the end result in an overburdened and unsustainable correctional system.

In relation to the question of how crime can best be reduced, the criminologists Jan Van Dijk, Wim Huisman, and Paul Nieuwbeerta (2014) provide a useful overview of different approaches based on different criminological theories, which we summarize in Figure 9.7. Each theory can be distinguished based on its underlying model of human behaviour, with the crucial question being: do criminal offenders act out of free will or are their actions determined by factors that they have little influence on? Depending on the answer that each theory provides to this question, we can order them on a scale from "free will" to "determinism".

At the top of Figure 9.7 we first see *classical criminal law*, which assumes that people commit crimes entirely out of their free will. According to this approach, each criminal makes an active choice to commit a crime without being forced or compelled by something outside of their control. The solution proposed by classical criminal law is to deter potential offenders from committing crimes via the threat of punishment.

One step down on the scale of free will versus determinism is *opportunity theory*, which does not deny the role of free will in explaining criminal actions, but additionally assumes that there will be more crime when there are more opportunities for crime. Therefore, this perspective advocates a combination of deterrence through punishment and the implementation of measures to reduce criminal opportunities (e.g., installing burglar alarms).

Free will

Theoretical perspective	*Proposed policy or action*
Classical criminal law	Deterrence by punishment
Opportunity theory	Reduction of opportunities / criminal law
Braithwaite	Reintegrative shaming
Labelling	Abolitionism / social support
Social control	Upbringing / education
Deprivation / strain	Deprivation policy
Self control	Upbringing / reduction of opportunities
Biosocial direction	Upbringing
Lombroso (positivism)	Imprisonment / adjusted work

Determinism

Figure 9.7 An overview of different criminological theories and their views on how crime can be reduced
Note: This scheme is an adapted version of a diagram by Van Dijk et al. (2014).

The criminologist John Braithwaite (1989), in turn, recommends so-called *reintegrative shaming*. His idea is that punishing criminals may further exclude them from society, increasing their chances of recidivism. He believes that it is more effective to reintegrate criminals into society rather quickly, and to let their close friends and relatives point them to their mistakes.

A related approach is derived from *labelling theory*, which states that criminal punishment has a stigmatizing effect on criminals, which may give rise to a negative self-image and eventually higher chances of recidivism. The implication is that providing criminals with social support makes more sense than punishing them. The most radical form of this approach is *abolitionism* – that is, the idea that punishment should be abolished altogether.

We next arrive at Hirschi's *social control theory* or *social bonding theory* that we already described in the previous section. Hirschi's proposed remedy to crime is to improve people's social bonds and commitment to society. Instruments that can be used in this regard include the social security system, providing educational resources, and ensuring plentiful job opportunities – all of this to prevent people from getting trapped in an isolated, dysfunctional underclass.

Moving further down the scale towards determinism, there is Merton's *relative deprivation theory* or *strain theory*, which we also discussed in the previous section. According to this approach, the best way to reduce crime is to invest in community cohesion and especially the improvement of problem neighbourhoods that suffer from concentrated disadvantages vis-à-vis the rest of society.

With *self-control theory* we have properly drifted away from the idea that engaging in criminal activities represents a free choice of individuals. The assumption of self-control theory is, instead, that criminals are naturally drawn to criminal activities, and that the only way to overcome these inclinations is to exercise strict self-control or avoid being exposed to any criminal temptations. To some extent, self-control can be taught via one's upbringing.

According to the *biosocial approach*, in turn, criminal behaviour is the result of an interaction between biological and social factors. This means that the best way to reduce crime consists of concerted action through both one's upbringing as well as medical or psychological treatment of potential offenders. Importantly, this approach is not fully deterministic insofar as it still assumes that it is possible to influence potential offenders so that they refrain from criminal activities.

The Italian lawyer Cesare Lombroso (2006[1876]), on the other hand, maintained a completely *deterministic perspective*, assuming that people are either born as criminals or not. Among other things, he asserted that criminals can be identified by a low forehead and strong jaw. The implication is that the only way to keep potential offenders from committing crimes is to imprison them or send them to work camps or similar restrictive facilities. However, it should be stressed that, while most of the theoretical approaches in Figure 9.7 seem to possess at least some merit, Lombroso's theory was already disproven early in the twentieth century.

The legalization of drugs as a potential solution to drug criminality

The production, distribution and use of illegal drugs is a worldwide problem. In addition to the health risks posed by certain illegal drugs (although many illegal drugs are in fact less addictive or physically harmful than alcohol or tobacco), society also suffers from the crimes involved in the illegal drug trade. Opinions on what ought to be done about this problem are heavily divided. Roughly speaking, we can distinguish two extreme camps in this debate: on the one hand, there are those who want to use law enforcement to interdict supplies and shut down drug trafficking networks; and on the other hand, there are those who want to legalize drugs.

To understand the position of those who advocate drug legalization, it is worthwhile to draw a parallel with the prohibition of alcohol in the US. The American government introduced a law prohibiting the sale of alcohol in 1920, and set up a Prohibition Bureau to monitor bootlegging activities. As a consequence of this policy, alcoholic beverages became scarcer and therefore more expensive. At first, this meant that alcohol consumption decreased, due to the higher prices. At the same time, however, these higher prices provided an incentive to criminal entrepreneurs to start distilling and trading alcohol illegally. This, in turn, had many negative consequences.

For one thing, many organized crime groups emerged that made large profits from the illegal trade in alcohol. This trade also involved a lot of violence, and many corrupt employees of the Prohibition Bureau were actually in on this trade, trying to obtain a share in the huge profits that were being made. Moreover, the prohibition led to a large increase in incarceration rates, and although the consumption of beer decreased, the consumption of hard liquors actually increased (since these were harder to interdict per volume of alcohol). In short, the prohibition of alcohol had many perverse effects, which eventually led to the repeal of the prohibition law in 1933.

What similarities are there between the prohibition of alcohol and the current problem of illegal drugs? First, because the supply of drugs is restricted by their illegality, prices are exceptionally high and this encourages criminals to get involved in the drug trade. Moreover, the lack of official dispute settlement mechanisms in the illegal market for drugs means that rival suppliers settle disputes through violence. From this perspective, legalization of drugs is likely to reduce criminality, as this would allow addicts and other drug users to get their fix from legal sellers, and there would no longer be an incentive for drug gangs to engage in violent turf wars. Therefore, law enforcement costs would presumably also decrease.

Another benefit of the legalization of drugs is that it becomes possible for governments to regulate the drug trade. Among other things, they could set and enforce certain quality standards, as well as require suppliers to provide better information to consumers. As a result of such measures, the number of deaths due to drug overdoses or consumption of poor-quality drugs can be significantly reduced. Moreover, when drugs are legalized, it becomes possible to levy taxes on drug sales, the proceeds of which can subsequently be used to address other problems.

Finally, the legalization of drugs might even facilitate peace in countries such as Colombia and Afghanistan that are seriously disrupted by violent and powerful drug gangs and mafias that undermine a peaceful society. Particularly dramatic is the war between drug cartels in Mexico. In 2017 alone, there were in Mexico 25,000 homicides with some relation to the illegal drug industry. The political scientists Guillermo Trejo and Sandra Ley (2018) argue in this context that drug violence has increased substantially since Mexico's transition to a multiparty democracy, due to unintended consequences of the democratic reforms, in particular the replacement of many state-level public officials. Prior to these reforms, corrupt state-level officials had been protecting the drug cartels' local monopolies, meaning that their replacement led to an increase in competition between rival drug cartels. Against this background, one might argue that the incentive to kill one another would presumably disappear if there was less to fight over – in other words, if the illegal drug trade was less lucrative. As such, legalization of drugs might help to reduce violence.

Of course, the full-scale legalization of drugs may also come with disadvantages and unintended consequences. For example, criminal entrepreneurs will presumably look for new markets once the trade in drugs is no longer profitable. The markets they might plausibly move into include cigarette smuggling, human trafficking and illegal trading in body parts. It is, therefore, highly likely that other forms of crime would increase in prevalence if drugs were legalised. Secondly, because the price of drugs would fall massively under legalization, drug consumption in the population at large might increase.

Indeed, the fact that, in recent decades, a considerable number of Americans have become addicted to opioids (including prescription painkillers, which are legal) suggests that mass epidemics of drug use are perfectly possible. As the economists Anne Case and Angus Deaton (2015) demonstrate, the *opioid epidemic* has in recent years contributed to a significant uptick in the mortality rate of white Americans. That said, by levying taxes on drug consumption, governments could try to prevent such increases in consumption, and the evidence so far from places where certain drugs such as marijuana have been legalized (e.g., Portugal, Canada, certain states in the US) indicates that there has been no increase in the consumption of these drugs since their liberalization (Dills, Goffard, and Miron 2017), while crime levels seem to have declined.

Whereas many people, therefore, claim that the advantages of legalization outweigh the disadvantages, this is clearly not the view of Rodrigo Duterte, who was elected president of the Philippines in 2016. Duterte escalated the war on drugs by stimulating extrajudicial killings of drug sellers. As a result, thousands of people were killed by paramilitary death squads in the first year of Duterte's presidency, threatening both public safety and the rule of law in the Philippines. Interestingly, the former president of Colombia, César Gaviria, argues that Duterte should avoid making the same mistakes as Colombia (Gaviria 2017). Over a period of decades, the Colombian authorities invested billions of dollars in a campaign to defeat the cartels and eradicate drugs. This campaign had the unintended consequence of pushing drugs and crime into neighbouring countries, and causing tens of thousands of civilian deaths – among them judges, politicians, police officers and journalists. Based on this experience, Gaviria's contention is that extrajudicial killings and vigilantism do not work. Instead, he advocates improving health conditions, fighting corruption, and decriminalizing drug use.

Organized crime

According to the 2017 Europol annual report, there are about 5,000 organized crime groups under investigation in the 28 member states of the EU. It is generally agreed that the activities of such organized crime groups – namely the production, distribution and sale of illegal goods and services – impose great costs on society, whether from an economic perspective (by stealing money or failing to pay taxes), a public health perspective (by importing dangerous drugs), or a human rights perspective (by human trafficking). Given these substantial societal costs as well as the distinct character of organized crime vis-à-vis stand-alone crimes, it is useful to provide a brief discussion of organized crime.

Donald Cressey, a consultant on the 1967 US President's Commission on Organized Crime, introduced the bureaucratic model of organized crime (Cressey 1969). Based on information obtained from trials of members of the Italian American mafia during the 1950s, Cressey concluded that there was a national crime enterprise operating in big cities across the US, known as *La Cosa Nostra* (Our Thing), the Mafia or the Syndicate. According to Cressey, this criminal enterprise had a large bureaucratic structure, not unlike a large company or government organization, consisting of so-called families, legal advisors, and an overall boss. Above the whole family system stood a commission, formed by the leaders of each family, that coordinated activities and solved disputes. Each family was itself also organized into a hierarchical and almost military structure, with under-bosses, lieutenants, section heads and lower functionaries, as well as soldiers at the bottom. The organization was bound together through oaths of loyalty and secrecy, and through extreme punishments for any violations of those oaths.

While Cressey's bureaucratic model of organized crime implicitly assumed that organized crime groups could grow ever larger and more powerful by taking on more employees and families joining forces, the criminologist Dwight Smith (1975) emphasized that criminal enterprises cannot expand unlimitedly, as there are practical bounds to the size of criminal organizations and their division of labour. This can be explained through the *principal-agent model* introduced in Chapter 2. Applying this framework, a leader of a criminal organization (the principal) needs trustworthy and skilled agents to execute complex tasks, but possesses only limited information on the actions of these agents, giving rise to monitoring problems. A particular challenge is that all agents have their own interests and incentives, which need not be consistent with the interests and goals of the leader and the criminal enterprise as a whole.

Among other things, any delegation of tasks implies a potential risk of the criminal organization being revealed and its members being arrested. This implies that the leader cannot simply entrust anyone in the organization with the most delicate tasks. Indeed, the leader can rarely trust individual agents outside his own family with anything more than routine tasks, because for agents without a direct kin relationship to the leader there is a much higher risk that they will pursue their own private interests, by selling the principal out to his competitors, or passing information to the police. Hence, it makes sense for the leader to keep his criminal organization limited in size, to surround himself with trustworthy people (preferably family members), and not to provide anyone with more information than is strictly necessary for executing their concrete tasks at hand. For complex tasks, it makes sense for the boss to maintain a so-called *patronage relationship*, giving out favours and benefits in exchange for the loyalty and devotion of the agent. For routine tasks, like courier services, hiring unattached manpower is preferable.

Even when organized crime groups originate from one particular criminal activity, over time they typically tend to become involved in a range of illegal activities: drug trade, weapons trade, extortion and protection rackets, trade in radioactive waste, smuggling of illegal migrants, trafficking of women and children for prostitution, trade in human organs, counterfeiting, money laundering, contract killing, trade in stolen artefacts, etc. This is true for all of the most well-known criminal organizations, such as the Sicilian mafia, *La Cosa Nostra*, the *'Ndràngheta* in Calabria, Mexican drug cartels, Nigerian criminal networks, the Japanese *Yakuza*, the Hong Kong triads, the Russian mafia, and a wide variety of other criminal groups.

The sociologist Manuel Castells (1998) furthermore argues that, under the influence of globalization, many criminal organizations are increasingly operating on a global scale. Indeed, most of the previously listed activities require international contacts and transnational movements. For this reason, criminal organizations often end up entering strategic alliances and dividing up markets. Moreover, in the age of globalization, criminal organizations have also been observed to increasingly engage in so-called *jurisdictional shopping*. Specifically, they seek to base their operations in countries where standards and investigations are relatively lax. Such jurisdictional shopping does not only apply to decisions on where to conduct certain criminal actions but also to the question of where to subsequently channel the revenues of these actions for the purpose of money laundering. However, as noted by the criminologist Federico Varese (2011), the globalization of criminal enterprises does not only make them bigger, more powerful and more efficient, but also more vulnerable. After all, by increasingly operating across borders and on a larger scale, there is an increased risk of the enterprise being brought down due to a mistake or betrayal by one weak link within the enterprise or one of its relations.

Over time, many different explanations have been advanced for the rise of organized crime groups. Indeed, as it turns out, the reasons for the emergence of organized crime can differ markedly from one context to another, and there is thus no "one-size-fits-all" explanation. Nevertheless, we can distinguish several factors that often play a role in the rise of organized crime.

For example, Varese (2014) points out that, at the macro level, the state is often absent or weak, characterized by little protection of private property rights, high levels of corruption, and an ineffective police force and justice system. All of this offers many opportunities to criminal entrepreneurs, while the risks of arrest and punishment are relatively low.

Local economic context represents another important explanatory factor. In particular, organized crime is more likely to emerge in an environment of high economic inequality or when there is a lot of poverty, especially within the lower social classes. Such circumstances may lead to feelings of indignation and make individuals more susceptible to recruitment by criminal entrepreneurs, who offer ambitious individuals an alternative path to richness, status and luxury. Similarly, people with a migration background are often also more likely to be recruited into criminal groups. Organized crime in American cities such as Chicago and New York was, for example, dominated by people of Irish and Italian extraction. Likewise, organized crime in Europe today features many individuals of Italian, Turkish or Russian origin, as well as migrants from the former Yugoslavia and the Balkans. The criminologists Frank Bovenkerk, Dina Siegel, and Damián Zaitch (2003) argue in this context that criminal groups operating in foreign countries recruit disproportionately from within their own ethnic group, as this allows them to appeal to prospective gang members' sense of ethnic identity.

The rise of organized crime in Russia after the collapse of the Soviet Union provides a clear illustration of several of the aforementioned points. According to Varese (2001), the Russian state was, firstly, incapable of steering the new market economy in the right direction, and secondly, equally incapable of enforcing its monopoly on violence. This situation gave numerous violent criminal groups a free playing field, which they exploited by starting to demand money from large as well as small business owners. This, in turn, resulted in a demand for protection. Since the state was incapable of providing such protection, the business owners instead had to rely on other criminal entrepreneurs or even the same ones as they were threatened by in the first place. As a consequence, criminal groups experienced a significant growth in their operations. This growth was further facilitated by the fact that unemployment in Russia was rampant during this period. Criminal entrepreneurs were, therefore, able to recruit many unemployed males from the lower strata of the population. Especially those who had been formerly employed in the army or intelligence services were popular recruitment targets, due to their training in violence. Over time, organized crime has increasingly penetrated many aspects of Russian society, as described in great detail by international relations scholar Mark Galeotti (2018). Among other things, there are intense relationships between corrupt state officials and organized crime groups.

Cybercrime

An important societal change that has provided a range of new opportunities for criminal entrepreneurs is the diffusion of new information and communication technologies through virtually all areas of society. A computer, an internet connection and many other interactive technologies can now be found in almost every Western household and, among other things, the majority of financial transactions are now digitalized. The internet especially offers a convenient place to commit crimes, as it has no borders, no overarching authority, and no harmonized security infrastructure, while it offers at the same time high levels of anonymity as well as speed and economies of scale when it comes to completing all kinds of transactions. As a result, the number of criminal offences committed through the internet or other digital channels – also known as *cybercrime* – has grown immensely in recent years.

The criminologist Miranda Domenie and her colleagues (2013) distinguish between two sorts of cybercrime. The first category comprises offences in which information and communication technologies constitute both the means and the end of criminal activity. One could think of hacking and the spreading of viruses, where computers are used to attack other computers. Criminal hackers are often referred to as *black hat hackers*, as opposed to *white hat hackers*, which comprise hackers with more benevolent purposes such as whistle-blowers and "hacktivists" attempting to demonstrate important public security threats. The second category of cybercrime encompasses offences in which information and communication technologies constitute a means but not the end of criminal activity. In such cases, criminals have co-opted old crimes for the digital world, where they benefit from a bigger playing field and weaker enforcement. Examples include financial and identity fraud, dissemination of child porn, cyber bullying, and online grooming.

Both the exact number of cybercrimes committed, and the exact damage they cause, are difficult to put a finger on. Among other things, reporting rates for cybercrime tend to be low, because many victims are unaware that they have been a victim, but also because they often do not know what the police can do for them. Moreover, companies may often be reluctant to report having fallen victim to cybercrime, as this could hurt their reputation and business operations – think of a major bank reporting a break-in in its online banking services.

Notwithstanding such measurement difficulties, it is evident that cybercrime occurs on an enormous and growing scale. For example, according to data for 2011 from the United Nations Office on Drugs and Crime, individual cybercrime victimization rates range from one to 17 percent of the online population, depending on the country and the type of cybercrime (UNODC 2013). More specifically, about ten percent of the online population had their email account hacked in 2011, while the average victimization rates for phishing, identity theft and online credit card frauds in that year were four percent each. All of these rates are higher than the average annual victimization rates for conventional crimes such as burglary (two percent), robbery (one percent), or car theft (one percent), and they are likely to have risen further since 2011. Private sector companies are also regular victims of cybercrime, with reported victimization rates in the range of two to 16 percent for crimes such as data breach due to intrusion or phishing.

Cybercrimes additionally impose huge costs on society, including direct costs such as money unlawfully withdrawn from bank accounts and the time and effort required to reset account credentials or repair computer systems. However, there are also many indirect costs, such as a loss of public trust in online banking or cybercrime defence costs related to the purchase of cybersecurity products and services. In this respect, Cybersecurity Ventures – a research platform on the cyber economy – estimates that the global cybersecurity market is worth about US$ 120 billion in 2017.

While some cybercrimes such as email account hacking and online credit card fraud are by now very well-known, there are constantly new forms of cybercrime popping up. For example, in recent years there has been a surge in so-called *ransomware attacks*, whereby hackers block computers and demand a ransom from victims to de-block their machines. There has also been a rise in cybercrimes that are not directly aimed at financial gains for the criminal involved, but rather are intended to hurt certain companies, governments or other institutions, for example by taking down their websites through so-called *DDoS attacks*.

With regard to the perpetrators of cybercrime, organized crime groups have entered the world of cybercrime in great numbers. The UNODC (2013) estimates that more than 80 percent of all cybercrime activities can be traced back to organized criminal structures as opposed to stand-alone individual acts. Such organized cybercrime is facilitated by very active and fastly expanding illegal markets on the *dark web* (an encrypted section of the world wide web that requires specific tools to access and where the identity or locations of users cannot be tracked), where one could obtain all kinds of products and services related to cybercrime. Relatedly, the sociologist Jonathan Lusthaus (2018) provides an illuminating description of the "industrialization" of the world of cybercrime – from a situation where a small number of technically skilled individuals committed one-off, individual acts of cybercrime to a highly organized and complex industry of cybercrime with many interconnections and collaborations among cybercriminals.

Recommended readings

- Graham Farrell (2013) tests a large number of explanations for the drop in crime rates that has been observed in most developed countries in recent decades. The explanations range from ones related to demographics to ones related to policing numbers and strategies, and from the impact of the legalization of abortion to the influence of incarceration. Farrell concludes that the security hypothesis discussed in the section "Crime statistics and trends" possesses the most explanatory power.
- David Kirk (2009) provides a study on the influence of neighbourhood environments and social surroundings on recidivism among ex-prisoners. He exploits a natural experiment resulting from Hurricane Katrina that destroyed many neighbourhoods in the city of Louisiana in 2005. Kirk finds that ex-prisoners who were forced to move away from their original neighbourhood upon their release were substantially less likely to commit new crimes than those who returned to the same criminal opportunities and peers that had led them to prison in the first place.
- Federico Varese (2011) describes the spread of organized crime groups across the world, whereby they leave their home grounds and attempt to take root elsewhere. Based on case studies of the moving experiences of, amongst others, the Sicilian mafia to New York, the Russian mafia to Italy, and the Taiwanese and Hong Kongese triads to mainland China, Varese explains why some relocations are successful while others do not work out.
- Jonathan Lusthaus (2018) charts how cybercrime has developed from small-scale activities by lone wolves to a highly organized, interconnected, complex and profitable global industry. Based on interviews with cybercriminals, security experts and law enforcers, Lusthaus analyses, among other things, how cybercriminals work together in contexts of anonymity, how certain environments are more conducive to cybercrime than others, and how the online and offline lives of cybercriminals are interrelated.

Bibliography

Agnew, Robert. 1992. "Foundation for a General Strain Theory of Crime and Delinquency". *Criminology* 30:47–87.

Bonger, Willem A. 1916[1905]. *Criminality and Economic Conditions* (translated by Henry P. Horton). Boston, MA: Little, Brown, and Company.

Bovenkerk, Frank, Dina Siegel, and Damián Zaitch. 2003. "Organized Crime and Ethnic Reputation Manipulation". *Crime, Law and Social Change* 39:23–38.

Braithwaite, John. 1989. *Crime, Shame and Reintegration*. Cambridge: Cambridge University Press.

Case, Anne, and Angus Deaton. 2015. "Rising Morbidity and Mortality in Midlife Among White Non-Hispanic Americans in the 21st Century". *Proceedings of the National Academy of Sciences* 112: 15078–15083.

Castells, Manuel. 1998. *End of Millennium*. London: Blackwell.

Cohen, Lawrence E., and Marcus Felson. 1979. "Social Change and Crime Rate Trends: A Routine-Activity Approach". *American Sociological Review* 44:588–608.

Cornish, Derek B., and Ronald V. Clarke. 1986. *The Reasoning Criminal: Rational Choice Perspectives on Offending*. New York, NY: Springer-Verlag.

Cressey, Donald R. 1969. *Theft of a Nation: The Structure of Organized Crime in America*. New York, NY: Harper and Row.

Dills, Angela K., Sietse Goffard, and Jeffrey Miron. 2017. "The Effects of Marijuana Liberalizations: Evidence from Monitoring the Future". *NBER Working Paper* 23779.

Domenie, Miranda L., Rutger Leukfeldt, Johan A. Van Wilsem, Jurjen Jansen, and Wouter Stol. 2013. *Slachtofferschap in een Gedigitaliseerde Samenleving*. Den Haag: Boom Lemma.

Farrell, Graham. 2013. "Five Tests for a Theory of the Crime Drop". *Crime Science* 2:5.

Galeotti, Mark. 2018. *The Vory: Russia's Super Mafia*. New Haven, CT: Yale University Press.

Gaviria, César. 2017. "President Duterte Is Repeating My Mistakes". *New York Times*, February 7th.

Hirschi, Travis. 1969. *Causes of Delinquency*. Berkeley, CA: University of California Press.

Kirk, David S. 2009. "A Natural Experiment on Residential Change and Recidivism: Lessons from Hurricane Katrina". *American Sociological Review* 74:484–505.

Lombroso, Cesare. 2006[1876]. *Criminal Man* (translated by Mary Gibson and Nicole Hahn Rafter). Durham, NC: Duke University Press.

Lusthaus, Jonathan. 2018. *Industry of Anonymity – Inside the Business of Cybercrime*. Cambridge, MA: Harvard University Press.

Massing, Michael. 1998. "The Blue Revolution". *The New York Book Review*, November 19th.

Merton, Robert K. 1938. "Social Structure and Anomie". *American Sociological Review* 3:672–682.

Pew Research Center. 2013. *King's Dream Remains an Elusive Goal; Many Americans See Racial Disparities*. Washington, DC: Pew Research Center.

Roeder, Oliver, Lauren-Brooke Eisen, and Julia Bowling. 2015. *What Caused the Crime Decline?* New York, NY: Brennan Center for Justice.

Smith, Dwight C. 1975. *The Mafia Mystique*. London: Hutchinson.

Trejo, Guillermo, and Sandra Ley. 2018. "Why Did Drug Cartels Go to War in Mexico? Subnational Party Alternation, the Breakdown of Criminal Protection, and the Onset of Large-Scale Violence". *Comparative Political Studies* 51:900–937.

UNODC. 2013. *Comprehensive Study on Cybercrime* (Draft, February 2013). New York, NY: United Nations.

Van Dijk, Jan. 1991. *Criminaliteit als Keerzijde: Een Theoretische en Empirische Verkenning van de Relaties Tussen Welvaart en Criminaliteit*. Arnhem: Gouda Quint.

Van Dijk, Jan, Wim Huisman, and Paul Nieuwbeerta. 2014. *Actuele Criminologie*. The Hague: SDU.

Van Wilsem, Johan A. 2003. *Crime and Context: The Impact of Individual, Neighborhood, City and Country Characteristics on Victimization*. Nijmegen: ICS Dissertation.

Varese, Federico. 2001. *The Russian Mafia: Private Protection in a New Market Economy*. Oxford: Oxford University Press.

Varese, Federico. 2011. *Mafias on the Move: How Organized Crime Conquers New Territories*. Princeton, NJ: Princeton University Press.

Varese, Federico. 2014. "Protection and Extortion". In: *The Oxford Handbook of Organized Crime*, edited by Letizia Paoli. Oxford: Oxford University Press.

Wilson, William J. 1987. *The Truly Disadvantaged: The Inner City, the Underclass, and Public Policy*. Chicago, IL: University of Chicago Press.

10 Corruption

Chapter overview

We begin this chapter by noting that corruption has a wide range of harmful impacts: it may destroy social trust, undermine the legitimacy of political institutions, distort public expenditures, reduce tax collection, impede economic growth, and increase socioeconomic inequality. We then discuss various definitions of corruption and present a typology of different types of corruption. Recognizing that corruption is difficult to measure, we review several common indicators, as well as the time trends and cross-country variation that they exhibit. The Corruption Perceptions Index (CPI) produced by Transparency International is the most prominent indicator. We proceed to articulate an explanation for the phenomenon of corruption, utilizing our familiar macro-micro-macro framework. Among other things, we explain how macro-level contexts can provide either weak or strong incentives for corrupt behaviour. At the micro level, the principal-agent-client model offers a valuable tool for analysing interactions between the parties involved. We conclude the chapter by discussing measures that can be taken to combat corruption.

Corruption as "the enemy within"

Corruption has a wide range of negative impacts on society: it may undermine social trust and the legitimacy of political institutions, distort the level of public expenditures, reduce tax collection, impede economic growth, and raise the level of socioeconomic inequality (Heath, Richards, and De Graaf 2016). The more widespread the corruption, the harder it becomes for citizens to trust one another or the government, the more likely it is that the government will engage in transactions that benefit themselves rather than society, and the more tax money will be lost by individuals or corporations bribing tax officials to look the other way. Furthermore, as rich people often have more opportunities than poor people to bribe or influence others, they usually benefit most from corruption – corruption can thus exacerbate pre-existing socioeconomic inequalities. In addition, economists have argued that corruption implies a severe impediment to economic development in the poorer regions of the world.

More generally, it is essential for a well-functioning society that civil servants, political leaders, judges, the police, and business people act in a correct and honest way. The state of affairs in which such behavioural standards are honoured can be regarded as a public good, insofar as everyone within society ultimately benefits from this, even though the individual actors involved may not be directly rewarded for their correctness and honesty. However, when individual actors do not act in a correct and honest way but rather engage in corrupt behaviours, the public good of an honest society is undermined. Citizens may accordingly lose their trust in other people and start to ignore rules and regulations themselves. From this perspective, corruption represents a public bad.

Well-known examples of corruption involve the behaviour of politicians such as former South African President Jacob Zuma, former German Chancellor Helmut Kohl, former Italian Prime Minister Silvio Berlusconi, and former Israeli Prime Minister Ehud Olmert, as well as the exploits of figures within FIFA, the world football association, or the International Olympic Committee (IOC). There are also numerous allegations of corporate corruption in, amongst others, the arms industry, the financial sector, and surrounding large-scale infrastructural projects.

Aside from such grand corruption, corruption often occurs in small-scale transactions among individual citizens, for example when people pay police officers to prevent a parking ticket or a local civil servant to have a building application approved. Although one might expect that only grand corruption could truly threaten society, many acts of such petty corruption can also have devastating impacts on the overall functioning of a society. For example, a recent study found that the presence of corruption and other rule violations in people's immediate social environment lowers their trust and intrinsic honesty (Gächter and Schulz 2016). In this context, Chinese President Xi Jinping has referred to corruption as "the enemy within". Indeed, the fight against corruption is a fight against an almost invisible enemy, as corrupt practices can be found in many spheres of society, but generally take place in secret. This also makes corruption a challenging phenomenon to study.

Over the years, a growing number of international organizations have launched campaigns against corruption. Examples include the UN, the Organisation for Economic Cooperation and Development (OECD), the World Trade Organization (WTO), the Organization of American States (OAS), the EU, the World Bank, and numerous NGOs. The most well-known among the latter is Transparency International, an NGO with its headquarters in Berlin, which was established in 1993 as part of the global fight against corruption. Moreover, an increasing number of countries have adopted legislation against corruption. All of these developments point to a broad consensus on corruption, namely that it represents a pressing societal problem with many harmful effects. It is also clear that corruption is a universal phenomenon, occurring in both rich as well as poor countries, although to different degrees. In many countries, the public and the media have also raised alarm regarding the problem of corruption, and follow corruption detection campaigns closely.

The extent to which corruption embeds itself within a society can be illustrated with an anecdote about the director of the 'Ndràngheta Museum in Calabria, Italy. The 'Ndràngheta is one of the richest and most powerful organized crime groups in Italy and even globally. The goal of the museum, located in a building confiscated from the 'Ndràngheta, is to inform the public on how the criminal and corrupt strategies of mafia organizations like that of the 'Ndràngheta can be counteracted. Strikingly, however, in 2016 the director of this museum was himself charged with corruption, having declared excessive expenses for private consumption goods. The fact that even the director of an anti-corruption museum engages in corrupt practices goes to show how deeply ingrained corruption is in Italian society.

Corruption as a concept emerged during the period of Western state formation described in Chapter 3, when modern bureaucracies with a strict separation of public and private interests were introduced. From this perspective, corruption is a Western-centric concept, and people from other cultures may well have rather different views about how the state and society ought to relate to one another. This provokes the question of whether it is possible to apply the same Western norms that reject corruption to certain developing countries, where socio-political relations tend to be much more personalized. Autocratic rulers have in this context often argued that several core elements of Western democracies are alien to the Asian or African culture, in which family relationships are very important and patronage relationships fulfil an important social role.

However, many of such cultural-relativist arguments were repudiated during the 1990s, with the rise of civil protest movements in various autocratic states. Social movements, based on principles of good governance, such as transparency, accountability, honesty, compliance with the law, and respect for human rights, have now spread throughout the world. Relatedly, the political scientists Richard Rose and Caryn Peiffer (2015) argue that the degree of cultural variation in attitudes towards corruption has been grossly overstated. According to their research, the majority of people in most parts of the world do, in fact, regard bribery and other types of corruption as unacceptable. Hence, arguments about the cultural-relativist nature of the public-private distinction are hard to maintain.

The difficulty of defining corruption

Although it is easy to state that corruption is the opposite of good governance, corruption is all but a straightforward object of study. Whereas everyone will be able to think of examples of corruption, and while the media regularly reports on corruption scandals, it is often hard to draw a strict line between what counts as corruption and what not. In other words, as also noted by the political scientists Bo Rothstein and Aiysha Varraich (2017) note, it is difficult to give a very precise definition of corruption. One of the reasons for this is that not all countries have legally mandated rules proscribing behaviour that would in other contexts be considered corrupt.

Regardless of which definition one adheres to, corruption presupposes a distinction between public and private interests. In a *modern bureaucracy*, as discussed in Chapter 3, a civil servant has to perform their tasks according to detailed rules and fixed procedures. While doing so, they must maintain a strict separation between public and private interests, and must apply rules without regard to which particular people are involved. As a side note, private interests should here be interpreted broadly. Politicians or civil servants do not only follow their private interests when they give themselves preferential treatment, but also when they favour other family members, friends, or members of their own ethnic group. If the benefits do not directly accrue to individuals but to an organization, for instance the cash register of a political party, we can speak of corruption as well.

When it subsequently comes to defining corruption, some scholars have proposed rather specific definitions of this concept. The sociologist David Jancsics (2014), for example, suggests a definition with four key conceptual elements:

1 Money, goods or other resources which belong to an organization are exchanged covertly in a way that benefit one or more persons who are not the formal owner.

2 At least one of the corrupt parties has formal contractual relations with the organization from which the resources are extracted.
3 Corruption happens between two or more corrupt parties – including one party who "sells" the resources and another party who compensates that first party for this.
4 A corrupt act is always a deviation from social rules or expectations of some kind, though not necessarily legal ones.

One advantage of this definition is that it is not restricted to just the actions of public officials, but also encompasses cases of corruption involving quasi-public or private parties. Furthermore, it contains both legal violations as well as more general abuses of trust, even if they are not strictly illegal. This is important, because in many countries corruption is not an accepted legal term, and therefore not explicitly mentioned in penal codes. The terms that more often appear in legislative texts include bribery, blackmailing, fraud, and theft, but those concepts are usually not uniformly defined in different countries or cultural contexts.

Possibly the most popular definition of corruption is the simpler and broader definition of corruption by the World Bank: "a corrupt practice is the offering, giving, receiving or soliciting, directly or indirectly, of anything of value to influence improperly the actions of another party". In recent years, many social scientists have embraced this broader approach to defining corruption (Beetham 2015; Lessig 2013). One reason for this is that social scientists are primarily focused on gaining insights into social processes. For this purpose, a broader definition of corruption – as opposed to a more specific or law-based one – represents a more productive starting point. Moreover, social scientists are often interested in international comparisons, which supersede specific national legislations. Hence, social scientists need a definition of corruption that is sufficiently broad so as to include all kinds of preferential treatments that are in some countries not (yet) part of the penal code. In this chapter, we also opt for a broad definition of corruption, following the World Bank definition quoted previously.

Having adopted such a broad approach, corruption can take numerous forms. To give the reader an indication of this, we list a selection of common examples of corruption that relate to civil servants, public officials and politicians:

1 Paying *grease money* to speed up the allocation of legal licenses or to evade complex regulations. In such environments, civil servants have an interest in making rules and procedures as complex and long-winded as possible.
2 Citizens and companies may bribe civil servants in an effort to reduce the amount of taxes, fees, fines or customs that they have to pay, or to acquire subsidies, licenses or loans from the government.
3 In order to obtain a government contract, such as for a large infrastructural project, companies may bribe the civil servants in charge of contracting.
4 Bribery to influence legislation or legal administration. This involves bribing judges to get a favourable verdict in a court case, bribing police officers so they refrain from reporting illegal activities, or bribing politicians so that they adopt certain laws.
5 Another way of influencing political decision-making is through the *revolving door phenomenon*. This concerns the situation where government officials, after leaving their public positions, become employees of companies that are directly affected by the government

department in which the official used to work, in the assumption that the former official can influence public policy in a direction favourable to their new employer.

6 *Nepotism* occurs when people in power use the privileges attached to their position to grant favours or assignments to close friends or relatives. One common practice is to give away prominent jobs in government to friends or relatives, even if their qualifications do not match those required for those jobs; another is to allocate preferential contracts to firms owned by family or friends.

At the national level, we can classify corruption by the degree to which it has penetrated society. In this regard, the United Nations Development Programme (UNDP 1998) applies a classification that distinguished between incidental, systematic, and systemic corruption.

The least severe situation concerns *incidental corruption*. This involves occasional cases of petty corruption and opportunistic actions by individuals or small groups. It typically concerns isolated behaviour by specific civil servants, and in the aggregate corruption is the exception rather than the rule. That said, incidental corruption can still affect many people and be very costly.

Systematic corruption is already more problematic for society, having a recurrent and organized character. This type of corruption is more deeply entrenched in society, involving large sums of money, and there is often a central role for high-level civil servants who exploit illegal opportunities. Nevertheless, it is still quite possible to combat systematic corruption, as removing the key players can make the corruption disappear.

This changes when the situation turns into one of *systemic corruption*. In this case, corruption has become an integral part of virtually all aspects of society. It has penetrated all economic and political institutions, affects all levels of employment and every government or business procedure, and is extremely difficult, if not impossible, to combat. This has to do with the fact that for eradicating systemic corruption it is not sufficient to remove the key offenders, and many politicians will in this setting be deeply entangled in corrupt activities themselves. Systemic corruption flourishes when public sector wages are too low to afford a reasonable living. Such circumstances offer strong incentives for malfeasance.

The existence of systemic corruption, which pervades all of society, is alarming. Notorious examples can be found in Southern Italy, Greece, various Eastern European countries, and countries in Latin-America, Africa, and Asia. In a number of countries, political rulers, together with some loyal elites, plunder the public treasury and expropriate lucrative sources of income such as mineral mines or oil or gas fields. When a new president is elected, he or she often promises to fight corruption, but corruption is so strongly embedded in society that such statements are often just rhetoric. In places with systemic corruption, members of the bureaucracy also have a stake in maximizing the number of rules and norms that citizens and companies have to comply with. After all, this provides them with additional opportunities for requesting bribes and other favours.

An illustrative recent example of systemic corruption is provided by Bill Browder (2015), who founded a large foreign investment fund (Hermitage Capital Management) in Russia after the collapse of the Soviet Union. Through his work, Browder discovered high levels of corruption within Russian business and government circles, including large-scale theft from partially publicly-owned companies. When Browder raised these issues in the media, he became victim of a corporate raid shortly after, whereby corrupt law enforcement officers seized all computers and documents within his office. Later it turned out that these seized documents were used by the corrupt law enforcers and their accomplices to start fake companies aimed at stealing public money via complex tax constructions. Browder and Hermitage were subsequently charged for this theft, while the corrupt individuals who were actually behind it were spending the stolen money on all kinds of luxury products, exotic travels, and expensive properties. While Browder had by this point already left Russia, his lawyer Sergei Magnitsky was arrested and eventually died in prison due to continuous maltreatment and abuse. Altogether, this case is a powerful illustration of how, in a systemic corruption environment, corrupt business people, politicians, judges and law enforcers all protect one another and enrich themselves at the expense of fundamental principles of honesty, fairness, and justice.

Measuring corruption

As already alluded to earlier, concealment is an essential pre-condition for corruption. In most countries, corruption is against the law, and considered morally reprehensible. Individuals that are involved in corrupt practices will thus generally try to keep their misbehaviour secret. This holds true for all parties involved in such practices, for example both the payer and the receiver of a bribe. One of the consequences is that there are no official statistics on the magnitude of corruption.

Does this mean that there is no way for social scientists to obtain any systematic insights on the spread of corruption? Fortunately, the answer is no, because – as already noted in Chapter 9 – there are more data sources at social scientists' disposal than just official statistics. In particular, social surveys allow researchers to directly ask citizens about a wide range of phenomena. Of course, directly asking citizens is not always equally helpful, and one might imagine that when someone is asked whether they have recently engaged in any corrupt behaviour, their answer will be in the negative no matter what. Nevertheless, social surveys can also ask respondents about whether they have been asked to be involved in bribery. Since such questions do not require respondents to implicate themselves in illegal or immoral behaviours, they are more likely to provide useful insights on the spread of corruption.

Figure 10.1 summarizes such data from the Global Corruption Barometer conducted by Transparency International, collected over the period 2006–2013. Focusing on the 30 countries that rank highest on the UN Human Development Index, the figure shows the percentage of respondents for each country who reported that they (or someone else in their household) were asked to pay a bribe for accessing certain services in the preceding year. As can be observed, Greece, Cyprus, Italy and the Czech Republic top this ranking, with bribery experience rates of over ten percent or even close to 20 percent (although in Italy there exist strong regional differences between the North and the South). At the bottom of this ranking we see all of the Nordic countries, with bribery experience rates of only about two percent. Of course, Figure 10.1 gives an incomplete overview of the overall degree of corruption, as it only relates to individual citizens paying bribes to access certain services. As such, grand corruption involving corporations and governments is not included.

Another source of information on corruption are corruption perception surveys. Questions on perceptions of corruption have been included in cross-national surveys such as the Global Corruption Barometer, the World Values Survey, and the International Social Survey Program.

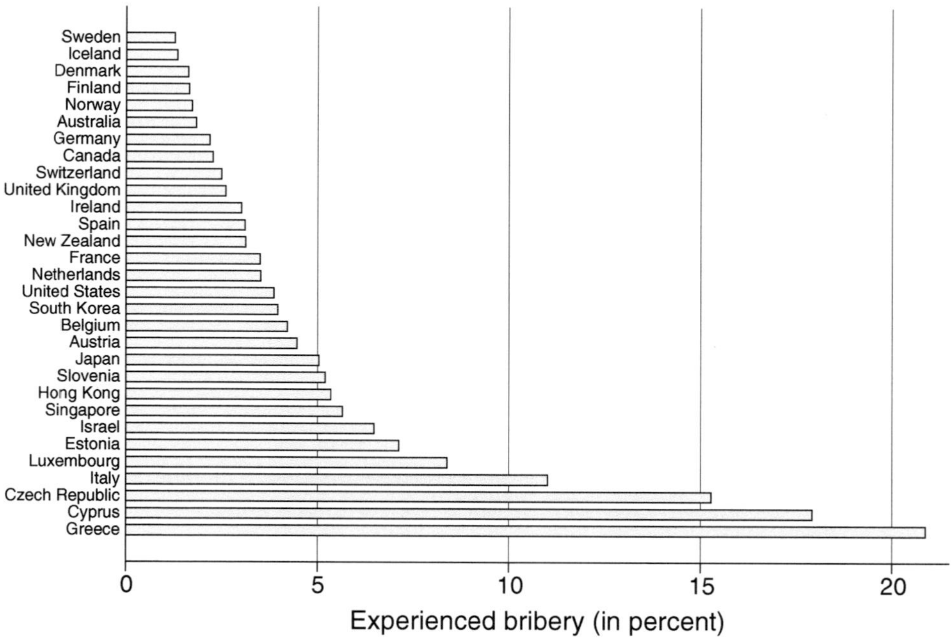

Figure 10.1 Experience of bribery across developed countries between 2006 and 2013

Note: Data are from the Global Corruption Barometer by Transparency International, pooled by country over the period 2006–2013. The figure is restricted to the 30 highest-scoring countries on the UN Human Development Index. Respondents were asked – separately for different types of government services (e.g., education system, medical services, police, judiciary, registry and permit services, utilities, tax revenue office) – whether they or any other household member had paid a bribe in any form in the past 12 months. The data points in this figure show the percentage of people who answered "yes" to any of these questions.

These surveys ask respondents how widespread they believe bribery and corruption to be in their country. As such, respondents' answers do not only pertain to their own, direct experiences with corruption, but comprise also their perceptions of corruption by, for example, high-level politicians or business executives. That said, corruption perceptions data suffer from several shortcomings of their own. Arguably the most important problem relates to *measurement equivalence* – that is, do different respondents have similar interpretations of what is meant by these perception questions? (Weber Abramo 2008). In this regard, the economist Benjamin Olken (2009) shows that there is a general correlation between individuals' perceptions of corruption and more objective measures of corruption, but that there remain serious disparities.

Another method for acquiring estimates of the amount of corruption is a victim survey (see Chapter 9). The idea here is that if one cannot obtain reliable information from the perpetrators, one may be able to obtain some information from the victims. Questions on victimization from corruption have been included in, amongst others, the European Social Surveys and the International Social Survey Program. These questions relate to petty or street-level corruption. Although victim surveys may, in some ways, be less problematic than perception surveys, important validity issues remain. For example, some people may acquire government contracts through corruption, but the people who were excluded from those contracts can only have suspicions that corruption took place. Similarly, while corrupt practices by political leaders harm practically the entire population, it is unlikely that any single individual will step forward and identify themselves as a victim. Also, the cross-national comparability of these surveys remains an issue (Heath et al. 2016).

Whereas all of the aforementioned surveys ask representative samples of the total population about their corruption experiences or their perceptions of corruption, another approach is to restrict surveys to specific subsamples of the population that can be expected to have particularly valuable insights into the issue of corruption. One particular group of people that is often targeted by such surveys are international businessmen. Evidently, such a survey can once again only gauge subjective assessments, but it has the advantage that all assessments are at least given by people who are more likely to encounter corruption in their daily activities and who may also have a sense of how different countries fare compared with one another. Since international organizations such as the World Bank began to advocate good governance as a core ingredient for successful development, several regular surveys among businessmen have been introduced.

The most prominent player in this regard is Transparency International, which compiles the Corruption Perceptions Index (CPI), which is derived from a number of surveys that ask businessmen about their perceptions and experiences with corruption across different countries. Based on these surveys, Transparency International assigns an integrity score on a scale from 0 to 100 to every country, such that higher scores correspond to higher levels of integrity and lower scores to higher levels of corruption.

Figure 10.2 shows trends in the CPI across eight countries. Something that immediately stands out in this figure is that most countries have not managed to improve their index scores much over time, with the exception of China. This can be taken as evidence that corruption

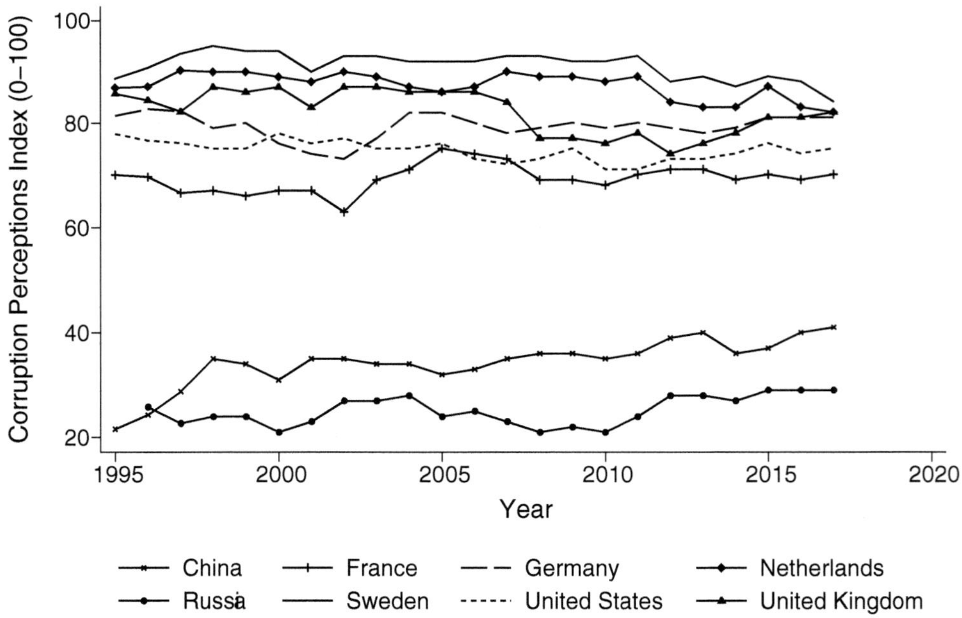

Figure 10.2 Trends in the Corruption Perceptions Index across a selection of countries, 1995-2017

Note: Data are from the Corruption Perceptions Index (CPI) by Transparency International, as compiled in their annual CPI reports. Higher CPI scores correspond to lower levels of corruption.

levels tend to be very stable over time and highly resistant to change, although some caveats are warranted. For example, when expressing their corruption perceptions, businesspeople are primarily making relative comparisons between countries at a single point in time, as opposed to comparisons to how things used to be in a given country. This might imply that if all countries in the world were making similar gains in terms of reducing corruption, this would not necessarily show up in their CPI scores. What is more, the underlying survey questions from which the CPI scores are derived exhibit some changes from year to year. However, notwithstanding such caveats, there clearly is more variation in CPI scores between countries, as compared to within countries over time. Countries from North-West Europe lead the pack in terms of integrity and lack of corruption, while Russia has consistently been the lowest scorer among these eight countries over the past 20 years.

Several scholars are sceptical about whether the CPI provides an accurate measure of corruption (Donchev and Ujhelyi 2014; Heywood and Rose 2014). Among other things, they argue that street-level and political corruption cannot be merged into one index. Moreover, critics claim that the surveys on which the CPI scores are based partly reflect attitudes to corruption within a given country, in addition to the actual incidence of corruption. Furthermore, as already mentioned, CPI scores are, strictly speaking, not comparable over time, since the specific data sources used for each country are not identical from year to year. Having said all of this, there are also scholars who defend the CPI as the best measure of corruption among many imperfect alternatives (Lambsdorff 2006; Uslaner and Rothstein 2012), and since 2012 Transparency International has improved its measurement methodology, making comparisons more valid.

Another method for studying corruption is the analysis of police investigations and legal inquiries. Some part of this information is, by definition, controversial and disputed: public prosecutors try to support their accusations with arguments and evidence, but the defendants will almost certainly deny the charges and attempt to discredit the evidence put forward. Nonetheless, insights can still be gained. For example, the political scientists Donatella Della Porta and Alberto Vannucci (1999) have conducted an analysis of corruption in Italy on the basis of documents from archives, court reports, and parliamentary investigations that were compiled as part of large-scale actions against corruption during the 1980s and 1990s. Obviously, however, such research is only feasible in countries where the legal authorities have actually taken action against corruption.

Finally, there is one category of people who can provide especially reliable information about corruption, and those are the people who have personal experience with it but are nonetheless willing to report on it. However, these kinds of people are a rare species. The term *whistle-blower* is used to refer to someone who reports secrets about illegal practices that they have been involved in. Through public accusations, the whistle-blower breaks the powerful, informal code of silence or *omertà* that exists within many organizations and communities. Therefore, organizations often react furiously when one of their employees publicly accuses particular colleagues or the organization as a whole. The accused organization is likely to accuse the whistle-blower of slander, and former colleagues may denounce the whistle-blower as someone who violates norms of mutual loyalty.

There are many examples of whistle-blowers whose revelations have had a big impact. A recent example is Edward Snowden, who in 2013 leaked classified information from the US National Security Agency (NSA) on numerous global citizen surveillance programmes.

Public reception to whistle-blowers is generally mixed. On the one hand, whistle-blowers are respected for having the courage to uphold certain ethical principles and for highlighting wrongdoing in complex situations, yet at the same time many people are reluctant to directly associate themselves to whistle-blowers. As a consequence, whistle-blowers usually do not receive much support and often end up miserable and isolated.

An example of a whistle-blower who risked everything to expose corruption is the former lieutenant of the Spanish army, Luis Gonzalo Segura. He denounced corrupt practices within the army and wrote a book about his shocking experiences – *A Step Forward* (translated title), published in 2014. Although the book received much attention, Segura has been struggling since leaving the army, among other things because he lost his house due to the huge legal fees he faced for his appeal against the disciplinary charges that were brought against him by the army.

This is, however, not an uncommon outcome. For example, Edward Snowden has been living in exile in Russia since his revelations, cut off from his friends and relatives and unable to return to his home country. Indeed, whistle-blowers are rarely able to pursue a successful career after their accusations. They may end up spending lots of money on court cases against their previous employers, and future employers seem unwilling to hire them, possibly because their actions (while laudable from a public perspective) signal a lack of loyalty and trustworthiness from the employer's perspective.

Over the last few decades, some countries have implemented legislation that aims to protect employees who report comprising information about their organization. This legislation is part of a broader agenda aimed at fighting corruption, and encourages employees to step forward as whistle-blowers, by protecting them against dismissal, transfers, demotions or other penalties. In the US, a new research commission was also established as part of this policy agenda, which has been assigned the task of investigating accusations made by whistle-blowers. Critics have pointed out, however, that this legislation may have a negative side effect, namely encouraging opportunistic behaviour on the parts of employees who – for whatever reason – hold a grudge against their employer.

Explaining corruption

In his theory of the modern bureaucracy, the sociologist Max Weber portrays corruption as a legacy of out-dated societal structures. In particular, he contrasts two governance structures: the *patrimonial bureaucracy* and the *modern bureaucracy* (Weber 1978[1925]). The patrimonial bureaucracy was the prevailing governance structure in old empires such as ancient China, and kingdoms in Asia, Africa, and pre-colonial America. Also the feudalist system in medieval Europe was a specific decentralized version of this governance structure. In these societies – where the political apparatus consisted of mercenaries, slaves or conscripts who were loyal to the autocratic ruler in exchange for money, protection or favours – there was no real distinction between public and private property. Only with the rise of modern bureaucracies was such a distinction introduced, making it possible to identify corruption as the breaking of norms by civil servants (see Chapter 3).

While many Western countries transitioned from patrimonial to modern bureaucracies already several centuries ago, for many developing countries this transition is still more recent or even ongoing, having only started following their independence from their colonizers. In the 1950s and 1960s, the dominant expectation among social scientists was that, once political independence had been achieved, and the construction of a modern state had begun, the population of these countries would automatically develop new loyalties towards their nation in addition to traditional family and clan interests. Moreover, it was believed that traditional values and norms such as in-group favouritism could be replaced by modern ones such as efficiency and professionalism, thereby eradicating corruption. However, as became clear in the post-colonial era, such expectations were overly optimistic. Following Weber's logic, social scientists have sought to explain the continued high prevalence of corruption in post-colonial states by referring to the persistence of patrimonial elements in their governance. The key idea is that civil servants in these countries have not fully adjusted to the modern bureaucratic system, so they still view their position within the government apparatus as a legitimate source of personal income.

In the remainder of this section, we aim to get a firmer grip on the question of how corruption can be explained. For this purpose, we employ a macro-micro-macro framework (see Chapter 2) to address when, where and under which circumstances corruption is likely to emerge. We successively discuss various social mechanisms that relate to the macro-to-micro, micro-to-micro, and micro-to-macro links in Figure 2.2.

Macro-level backgrounds and situational mechanisms

One macro-level background that will positively affect corruption is the quality of the state. Many countries with low CPI scores fall into the category of *weak states* – with an inefficient and ineffective government apparatus – and the ones with the lowest CPI scores tend to have a completely collapsed governance structure, where the government is so weak that it has lost all control over the country. The latter class of countries are known as *failed states*. Those countries are often characterized by civil conflict, they have no functioning public sector, and their leaders are more concerned with pursuing their own interests than the public good.

Such a macro-level context will inevitably have grave consequences at the micro level, among other things triggering belief-formation mechanisms such as *self-fulfilling prophecies*. That is, in a failed state, citizens will have low expectations as to whether the government will fulfil its public duties, and they will think it is normal that bribes have to be paid in all transactions. Based on such beliefs, individual citizens will be ready to request or pay bribes at every transaction they are involved in. They will thus maintain and reinforce a situation of widespread corruption, which further undermines the state's capacity and strengthens citizens' beliefs that corruption is an intrinsic part of daily life. Through such a vicious circle society remains firmly based in a self-perpetuating high-corruption equilibrium, where government services are not provided as standard, but as favours in return for bribes, and where the atmosphere among the population is characterized by suspicion and distrust.

Similar feedback mechanisms can help to explain why other countries, such as the Nordic countries, are able to maintain low-corruption equilibria. This is illustrated with a macro-micro-macro scheme in Figure 10.3. Starting off from a low initial level of corruption at the macro level, individual actors in these countries know what to expect from one another as well as the government. They know that honest behaviour is the norm and, as a result, they exhibit high levels of social trust. Given these high trust levels, individual actors will approach others in an honest and principled manner in their interactions. After all, they know that those others will likely do the same. The macro-level consequence of all these micro-level interactions will thus

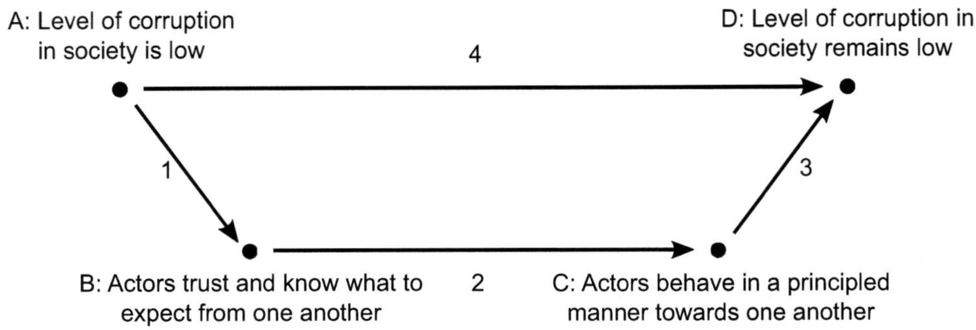

Figure 10.3 Illustration of how a low-corruption equilibrium can sustain itself

be that the overall level of corruption remains low. So, here we observe a positive case of the self-fulfilling prophecy – a virtuous circle.

High-corruption and low-corruption equilibria both tend to be rather stable. That is to say, small deviations from the dominant social norm in each environment will not easily lead to a different equilibrium. If a few people in a failed state, against the dominant social norm of paying and requesting bribes in every transaction, start to act honestly, this will only have a marginal effect on the overall level of corruption, and after a while these few honest actors will probably give up and resume their corrupt behaviours. After all, as Della Porta and Vannucci (1999) convincingly show in their study of political corruption in Italy, there is a high price to being honest in a corrupt society: honest politicians are excluded from governmental roles by their corrupt colleagues, and honest businessmen are excluded from governmental contracts. Similarly, if a few people in a well-functioning state, against the dominant social norm of acting honestly, start to engage in corrupt actions, this will also only have a marginal effect on the overall level of corruption, and the majority of the population will thus remain trusting and non-corrupt in their behaviours.

However, in some cases it is possible for a country to slip from a low level of corruption to a situation of widespread corruption. These dynamics are illustrated in Figure 10.4, again by way of a macro-micro-macro scheme. We can, furthermore, draw a connection with Schelling's *tipping points model* outlined in Chapter 2. While we stated earlier that small increases in the frequency of corrupt behaviour will generally only have little impact on the overall level of

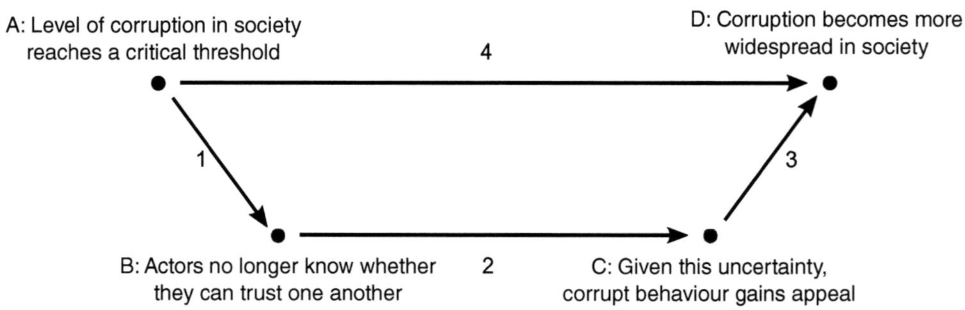

Figure 10.4 Illustration of how a rise in corruption can set off a self-reinforcing spiral

corruption in well-functioning societies, this is only true up to a point. If the increase in corruption exceeds a certain critical threshold (a tipping point), then the individual actors who previously all trusted one another will start to doubt whether their trust is actually justified. By this point, they will probably all have come across corruption at some point, and they will start to wonder whether corruption is actually more widespread than they always thought. Given this uncertainty, individual actors will start to consider engaging in corrupt behaviour themselves, since in a corrupt society those who do not engage in corruption are worst-off (for example, they have to wait the longest for particular services or pay the most for them). In aggregation, this will at the macro level translate into a rise in corruption. This will then, in turn, influence social norms and individual actors' expectations, thus setting off a cascade that eventually leads the country to a high-corruption equilibrium.

Micro-level interactions and action-forming mechanisms

It is worthwhile to elaborate on the micro-level interactions that play out when there is widespread corruption in society. For this purpose, we can make use of the *principal-agent model* discussed in Chapter 2. As discussed there, the principal-agent model applies to situations where some kind of superordinate (the principal) needs to delegate certain tasks to a subordinate (the agent), while being limited in the extent to which they can monitor the behaviour of the subordinate. The subordinate, in turn, has interests of their own that do not necessarily align with the interests of their superordinate, potentially giving rise to a conflict of interest between the two parties.

With respect to corruption, it makes sense to extend the principal-agent model by adding a third party – a client with whom the agent interacts. We thus arrive at a *principal-agent-client model* (see also Groenendijk 1997). This model enables an in-depth analysis of the incentives and motives of the parties that are involved in the corruption process. We assume here that corruption refers to a situation in which the principal entrusts an agent with certain authority, but this agent takes bribes from a third party (the client) for deviating from the rules of behaviour that he had agreed upon with the principal.

One crucial element of these dynamics is that the different parties in this framework each have their own interests, which need not align with each other's. Second, the principal is unable to monitor exactly what is happening between the agent and client. As such, the principal is the less-informed party, the agent is the well-informed party, and the client is the party that conspires with the agent. One could, for example, think of a scenario in which a minister (principal) puts a civil servant (agent) in charge of collecting tenders for a major infrastructural project, where the civil servant accepts bribes from a particular contracting company (client) to give them the job.

Figure 10.5 summarizes the interactions that take place between the principal, the agent, and the client. As indicated by arrow (1), the principal supervises the agent and sets rules and incentives. As indicated by arrow (2), the principal receives information from the agent about their efforts and results, yet cannot directly observe what takes place between the agent and the client. As indicated by arrow (3), the agent interacts with the client and can negotiate with them about services and contracts. As indicated by arrow (4), the client pays the agent for any goods or services exchanged and may also try to exert influence on the agent's behaviour. As indicated by arrows (5a) and (5b), the client can under certain circumstances reach out to the principal – either through private or public channels – thereby by-passing the agent. For example, if the

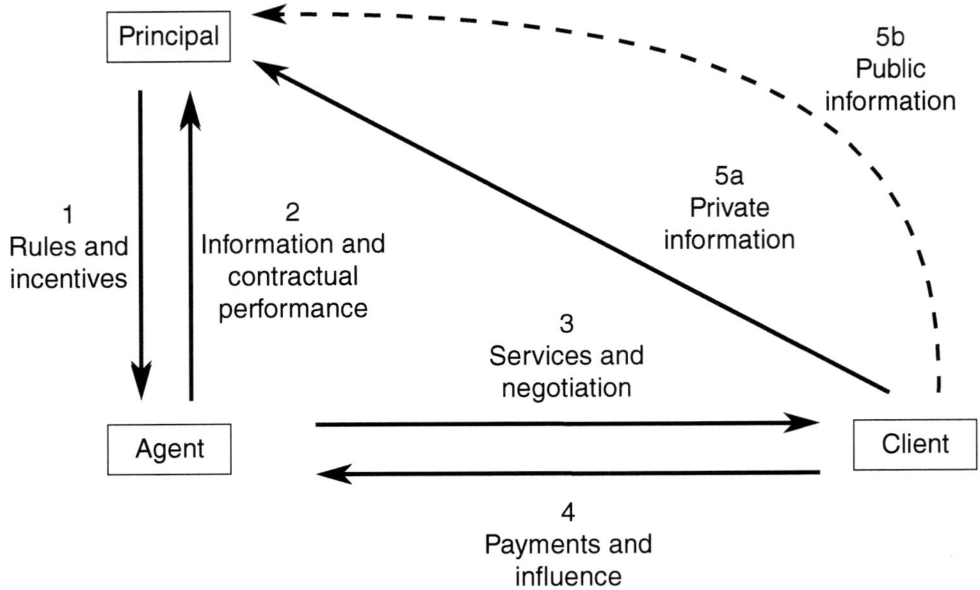

Figure 10.5 The principal-agent-client model and the scope for corruption

client is asked for a bribe by the agent but refuses to be a part of such practices, they might directly contact the principal (5a) or look for publicity in the media (5b). In this context, it will usually be in the interest of the principal to minimize any media attention; and when there is widespread corruption, the principal is likely to be corrupt as well, making the direct information channel less attractive to the client.

Let us now, using the principal-agent-client model, zoom in on the incentives and motives of the various actors involved. To begin with, the principal wants to monitor the agent's behaviour. In this regard, they can choose between two basic strategies:

1 Meticulously monitoring the agent's behaviour. A drawback of this strategy is that it imposes high costs upon the principal (in terms of time and effort). Moreover, it may cause friction with the agent, which may negatively affect the agent's productivity.
2 Monitoring the agent's behaviour less strictly. This strategy gives the agent more freedom and discretion, which is good for the relationship between the principal and the agent, but simultaneously makes effective control more difficult.

The agent, in turn, can choose between roughly three strategies as far as their relationship with the principal is concerned:

1 Fully informing the principal about everything that they do, and fully complying with the rules and behavioural guidelines as set out by the principal. A disadvantage of this strategy is that the agent does not retain much behavioural freedom and discretion, which may hinder the execution of their formal tasks.

2 Operating with a high degree of discretion. This may enable the agent to perform their tasks more efficiently, but it will entail disobeying certain rules set by the principal.
3 In case the organization to which the principal and the agent belong is corrupt, the agent has the option to become a whistle-blower.

When it comes to his relationship with the client, the agent can choose between the following three basic strategies:

1 Acting in line with the guidelines set out by the principal, and keeping distance between themselves and the client by approaching the client in an impersonal and impartial way.
2 Prioritizing networking and good contacts, cultivating a personal relationship with the client, and developing a thorough understanding of the client's situation. This strategy may provide mutual benefits to both the agent and the client.
3 If the agent wants to gain extra money, they might request a bribe from the client in exchange for speeding up procedures or providing preferential treatment. The incentives for corrupt actions are influenced by the overall level of corruption.

In their interactions with the agent, the client can, finally, choose between two core options:

1 Maintaining some distance from the agent, letting the process or transaction be governed by formal rules and impersonal relations. If the client is treated incorrectly by the agent (e.g., asked for a bribe), they might also inform the principal about this corrupt behaviour, through public or private channels.
2 Striving to promote their personal interests vigorously, building a personal relationship with the agent, and asking the agent whether there is anything the client can do in order to get what they want. This may involve offering or agreeing to pay a bribe.

Given this constellation of interests and strategies, the agent and the client could agree on a transaction in which the client pays the agent a sum of money in exchange for a favour. The agent will be well aware that the act of accepting bribes violates the principles of proper public conduct. The agent will also incur personal costs by engaging in corrupt behaviour, in the form of a bad conscience over having dishonoured the norms of good behaviour, as well as in the form of the risk of being caught and punished. Nevertheless, if the bribe offsets the moral objections and the risks involved, the agent will still commit the corrupt behaviour.

The advantage of the principal-agent-client model is that it illustrates that corruption is a matter of trade-offs and choices in micro-level situations. That said, it is important to reiterate that these micro-level trade-offs are heavily influenced by macro-level factors such as the overall level of corruption. After all, the more widespread the corruption is, the smaller the risk of being caught for corrupt agents and clients, and the higher the relative costs for those that remain honest and do not engage in corrupt behaviour (in terms of additional waiting times or increased prices for certain services, or in terms of bribes that one could have asked for but did not). Moreover, while we assumed in our earlier discussion that principals have an interest in controlling the behaviour of agents, this may in fact not apply in cases of widespread corruption, in which the principals themselves are also corrupt.

Micro-to-macro aggregation mechanisms

All else being equal, it is detrimental for clients to have to pay bribes. This becomes clear if we consider the situation of entrepreneurs bribing politicians and civil servants for certain favours. When an increasing number of entrepreneurs start to bribe politicians and civil servants, simple market dynamics will imply that the politicians and civil servants can start asking for larger bribes and that the favours they provide lose some of their value (since nearly everyone now pays bribes and thus has access to these advantages). In short, widespread corruption implies that entrepreneurs will have to pay increasingly large bribes for increasingly useless favours. As such, all clients are worse off when corruption is widespread than if it were absent.

So why would the clients not collectively disengage from corrupt practices? As Della Porta and Vannucci (1999) demonstrate, the answer has to do with a *free-rider problem* that makes it nearly impossible to unite a large number of entrepreneurs in collective action against corruption. It is in this context useful to recall that a low level of corruption can be regarded as a public good – or, vice versa, a high level of corruption can be regarded as a public bad. The public good of a low-corruption society can only be attained if many individual actors all work together to eradicate corruption. However, for each individual actor it will be more attractive to continue engaging in corrupt practices while others are bringing down the overall level of corruption. With every actor applying this same logic, in the end nobody is willing to stop their corrupt behaviours and the total level of corruption in society remains the same.

This outcome is reinforced by the fact that it is especially costly to abstain from corruption if everyone else is involved in corruption. For example, if you are an honest entrepreneur but all of your competitors are corrupt, you might as well close up shop straight away. From this perspective, entrepreneurs will only be willing to refrain from corruption if they have a guarantee that others will do the same. However, such a strategy of conditional honesty cannot become a stable equilibrium, because entrepreneurs lack information on the behaviour of other actors within the clandestine "market for corruption", and a history of corruption will additionally make entrepreneurs very distrustful of one another.

That said, there have been cases in which highly corrupt systems collapsed or witnessed a significant decline in corruption. A prime example concerns Italy in the 1990s, following the so-called *Clean Hands trials* (Della Porta and Vannucci 1999). These were not instigated by the victims of corruption, but rather by a judge (Antonio Di Pietro) who caught and charged a politician for corrupt practices. When some of this politician's associates ended up in prison, others came to expect that their names would soon be given to the authorities too. Politicians and entrepreneurs who had been engaged in corruption thus became scared and decided to turn themselves in, in the hope that this would translate into reduced sentences. Consequently, the legal authorities received a torrent of confessions, and began working together to put the confessors on trial and to catch more criminals by combining information from the various confessors.

Once again, we see here a case of Schelling's *tipping points model*. With every corrupt individual that was caught or turned themselves in, the risk of arrest for all other corrupt individuals rose significantly. As a result, once the number of arrests reached a certain point, there was a huge spike in the number of corrupt individuals that turned themselves in. However, later in the 1990s, the political leaders in Italy terminated the Clean Hands campaign. This happened when the legal inquiry started to increasingly shift towards the alleged corrupt practices of these political leaders themselves.

What can be done about corruption?

Since the 1990s, the anti-corruption movement has gained momentum throughout the world. Promoting good governance has become one of the core targets of international organizations such as the World Bank and the UN. Moreover, Transparency International's annual publication of the Corruption Perceptions Index has put pressure on governments with low CPI scores to improve the reputation of their country. In many of the more corrupt countries, it is now very common that each time a new leader assumes power they announce that the fight against corruption is one of their core priorities. Nevertheless, despite the introduction of, for example, special departments, anti-corruption ministers, investigative commissions and a lot of rhetoric, very few governments have succeeded at realizing significant change. Several anti-corruption ministers have even been accused of corruption themselves.

In view of these disappointing outcomes, the question arises of which actions will be truly effective on the road to eradicating corruption. Looking at the specific recommendations of organizations such as the World Bank, the UN, and Transparency International, we can distinguish at least five fruitful pathways that may help countries getting closer to this goal.

The first pathway is to promote government transparency. Independent auditing agencies should be tasked with evaluating public budgets, which should be published for scrutiny by the general public. Freedom of the press should be nurtured so as to ensure that scandals are faithfully reported to the public when they arise. In Ukraine, a country known for its high level of corruption, a position of Commissioner for Anti-Corruption was installed in 2009 and in 2014 the government launched the National Anti-Corruption Bureau. One of the mandates of this bureau is to collect information about the financial circumstances of high officials and to release this information to the general public. It quickly became apparent that certain officials had amassed huge wealth through illicit activities while in office. By 2016, President Petro Poroshenko, who had initially called for more transparency himself, came to the defence of corrupt officials. This underlines that transparency alone is not enough to eradicate corruption.

A second pathway is to strengthen legislation, implement systematic rules, and apply them consistently. As Transparency International frequently points out, effective law enforcement is essential to ensure that corrupt officials are punished, thereby breaking the cycle of impunity. Given that we live in a highly globalized world nowadays, strengthening the international legal framework for corruption control can be particularly important in this regard. In 2005, the UN Convention against Corruption (UNCAC) came into force and was ratified by a vast majority of UN members. However, since the UN has no enforcement power, the effectiveness of the UNCAC strongly depends on national monitoring to assess compliance. On a related note, some countries have already adopted legislation that forbids their citizens from engaging in bribery abroad. For example, in 1977 the US adopted the Foreign Corrupt Practices Act (FCPA), which penalises the payment of bribes by American citizens or companies to foreign government officials, political parties, and politicians. In 2002, the UK adopted an act with a similar scope.

A third pathway is to make the general public aware that they have the right to a non-corrupt state, and to empower them to demand greater government accountability. Community monitoring initiatives can be useful for detecting corruption and, with increasing access to the internet, these initiatives can connect activists from dispersed locations into a single hub. The public can then play an active role in tracking down and communicating cases of corruption.

A fourth pathway is to restrict the access of corrupt actors to international financial markets. For this purpose, it is important that governments prohibit their banks to accept money flows from suspicious origins. There are currently still many examples of banks being involved in international money laundering, knowingly and willingly. In 2016, the *Panama Papers* – 11.5 million leaked documents revealing how financial institutions facilitate corrupt transactions – provided some insight into this matter. This leak was important for stimulating new anti-corruption measures from various governments, although other governments seem to have conveniently ignored the information laid bare.

In the same spirit as the fourth pathway, Bill Browder (see the section "The difficulty of defining corruption") has been lobbying with numerous governments for the adoption of so-called *Magnitsky Acts*, named after his lawyer Sergei Magnitsky, who died in Russian prison after helping to expose fraud and corruption by Russian state officials. The idea of a Magnitsky Act – which can be applied to perpetrators of corruption as well as human rights violations – is that governments can hit foreign officials involved in corruption where it hurts them the most: namely by restricting the extent to which these foreign officials can enjoy the luxurious lifestyles which they finance through their corrupt activities.

Concrete measures that governments could take as part of a Magnitsky Act include denying corrupt foreign officials future access to banks and other financial services in their country, the freezing of any financial assets that corrupt foreign officials hold in their country (so that these funds can no longer be used), and imposing restrictions on corrupt foreign officials' entry into their country. The US already adopted such a law, specifically aimed at corrupt and fraudulent Russian officials, in the wake of Magnitsky's death. Moreover, the UK adopted in 2018 the Sanctions and Anti-Money Laundering Bill, which is founded on the same principles, and which can be invoked against corrupt officials or human rights violators from any country in the world.

A fifth pathway to combat corruption is to put external pressure on governments of corrupt countries to implement reforms. As mentioned previously, many international organizations, NGOs and other governments are already quite active on this front. However, pressure can also be exerted through other channels, such as international capital markets. Indeed, countries with widespread corruption usually find it difficult to attract foreign capital, and when they succeed at curtailing corruption, they may benefit from more foreign investment.

Finally, the principal-agent-client model discussed in the previous section also offers a number of direct suggestions on how to alter the incentives and opportunities of individual actors in order to reduce corruption. Among other things, civil servants tend to respond strongly to monetary incentives in their decisions whether or not to engage in corruption. From this perspective, raising the salaries of civil servants might make the corruption option less attractive to them. Second, the likelihood of corrupt behaviour tends to decrease as the likelihood of being caught increases. In this light, governments could for example think of additional ways to empower and support whistle-blowers, thereby increasing the chances that corrupt actors get identified and arrested. Third, because close relationships between agents and clients can open the way to illicit transactions, it can be beneficial to impose more distant relationships between agents and clients. New technologies may be able to facilitate this process, as they make repeated personal interactions less needed. For example, organizing more transactions through the internet as opposed to in person can be a successful tool in reducing corruption (Andersen et al. 2011).

Recommended readings

- Anthony Heath, Lindsay Richards, and Nan Dirk de Graaf (2016) offer a broad overview of what social science and especially sociology as a discipline have to offer to the study of corruption. Focusing on corruption in the developed world, they discuss cross-country variation and trends in corruption, based on different data sources and measures. They also look at the predictors of corruption at the national level and discuss a variety of theoretical approaches to corruption, including the principal-agent-client model.
- Richard Rose and Caryn Peiffer (2015) provide a comprehensive study of the topic of paying bribes to public officials, drawing on survey data from more than a hundred countries. Among other things, they chart cross-country variation in people's experiences with paying bribes, their perceptions of how common bribes are, as well as their views on the acceptability of bribes. One of their conclusions is that the majority of people in most parts of the world regard bribery as unacceptable.
- Donatella Della Porta and Alberto Vannucci (2012) go beyond merely describing corruption and dig into the invisible codes and mechanisms that govern the relationships between "corrupters" and "corruptees". In doing so, they rely on a wide range of data, including judicial sources, data from Transparency International, but also the everyday news. Throughout the book they make cross-country comparisons to illustrate how macro-level contexts and micro-level behaviours mutually influence each other.

Bibliography

Andersen, Thomas B., Jeanet Bentzen, Carl-Johan Dalgaard, and Pablo Selaya. 2011. "Does Internet Reduce Corruption? Evidence from US States and Across Countries". *World Bank Economic Review* 25:387–417.

Beetham, David. 2015. "Moving Beyond a Narrow Definition of Corruption". Pp. 41–46 in *How Corrupt is Britain?*, edited by David Whyte. London: Pluto Press.

Browder, Bill. 2015. *Red Notice – How I Became Putin's No.1 Enemy*. London: Bantam Press.

Della Porta, Donatella, and Alberto Vannucci. 1999. *Corrupt Exchanges: Actors, Resources, and Mechanisms of Political Corruption*. New York, NY: Aldine de Gruyter.

Della Porta, Donatella, and Alberto Vannucci. 2012. *The Hidden Order of Corruption: An Institutional Approach*. Farnham: Ashgate.

Donchev, Dilyan, and Gergely Ujhelyi. 2014. "What Do Corruption Indices Measure?". *Economics and Politics* 26:309–331

Gächter, Simon, and Jonathan F. Schulz. 2016. "Intrinsic Honesty and the Prevalence of Rule Violations Across Societies". *Nature* 531:486–499.

Groenendijk, Nico. 1997. "A Principal-Agent Model of Corruption". *Crime, Law & Social Change* 27:207–229.

Heath, Anthony, Lindsay Richards and Nan Dirk De Graaf. 2016. "Explaining Corruption in the Developed World: The Potential of Sociological Approaches". *Annual Review of Sociology* 42:51–79.

Heywood, Paul M., and Jonathan Rose. 2014. "'Close but no Cigar': The Measurement of Corruption". *Journal of Public Policy* 34:507–529.
Jancsics, David. 2014. "Interdisciplinary Perspectives on Corruption". *Sociology Compass* 8:358–372.
Lambsdorff, Johann G. 2006. "Measuring Corruption – The Validity and Precision of Subjective Indicators (CPI)". Pp. 81–99 in *Measuring Corruption*, edited by Charles J. Sampford, Arthur H. Shacklock, Carmel Connors, and Fredrik Galtung. Aldershot: Ashgate
Lessig, Lawrence. 2013. "Institutional Corruption Defined". *Journal of Law Medicine and Ethics* 41: 553–555.
Olken, Benjamin A. 2009. "Corruption Perceptions Versus Corruption Reality". *Journal of Public Economics* 93:950–964
Rose, Richard, and Caryn Peiffer. 2015. *Paying Bribes for Public Services: A Global Guide To Grass-Roots Corruption*. Basingstoke: Palgrave Macmillan.
Rothstein, Bo, and Aiysha Varraich. 2017. *Making Sense of Corruption*. Cambridge: Cambridge University Press.
UNDP. 1998. *Corruption and Integrity Improvement in Developing Countries*. New York, NY: United Nations.
Uslaner, Eric M., and Bo Rothstein. 2012. "Mass Education, State-Building and Equality: Searching for the Roots of Corruption". Working Paper 2012:5, Quality of Government Institute, University of Gothenburg.
Weber Abramo, Claudio. 2008. "How Much do Perceptions of Corruption Really Tell us?". *Economics Open-Access* 2:1–56.
Weber, Max. 1978[1925]. *Economy and Society: An Outline of Interpretive Sociology* (Wirtschaft und Gesellschaft: Grundriss der Verstehenden Soziologie). Berkeley, CA: University of California Press.

11 The fragility of the financial system

Chapter overview

Well-functioning financial markets represent a public good, yet problems often arise in these markets, throwing large sections of society into disarray. This chapter starts with a review of various market crashes throughout history, including the financial crisis of 2008, the Great Crash of 1929, but also the Tulip Mania of 1637. To better understand these events, we consider how individual actors make decisions under conditions of risk and uncertainty, referring to various cognitive biases and concepts such as bounded rationality and Black Swan events. We then proceed by explaining what happens at the macro level when individual actors interact. In this respect, we highlight the role of social contagion mechanisms and tipping points. Next, we shift our discussion to the behaviour of banks and other financial institutions, and especially their incentives for excessive risk-taking. Finally, we discuss how the complexity and interconnectedness of the financial system give rise to systemic weaknesses, and make it difficult for governments and regulatory authorities to effectively intervene. Among other things, we outline moral hazard problems that occur when banks are considered too-important-to-fail.

Bubbles and crashes throughout history

Well-functioning financial markets and institutions potentially bring great benefits to society. They enable actors with a surplus of money to gain interest on their savings or to make profits through investing their money. At the same time, they enable other actors with a shortage of money to borrow, thus allowing them to realize projects that they would otherwise have had to leave unfulfilled. Financial markets and institutions play a crucial role in bringing both of these parties together. Moreover, they often do so in ways that reduce the risks for each party involved. As such, the financial system helps to make more efficient and effective use of the funds that are available in the economy, thereby stimulating economic growth and prosperity. Importantly, it is not just the actors who want to invest their money, or who are seeking money, that benefit from the financial system, but society as a whole. After all, every member of society could, in principle, benefit from the additional economic growth that is generated or the technological innovations that are made possible through the help of financial markets and institutions. In short, a well-functioning financial system has many characteristics of a public good.

That said, the financial system is also vulnerable in many ways. In this regard, the economist John Maynard Keynes (2010[1930]:126) described the financial system as "a delicate machine, the working of which we do not understand". When the financial system crashes, many people suffer. People with savings or investments may lose part of their money, financial institutions may collapse, and economic growth may be stalled for a prolonged period, resulting in increased unemployment and public budget cuts. Such crises can also destroy people's trust in financial markets and institutions, which in turn may take a long time to rebuild. Interestingly, financial crises represent a recurrent phenomenon, showing up at more or less regular intervals throughout history. The fact that such recurrent episodes display many parallels suggests that some common forces are behind them. Next we discuss several prominent crashes that have taken place over the past centuries, generally preceded by so-called bubbles in which financial markets were booming and prices of financial products skyrocketed.

The Tulip Mania of 1637

One of the earliest known bubbles occurred in the Netherlands in the seventeenth century around the trade of tulip bulbs. It is important to stress that we are talking here about a relatively benign bubble that did not result in major economic losses for anyone involved when it ultimately burst. However, aside from the fact that it is a fascinating story, it is useful to discuss the Tulip Mania because it lays bare some of the underlying dynamics that are also relevant for bubbles and crashes that came later, and that did result in significant distress and chaos. The economic historian Peter Garber (1989) has studied the Tulip Mania extensively, and here we draw upon his research.

As Garber notes, tulips are originally from Turkey and only made it to Western Europe around the middle of the sixteenth century. The tulip was pretty much immediately accepted by the wealthy elites of Western Europe as a beautiful and rare flower, a proper asset to one's garden, and a sign of status. As a result, an active market for tulip bulbs quickly came into existence, and the Dutch were at the forefront of this market, being extremely prolific in the development of new tulip varieties. Since tulip bulbs were able to yield flowers every year, they represented an investment rather than a product meant for simple, short-term consumption. Interestingly, the highest prices were paid for diseased bulbs affected by a virus that in some cases created beautiful patterns on the tulip. However, this blight also meant these beautiful bulbs had a reduced reproduction rate, ensuring their rarity status and justifying their high prices.

One of the consequences of these high prices paid for rare varieties was that tulip bulbs became a popular object of financial speculation, with many new traders entering the market. These new entrants were not so much interested in the tulip bulbs as such, but were rather hoping to make money by buying bulbs and then later selling them at a profit. As a result of this increased demand, the prices of tulip bulbs rose and became an object of interest in and of themselves, thus to some extent their trading value became divorced from the "objective value" of the underlying product.

The speculative trade in tulip bulbs flourished especially in pubs and a so-called *futures market* developed. This meant that people started to trade promises to buy or sell a given bulb at a given price at some point in the future. For example, person A could promise to sell a certain bulb to person B for one guilder in six months' time. If then, after six months, the market price of that bulb was less than a guilder, person A would make a profit when this contract was executed; if, on the other hand, the market price was more than a guilder, person A would make a loss and person B would take a profit. Since person A could simultaneously, for example, also make a promise to *buy* that same type of bulb for half a guilder from person C in six months, and also engage in many other futures contracts, this market was really about making bets and, generally speaking, did not even involve the actual transfer of tulip bulbs.

This futures market had several noteworthy features that made it particularly prone to speculation. Aside from the fact that no actual tulip bulbs were exchanged, there was also no collateral needed – for example, one could promise to buy a certain bulb without needing to prove that one had the money required to do so. Moreover, as this trade often took place in pubs, much of it was, in the end, only about the participants' "wine money" – that is, debt and credit accounts the speculators held with their publican. This imposed a serious cap on the losses that speculators could actually incur, as they were not obliged to pay back any losses that exceeded their wine money. This all meant that people gradually started to make increasingly large bets on tulip bulb prices, because there was no real risk involved.

In the meantime, in addition to betting on the future price for rare tulip bulbs, people had started to speculate on common tulip bulbs. As a result, common tulip bulbs also became more expensive, even though their rarity did not warrant any price increases. In January 1637, the market really heated up, with the price of many common bulbs rising by a factor of 20 to 30. For example, while the *Witte Croonen* variety sold for 128 guilders per pound in the beginning of January, its price had exploded to 3,336 guilders per pound by the first week of February. However, shortly after this explosive rise the market crashed and the prices of tulip bulbs plummeted, with the price of the *Witte Croonen* variety, for example, falling to only five percent of its peak value within a week.

In short, after a period of gradually increasing prices and then accelerated price increases, during which the bubble grew and grew, it eventually burst and caused a spectacular crash in bulb prices. One of the interesting things behind these price trends – and indeed behind many later bubbles and crashes – is that it is unclear what exactly made the tulip bubble burst and set off the downward spiral in price levels. However, what is clear is that once the prices stopped increasing and started to drop, the same type of social dynamics that had made the prices increase in the first place also made them come down with astonishing speed. While people were initially keen to enter the market simply because they saw that many others did so, once the prices stalled, suddenly everyone wanted to get out of the market. This tendency of individual actors to follow – sometimes almost blindly – the behaviour of other actors is sometimes referred to in terms such as *herding behaviour, social contagion*, and *mob psychology*, and gives rise to *feedback loops* and *self-fulfilling prophecies*.

The Great Crash of 1929

While the Tulip Mania can be considered a fairly whimsical episode without serious harm done to anyone involved – Peter Garber elsewhere (1990:39) describes it as "little more than a midwinter diversion among tavern regulars mimicking more serious traders" – later bubbles and crashes have certainly been far less whimsical and inconsequential. Indeed, if we fast-forward three centuries, we arrive at one of the defining events of the twentieth century, namely the Great Crash of 1929. This was the bursting of the stock market bubble that had been building up during the 1920s. While only a relatively small and wealthy portion of the population directly suffered from this event, the global economic depression that ensued threw millions of people into poverty and played a key role in the lead-up to the Second World War.

The Great Crash and the preceding stock market bubble are illustrated in Figure 11.1. This figure shows the inflation-adjusted trend in stock prices for the period 1881–1931 as well as the ratio between these stock prices and the average earnings of the underlying companies in the previous ten years, which are an indicator of how much dividend one can expect to earn on one's stock holdings. In this context, a stock represents a share in a company's future profits, which are distributed among stockholders through dividends. As Figure 11.1 shows, stock prices began to rise in the 1920s as general optimism started to build after the economically tough 1910s. The economy was booming in these years, so from that perspective there was good reason for stock prices to go up. As investors expected companies' profits to go up, they were keen to join in on these gains.

Yet, as stock prices were steadily increasing this attracted a new kind of investor to the market. These investors did not just want to share in the profits of the underlying companies, and were not even interested in longer-term stock ownership, but saw an opportunity to make money in the short run by buying stocks and subsequently selling them at higher price. As a consequence, the actual value of the underlying business and their expected future profit streams became much less relevant. In addition, the optimism regarding stock price trends gave rise

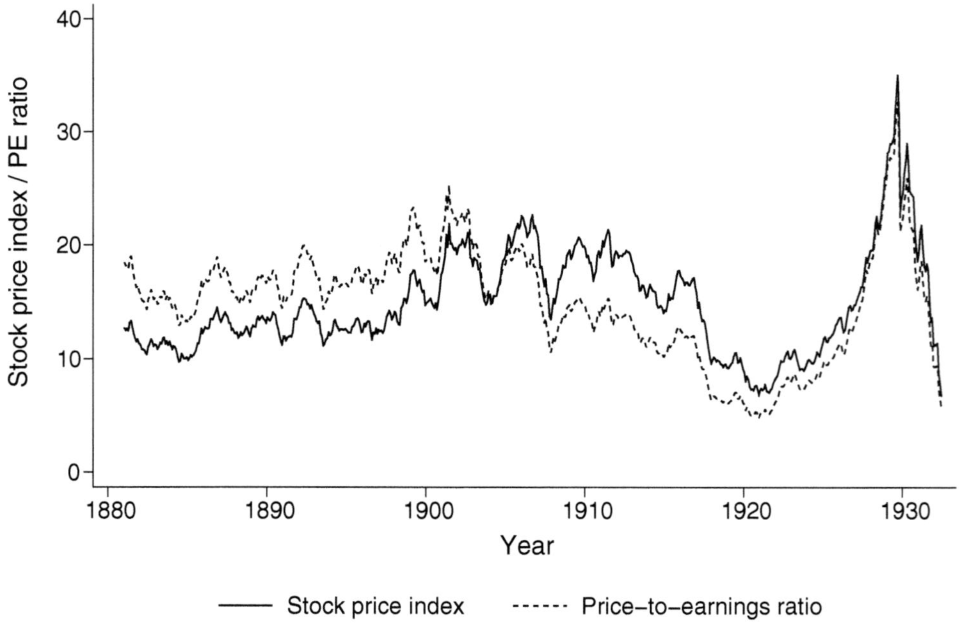

Figure 11.1 Stock prices and the price-to-earnings ratio in the United States, 1881-1931

Note: Data are from Robert Shiller's US Stock Markets 1871-Present and CAPE Ratio dataset, available online via http://www.econ.yale.edu/~shiller/data.htm. All figures have been adjusted to 1920 price levels. The stock price index is Standard & Poor's Composite Index, which is nowadays called S&P 500. The price-to-earnings ratio is defined as the current stock price index divided by the earnings (averaged over the preceding ten years) of the companies listed in the index.

to a *self-fulfilling prophecy*: investors expected rising prices, therefore entered the market or expanded their stakes, and with many investors applying this same logic, prices did indeed rise as a result. The similarities with the Tulip Mania are obvious.

As with many bubbles, the rising trend in prices was bolstered by financial innovations of which the consequences were not necessarily fully understood yet. In particular, the foundation of *investment trusts* was important. This meant that instead of investing directly in individual companies, people could put their money in trusts that invested it on their behalf. Advantages of this practice were that the investment trusts could maintain bigger, more diversified portfolios, thereby reducing the overall risk of one's investment, and offered professional expertise and market analysis. As a result, many smaller investors now entered the market, stimulated also by the belief that everyone should have the opportunity to be rich – a belief promoted by, among others, the Democratic Party.

All of these forces jointly led to a steep rise in stock prices in the late 1920s. The economist John Kenneth Galbraith (1961[1954]:19) later referred to these events as a "speculative orgy", which he describes as "one of the suicidal tendencies of the economic system". It is also relevant here to stress, as Figure 11.1 shows, that the steep increase in stock prices was paralleled by an equally steep increase in the price-to-earnings ratio. This demonstrates that the earnings of the underlying companies did not necessarily justify the steep increase in stock prices, and that the latter was more likely driven by speculation (that is, people buying stocks based on the expectation that stock prices would continue to rise). Indeed, the economist Robert Shiller (2000:xii) describes bubbles as situations "in which temporarily high prices are sustained largely by investors' enthusiasm rather than by consistent estimation of real value".

Despite the firm belief that stock prices would continue to rise, there came a point where prices had risen so much that nobody either wanted or was able to buy any more stocks. This exhaustion of the market meant that prices stopped rising. This was a crucial development, since so many people were in the market based on the expectation that prices would continue to rise and that they could make a profit re-selling their stocks at a later date. With prices no longer rising, this no longer seemed possible and suddenly everyone wanted to sell their stocks. By no means was this a coordinated process: all individual investors simply wanted to get out before the prices dropped even further. Yet with almost every investor applying the same logic, the prices could only go down and the result was the huge crash of the autumn of 1929. The turnaround in investors' mood was spectacularly quick. As Galbraith (1961[1954]:153) notes, "within a few days something close to universal trust turned into something akin to universal suspicion".

Nevertheless, as Figure 11.1 shows, the crash did not represent a straight-line drop, but rather one with some upward spikes also. This reflected that many people remained optimistic – perhaps out of wishful thinking – that the market would recover. For example, Irving Fisher, one of the first neoclassical economists, who on the eve of the crash had noted that "stock prices have reached what looks like a permanently high plateau", in late October, when prices had already dropped by twenty percent, still maintained that this decline had merely been the "shaking out of a lunatic fringe". Likewise, the Harvard Economic Society still argued in May 1930 that the market remained fundamentally strong and sound "despite existing irregularities". However, in the end, such statements were insufficient to counterbalance the panic that had replaced the previously optimistic mood. Consequently, the stock market lost about one-third of its value between September and November 1929, and within three years only 15 percent of the September 1929 value was left.

Reflecting several decades later on the Great Crash, Galbraith (1961[1954]) noted that speculative episodes like this require a pervasive sense of confidence and optimism. He furthermore argued that such episodes will always end the same way (that is, with a big crash), with the only question being how long the bubble will last. Yet, he argues that similar episodes will also always reoccur, with the length of the interval in between roughly indicating how long it takes to forget what happened before. In Galbraith's (1961[1954]:188) words, "A speculative outbreak has a greater or less immunizing effect. The ensuing collapse automatically destroys the very mood speculation requires. (. . .) [Yet] with time and the dimming of memory, the immunity wears off".

The Credit Crunch of 2007–2010

It is tempting to conclude that there indeed had been a significant dimming of memory before the next big financial crisis occurred in the late 2000s. This crash had its origin partially in the American housing market, where a bubble had been brewing since the late 1990s. This is illustrated in Figure 11.2, which plots the development of the real (that is, inflation-adjusted) house price index since 1953, where an index score of 100 corresponds to the 1953 benchmark. For most of the second half of the twentieth century real house prices oscillated around this benchmark, but from 1998–2005 real house prices rapidly rose by as much as 70 percent.

One of the factors contributing to this boom was that many people who had previously been unable to afford to buy a home now entered the housing market in massive numbers, and took out so-called *subprime mortgages*. In doing so, they were encouraged by the reigning

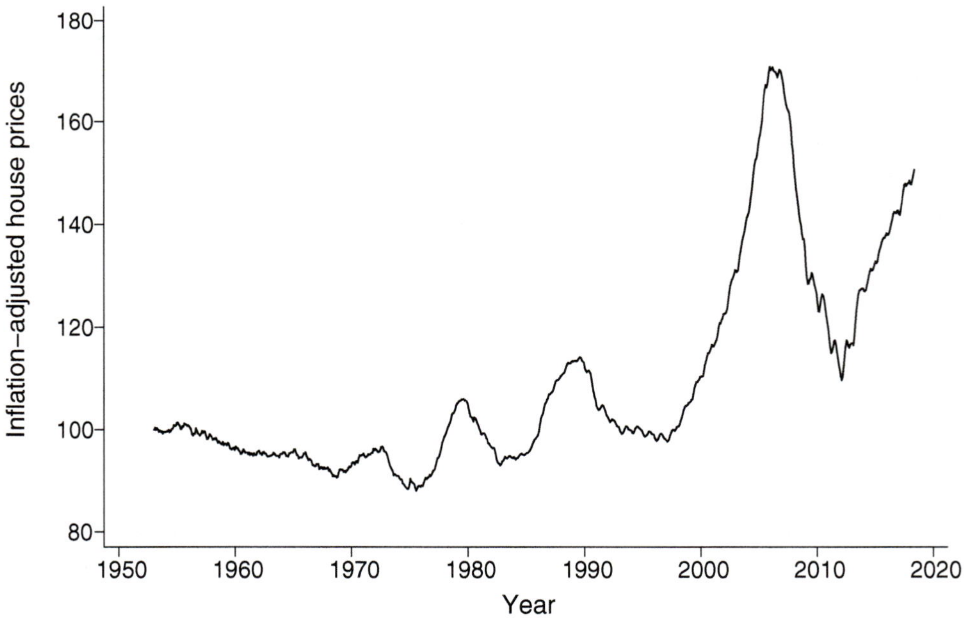

Figure 11.2 Trends in inflation-adjusted house prices in the United States, 1953-2018

Note: Data are from Robert Shiller's US Home Prices 1890-Present dataset, available online via http://www.econ.yale.edu/~shiller/data.htm. The inflation-adjusted house prices are tracked with 1953 as benchmark, with the index number for 1953 equalling 100.

political elites. For example, in October 2002 American president George W. Bush stated, "We can put light where there's darkness, and hope where there's despondency in this country. And part of it is working together as a nation to encourage folks to own their own home." One year later, he signed into law the *American Dream Downpayment Initiative*, which was meant to help families with their down payment and closing costs on property purchases, justifying this act by stating that "the dream of homeownership should be attainable for every hardworking American". In other words, while in the 1920s there was a widespread belief that everyone should have the opportunity to become rich, the early 2000s were characterized by a widespread belief that everyone should be able to own a home.

There were two other factors that made it possible for these new homeowners to enter the market. First, there was the very fact that house prices were rising swiftly. As a result, financial institutions were quite happy to extend mortgages to these new borrowers, knowing that the underlying real estate would transfer to them in case of a default. The borrowers, in turn, could benefit from the rising house prices by renegotiating their mortgages, making it easier to pay them back. Second, an important financial innovation had taken place in the form of the *securitization* of mortgages. In a nutshell, this practice implied that various mortgages, but also other debt contracts, were combined into a single package, which was subsequently sold as a bond or collateralized debt obligation (CDO) to investors, who thereby became entitled to the interest payments and other cash flows related to the mortgages within the package. The packaging of multiple mortgages meant that default risks were pooled, thus making these packages – at least under fair-weather circumstances – less risky than individual mortgages. Hence, they became popular investment vehicles, allowing mortgage providers to increase their supply of mortgage lending.

Not unlike the futures market introduced in seventeenth century Netherlands, and the investment trusts that made their entrance in the 1920s, these *mortgage-backed securities* carried a lot of promise. Yet, notwithstanding the opportunities they opened up, the working of these mortgage-backed securities was not fully understood by most people. Indeed, because the packages typically combined mortgages of various quality (as defined by default risks etc.) and had limited transparency, even experts struggled to monitor the risks involved. As became painfully clear in the crisis of the late 2000s, this meant that these packages carried a huge threat to the financial system as a whole.

In particular, problems started to emerge when the American housing market began to stagnate from the end of 2005 onwards. The immediate effect was that many subprime borrowers, who were dependent on continuously rising house prices, ran into trouble with paying off their mortgages. While in the "old world" the resulting burden of this would simply have been carried by the mortgage providers, who would witness defaults on their mortgage lending, things were different now due to the substantial rise in mortgage-backed securities, which had penetrated many parts of the financial system.

If these mortgage-backed securities had been totally transparent, it would still have been fairly straightforward who would have needed to take these losses (that is, the investors at the end of the chain). However, given their complex and impenetrable character, it had become entirely unclear who was at risk precisely. Since it was practically impossible for investors to make out which bonds and CDOs had suffered losses and to what extent, they became highly suspicious, withdrawing funds they had invested and being unwilling to invest any more in mortgage-backed securities. These kinds of confidence problems also spread to other parts of the financial system with, among other things, the market for interbank lending freezing up.

In short, the confidence and trust issues set off by poorly performing mortgage-backed securities had a paralyzing impact on the financial system. These developments had a particularly big impact on investment banks (that is, banks that do not take deposits but rather help clients – often corporations – raising financial capital or assisting them with mergers and acquisitions). Since investment banks rely heavily on short-term financing, they were suddenly in serious trouble when credit markets dried up. The first clear sign of this was that the investment bank Bear Stearns had to be taken over by JPMorgan Chase in the spring of 2008 in order to avoid bankruptcy.

Another investment bank entering rough waters was Lehman Brothers, which had been the largest producer of securities based on subprime mortgages in the preceding years. Inevitably, they incurred severe losses on their holdings of these securities, while they were simultaneously – like any other investment bank – highly dependent on short-term finance and thus lenders' confidence. Yet, following the near bankruptcy of Bear Stearns, there was very little confidence left in the market and investors were getting increasingly nervous, fuelled by rumours that Lehman Brothers was going to be the next investment bank to collapse. The public authorities therefore tried to stimulate other market parties to take over Lehman, but as these attempts failed, the question increasingly became whether the central bank or the state would step in to save Lehman from bankruptcy.

There was at this point a high level of confidence in the market that the government would indeed intervene and not allow a large player like Lehman Brothers to collapse. This confidence was built up ever since the failure of a large American bank in 1984 – the biggest bank failure in history until then. The idea was that the state would not allow such an event to happen again. Be that as it may, the state in the end did not step in and Lehman Brothers had to file for bankruptcy on 15 September 2008. Whether this lack of intervention reflected an underestimation of the consequences, or rather a fear that if this bank were bailed out many others would follow, is unclear to this day.

As a consequence of Lehman's bankruptcy, institutions and investors with direct ties to Lehman (of which there were many) suffered huge losses. However, there were also large indirect effects – among other things there was the fear and rumours that other banks were facing similar problems and could also fall. Moreover, investors had got the impression that the US authorities had lost control of what was happening. The ensuing panic and crisis of confidence in the financial system led to stock markets taking a big hit in the autumn of 2008 and many investors losing great amounts of money. These events subsequently marked the beginning of the *Great Recession*, the aftermath of which is still very much felt in many parts of the world.

Bounded rationality, Black Swans, and cognitive biases

Although separated by up to four centuries, the three historical episodes discussed in the previous section exhibit striking similarities. Each of them initially features rising prices driven by a pervasive sense of optimism, new players entering the market, and financial innovations, yet each of them subsequently also features an impressive crash in which optimism rapidly turns into suspicion and distrust, leaving behind a market that only represents a fraction of its peak value. The recurrent character of these crashes combined with the harm they bring about raises the question of why we do not seem to learn from our past experiences. As mentioned, Galbraith (1961[1954]) points in this regard to our limited memory. However, is there perhaps more going on? To shed light on this question, this section zooms in on the behaviour of individual actors in financial markets. We focus here on investors, saving a discussion of the behaviour of financial institutions, governments, and regulators for the section "Financial institutions' risk-taking and government intervention".

A first point to note is that, despite the strong similarities between the three episodes described in the previous section, they each also have their unique circumstances. This is particularly apparent regarding the financial innovations that pop up in each episode: in seventeenth century Netherlands there were no investment trusts yet and in the 1920s mortgage-backed securities were still nowhere to be found. These innovations opened up many opportunities and thus played a significant role in explaining the market booms in the 1920s and 2000s, but at the same time the risks they involved were not immediately fully understood.

We can draw a link here with the concept of *bounded rationality* (Simon 1947) introduced in Chapter 2. This means that people's behaviour may deviate from what is optimal given their preferences due to limits they face in acquiring and processing all the information that is relevant to come to an optimal course of action. As a consequence, people may get things wrong in complex situations. This is what happened in the 2008 financial crisis with investors' valuations of mortgage-back securities: packaging together mortgages with varying durations, interest rates and risk levels, meant that even the most expert investors struggled to estimate the risks involved in these securities. Indeed, rating agencies often gave such packages an AAA rating, suggesting that they were almost as safe an investment as government bonds, even though many of them later turned out to contain subprime mortgages that lost pretty much all of their value when the housing bubble burst.

Notwithstanding the role of bounded rationality, which can explain why people get complex problems wrong, human behaviour also exhibits cognitive biases that imply that we get even utterly simple problems wrong. As the social psychologist Daniel Kahneman (2011) demonstrates, this is especially true for situations that are subject to risk and uncertainty, which is exactly the environment that investors usually find themselves in. In this context, Kahneman distinguishes two distinct systems of thinking that we can rely on: *System 1* (thinking fast) and *System 2* (thinking slow). The economist Andrei Shleifer (2012:3) summarizes System 1 as "intuitive, automatic, and effortless: it answers questions quickly through associations and resemblances", and additionally states that it is non-statistical and gullible. System 2, on the other hand, is "what economists think of as thinking: it is conscious, slow, controlled, deliberate, effortful, statistical, suspicious, and costly to use".

Kahneman argues that in many situations, including very consequential ones, people do not go through the effort of engaging System 2, but rather revert to System 1. This also applies to investors. For example, when Robert Shiller (2000) asked investors in a survey what motivated their predictions on the direction in which the stock market would move, the majority referred to things such as intuition, gut feeling, historical evidence, and common sense, or market psychology. This was not only true for private investors but also for institutional investors such as pension fund managers. In this context, already in the 1930s, Keynes noted that many economic decisions probably result from "animal spirits" (spontaneous urges, gut instincts) as opposed to formalized, quantitative cost-benefit analyses.

One particularly prominent expression of System 1 thinking in the financial sphere concerns the *representativeness heuristic*. The underlying idea is that when people are confronted with an unfamiliar problem, they attempt to solve it by looking for resemblances with more familiar situations. So, before solving the actual problem, we represent it in our minds, and, as a typical System 1 process, we do this quickly and automatically. Investors considering whether or not to invest in a certain company, for example, are likely to quickly draw connections with the performance of other companies in the same industry or with the past performance of the company in question. Especially the latter type of connection – that is, *extrapolation*: the expectation that an ongoing trend will continue – is widely applied among investors and plays a crucial role in the emergence of bubbles. However, while extrapolation may often provide an efficient shortcut to making decisions, and does not always need to result in harmful outcomes, it obviously ignores that what goes up must come down, and that past results provide no guarantee of future success. In short, when we represent a problem using our System 1 thinking, we draw on things like our perception of the problem and our memory of other problems, but in this process not all of the decision-relevant information will come to mind and this will subsequently lead to errors.

The influence of the representativeness heuristic is one of the reasons why people are often overconfident (also known as the *overconfidence bias*) as well as overly optimistic about the expected success of their decisions. Indeed, by connecting problems that come up to familiar situations and patterns that seem similar, we will often fail to take into account specific complexities of the new problem, giving rise to a false sense of knowledge and control. After all, when looking for similarities with familiar situations, we are inevitably bound by the situations that we know of and we often easily forget that there are many other potential situations that we do not know of.

Kahneman (2011) introduces in this context the concept of *What You See Is All There Is (WYSIATI)*. We clarify this concept in Table 11.1, which provides a typology of phenomena by one's degree of knowledge about them (that is, whether we know something or not) and one's degree of knowledge awareness (that is, whether or not we know whether we know something). This knowledge awareness can also be interpreted as second-order knowledge. In this classification, we have four types of phenomena: *Known Knowns* (e.g., I know that I know the answer to the question "what is two times two?"), *Known Unknowns* (e.g., I know that I do not know how warm it will be in a hundred days), *Unknown Knowns* (e.g., if someone has implicitly shared their PIN code with me, but I did not realize), and *Unknown Unknowns* (e.g., events that elicit the response "who could have ever guessed?" when they happen). Kahneman notes that when people make decisions, they primarily rely on Known Knowns, they sporadically take into consideration Known Unknowns, but that they appear largely oblivious to Unknown Unknowns. The existence of Unknown Unknowns thus implies that people think they know more about the world than they actually do and that they tend to be overconfident about their decisions.

The statistician and former trader Nassim Nicholas Taleb has written extensively about the general influence of Unknown Unknowns as well as people's struggle in dealing with these phenomena, in his book *The Black Swan* (2010) and elsewhere. Taleb uses the term *Black Swan*

Table 11.1 A typology of phenomena by our knowledge about them

		Degree of knowledge	
		Known phenomenon	**Unknown phenomenon**
Degree of knowledge awareness	**Aware**	Known Knowns	Known Unknowns
	Unaware	Unknown Knowns	Unknown Unknowns

to refer to extreme events with a major impact that we generally fail to predict before they take place. The metaphor is derived from the belief commonly held up to the late seventeenth century in the Western world that all swans were white, which was in 1697 disproved in the blink of an eye as Dutch explorers saw a black swan in Australia. As Taleb (2010:xxi) notes, this story "illustrates a severe limitation to our learning from observations or experience and the fragility of knowledge. One single observation can invalidate a general statement derived from millennia of confirmatory sightings of millions of white swans."

According to Taleb, many important historical events represent Black Swans, ranging from the consequences of the assassination of Archduke Franz Ferdinand of Austria in 1914 and the precipitous collapse of the Soviet bloc in the late 1980s to the spread of the internet and the terrorist attacks of 9/11. Importantly, Taleb argues that with the world growing ever more complex, Black Swan events are becoming increasingly common, making what we do not know more important than what we know. That is, Known Knowns are losing importance and Unknown Unknowns are gaining relevance.

The Black Swan logic can be readily applied to the occurrence of financial crises in general and certainly also the most recent one of 2008. Indeed, the risk assessments of investors, financial institutions, regulators and governments in the period leading up to this crisis were very much based on Known Knowns and Known Unknowns, but did not sufficiently factor in risks that fell outside the realm of previous observations and experiences. At the same time, such risks were abundantly present in the complex environment of the twenty-first century financial system, containing new types of securities and increasingly interconnected financial institutions. Previous experiences and knowledge derived from past observations only provided limited guidance on how to deal with these new circumstances. This meant that very few people saw the crisis coming.

Taleb criticizes in this context the dominant usage of the *bell curve* in estimating risks. This curve (see Figure 11.3) depicts a normal probability distribution, in which the most likely events are located near the centre (the mean outcome), with the likelihood of occurrence dropping fast as one moves away from the centre. As a result, extreme outlier events get assigned miniscule probabilities and are often deemed impossible and thus ignored altogether. Taleb considers the widespread usage of bell curves a major analytical flaw, even labelling it as a "great intellectual fraud". He argues that, especially as our world is growing more complex and interdependent, extreme outliers are much more likely to occur than the bell curve suggests, as possibilities abound in which one minor event can set off a powerful chain of subsequent reactions. For example, the 2005 slow-down of the American housing market did not only affect home owners in the US, but investors around the world who were holding securities containing US subprime mortgages, and the demise of one bank (Lehman Brothers) had huge spillover effects on other financial institutions, pushing the whole financial system into disarray.

Interestingly, while people struggle to prospectively predict Black Swan events, we tend to be very good at retrospectively rationalizing ("postdicting") them, aided by the benefit of hindsight. Indeed, aside from rarity and extreme impact, Taleb considers this the third characteristic of Black Swans. He notes (2012:385), "There will be after every event many more postdictors than true predictors, people who had an idea in the shower without taking it to its logical conclusion, and, given that many people take a lot of showers, say, nearly twice a day (if you include the gym or the episode with the mistress), they will have a large repertoire to draw from."

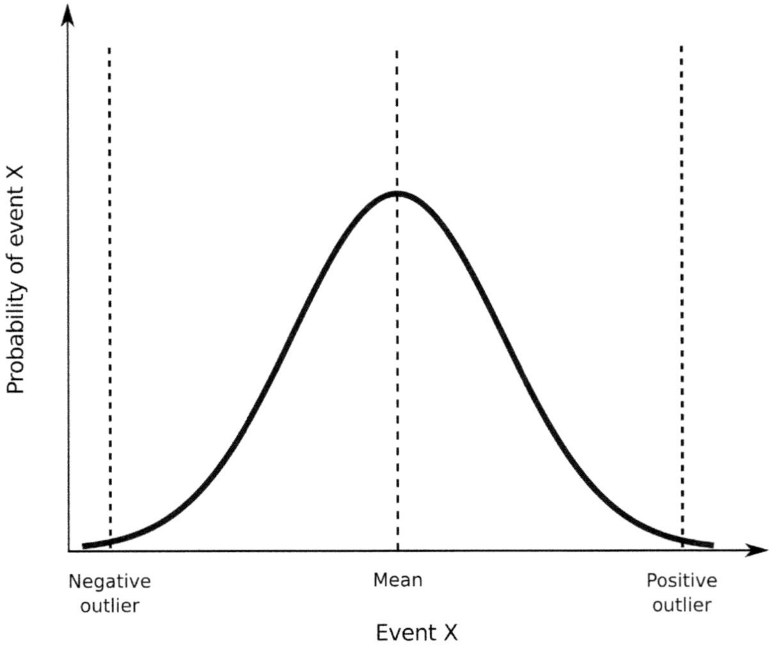

Figure 11.3 Illustration of the bell curve

Note: The graph plots the probability of an event X occurring, where X could, for example, refer to a change in stock prices.

Such *hindsight bias*, whereby an event appears to be understood after its occurrence, encourages a view of the world as more predictable than it actually is, adding to people's overconfidence and under-appreciation of the role of chance. This very illusion of predictability makes us more vulnerable when it comes to future Black Swans and may help to explain why financial crises keep occurring throughout history.

Before closing this section, we should spend a few words on how people (and investors in particular) tend to deal with gains and losses. Gains are generally associated with positive mental experiences, giving people a sense of satisfaction, joy, pride and accomplishment. All of these mental states also have a certain addictive element. This is especially apparent among gamblers, who are often tempted to continue betting when they are "in the winning mood" or having "hot hands", but many investors are not immune to these thoughts either. This tendency is reinforced by the fact that previous gains make one wealthier. As Shiller (2000:57) states, people may consequently feel like they are "playing with the house money" and thus have less to lose. Related to the earlier discussed overconfidence bias and the illusion of control, there is also a tendency among investors to attribute any gains to their own abilities and intellect, even though gains often occur in a rising market that "lifts all boats" (Shiller 2000:59). This tendency can further increase one's appetite to continue trading once one is winning. Finally, the experience of seeing others make gains while being a bystander oneself can evoke feelings of envy and fuel a desire of wanting to get in on it too.

Losses, in turn, involve a completely different ball game. Aside from implying a worsening of one's financial position, they give rise to feelings of sadness, disappointment, regret, and sometimes failure. It is, furthermore, not uncommon for people to experience difficulty in accepting losses. Kahneman (2011) has, through his experiments, for example, shown that human behaviour is subject to *loss aversion* and a *sunk cost fallacy*. Loss aversion means that people have a stronger preference for avoiding losses than they have for making gains. In more technical terms, the amount of compensation that they would like to receive for a loss of a given amount is more than what they are willing to pay for a gain of the same amount. An interesting implication is that people's valuation of a good increases once they have it in their possession. For example, while one may only be willing to pay US$ 20 to obtain a share in a certain company, once one has become the owner of that share, one is only willing to part with it for US$ 30. The sunk cost fallacy is a related phenomenon, which states that people cannot see their current decisions around a certain good separately from their prior investments in it. Rather than considering these prior investments a sunk cost (that is, one that we cannot do anything about anymore), people will often try terribly hard to make up for any losses and make their initial investment "worth it". As a result, they may end up throwing good money after bad and continuing to put money in enterprises that have already gathered significant losses. Both loss aversion and the sunk cost fallacy help to explain why investors often stay longer in the market than they should from a rational point of view.

The social dynamics behind "irrational exuberance"

Having laid out some of the characteristics of the behaviour of individual actors in financial markets, we can now assess what happens when these actors interact with one another. In particular, we focus on the social dynamics underlying financial bubbles and the crashes that follow sooner or later. In this context, the former chairman of the American central bank Alan Greenspan coined the phrase "irrational exuberance" in the midst of the *dot-com bubble* in the 1990s, when financial markets were booming owing to a huge sense of optimism regarding how the internet could transform the economy. Greenspan used this catchphrase to describe the collective behaviour of investors at the time. Notwithstanding that one may debate to what extent the exuberance that could unmistakably be observed was indeed irrational, it is interesting to unpack the social interactions underlying this macro-level phenomenon.

Most bubbles contain an element of *social contagion* or *feedback loops*. Figure 11.4 illustrates the fundamentals of how these dynamics play out by way of a macro-micro-macro scheme. The macro-level starting point is a rising trend in the market, reflected by rising prices and possibly an increasing number of people entering the market (point A in Figure 11.4). The reasons for this initial trend can be anything (e.g., expectations of the positive impact of a new technology on the economy or people having more money to invest as they get richer), yet regardless of these original instigators, the trend may subsequently take on a life of its own. That is, individual actors will observe the rising trend and interpret it as a signal of where the market is heading (point B in Figure 11.4). In doing so, they apply the representativeness heuristic described in the previous section, and particularly the method of extrapolation: they model the problem of what *will* happen to the market as being similar to what *has been* happening to the market. Based on this,

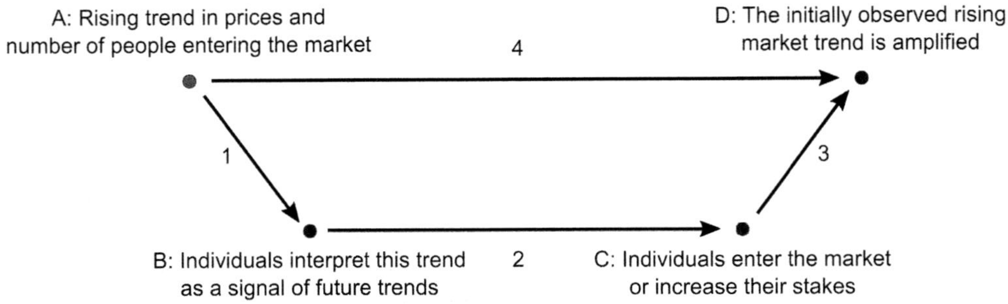

Figure 11.4 Social contagion and feedback loops behind financial bubbles

individual actors will decide to enter the market or increase their stake in the market (point C in Figure 11.4). In this decision, the gains that one has already made or that one has witnessed others making will likely also play a role. With many individual actors applying the same logic and course of action, the resulting macro-level outcome will be an amplification of the initially observed trend – that is, an accelerated rise in prices (point D in Figure 11.4). This outcome will subsequently serve as the starting point of a new macro-micro-macro cycle. As such, the social contagion process or feedback loop summarized in Figure 11.4 sets off a cascade of rising prices.

One of the core lessons to be drawn from this discussion is that potential investors in financial markets are influenced by one another, with powerful implications for market trends. Indeed, once we take into account such interdependencies and the feedback loops they produce, we can explain many developments that are regularly observed in financial markets. This not only applies to bubble episodes but also to more complex fluctuations that are often attributed to random volatility. For example, the Dutch economist Cars Hommes combines insights from *chaos theory* (a branch of mathematics dealing with nonlinear, unstable systems) with an enriched model of economic behaviour (recognizing that individual actors are boundedly rational, differ in their preferences) to show that many trends in financial markets are not as random as they may appear at first glance.

Yet, why are investors so strongly influenced by one another? The solution to this puzzle very much relates to the complexity of the financial system. Indeed, in complex environments involving lots of risk and uncertainty, it is very difficult for individual actors to determine what their optimal course of action is. Given these difficulties, they may look for clues in the behaviour of other actors. Shiller (2000) argues that in our everyday living we have learned to put a great amount of trust in the judgment of experts or a large group of people in general, even when these judgments completely contradict one's own matter-of-fact judgment.

He draws a link here with the famous *Asch experiments* from the 1950s (conducted by the social psychologist Solomon Asch). In these experiments, a subject was placed in a group of about eight other people, who were confederates to the experiment. All of these individuals were subsequently asked a set of simple questions, starting with the confederates and finally reaching the subject of interest. The confederates had been instructed to deliberately give wrong answers. Listening to all these answers and observing the unanimity among the confederates, the subject of interest ended up also giving wrong answers in one out of three cases. Later on, the same outcome was found in a setting in which individuals were part of a group that they never saw and would never see, and in which they could post their answers anonymously. The suggestion is that the subjects ended up giving incorrect answers because they simply could not believe that all other group members were wrong.

Similarly, the equally famous *Milgram experiments* from the 1970s (named after the social psychologist Stanley Milgram) show that people often believe whatever experts say to be right, even if it does not seem right to them personally. In these experiments, the subject of interest was asked to administer electrical shocks to another individual, with the shocks gradually increasing in intensity. There were no real electrical shocks, but the supposed victim – a confederate to the experiment – simulated extreme amounts of pain. However, when the experimenter assured the subjects that no permanent damage was done, all of the subjects proceeded to give shocks of at least three hundred volts.

According to Shiller, if individuals are already so willing to rely on other people's judgments in relatively straightforward situations such as in the Asch and Milgram experiments, it is no surprise that they also put a lot of trust in other people's judgements when it comes to risky and uncertain environments in the financial sphere. In some way, such imitating of others can also be considered a form of *free-riding*. After all, by relying on other people's judgment, one can avoid having to engage in costly System 2 thinking oneself. This may especially seem an attractive strategy when the other people in question are highly reputed researchers or authorities such as rating agencies. That said, if all investors apply the free-riding logic, the resulting market outcomes are obviously built on very fragile foundations. This is only more so given that supposed experts (for example, the economist Irving Fisher in the 1920s and the rating agencies in the lead-up the 2008 crisis) also get some things massively wrong.

Shiller (2000:71) additionally highlights the role of the media in social contagion dynamics, as the "essential vehicles for the spread of ideas". He points out that the media are particularly keen to cover financial markets as they provide them with a constant stream of news and are interpreted as "a barometer of the status of the nation". As such, financial markets offer a lot of potential to capture the public's attention, which is crucial for the longer-term survival of media companies. In their way of reporting about financial markets, the media can amplify existing market trends by drawing the public's attention to these very trends, by making comparisons with similar trends in the past, or by broadcasting the trading strategies or market judgments of other people.

Coming back to the phrase irrational exuberance, it is important to stress that the underlying behaviour of individual actors is not necessarily irrational – although it may well be. Indeed, someone going through the costly process of making their own valuation and risk assessment of the market may well conclude that it is optimal to follow the behaviour of other players in a booming market. Even though this individual may realize that the market is fundamentally overpriced and that many investors are engaging in *herding behaviour*, they may still want to take advantage of the rising market by making some short-term speculative gains. However, although such behaviour may be rational from an individual point of view, the resulting collective behaviour of the market as a whole does seem irrational, as more often than not the proverb "what goes up, must come down" applies.

Although it is difficult, if not impossible, to predict when exactly the reversal of the trend will occur; that it will occur is a near certainty. Once the market starts to slow down, things may go from bad to worse at high speed. This is particularly clear when we consider the stock market. Recall that the gains of long-term stock ownership primarily reflect the paying out of dividends, whereby shareholders share in companies' profits. With rising stock prices, it becomes increasingly unlikely that the expected future stream of dividends can justify them. At the same time, the flow of speculative capital pumped into the market by investors who are not interested in longer-term dividends but rather aim to resell their shares in the short run will inevitably start to dry up at some point. This is when the market is approaching its *tipping point*.

At this stage, the smallest bit of negative news or even just some random negative fluctuations in the market can set off a powerful chain reaction with big consequences (see also our discussion of Thomas Schelling's segregation dynamics in Chapter 2). Indeed, once prices stop rising or start to decline, speculators see the rationale for their investments vanishing. After all, their main goal was to exploit increases in the price of stocks. As a result, at least some of them will start to sell at least some of their shares, which will then rapidly bring stock prices down, due to very similar social contagion dynamics as explained the initial market boom. Generally speaking, this fall will occur with a few bumps as some people, almost against one's better judgment, will increase their stakes in the market, speculating on a speedy recovery. Here we see loss aversion and the sunk cost fallacy coming into play.

In the end, when the bubble has fully disintegrated, those investors who were sufficiently early in entering and exiting the market may still have made some profit. Conversely, those who entered and exited later are likely to have incurred losses. Importantly, however, the crash will have important spillovers beyond these direct impacts on investors, as it will depress, among other things, investor confidence and consumer spending, thus imposing a drag on the overall economy.

Financial institutions' risk-taking and government intervention

While much of our preceding discussion has centred on the behaviour of investors, we now turn to the behaviour of financial institutions and public authorities. Although these players share many aspects of investors' behaviour – such as being subject to high risk and uncertainty and being heavily influenced by other players' actions – their behaviour also exhibits features that warrant a separate analysis. This is especially true in light of frequently made claims that financial institutions and public authorities are to blame for financial crises, by respectively engaging in too risky or even fraudulent behaviour, or failing to keep a close enough check on the financial system.

The incentives of financial institutions and the 'Skin in the Game' problem

The behaviour of financial institutions can be illuminated by modelling it as a *principal-agent problem*. We can set up this model in different ways, depending on the relationships that we are primarily interested in. Focusing on banks, for example, we could in one constellation portray banks as agents who are entrusted by customers (the principals) to manage their money, yet we could also model the chief executives of a bank as agents who are running the company on behalf of its shareholders (the principals). In both cases, the principals delegate certain tasks to the bank, or its management, in exchange for certain remunerations, such as account fees or salaries. Crucially, as for any principal-agent problem, there exists an information asymmetry between the agent and the principals. This implies that the principals cannot fully monitor all of the actions of the bank employees and managers, thus providing the latter with a certain level of discretion.

Figure 11.5 illustrates the setting between bank managers as agents with the banks' shareholders as their principals. The shareholders' goal is the maximization of the bank's profits while safeguarding its continuity. Since profit making requires certain risks, there exists an inherent trade-off between these two aims and, depending on shareholders' time horizon, they will give more weight to either short-term profits or longer-term continuity. Regardless of their specific goals, shareholders will expect from the bank managers that they run the company in line with these goals. In return, the managers receive a financial reward. These rewards are often structured in such a way as to incentivize the managers to act in line with the shareholders' interests. For example, managers can earn bonuses depending on how much profit the bank makes or they get part of their reward in the form of shares of the bank, making them partial owners of the bank themselves.

The main ways through which bank management reports back to the shareholders on their activities include annual and quarterly reports, shareholder meetings, and press releases. Although there are certain official standards that annual and quarterly reports are required to live up to, bank managers still have a great amount of discretion in what information makes it to the shareholders. As such, there is limited transparency on the actions of bank managers and a limited scope for effective monitoring by the shareholders. This statement is only becoming more relevant as the financial system is growing ever more complex, with financial products that are difficult to grasp and banks being increasingly interconnected with one

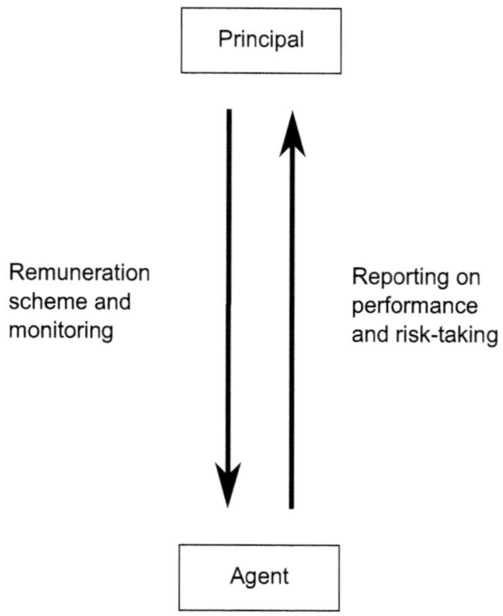

Figure 11.5 The principal-agent relations between bank shareholders and bank managers

another, globally active, and engaged in different types of activities – for example, deposits and lending, insurance, investment banking.

One of the potential outcomes of these principal-agent interactions is that bank managers exploit their discretion vis-à-vis their shareholder by engaging in excessive risk-taking. Although bank managers' reward structures are meant to make their incentives compatible with the interests of their shareholders, there remains a substantial discrepancy between the potential upsides and downsides that managers face by their risk-taking. Taleb (2012) speaks in this regard of the *Skin in the Game problem*. In his view, bankers do not have "skin in the game", as they stand to gain a lot if their risk-taking works out positively (that is, big bonuses through their performance pay contracts) but experience no real harm if their risk-taking results in major losses. To be sure, this would translate into smaller bonuses and might stain their reputation, but other than that, bank managers pay no real price as the banks' shareholders bear the brunt of their mismanagement. As Taleb points out, this asymmetric risk burden implies that bank managers have access to "free options". In contrast, he notes that in medieval Catalonia the tradition was to behead bankers in front of their own banks if their banks collapsed, but that nowadays only the mafia employs such strategies to remove the "free options".

Aside from excessive risk-taking, a number of banks have in the past also engaged in behaviour that can simply be labelled *fraud*. For example, there is evidence that numerous mortgage providers knowingly made borrowers take on loans they could not afford (Appelbaum 2015). This mainly occurred through so-called stated income loans, for which the mortgage provider was not obliged to verify the income stated by the prospective borrower. In some cases, mortgage brokers coached mortgage applicants to overstate their income in order to meet the minimum requirements to receive a loan or to qualify for a larger loan, yet there is also evidence of mortgage brokers overstating the income of mortgage applicants without even telling them. Moreover, numerous banks have been accused of mis-selling mortgage-backed securities in the lead-up to the 2008 financial crisis, making "materially false" statements about the quality of the mortgages that were bundled into these packages (Braithwaite, Scannell, and McCrum 2011). On top of this, the two largest rating agencies in the world – Standard & Poor's and Moody's – have settled lawsuits that accused them of being directly influenced in their ratings of these mortgage-backed securities by the investment banks that issued these securities and paid Standard & Poor's and Moody's for rating them (Freifeld 2017). Notice the conflict of interest here: the rating agencies were paid for their ratings of mortgage-backed securities by the investment banks that wanted to sell these mortgage-backed securities. Another well-known case of fraud in the financial sector is the *LIBOR scandal*, in which several major banks illegally manipulated the interest rates at which they could borrow from one another.

Overall, it seems justified to conclude that both excessive risk-taking and fraudulent behaviour by financial institutions played an integral part in causing the 2008 financial crisis.

Too-important-to-fail and moral hazard

The fact that financial institutions face incentives for excessive risk-taking, combined with the immense societal costs associated with a collapse of individual financial institutions, or even the financial system as a whole, provide good reason for governments to keep a close eye on financial markets and institutions. However, this is much easier said than done. One of the reasons is a lack of transparency around the activities of financial institutions. There is in this regard a fundamental information asymmetry between financial institutions and regulatory authorities. Despite the former reporting extensively on their activities in published annual reports and so on, they can keep a lot of information that is important for regulators under the carpet, especially as financial products and markets are growing more complex. In the lead-up to the 2008 financial crisis, for example, regulatory authorities had only limited awareness of banks' holdings of troubled or toxic assets, as well as of their degree of interconnectedness. As a result, public authorities were rich in terms of information, but poor in terms of insight and control.

Aside from setting regulatory standards to reduce the risk of financial institutions getting into trouble, a core question for public authorities is what to do if financial institutions do, nonetheless, get into trouble. This was the dilemma faced by the US Government and central bank when Lehman's faced rough weather in 2008, as well as the dilemma of many other governments when they were confronted with banks at risk of collapsing in the following year. The traditional wisdom on this topic is that no rescue is required as long as the bank or company in question is a small player. In that case, a bank failure will lead to harm for a relatively small group of owners and customers, but there is no *systemic risk* insofar as it is unlikely that the bank's failure will have broader spillovers for the financial system and the economy a whole. On the other hand, big banks in trouble do need to be bailed out according to this traditional wisdom. After all, if they fail, a large number of customers will be affected, which in turn represents a threat to the overall economy. These banks are, in other words, considered *too-big-to-fail.*

However, with the financial system turning more complex and interconnected, this conventional wisdom needs to be qualified. Banks and other financial institutions are nowadays interwoven with one another in so many ways, that even the failure of small players represents a major contagion danger. In addition to the size of banks, one therefore also needs to take into account the network structure of the financial system and the position of individual players therein. As the economists Stefano Battiston, Cars Hommes and their colleagues (2016) argue, the issue of *too-central-to-fail* may even be more important than the issue of too-big-to-fail. Others also use the term *too-important-to-fail.* Regardless of the exact term used, a greater attention for the dependencies between banks and other financial institutions is much-needed as research has shown that the global financial network can collapse even if many individual players appear in a healthy state (Battiston et al. 2012). Indeed, this is one of the big lessons of the 2008 financial crisis.

It should be noted, however, that government intervention in the form of bailing out systemically important banks comes at a cost. These costs are not restricted to the billions of taxpayers' money that are required for such operations – for example, in 2010 the US government spent about US$ 135 billion on the bailout of Fannie Mae and Freddie Mac, two large producers of mortgage-backed securities. Importantly, the very act of bailing out struggling banks or other companies generates expectations on how the government will act in similar situations in the future and thereby alters the incentives faced by banks and other financial institutions. After all, if banks know that the government will come to their rescue when business turns bad, this changes the risk structure they face. Knowing that, in the end, the taxpayers will bear the costs of failure encourages banks to take more risks, thereby making it more likely that a bailout will eventually indeed be necessary. In Taleb's (2012) language, the possibility of a bailout reduces banks' skin in the game, making excessive risk-taking more of a free option.

In short, the expectation that governments will bail out financial institutions if needed creates a *moral hazard* problem. That is, given this expectation, financial institutions have incentives to behave opportunistically at the expense of the government and taxpayers. In doing so, they are facilitated by the fact that public authorities can only to a limited extent monitor the exact risks that financial institutions are taking. The moral hazard problem is aggravated by the network structure of the banking system, which typically is characterized by a core-periphery pattern (Battiston et al. 2016). The core of the banking system consists of a relatively small number of large banks that are densely interconnected and very similar when it comes to their business and risk models. This means that when one of these banks gets into trouble, the others will probably do so as well. As a consequence, the failure of one bank "can trigger a domino effect that propagates through the system and propels it into a crisis state" (Battiston et al. 2016:818).

The network structure of the banking system hence makes it more necessary for the government to step in if an individual bank is on the verge of collapse, which in turn gives banks more reassurance that they can take on extreme risks in the pursuit of large profits. Governments are thus left in a Catch-22 state: if they commit to rescuing a bank, they encourage other banks to take on more risk and may have to bailout another one the next day, yet if they do not rescue the bank in question, the whole system can topple over. The then US Secretary of the Treasury Hank Paulson was well aware of this troublesome position in the lead-up to the collapse of Lehman Brothers. In a phone call in the week before this collapse, he allegedly exclaimed with dismay, "I am being called Mr. Bailout. I cannot do it again." (Wessel 2010:14).

Needless to say, the resulting situation is problematic from a social justice perspective. Taleb (2012) provides a powerful illustration of this point. He notes that while banks have lost more money during the 2008 financial crisis than they have ever made in their history, the costs of this have been distributed unequally and unfairly. People who invested money in these banks have lost a great amount and the same is true for taxpayers, in light of the large-scale bailouts that were needed. On the other hand, the people who managed these banks in the lead-up to the crisis have not lost anything but instead been paid billions in compensation. In other words, "society pays for the losses of the bankers, but gets no bonuses from them" (Taleb 2012:398).

In response to the 2008 financial crisis, there has been a rise in new regulations aimed at preventing another such crisis. For example, in 2010 President Barack Obama signed into law the *Dodd-Frank Wall Street Reform Act*, which was designed to, among other things, intensify the monitoring of financial institutions (including hedge funds, insurance companies and rating agencies, which were previously largely unsupervized), increase regulation regarding mortgage lending, and curb the influence of complex and risky securities. Moreover, the *Basel III standards* were developed, as an international regulatory framework to make financial institutions more resilient by strengthening bank capital requirements, applying more frequent stress testing, and related measures.

Yet, it is questionable whether such regulatory initiatives will be able to prevent a future financial crisis. For one thing, in May 2018 President Donald Trump approved a large rollback of what he called the "Dodd-Frank disaster", relieving banks and other financial companies from a large amount of the regulations that the Dodd-Frank act had imposed on them. More fundamentally, it is important to realize, in light of our earlier discussion of Black Swans, that while regulations such as the Dodd-Frank act and the Basel III standards might possibly have prevented or alleviated the 2008 financial crisis, they may not be equally successful at combating the next crisis, which will inevitably be different in some respects.

A more ambitious plan is provided by Battiston et al. (2016), who advocate the development of a global policy dashboard that incorporates insights from *complexity science*. In particular, they call for "an online, financial-economic dashboard that integrates data, methods, and indicators. . . [to] monitor and stress-test the global socioeconomic and financial system in something close to real time, in a way similar to what is done with other complex systems, such as weather systems" (Battiston et al. 2016:819). Critically, such a dashboard would appreciate the highly interactive and interconnected nature of the financial system and thus be able to better map contagion dangers. Among other things, such a dashboard would ideally also include information on business interactions between banks, which is currently still entirely off the radar of regulators, compromising reliable estimations of systemic risks. While such a dashboard may sound utopian, Battiston and colleagues show that progress in this direction is already underway. They cite an analysis of the Dutch banking network as an example (Squartini, Van Lelyveld, and Garlaschelli 2013). This example demonstrates that if we were to model this network in a way that each bank has the same number of connections as they have in the real world, as opposed to applying the standard assumption that all banks have the same number of connections, one could have detected the impending crisis already in 2005. Making our economic models more realistic and exploiting insights from complexity science could therefore help in discovering early warning signals and approaching tipping points.

Recommended readings

- John Kenneth Galbraith (1961[1954]) provides a wonderfully accessible and colourful description of the Great Crash of 1929, which has clear parallels to other crisis episodes throughout history. Benefitting from the value of hindsight, he takes the reader step by step through the unfolding of events, with the book almost reading like a novel.
- Robert Shiller (2000) writes about the "irrational exuberance" on the stock market at the time of the dot-com bubble in the late 1990s. He explains how this phenomenon can only be understood if we take account of numerous psychological and sociological mechanisms in addition to standard economic models.
- Nassim Nicholas Taleb (2010) draws our attention to one of the major pitfalls in our thinking, namely our failure to appreciate both the likelihood and impact of improbable extreme events. In his characteristic language, Taleb discusses the relevance of Black Swan events across a range of life domains.
- Stefano Battiston, Cars Hommes, and their colleagues (2016) provide a brief, yet very illuminating, discussion of the challenges related to government intervention in an increasingly complex financial system. This interdisciplinary study not only highlights the problems involved, but additionally proposes potential solutions.

Bibliography

Appelbaum, Binyamin. 2015. "How Mortgage Fraud Made the Financial Crisis Worse". *New York Times*, February 12th.

Battiston, Stefano, Domenico Delli Gatti, Mauro Gallegati, Bruce Greenwald, and Joseph E. Stiglitz. 2012. "Liaisons Dangereuses: Increasing Connectivity, Risk Sharing, and Systemic Risk". *Journal of Economic Dynamics and Control* 36:1121–1141.

Battiston, Stefano, J. Doyne Farmer, Andreas Flache, Diego Garlaschelli, Andrew G. Haldane, Hans Heesterbeek, Cars Hommes, Carlo Jaeger, Robert May, and Marten Scheffer. 2016. "Complexity Theory and Financial Regulation". *Science* 351:818–819.

Braithwaite, Tom, Kara Scannell, and Dan McCrum. 2011. "Banks Sued over Mortgage Deals". *Financial Times*, September 3rd.

Freifeld, Karen. 2017. "Moody's Pays $864 Million to U.S. States over Pre-Crisis Ratings". *Reuters*, January 14th.

Galbraith, John Kenneth. 1961[1954]. *The Great Crash 1929*. London: Penguin Books.

Garber, Peter M. 1989. "Tulipmania". *Journal of Political Economy* 97:535–560.

Garber, Peter M. 1990. "Famous First Bubbles". *Journal of Economic Perspectives* 4:35–54.

Kahneman, Daniel. 2011. *Thinking, Fast and Slow*. New York, NY: Farrar, Straus and Giroux.

Keynes, John Maynard. 2010[1930]. "The Great Slump of 1930". Pp. 126–134 in: *Essays in Persuasion*, John Maynard Keynes. London: Palgrave Macmillan.

Shiller, Robert. 2000. *Irrational Exuberance*. Princeton, NJ: Princeton University Press.

Shleifer, Andrei. 2012. "Psychologists at the Gate: A Review of Daniel Kahneman's 'Thinking, Fast and Slow'". *Journal of Economic Literature* 50:1–12.

Simon, Herbert A. 1947. *Administrative Behavior: A Study of Decision-Making Processes in Administrative Organization*. New York, NY: Macmillan.

Squartini, Tiziano, Iman van Lelyveld, and Diego Garlaschelli. 2013. "Early-Warning Signals of Topological Collapse in Interbank Networks". *Scientific Reports* 3, no. 3357.

Taleb, Nassim Nicholas. 2010. *The Black Swan – The Impact of the Highly Improbable* (2nd edition). New York, NY: Random House.

Taleb, Nassim Nicholas. 2012. *Antifragile – How to Live in a World We Don't Understand*. London: Allen Lane.

Wessel, David. 2010. *In FED We Trust – Ben Bernanke's War on the Great Panic*. New York, NY: Three Rivers Press.

12 Global warming and climate change

Chapter overview

There is perhaps no context where the conflict between individual incentives and collective responsibility is clearer than that of the natural environment. Since the 1970s, degradation of the environment has been recognized as one of the foremost problems facing human society, and the environmentalist movement has been the driving force behind many far-reaching public policies. In this chapter, we discuss common-pool resources that relate to the environment, and especially renewable resources that are at risk of overexploitation, such as forests, oceans, and the atmosphere. We focus on global warming as a change to the atmosphere that poses many threats. We show that, although sustainable resource management is possible under certain circumstances, it is particularly difficult to achieve with regard to the atmosphere as a global common-pool resource. Indeed, individual actors face strong free-riding incentives when it comes to combating global warming. We subsequently address what should be done to slow global warming and what are the most suitable policy tools in this respect. Finally, we turn to the obstacles that hinder successful international cooperation to attenuate climate change.

Global warming as a major threat

The signing of the 2015 Paris Agreement signalled worldwide recognition of the threat posed by environmental degradation, being the first time in history that practically all nations in the world made a collective agreement to combat climate change. One of the most alarming trends with respect to environmental degradation is that of *global warming*: the staggering rise in global temperatures since the start of the twentieth century, which has accelerated since the 1960s. Figure 12.1 shows the increase in global temperature since 1850. It is telling that 24 of the 25 hottest years over this period have occurred since 1990. The increasing number of heatwaves, forest fires, hurricanes, floods, and droughts are examples of the consequences of this trend, and these symptoms will most likely gain in frequency and intensity going forward.

Although environmental problems have plagued societies for some considerable time, it was not until the 1970s that the problem of environmental degradation first received widespread

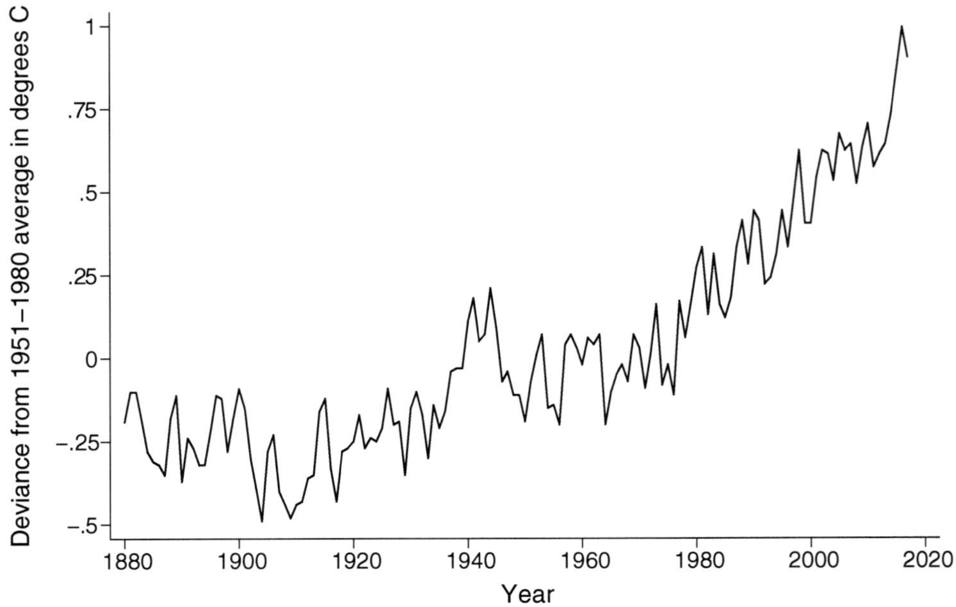

Figure 12.1 The rise in global temperatures since 1880

Note: Data are from NASA's Global Climate Change website and downloadable via https://climate.nasa.gov/vital-signs/global-temperature/. The rise in global temperatures is measured using the annual deviance from the average global temperature over the 1951-1980 period, in degrees of Celsius.

public attention and was recognized as a serious societal problem. Over the years, rising concerns about environmental degradation have led to the implementation of far-reaching public policies such as fuel taxes, the emergence of new political parties, the establishment of highly influential non-governmental organizations (NGOs) such as Greenpeace, and the establishment of the Intergovernmental Panel on Climate Change (IPCC).

From the inception of the modern environmentalist movement in the 1970s, economic growth, large-scale industrialization and population growth were identified as the three ultimate causes of environmental degradation. This reasoning is captured in the so-called *IPAT equation*, which was developed by the environmental scientists Barry Commoner, Paul Ehrlich and John Holdren. This equation states that the total environmental impact of human activity *I*, is equal to the product of three factors, namely population *P*, affluence *A*, and technology *T*. In short: $I = P * A * T$. Since the dawn of the industrial revolution, all three factors have changed dramatically. World population has risen from 1 billion to 7.6 billion (see Chapter 5). GDP per capita in economically advanced counties has increased from around US$ 1,000 to more than US$ 40,000. Myriad new technologies have been invented: asphalt, airplanes, nuclear power, solar energy and electric cars. Some of these technologies have a beneficial or neutral impact on the environment, yet many of them undermine the quality of the environment.

The publication of the 1972 *The Limits to Growth* report by the American scientist Dennis Meadows and his colleagues (Meadows et al. 1972) has proved to be of great importance for the development of the environmentalist movement. Its central conjecture was that, if left unchecked, economic growth would ultimately undermine the *carrying capacity* of the globe – that is, the number of people that our planet could support. This conjecture was based on a model of the global economic system that comprised five key factors and their interactions with one another: population, industrialization, food production, consumption of non-renewable resources, and pollution. At the time of the report, all of these factors were displaying rising trends and the expectation was that these trends would continue to follow an *exponential* pattern of ever-accelerating growth. The resulting projections implied that during the first part of the twenty-first century the industrial sector would have expanded massively, pollution would have reached unprecedented levels, and non-renewable resources such as petroleum would be all but exhausted. At the same time, Meadows and his colleagues forecasted that improvements in technology, as a potential counterbalance to these exponential trends, would only occur at a *linear* rate. This would make the system as a whole unsustainable.

Given its alarming conclusions, it is no surprise that the *The Limits to Growth* report started a heated debate within the Western world. Essentially two camps could be distinguished. First, the anti-growth movement, consisting of a large number of non-governmental organizations and informal initiatives, which argued that economic growth should be limited or even reduced to zero. Second, the pro-growth movement, consisting mainly of economists and business people, who accused the anti-growth movement of neglecting the role of technological progress, and who argued that economic growth was, in the long run, perfectly consistent with protection of the environment.

The second camp became dominant during the period of high inflation and mass unemployment in the late 1970s and early 1980s. In those years, environmental concerns took a back seat as reducing inflation, becoming globally competitive and kick starting the economy re-emerged as the top priorities for governments. Nonetheless, during the late 1980s, environmental problems returned to the forefront of the policy agenda. In 1987, another major report, *Our Common Future*, was published, this time on behalf of the United Nations, under the leadership of former Norwegian Prime Minister Gro Harlem Brundtland (World Commission on Environment and Development 1987). This report not only outlined the causes of global environmental problems, but also put forward an all-encompassing solution based around the concept of *sustainable development*. This conceives of economic growth that meets the needs of the current generations without harming the ability of future generations to meet their own needs. As such, Brundtland's report mitigated the sharp divide between the anti-growth and pro-growth movements.

Shortly after the publication of Brundtland's report, the UN founded the *Intergovernmental Panel on Climate Change* (IPCC), bringing together climate-change scientists from throughout the world. By the start of the twenty-first century, an overwhelming amount of evidence had been gathered suggesting there was a process of global warming going on that was caused by human influence. In 2007, the IPCC received the Nobel Peace Prize for their efforts in increasing public knowledge about man-made climate change as well as laying the foundations for potential counteracting measures. They shared the prize with former US Vice President Al Gore, who had been campaigning for many years for increased attention for climate change, most notably through his 2006 documentary *An Inconvenient Truth*.

In their most recent synthesis report, the IPCC (2015) concludes that it is extremely likely – that is, at least for 95 percent certain – that humans are to blame for global warming and therefore climate change. In particular, global warming is to a large degree caused by human-driven increases in the concentrations of *greenhouse gases* in the atmosphere. These gases permit the inflow of solar energy but impede the outflow of heat radiation, thereby increasing the total amount of heat within the atmosphere. Most significant among the greenhouse gases in the atmosphere are carbon dioxide (CO_2), methane (CH_4), and nitrous oxide (N_2O), and their growing concentrations in the atmosphere can be linked to increased usage of fuel-based transportation methods, industrial activity, and food production, among other things. Since most of these gases are long-lived, remaining semi-permanently in the atmosphere, it is easy for their concentration in the atmosphere to increase and extremely difficult to reverse such trends. Therefore, greenhouse gas emissions cast a big shadow over the future of the planet.

As an illustration, Figure 12.2 provides an overview of the increase in carbon dioxide levels in the atmosphere since 1850. It shows a staggering increase from about 1950 onwards. About half of the total greenhouse gas emissions can be attributed to the burning of fossil fuels for energy and the rest to chemical industry, burning of tropical rain forests, agriculture, and cattle farming.

One of the most damaging results of global warming is that sea levels will rise due to the melting of polar ice caps and mountain glaciers. Other adverse consequences include increases in the frequency and intensity of tropical storms and the more problematic distribution of rainfall, with some areas suffering from excessive rainfall and others from severe droughts. Insofar as global warming is an unintended consequence of human production and consumption activities, it constitutes a negative externality. That is, it is an unintended by-product that people do not take into account when planning these activities.

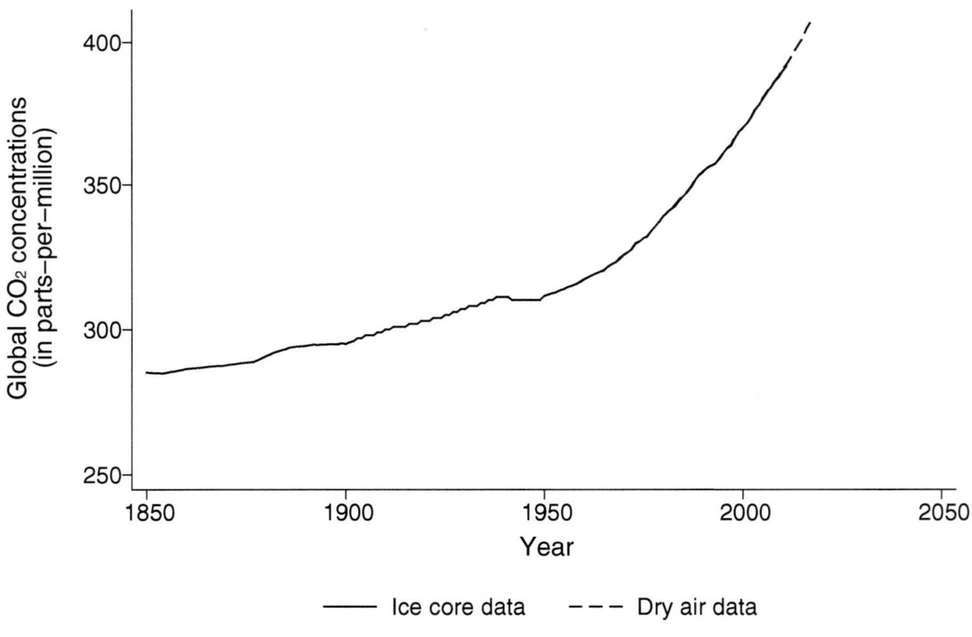

Figure 12.2 The concentration of carbon dioxide (CO_2) in the atmosphere since 1850

Note: The data from 1850-1959 are from Etheridge et al. (1996), who obtained these data by measuring the CO_2 levels in samples of air trapped in ice core samples extracted from three sites in Antarctica between 1987 and 1993. Additional ice-core data from 1960-2011 are from NASA and downloadable via https://data.giss.nasa.gov/modelforce/ghgases/Fig1A.ext.txt. Dry-air data from 1959-2017 were measured at the Mauna Loa Observatory and collected by the Earth System Research Laboratory within of the US Department of Commerce. These data are downloadable via ftp://aftp.cmdl.noaa.gov/products/trends/co2/co2_annmean_mlo.txt.

The atmosphere as a global common-pool resource

In Chapter 1, we demarcated several types of goods, one of which was termed *common-pool resources* (CPRs), which have the twin properties of rivalry and non-excludability. Rivalry means that one individual's consumption of the good reduces what is left for others to consume. Non-excludability means that it is generally not possible, or only at extreme costs, for some individuals to prevent others from consuming the good. Examples of common-pool resources are oil fields, grazing lands, fresh water resources, fish stocks, and tropical rain forests.

Similarly, the atmosphere can be regarded as a common-pool resource. More specifically, it constitutes a *global* common-pool resource, as, among other things, a global dump for greenhouse gases that are emitted through industrial and agricultural production, fuel-based modes of transport, domestic energy usage, and so on. While the atmosphere has a large capacity to store such gases, this capacity is not unlimited, and therefore the atmosphere is subject to the risk of overexploitation. Like other common-pool resources, the atmosphere has a non-excludable and rivalrous character. That is, anyone can, in principle, emit greenhouse gases into the atmosphere, but each emission unit does reduce the atmosphere's storage capacity as well as its ability to maintain a stable climate.

The atmosphere represents a renewable resource to the extent that it can regenerate itself, as greenhouse gases dissipate from the atmosphere after a certain time. However, as mentioned earlier, many greenhouse gases have a long lifespan, meaning that any cleansing of the atmosphere is necessarily a very slow process. In addition, the atmosphere is linked to other common-pool resources such as oceans and forests, which are capable of removing certain greenhouse gases such as CO_2 from the atmosphere and storing them in their biomass. However, these "carbon sinks" are limited in their capacity to clean the atmosphere. For example, the oceans are getting saturated with CO_2, diminishing their ability to soak up any more. Moreover, global forest stocks are themselves a threatened common-pool resource: the UN Food and Agriculture Organization (FAO) estimates that every year 18 million acres of forest – roughly the size of Panama – disappear.

In general, two different outcomes may arise regarding common-pool resources (Gardner, Ostrom, and Walker 1990). First, the fact that resource users compete with one another in terms of their usage of the resource implies that there is a danger of overexploitation and eventual depletion of the resource. No matter how high the short-term profits, this means that the future productive value of the resource is destroyed and can thus be regarded a suboptimal outcome. Second, resource users may succeed at establishing a set of institutional arrangements that bind them to certain rules when it comes to their usage of the resource. Such rules can help to ensure that the productive capacity of the resource remains intact.

The political scientist and Nobel Prize laureate Elinor Ostrom (1990) has done a great amount of research on common-pool resources and how they should be managed. She makes a distinction between the ecosystem of the resource on the one hand and the resulting stream of consumption units on the other. Ostrom's research demonstrates that institutional arrangements regulating the use of a common-pool resource are crucial to the fate of the resource. They determine whether the interaction between actors and ecosystems can result in sustainable resource yields. However, the degree to which sustainable institutional arrangements can be achieved depends on the physical conditions and the ownership structure of the underlying resource.

Institutional arrangements and ownership structures

If a common-pool resource has an *open-access* character (that is, it is not owned by anyone), it is likely to be depleted after a certain amount of time, due to the *tragedy of the commons* (see Chapters 1 and 2). The core of this problem is that while all resource users directly and immediately benefit from using the resource, the costs of using the resource are shared among all users and only occur in the future. Individual users consequently do not fully take into account the impact of their resource usage on the productive or regenerative capacity of the resource. As a result, they end up using more of the resource than is optimal. To prevent this outcome and to achieve a sustainable usage of a common-pool resource, it is crucial that effective practices of resource management are implemented. Two public goods come into play here: first, the rules and norms that enable sustainable management of the common-pool resource, and second, the cooperation among individuals that is necessary to establish such rules and norms in the first place.

However, as seen in Chapter 2, these public goods can by no means be taken for granted. In many cases where public goods are clearly beneficial to society, rational self-interested individuals will often not voluntarily cooperate to provide such public goods. This is because individuals often do not take into account the effects of their behaviour on others, whether it concerns the benefits that others experience if one contributes to the public good or the harm experienced by others if one does not contribute. Without taking into account these *externalities*, the *dominant strategy* for individual actors will be to refrain from contribution to the public good. As such, it seems a huge challenge to get individual actors united behind a set of rules and norms that could ensure sustainable management of common-pool resources.

Nevertheless, according to Elinor Ostrom (1990), this conclusion is too pessimistic. She notes that not all common-pool resources have an open-access nature and that in cases where the physical characteristics of the resource allow for alternative ownership structures, there is more potential to achieve sustainable resource management. Indeed, different ownership structures will have different effects on the economic behaviour of the resource users. One of Ostrom's primary conclusions is that, in many parts of the world, some of the most successful institutions have arisen through a self-organizing process at the local level. These institutions generally have the character of *communal ownership*. This involves a system of rules governing the exploitation of the resource that apply to all members of some local community and that each community member voluntarily abides by. The most important function of these rules is to prevent free-riding behaviour.

Such communal resource management systems are widely practiced by local communities and often remain extant over many years, and sometimes even over many centuries. Prominent examples include irrigation communities, where different farmers want to use water from the same water resource to irrigate their land, and cattle grazing communities, where different farmers or shepherds share the same grazing lands. One of the keys to success of the most effective communal resource management schemes seems to be that individual actors can observe how much effort others are making toward some common objective. This information makes it possible to reward those who put in extra effort, while those who shirk their responsibilities can be punished. In general, such monitoring and sanctioning is easier to realize within smaller communities of resource users.

Another ownership structure is *state ownership*. In principle, state ownership applies to all land and resources within a certain territory that are not privately owned. Since the 1970s, industrialized countries have built up comprehensive regulatory apparatuses for monitoring the use of natural resources within their territories. For example, most advanced countries now have rules about what sort of structures can be built in certain locations and how industrial effluence must be disposed. The implementation of environmental regulations is not without difficulty, however: the supervisory problems inherent to the *principal-agent model*, which we discussed in Chapter 2, often arise within this context. As an illustration, it may be difficult for the state to check whether every citizen complies with rubbish disposal standards.

According to many liberal politicians and economists, the most suitable way to manage common-pool resources is through *private property rights*. The idea is that when a resource is not owned by anyone, or is owned by everyone collectively via the state, individual actors have little incentive to use it frugally. Also in the case of communal ownership, free-riding behaviour remains a serious threat, which can only be effectively combated if there are effective monitoring and sanctioning options. On the other hand, when a resource is owned by a single individual, they have a powerful incentive to use it frugally, as they are the only one who stands to lose from overexploitation of the resource.

Proponents of private ownership usually argue that environmental problems can be solved by allowing the various parties involved to negotiate with one another, either through the market or via the courts. Indeed, the *Coase theorem*, devised by the economist Ronald Coase (1960), states that, in the absence of any transaction costs and with perfect information on the benefits and costs of particular actions, bargaining between private parties will lead to the most efficient allocation of property rights – regardless of how those rights are initially distributed by the state. Under these conditions, the different parties involved can compensate one another in such a way that everyone is satisfied with the eventual outcome.

For example, suppose a factory is emitting pollution into a nearby lake, which is owned by an individual. If the pollution is generated by an extremely efficient production process, the factory owners will be earning a lot of money, and will therefore be able to compensate the individual for the clean-up costs. In that case, the owner of the lake will find that it is worth his while to allow production to continue. However, if the pollution is generated by an inefficient production process, the factory owners will not be earning much money, and will therefore not be able to pay the individual for the clean-up costs. In that case, the owner of the lake will find that it is in their interest to prevent production from continuing and no pollution will occur.

Of course, in many situations the two underlying requirements of the Coase theorem (that is, no transaction costs and perfect information on costs and benefits) are not met. For example, if the factory and lake owner referred to earlier have to draw up a contract outlining their agreement, this will already entail significant transaction costs. Moreover, it is often unclear who exactly is harmed by certain actions and by how much. For instance, in the previous example it may not only be the lake owner who is harmed by the pollution, but also people who spend their holidays by the lake or people who simply care about the well-being of rare fish living in the lake. In addition, the pollution caused by the factory may affect people over a very large distance. Clearly, to the extent that it is then still possible to determine who exactly is negatively affected, it is even harder to determine how much damage they experience, let alone get them all around the negotiating table to agree on a fair compensation.

Institutional arrangements concerning the atmosphere

Access to the atmosphere as a global common-pool resource is extremely difficult to regulate and enforce. Indeed, while our earlier discussion shows that communal, state, and private ownership structures provide potential for sustainable resource management, these ownership structures are practically infeasible as far as the atmosphere is concerned. The fact that we are dealing with a *global* common-pool resource is, from this perspective, of critical importance. This means that the resource cannot be managed by a self-contained local community. Neither can it be managed by different states in isolation, as problems related to the atmosphere and their causes transgress state boundaries. For example, CO_2 emissions in the US will not just affect the quality of the atmosphere right above American territory, but rather the global atmosphere, and the same is true for CO_2 emissions elsewhere. In general, the global character of the atmosphere implies that all citizens of the world are involved, as potential culprits as well as victims of greenhouse gas emissions. This makes it well-nigh impossible to agree on common rules, monitor everyone's behaviour, and avoid free-riding.

Theoretically, one could think of assigning a system of private property rights to the atmosphere, whereby individual actors can trade shares in the atmosphere with one another, with only those actors owning a share being allowed to pollute the atmosphere. To obtain these shares, the polluters would need to compensate those who do not want any pollution of the atmosphere. This idea shares some similarities with the concept of *tradable emission permits* or a *cap-and-trade system*, as implemented for example in the European Union Emission Trading Scheme since 2005. This scheme consists of three components: first, an overall cap is set on the total amount of greenhouse gas emissions that are allowed; second, individual emission permits are auctioned off or allocated across factories, power stations, and other polluters; third, all these parties can trade the permits with one another.

However, in order to assign private property rights to the atmosphere as a whole, such a system would need to be vastly extended, covering the entire world and all types of greenhouse gas emissions, not just industrial emissions. This, in turn, would involve all kinds of complexities. For example, it is not straightforward how the emission permits would need to be distributed initially. If one were to auction them off, rich countries would obviously be greatly advantaged in obtaining them vis-à-vis poor countries. Yet, if one were to assign them based on current emission levels or equal allocations, the eventual outcome may still be that rich countries end up buying out the poor countries and owning the majority of permits. This outcome would be undesirable insofar as a certain level of greenhouse gas emissions may help poor countries to develop. Moreover, this outcome would also be unfair to the extent that most rich countries have indeed emitted large amounts of greenhouse gases in the process of becoming rich. Another problematic issue, in light of the uncertainty regarding the precise timing and magnitude of climate change, would be how to determine the overall emission cap for the world as a whole. Finally, even if one were somehow able to roll out such a global emission permit system, the transaction costs and informational demands involved in such a system would likely violate the Coase theorem, suggesting that an optimal level and distribution of pollution may still not be reached.

Historically, it took a long time before people started to properly realize that greenhouse gas emissions had a major impact on the atmosphere and global warming. This observation reveals another complexity of the atmosphere as a global common-pool resource. In contrast to common-pool resources for which sustainable management structures have successfully been implemented (such as community-level irrigation systems and grazing lands), people cannot easily observe the consequences of their polluting behaviour. For example, looking at the trend in global temperatures plotted in Figure 12.1, there is an unmistakable increase, but the overall magnitude of this increase is relatively small (that is, a rise in global temperatures of less than one degree Celsius over the past 50 years), such that people are unlikely to notice it in their everyday lives. At the same time, the stock of greenhouse gas emissions already built up in the atmosphere, combined with the fact that this stock can only slowly dissipate and that we are even still adding to it, implies that over the coming decades there will be further temperature increases. In short, the gradual nature of global warming and the time it takes for the consequences of greenhouse gas emissions to materialize increase the risk of any required action being postponed, despite abundant evidence suggesting that the consequences will be disastrous in the long run.

Government intervention to address global warming

Since the emergence of the IPCC in the late 1980s, there has been an increasingly strong consensus among scientists about the nature of the global warming problem. More specifically, the vast majority of scientists nowadays agree that: first, global temperatures have in recent decades been rising faster than ever before (see Figure 12.1); second, this accelerating trend can be directly linked to human activities, in particular the emission of greenhouse gases (see Figure 12.2); third, global warming will have negative consequences for our planet, both in terms of economic impact and the degradation of ecosystems and the environment; fourth, these impacts will be unequally distributed throughout the world, with the biggest damages concentrated in low-income and tropical regions; and fifth, the rising trend in global temperatures will continue for the foreseeable future.

The reason for this fifth point is that the intensity of global warming is proportional to the *stock* of greenhouse gases in the atmosphere, which has been building up over many years with steadily increasing *flows* of greenhouse gases into the atmosphere. At the same time it is difficult to significantly speed up the outflow of greenhouse gases from the atmosphere. These gases have a long life span, and while ecosystems like oceans and forests could absorb greenhouse gases out of the atmosphere, the oceans are already getting saturated with greenhouse gases and the number of trees in the world is in decline. There are also technological innovations that could help in removing greenhouse gases from the atmosphere (such as installations that compress CO_2 emitted by factories into a supercritical fluid, which is subsequently stored deep underground), yet for the moment such technologies still operate at inefficiently high costs. Altogether, this means that the current inflow of greenhouse gases into the atmosphere greatly exceeds the current outflow, and that the stock of greenhouse gases in the atmosphere will continue to grow for the foreseeable future, even if we somehow manage to curtail the inflow of greenhouse gases.

Despite the broad consensus on the five points just discussed, debates on global warming also remain subject to an enormous degree of uncertainty. For example, while we know that global warming is likely to continue given the projected development of the stock of greenhouse gases in the atmosphere, we do not exactly know how fast temperatures will continue to rise. After all, the relationship between the atmospheric concentrations of greenhouse gases and climate change is not a simple linear one, and given the unprecedented concentration of greenhouse gases in the atmosphere we are very much in uncharted territory. One specific possibility might be that, if greenhouse gas concentrations continue rising beyond their current levels, there will at some point be a tipping point, leading to sudden catastrophic changes in our climate.

Similarly, the estimates of the economic impact of global warming vary widely. For example, the economist and Nobel Prize laureate William Nordhaus (2010) forecasts that if we do not intervene, the economic damages of climate change will amount to US$ 12 trillion in 2095 (that is, 2.8 percent of global income), assuming a rise in global temperature of 3.4 degrees Celsius compared to 1900. Yet, according to another economist – Nicholas Stern, who led the British investigation that resulted in the highly influential *Stern Review on the Economics of Climate Change* – the consequences of global warming are much more devastating. More specifically, the Stern (2007:xv) concludes that, "... if we don't act, the overall costs and risks of climate change will be equivalent to losing at least five percent of global GDP each year, now and forever. If a wider range of risks and impacts is taken into account, the estimates of damage could rise to 20 percent of GDP or more." The report goes on to argue that, "Our actions now and over the coming decades could create risks of major disruption to economic and social activity, on a scale similar to those associated with the great wars and the economic depression of the first half of the 20th century."

In short, although we have learnt a great deal in the past decades about the nature of global warming and its potential consequences, there are still many unknowns. Some of these concern *Known Unknowns* (for example, we know that we do not know how exactly greenhouse gas concentrations and climate change are linked, and we know that we do not know how fast exactly more environmentally-friendly technologies will become available), but importantly, there may also be *Unknown Unknowns* that will have a far-reaching impact (see Table 11.1). Indeed, as we noted in Chapter 11 that the financial system is a highly complex system, the working of which is difficult to grasp and predict, the same is certainly true for the climate system and its interactions with the economic system. The crucial question for governments to consider, given on the one hand the knowledge that we have about global warming yet on the other the large uncertainty that remains, is: what can and should be done to prevent or minimize any global warming and the damage that result from it?

By how much should we reduce greenhouse gas emissions?

The first question that follows from the core policy question of what to do about global warming is by how much we should aim to reduce greenhouse gas emissions. Because greenhouse gas emissions are the main culprit of global warming, it is evident that some effort should be made to reduce these emissions. The question of how much of a reduction is needed is, however, a subject of intense debate. From an economic point of view, some sort of balance will need to be found between the costs involved in reducing greenhouse gas emissions (in terms of curtailing industrial production or certain transportation methods, switching to cleaner technologies, and introducing taxes or other policy tools) and the costs involved in *not* reducing greenhouse gas emissions (in terms of additional rises in global temperature and the associated damage to our planet). In other words, the costs of slowing climate change need to be balanced against the damage caused by more rapid climate change.

From this perspective, the *Kyoto Protocol*, which was adopted in 1997 and has been influential in shaping environmental policies in many Western countries over the past 20 years, has often been criticized for doing too little to slow down global warming. In particular, critics argue that the emission reduction targets set by the participating countries are way too low compared with the future damage associated with climate change. At the other extreme, more rigorous proposals such as by the Stern Review and those proposed by Al Gore, which advocate immediate and sharp reductions in greenhouse gas emissions, have also been subject of criticism. The idea is that these proposals want to achieve too much in too little time, implying inefficiently high emission reduction costs in the short run. Of course, any such balance judgments are in principle disputable in light of the aforementioned uncertainties regarding the costs of (preventing) global warming. In addition, there may be philosophical arguments that override economic arguments.

One factor that is especially important from both an economic and a philosophical point of view concerns the choice of a *time discount rate*. This time discount rate determines how the interests of current and future generations are weighed against each other. As such, it captures the intertemporal trade-off between the costs of any emission reduction policies that we adopt today vis-à-vis the benefits they yield in the future. Because most of the biggest impacts of climate change or emission reduction policies occur far in the future, the choice of an appropriate time discount rate plays a central role in answering the question of how much emission reductions we should aim for.

The higher the discount rate, the more value is attached to the interests of current generations as compared with the interests of future generations. If we pick a time discount rate of zero, this implies we care as much about any future generation as we care about our current generation. The result of such a discount rate is that we will be much more willing to take on serious emission reduction costs today in order to prevent the harmful consequences of global warming for future generations. Conversely, if we apply a positive discount rate, this implies that we care most about our own generation and less and less about other generations as they go further into the future. As a consequence, we would opt for a lower level of emission reductions under a positive discount rate than under a zero discount rate, and this difference will widen as the discount rate gets more positive.

Clearly, concerns of intergenerational justice come into play when deciding on which time discount rate to apply. For example, if we were to apply John Rawls's theory (see Chapter 2), we would try to optimize the well-being of the generation that will be worst off, in line with the *maximin principle*. After all, reasoned from behind a "veil of ignorance", no individual would know in which generation they would end up, giving them reason to invest in making their worst possible destination as good as possible. In addition to people's economic circumstances, environmental circumstances and values could be included in such an optimization process. That said, such intergenerational judgments will still suffer from incomplete and uncertain information on the circumstances that each generation will be confronted with. Moreover, as noted by Nordhaus (2008), there is a gap between such philosophical reflections and actual intertemporal decision-making insofar as the current generation cannot tie the hands of future generations. In Nordhaus's (2008:176) words, "each generation is in the position of one member of a relay team, handing off the baton of capital to the next generation and hoping that future generations behave sensibly and avoid catastrophic choices such as dropping or destroying the baton".

Returning to a more economic viewpoint, any reductions in greenhouse gas emissions should ideally satisfy the principles of *where-efficiency* and *when-efficiency*. The idea behind where-efficiency is that the costs of reducing greenhouse gas emissions by one extra unit should be equalized across all countries and all sectors of the economy. If this is not the case, the world could benefit from shifting some emission reductions across countries or across sectors. To give a hypothetical example, if it would cost the EU US$ 100 to reduce emissions by one extra unit, but the US only US$ 20, it would be efficient to shift some emission reductions from the EU to the US. The world as a whole would gain from such a shift, either by achieving the same emission reductions at lower costs, or by keeping the costs constant but achieving greater emission reductions. Such shifts remain efficiency-enhancing as long as the costs of emission reductions remain lower in the US. Nevertheless, for any given country it will gradually become more difficult and thus more expensive to reduce emissions by one more unit if one already abates a lot. Therefore, as one will continue to shift emission reductions from the EU to the US, there will come a point where both regions face the same cost of abating one extra unit. That is the point when where-efficiency has been reached. This same logic can be applied to different sectors of the economy, such as airplane travel and electricity production.

The principle of when-efficiency requires that any emission reductions are efficiently distributed over time. This concept of efficiency is generally more difficult to realize than where-efficiency, as it extends to the future and thus incorporates much more uncertainty. Moreover, it is dependent on the time discount rate that one assumes. That said, Nordhaus (2008) argues that meeting the when-efficiency criterion will generally require a so-called "policy ramp", involving modest rates of emission reductions in the short run that gradually build up to sharper reductions in the medium and long run. One of the reasons for this is that it will be more costly to attain a given amount of emission reductions today than at some point in the future. This is, among other things, because the latter scenario allows for more adaptation, such as in the form of technological innovations. For example, it will be cheaper to reduce CO_2 emissions from airplane travel once we have a technology available that allows for flying based on solar energy. To be sure, such a technology currently still represents a fantasy, but in other areas of the economy solar energy has already been introduced.

How can we reduce greenhouse gas emissions?

Once governments have decided by how much they want to reduce greenhouse gas emissions, the next question is how they can achieve these targets. In this regard, policymakers face a plethora of options, ranging from imposing restrictions on emissions, levying taxes on activities that are high in emissions, subsidizing environmentally-friendly behaviours, introducing certain minimum technological standards, or stimulating technological innovation more generally. Governments regularly apply all of these measures, but the ones that receive most attention are quantitative emission targets and emission taxes.

The working of quantitative emission targets is relatively straightforward. Based on the overall level of emission reductions that the government wants to achieve and a certain algorithm whereby these reductions are distributed across different actors, the government imposes limits on how much greenhouse gases actors may emit. Such a system also includes a monitoring mechanism that allows governments to check whether individual actors comply with these targets – which may be more or less effective – and a sanctioning mechanism that allows governments to punish those actors that do not comply. Nevertheless, such a system often involves inefficiencies and is therefore usually adapted to a *cap-and-trade system* (see the section "The atmosphere as a global common-pool resource"), in which different actors are allowed to trade their emission quotas with one another. This ensures, for example, that industries for which it is very expensive to reduce their emissions can buy additional emission quotas from industries that can more easily reduce their emissions. Thus, the cap-and-trade system satisfies the principle of where-efficiency.

Emission taxes, in turn, are based on the idea of internalizing the externalities of the behaviour of individual actors for the environment. Recall here that individual actors often do not fully take into account the negative consequences of their behaviour on the environment when planning their actions. As such, they may decide to go to work by car, without fully accounting for the CO_2 emissions that this behaviour will generate and their impact on the global warming problem. The point of emission taxes is to put a price tag on these additional CO_2 emissions, in order to make sure that individual actors consider their "carbon footprint" when deciding on their actions. In this way, emission taxes are expected to make actors more aware of the negative externalities of their behaviour and thus reduce their emissions. The underlying idea is that people respond to incentives, and that there are few incentives that are more powerful than prices. Alternatively phrased, the levying of an emission tax can also be regarded as the removal of an implicit subsidy on behaviour that is harmful for the environment.

Quantitative emission targets, and especially cap-and-trade systems, tend to be most popular among policymakers, and form an integral part of many international treaties related to global warming, such as the Kyoto Treaty and the Paris Agreement (see the next section for more details). Compared to emission taxes, they impose harder constraints on greenhouse gas emissions and are thus thought to keep a closer check on the concentrations of greenhouse gases in the atmosphere and changes in global temperature. However, as Nordhaus (2008) points out, this advantage is largely illusory, given the considerable uncertainties on the climatic consequences of certain amounts of greenhouse gas emissions or concentrations. Any specific emission target is, as a consequence, somewhat arbitrary and may need updating as more knowledge of the climate system is acquired. Moreover, time has shown that tradable emission quotas are subject to excessive price volatility and have failed to deliver on their promise of ensuring where-efficiency.

Still, policymakers tend to prefer quantitative targets over emission taxes. This partially reflects that quantitative targets are believed to be more realistic to achieve. Indeed, in the political sphere there is often a taboo on introducing taxes that make life more expensive, as politicians fear that voters will punish them for this. Especially in countries with a dominant liberal or libertarian ideology, such as the US, the word "tax" almost has the status of a swear word. That said, emission taxes also have a clear set of advantages over quantitative targets (Nordhaus 2013).

To begin with, taxes have the benefit of raising revenues for governments, which can subsequently be used to soften the impact of emission taxes on low-income households, subsidize research on low-carbon technologies, help poor countries shift away from using fuels that are high in carbon content, or simply make citizens better off by reducing taxes in other areas of the economy. In addition, emission taxes represent a simpler policy instrument than emission quotas – it suffices to agree on one international tax rate for emissions as opposed to specific emission quotas for each and every country or region – and they are usually better understood by the governments that need to administer them.

Furthermore, emission taxes are much less susceptible to corruption and *rent-seeking* than emission quotas. The reason is that emission quotas create scarcities where previously none existed.

This artificial scarcity encourages individual actors to engage in unproductive or even corrupt behaviour to obtain these quotas, such as lobbying or paying bribes to government officials (see Chapter 10). More generally, the existence of so-called resource rents is known to increase the likelihood of civil wars and to reduce economic growth. This phenomenon is known as the *resource curse* and is illustrated by the history of many resource-rich countries on the African continent. With emission taxes, all of these problems are less likely to occur because they do not impose any explicit cap and thus do not introduce any artificial scarcities.

As mentioned earlier, however, emission taxes and quotas are not the only policy tools that governments use for achieving emission reductions. Aside from a hybrid of these two tools (a *cap-and-tax system*), the main alternative consists of subsidizing behaviours that can reduce greenhouse gas emissions. For example, people can be subsidized to change their car for a bike or public transport, to install solar panels on their roof, or to eat less meat. Yet, as Nordhaus (2008) explains, governments are generally better advized to focus their attention on other policy tools, as there are simply too many clean activities to subsidize. There are not enough resources to subsidize all of these behaviours and they require, rather than generate, public revenues. Moreover, it would be highly complicated to calculate an appropriate subsidy for each activity, and producers or suppliers of clean products or services may even end up in an unproductive lobbying race to get their products or services subsidized.

Some subsidies for "clean" or "green" behaviour may even end up having perverse effects. A prime example concerns subsidies for the use of biofuels, in particular bio-ethanol, which is made from cereals or sugar beets. In the early 2000s, biofuels were hailed as providing an opportunity to move away from fossil fuels and their deleterious impact on greenhouse gas concentrations in the atmosphere. However, with bio-ethanol gaining popularity among car users, research has increasingly started to point at its dark sides. At the core of the problem lies the fact that bio-ethanol is quite inefficient in its production process. That is, one needs a huge amount of cereals or sugar beets to produce a rather modest amount of bio-ethanol. As a result, a large amount of agricultural land that could otherwise have been used to produce food has been turned into bio-ethanol production grounds, and in countries such as Brazil great amounts of forest have been cut or burnt down to make way for this production. If we take into account this deforestation, the striking result is that bio-ethanol may on balance even imply *bigger* greenhouse gas emissions than do fossil fuels – let alone the fact that its production also competes with feeding a growing global population, leads to losses in biodiversity, and threatens indigenous rights in various places.

According to Nordhaus (2013), one key exception to the general rule that subsidies are inefficient for combating climate change concerns subsidies to stimulate inventions and innovations. These have the potential to result in cleaner technologies that allow us to reduce our greenhouse gas emissions, while at the same time being subject to positive externalities. That is, any investments in innovation have benefits that extend beyond the people making these investments. In this case, a subsidy can help investors to internalize these positive externalities, resulting in greater investments than they would otherwise have made, thereby benefiting society as a whole.

That said, Nordhaus also makes the argument that any politician who on the one hand speaks eloquently of the perils of global warming and advocates that the nation should take decisive actions to slow climate change, but on the other hand only proposes subsidies and no taxes to achieve this goal, is not really serious about this cause. Such a politician is apparently willing to propose less efficient climate change policies in order to prevent falling from grace with their voters. They are unwilling to put their neck on the line, or in Nassim Nicholas Taleb's (2012) language, they have no skin in the game (see Chapter 11).

International climate treaties and the free-riding problem

International politics around climate change since the 1990s has been mainly shaped by the *Kyoto Protocol* adopted in 1997. Its goal was for countries to commit to binding emission quotas, with developed countries bearing the brunt of this burden, reflecting that they have a disproportionate responsibility for the global warming to date and can afford greater emission reductions. However, when the protocol came into force in 2005, only 37 industrialized countries committed to reducing their greenhouse gas emissions. This was after the US and several other countries had pulled out of the treaty in 2001, as they did not agree with the emission quotas set for the different countries. Since the targets set were at the same time still rather modest from the perspective of combating global warming, the Kyoto Protocol never became a real success.

After failing to secure a new global agreement on emissions reductions in Copenhagen in 2009, a new landmark treaty was negotiated under the flag of the United Nations in 2015: the *Paris Agreement*. This treaty is historical insofar as it includes all countries in the world, including many countries that did not take part in the Kyoto Protocol. It formally expresses the aim of restricting the rise in global temperature to no more than two degrees Celsius above preindustrial levels, promising to "endeavour" to limit this rise to only 1.5 degrees Celsius. However, the Paris Agreement does not set out emissions reduction targets that have legal force. Rather, it emphasizes consensus-building and encourages individual nations to establish their own emission reduction targets. As one may imagine, such a procedure does not necessarily result in the most ambitious targets. Indeed, calculations by the Danish economist Bjorn Lomborg (2016) suggest that, even if all the treaty's promises were fulfilled, the reduction in the increase in global temperature would fall short of the reduction that the IPCC says is necessary to avert the most harmful effects of climate change. What is more, in November 2017 President Donald Trump announced that the US – as one of the biggest greenhouse gas emitters – would withdraw from the agreement.

The withdrawal of the US is a big blow for the Paris Agreement. First, it could undermine the broad-based international cooperation on which the agreement is based, possibly encouraging other countries to also withdraw, thus setting off an unravelling process. We can draw a link here with the *critical mass models* of collective action discussed in Chapter 2: longer-term cooperation may only be maintained if there is a certain minimum number of participants. Second, a lack of cooperation from one or more countries implies major increases in the costs of slowing down global warming for all other countries. This relates to the earlier introduced concept of where-efficiency and the fact that the costs of reducing greenhouse gas emissions are low for any initial reductions but rise sharply for larger reductions. From this perspective, it is far cheaper to achieve a certain climate target by all countries doing a little, than by bigger reduction efforts among a smaller set of countries. In this context, Nordhaus (2008) estimates that if all of the biggest emitters were included in a treaty (covering as much as 75 percent of all global greenhouse gas emissions), it would still be 70 percent more expensive to achieve a given climate target than when all countries were concluded. Yet, if we look at the incentives that actors (here: countries) face, it comes as no surprise that it is challenging to establish and maintain a global climate treaty.

Free-riding and the game theory of global climate deals

At this point in the book it should be clear that free-riding problems occur in a wide range of situations with public good characteristics. Yet, in the case of combating global climate change, the incentives for free-riding are particularly strong, and it is particularly difficult to mitigate the free-riding problem.

The incentives for individual countries to free-ride originate from the fact that the costs of reducing greenhouse gas emissions are very much felt locally, while the benefits of such reductions in the form of slowing global warming are widely dispersed and indeed truly global. The combination of local costs and dispersed benefits imply strong free-riding incentives. That is, countries have an incentive to rely on the emission reductions of other countries without taking any serious steps themselves. Alternatively, they may decide to formally participate in a climate treaty, but cheat in terms of their compliance, by hiding some of their greenhouse gas emissions or overstating any emission reductions.

Interestingly, combating global climate change does not only involve incentives for *free-riding between countries* but also for intertemporal free-riding or *free-riding between generations*. This is because the biggest damages of climate change are located well into the future. As a result, current generations can decide to take a back seat when it comes to reducing greenhouse emissions, but still enjoy a high standard of living themselves, while leaving the associated environmental damages and the costs of slowing down global warming for future generations.

The reason why free-riding with respect to global climate deals is especially difficult to overcome relates to the absence of an overarching authority that can force individual countries to participate and comply. In national or local arenas, on the other hand, a higher-level authority is often available. For example, national governments can force individual citizens to contribute to public infrastructure, national defence, and the prevention of crime by making them pay taxes under the threat that they will be prosecuted if they fail to do so. As Nordhaus (2015) points out, however, such use of force by a higher-level authority is impossible in our system of international law, where nations have the right of political self-determination, where states are legally equal, and where states are free to manage their internal affairs without intervention by other states. The implication of these principles is that participation in a climate treaty is in the end an entirely voluntary choice, without any direct options to force individual countries into participation.

Some of the difficulties in achieving international climate treaties can be illustrated using *game theory*, which models interactions between actors (here: countries) where the outcomes for each actor depend on the behaviour of the other actors involved. Tables 12.1 and 12.2 show two stylized game theoretic settings for the simple case in which only two countries (Country A and Country B) are involved in the climate treaty negotiations. The two scenarios differ by how costly they assume climate change to be. In each situation, each country has the choice between

Table 12.1 The incentive structure behind climate deal negotiations (set-up 1)

		Country B	
		Reduce emissions	Do nothing
Country A	Reduce emissions	0 ; 0	–10 ; 2
	Do nothing	2 ; –10	–5 ; –5

Note: The numbers in each cell reflect the societal payoffs for, respectively, Country A and Country B.

two strategies: either they can decide to reduce their greenhouse gas emissions, or they can decide to do nothing. The cells within Tables 12.1 and 12.2 depict the overall societal payoffs for each country, which depend on their own strategy as well as the strategy followed by the other country.

Starting with Table 12.1, the benchmark outcome is the scenario in which neither of the countries take any steps to reduce their greenhouse gas emissions (the bottom-right cell in Table 12.1). In this scenario, both countries suffer a negative payoff of -5, reflecting that uncontrolled greenhouse gas emissions will undermine the quality of the natural environment and countries' future production capacities. On the other hand, if both countries engage in concerted action to reduce their greenhouse gas emissions, they both face a payoff of 0 (the top-left cell in Table 12.1). This scenario reflects a break-even situation in which countries incur certain costs today in terms of reducing their greenhouse gas emissions in order to prevent future deteriorations of the environment and their production capacity.

However, the battle against climate change is only properly effective if both countries participate and reduce their greenhouse gas emissions; otherwise only part of the environmental benefits are realized. This situation occurs when Country A and Country B follow a different strategy (the bottom-left and top-right cells in Table 12.1). In those cases, the country that does not reduce its greenhouse gas emissions will on balance actually be better off than in the situation in which both countries follow that course of action. Taking the bottom-left cell of Table 12.1 as an example, the natural environment and future production capacity of Country A will be compromised compared to the situation in which both countries reduce their emissions, but things will not be as bad as in the situation of neither countries making any emission reductions. This relative gain compared to the benchmark scenario is entirely the result of the emission reductions of Country B, with Country A making no sacrifices and thus being able to still enjoy greater consumption today. Conversely, Country B is the big loser in this case, as they do make sacrifices in the form of emission reductions, but only get little in return in terms of the quality of their natural environment and their future production capacity. Therefore, Country B is in fact worse off than in the scenario in which both countries do nothing.

Studying the payoffs in Table 12.1, one can see that both Country A and Country B have a *dominant strategy* that consists of doing nothing. That is, given the behaviour of the other country, it will for each country always be more advantageous to do nothing. For example, if Country B *does* reduce their emissions, Country A can have a bigger payoff when they do not reduce their emissions than when they do. And if Country B *does not* reduce their emissions, Country A will still have a bigger payoff when they do not reduce their emissions than when they do. Given that the same applies to Country B, the most likely outcome is the scenario in which neither country reduces their emissions (the bottom-right cell in Table 12.1).

This scenario represents a *non-cooperative Nash equilibrium* insofar as neither of the countries can improve their payoffs from this situation by unilaterally changing their behaviour. Nevertheless, the equilibrium is suboptimal in the sense that both countries would be better off if they jointly reduced their greenhouse gas emissions. Yet, given the free-riding incentives enclosed within this set-up and the fact that international climate treaties are voluntary in nature, the more optimal equilibrium in which both countries reduce their emissions is hard to sustain. Note the similarities between this situation and the *prisoner's dilemma* discussed in Chapter 2.

The exact way in which the climate deal negotiations unfold hinges on the particular set-up of the game. In this regard, Table 12.2 displays a slightly altered version of the game in Table 12.1, assuming that climate change is more costly. As a consequence, the payoffs for each country in every scenario other than the one in which both countries reduce their emissions are ten points lower. The implication of this change is that both countries no longer have a dominant strategy. Indeed, if Country B does nothing, it will still be best for Country A to do the same, yet if Country B decides to reduce their greenhouse gas emissions, the best response for Country A will now be to reduce their emissions too (and vice versa).

This set-up gives rise to two stable equilibria: as before, one in which none of the countries reduce their greenhouse gas emissions (the bottom-right cell in Table 12.2), but now also one in which both countries reduce their greenhouse gas emissions (the top-left cell in Table 12.2). Although both equilibria are stable in the sense that no country can improve their payoff by unilaterally changing their behaviour, it is clear that they are not equally desirable, with the cooperative equilibrium resulting in higher payoffs for both countries. However, if the countries are for some reason stuck in the non-cooperative equilibrium, it can be difficult to escape this situation without any form of coordination. For this reason, this type of game is often referred to as a *coordination game*.

The games displayed in Tables 12.1 and 12.2 represent major simplifications of what real-world climate treaty negotiations entail, but can be extended in ways to make them more realistic. While some of these extensions may make the achievement of cooperation more likely, for others the reverse is true. One obvious extension concerns the number of countries involved. Rather than just two countries, real-world climate negotiations such as the ones underlying the Kyoto Protocol and the Paris Agreement involve a far greater number of countries. In general, this increase in the number of players threatens the achievement of cooperation. Recall in this context Mancur Olson's argument that collective action is more difficult to achieve in larger groups (see Chapter 2). Among other things, this is because individual defections may more

Table 12.2 The incentive structure behind climate deal negotiations (set-up 2)

		Country B	
		Reduce emissions	Do nothing
Country A	Reduce emissions	0 ; 0	–20 ; –8
	Do nothing	–8 ; –20	–15 ; –15

Note: The numbers in each cell reflect the societal payoffs for, respectively, Country A and Country B.

easily go unnoticed, because there will likely be more communication challenges, and because group norms and social control are harder to maintain.

Another factor that complicates real-world climate deal negotiations is the fact that countries differ from one another in many ways, including their economic endowments and what they stand to gain from a climate treaty. This gives rise to deviations from the games presented in Tables 12.1 and 12.2, which are characterized by symmetric payoffs for both countries involved. In general, inequalities in endowments and payoffs make it more difficult to achieve and sustain cooperation, as the interests and objectives of the different parties do not tend to align well under these circumstances. It is particularly hard to get both rich and poor countries united behind a global climate deal, as rich and poor countries differ markedly in their reliance on dirty technologies, access to cleaner technologies, and their opportunities to abate greenhouse gas emissions.

A related challenge stems from the inherent uncertainty of the global warming problem. While it is pretty much certain that global warming is driven by greenhouse gas emissions, there remains a lot of uncertainty as to how severe the damage will be and how it will be distributed across nations, among other things. Such uncertainty makes cross-country cooperation less likely insofar as different countries may have different conceptions of the stakes involved. For instance, if in Table 12.2 one of the two countries expects climate change to be less of a problem, it will be harder for the two countries to coordinate their actions such that they end up in the cooperative rather than non-cooperative equilibrium.

Despite these threats to achieving international cooperation, real-world climate deal negotiations also have certain characteristics that might make cooperation more likely than in the simple games displayed in Tables 12.1 and 12.2. First, while those tables summarize one-shot games in which the countries only have to make one decision that will determine their fates for the remaining future, real-world negotiations concern repeated interactions with no clear endpoint. One of the implications is that countries face stronger incentives to invest in cooperation. After all, it is less attractive for a country to try to extract some gains at the expense of another country if they know that they will meet that other country again in the near future to negotiate about the same or other issues. Moreover, repeated interactions allow countries to develop stronger bonds with one another as well as to learn about each other's interests and motivations, and what works and does not work to achieve cooperation.

Another important characteristic of real-world climate deal negotiations is that countries have plenty of opportunities to communicate with one another. This is a crucial difference vis-à-vis the prisoner's dilemma discussed in Chapter 2, where the prisoners ended up in a suboptimal equilibrium because they were unable to communicate with one another. The availability of communication options means that there is more potential for countries to reach a climate agreement, as they can share their objectives with one another, try to persuade one another, and keep each other accountable. As such, communication can make countries refrain from becoming a free-rider. On a related note, countries may also resort to punishment or counteraction towards other countries that are unwilling to participate in a climate agreement or that do not comply with its standards.

In this context, Nordhaus (2015) proposes so-called *climate clubs* as a way to arrive at international climate agreements that can really make a difference in terms of slowing global warming. In a nutshell, these climate clubs provide a solution to the free-riding problem by imposing sanctions on those countries that do not take part in the climate agreement. In particular, the idea is to link the "climate game" to the "international trade game" and punish non-participants in the climate agreement by levying tariffs on all their imports into the club region. For instance, if the US were to pull out of a climate agreement encompassing all countries of the European Union, this would imply that the US subsequently have to pay increased taxes on all their imports into the European Union.

Because international exports generally have such high payoffs for countries, these import tariffs effectively remove the free-riding incentives of individual countries and thus stimulate countries to join the climate agreement and, once joined, not to defect. Furthermore, in contrast to other sanctions from which both the country that imposes them and the country that is subject to them suffer, these import tariffs do harm the country that the tariffs are targeted at but they benefit the country that imposes them. This makes the imposition of the tariffs a credible threat. In short, Nordhaus (2015:1362) notes that import tariffs to non-members of the climate clubs can provide the "economic glue to hold a cooperative coalition together". Having said that, it is currently still impossible to introduce climate clubs, as they conflict with current international-trade law and risk resulting in trade wars, with countries imposing escalating sanctions on one another. For this reason, Nordhaus proposes a set of "climate amendments" to international-trade law that allow for tariffs on countries that do not participate in a climate treaty, and that prohibit retaliation against countries that invoke these tariffs.

Recommended readings

- Elinor Ostrom (1990) studies how natural common pool resources can best be governed. Relying on numerous real-world examples of successful and unsuccessful governance, she lays out the conditions under which common pool resources can be sustainably managed. Ostrom presents a relatively optimistic outlook, showing that the "tragedy of the commons" does not always need to unfold. In particular, she demonstrates that common pool problems can sometimes be solved by community-based voluntary organizations, without any state intervention.
- The Intergovernmental Panel on Climate Change is the leading authority on the study of the causes and consequences of global warming. Their latest synthesis report (IPCC 2015) provides an accessible summary of the state-of-the-art knowledge regarding climate change, including a vast amount of charts. Among other things, the report outlines the links between human activities and global warming, provides forecasts of future climate change and the risks involved, and discusses potential adaptation and mitigation pathways.
- William Nordhaus (2013) analyses the economic and political debates surrounding climate change in all their facets, from the origins of global warming in terms of personal and commercial energy usage to political reactions to global warming in the form of taxes, subsidies and quotas to slow down the emissions of greenhouse gases. He explains the steps that are necessary to combat climate change, why earlier policy interventions such as the Kyoto Protocol have failed, and which policy tools will be most effective going forward.

Bibliography

Coase, Ronald H. 1960. "The Problem of Social Cost". *Journal of Law and Economics* 3:1–44.

Etheridge, David M., L.P. Steele, R.L. Langenfelds, R.J. Francey, J.M. Barnola, and V.I. Morgan. 1996. "Natural and Anthropogenic Changes in Atmospheric CO_2 over the Last 1000 Years from Air in Antarctic Ice and Firn". *Journal of Geophysical Research: Atmospheres* 101:4115–4128.

Gardner, Roy, Elinor Ostrom, and James M. Walker. 1990. "The Nature of Common-Pool Resource Problems". *Rationality and Society* 2:335–358.

IPCC. 2015. *Climate Change 2014 – Synthesis Report. Contribution of Working Groups I, II and III to the Fifth Assessment Report of the IPCC*, edited by The Core Writing Team, Rajendra K. Pachauri, and Leo A. Meyer. Geneva: IPCC Publication.

Lomborg, Bjorn. 2016. "Impact of Current Climate Proposals". *Global Policy* 7:109–118.

Meadows, Donella H., Dennis L. Meadows, Jørgen Randers, and William W. Behrens III. 1972. *The Limits to Growth – A Report for the Club of Rome's Project on the Predicament of Mankind*. New York, NY: Universe Books.

Nordhaus, William D. 2008. *A Question of Balance: Weighing the Options on Global Warming Policies*. New Haven, CT: Yale University Press.

Nordhaus, William D. 2010. "Economic Aspects of Global Warming in a Post-Copenhagen Environment". *Proceedings of the National Academy of Sciences* 107:11721–11726.

Nordhaus, William D. 2013. *The Climate Casino: Risk, Uncertainty, and Economics for a Warming World*. New Haven, CT: Yale University Press.

Nordhaus, William. 2015. "Climate Clubs: Overcoming Free-Riding in International Climate Policy". *American Economic Review* 105:1339–1370.

Ostrom, Elinor. 1990. *Governing the Commons: The Evolution of Institutions for Collective Action*. Cambridge: Cambridge University Press.

Stern, Nicholas. 2007. *The Economics of Climate Change – The Stern Review*. Cambridge: Cambridge University Press.

Taleb, Nassim N. 2012. *Antifragile: How to Live in a World We Don't Understand*. London: Allen Lane.

World Commission on Environment and Development. 1987. *Our Common Future* (The Brundtland Report). Oxford: Oxford University Press.

13 Secularization, religious fundamentalism, and religious extremism

Chapter overview

The global religious landscape has undergone major changes in recent decades, which pose critical challenges to many societies around the world. In this chapter, we review several of these changes and challenges. We start by explaining how religious communities can be regarded as public goods that fulfil important functions – not just to their members, but to society as a whole. We next describe, for the two largest Abrahamic religions (Christianity and Islam), various trends and phenomena that have the potential to undermine this positive contribution to society, and to give rise to public bads. In particular, we focus on three phenomena: secularization, whereby an increasing number of people disengage from religion and religious institutions; religious fundamentalism, which involves a very strict adherence to the rules and teachings of a religion; and religious extremism, which translates fundamentalist views into extreme actions that most people do not consider reasonable or acceptable, such as violence and other human rights infringements. We stress, however, that the origins of religious violence and religion-based human rights transgressions lie in people's interpretations of holy scriptures, rather than in the holy scriptures themselves.

Religious landscapes in flux

In the first few decades after the Second World War, it seemed as though Western countries were going through an irreversible process of *secularization*, with an increasing number of people giving up their religious beliefs and leaving religious communities. Although such secularization trends are still ongoing, religion has returned to the forefront of public debate in recent decades. Factors that play a role in this regard include the rise of *religious fundamentalism* in certain subsections of the population (involving very strict and often literal interpretations of religious texts), the arrival of immigrants with different religions from the native population (see Chapter 6), and various terrorist attacks and other atrocities committed by people claiming to act in the name of religion.

Also in other parts of the world religion has maintained a key role in society or re-emerged as an important societal phenomenon. This is particularly clear for various regions in Africa, the Middle East, and East Asia, where there has been a surge in *religious extremism* – that is, extreme interpretations of holy texts that are translated into equally extreme actions, which are considered not normal, unreasonable, and unacceptable by most people. Such religious extremism – which can, by the way, also be found within many Western societies – often entails violence and other human rights infringements (e.g., forbidding people to switch religion or leave church), and takes a central place in many wars and conflicts around the world.

A prominent recent example of religious extremism involves the Islamic State of Iraq and Syria (ISIS), whose members adhere to a radical interpretation of Sunni Islam. As do many other extremist groups, ISIS rejects the distinction between the private sphere and the public sphere, as well as the separation between church and state. These views are derived from the idea that the rules for how society ought to be governed are laid out in religious texts, and that these rules constitute the revealed word of God. Moreover, religious extremists generally want to impose their rules and prescriptions on the rest of society, considering their own beliefs superior to those of others. As such, they reject democracy, as well as social norms such as tolerance, open debate, and compromise with those who hold different views. In doing so, they act in conflict with the UN's Universal Declaration of Human Rights, which prescribes that every individual has a right to freedom of religion, freedom of thought and conscience, freedom of opinion and expression, and protection against force and oppression.

Religious communities as public goods

Religion and religious communities have the potential to deliver numerous benefits to individuals and society as a whole. Most fundamentally, religion can offer believers comfort and salvation from the existential fears of humans over despair and death. It can also shed light on the meaning of life, provide individuals with inspiration, and teach them useful lessons on how to behave in everyday life. Furthermore, religious communities often serve an important social function to their members, representing a source of social support and identity, and offering a platform for social interactions and the development of friendship ties. Indeed, research indicates that there is a positive link between religiosity and life satisfaction and that this link is for the most part explained by the social benefits that religious communities offer (Lim and Putnam 2010).

As such, religious communities can play a key role in strengthening social cohesion in society and preventing individuals from social isolation. Importantly, however, such benefits do not only accrue to people who are members of religious communities – if there are active religious communities, this can also have positive spillover effects on society at large. For instance, it has been shown that overall rates of volunteering are higher in countries with higher religiosity levels, as religious individuals tend to volunteer more for both religious as well as secular causes and are often successful in also drawing their non-religious friends and acquaintances into volunteering activities (Ruiter and De Graaf 2006). In other words, religious communities have benefits that extend beyond their own group boundaries. Indeed, many religions have explicit social norms that their adherents should make a positive contribution to society as a whole, for example by helping vulnerable groups such as the poor, the homeless, or the disabled, or by donating to charity.

At the same time, however, being affiliated to a religion may impose substantial costs on believers – where "costs" should be interpreted broadly so as to also comprise non-pecuniary costs. For example, they must devote time to prayer, participate in rituals, follow certain rules, contribute to the running of their religious community, and in some cases it may also be required to make certain sacrifices, adhere to certain dietary prescriptions, or to adopt certain physical symbols. Given all of these costs, one may easily wonder why people join religious communities, and why they show such devotion to the tenets of their faith. In most cases, the answer to these questions will simply be that religious adherents perceive the benefits of their religious affiliation to exceed the costs involved.

Religious communities and organizations have certain public good characteristics insofar as they deliver certain benefits to their members (and indeed society at large) that are not directly tied to members' specific contributions to the community. One can think of the promise of an afterlife or social benefits that result from being part of the community. For individual actors it may be appealing to join a religious community in order to gain access to these benefits but to subsequently not give anything back to the community. From this perspective, religious communities are subject to a *free-rider problem*. This raises the challenge of how religious organizations can make sure that all of their members make a valuable contribution to the community.

The sociologist Michael Hechter (1987) points in this context to three available tools: monitoring, sanctioning, and providing so-called "immanent exclusive collective goods", which are only available to actively contributing members. Believers, in turn, can signal their commitment to the community by openly incurring certain costs (e.g., doing volunteer work, making sacrifices, following certain dietary and clothing requirements). As a reward for their efforts, the believer acquires status, protection, and comfort from the community, as well as spiritual support and the promise of an eternal life after death.

An interesting related phenomenon is that churches that impose stricter conditions upon their members tend to be the most resilient and tend to grow most rapidly. Initially, one would think of this as a paradox, given that one would probably expect fewer people to be attracted to organizations that are more demanding of their members. However, the economist Laurence Iannaccone (1994) demonstrated that this situation actually makes sense if we think of a religious community as a public good, and of a church doctrine as a tool to protect this public good.

In this setting, individual church members want comfort and support from the religious community, but are to some extent reluctant to incur the costs of providing such goods themselves. To prevent such free-rider behaviour, a strict church carefully monitors the behaviour of individual members through methods of social control. In particular, strict churches use methods such as preventing members from forming ties with outsiders, and delineating group membership via dietary and testamentary prescriptions. Since such strictness prevents free-rider behaviour, it increases the overall level of public goods provided within the religious community. This, in turn, means that these strict churches tend to have high levels of commitment to the community, and that these churches are relatively popular among prospective members.

It is clear that, given the social dynamics described above, different initial conditions may bring about very different kinds of religious organizations. Within each major world religion there are open organizations, which have usually not solved the free-rider problem, as well as small closed organizations, in which leaders impose stringent conditions on their members. Relatedly, there is also a decent degree of religious diversity within many countries. This especially holds for countries where the state does not favour any particular church. Conversely, in countries where one particular religious denomination is closely connected to the state, religious diversity within society tends to be quite limited. As such, institutions such as the state can leave a significant mark on the religious landscape of society.

When religious communities turn into public bads

Religious fundamentalism is regularly covered in the media. Typically, fundamentalists think that mainstream adherents of their religion have lost the ideological purity and they want to recapture that ideological purity. For this purpose, they advocate a return to a very strict and often literal interpretation of the holy scriptures of their religion. According to the religion scholar Bruce Lawrence (1989), religious fundamentalists hardly permit any criticism of their symbols, practices, beliefs or doctrines, and often demand that prescriptions derived from holy texts are publically acknowledged and legally enforced. Fundamentalism can thus be a source of violent extremism. At this stage, we can no longer speak of religious communities as public goods that deliver numerous benefits to society. Quite the contrary, radicalized religious groups that employ violent extremism are more aptly portrayed as public bads.

That said, it is important to remember that not every fundamentalist is necessarily also an extremist (Berman 2009). Roughly speaking, the former simply has to do with going back to the historical and written fundamentals of a religion, while the latter goes a step further and derives extreme implications from these fundamentals that most other people (including many fundamentalists) would regard as unreasonable and unacceptable. In many cases, these extreme implications involve violence and human rights transgressions.

Although fundamentalism can apply to any religion, the term originated in the late nineteenth and early twentieth centuries in the US. Fundamentalism arose there through Christian groups that advocated returning to the core doctrines – the fundaments – of Christian belief, as enshrined in the Bible. They also wanted to abolish the secular independence of the state from Christian beliefs. The fundamentalist movement was a reaction to theological liberalism, and its followers espoused a literal interpretation of Biblical stories and took the prescriptions found in the Bible as the benchmark for their behaviour in everyday life.

In the 1980s, the term Islamic fundamentalism began to gain currency within the Western world. While this term is regularly used in association with statements about violent atrocities, it is important to separate Islamic fundamentalism (covering people who favour a strict interpretation of the Quran) from Islamic extremism (covering people who commit violence, human rights infringements, and other extreme actions in the name of Islam). In addition to these terms, the French scholar Oliver Roy (1994) also coined the term *Islamism* to refer to the belief in Islam as an ideology and political programme, and more recently, the term *Jihadism* was coined in Western languages to describe violence committed in the name of Islam (Hammer and Rothstein 2012). Finally, the term *political Islam* is now often used to refer to all kinds of activities by individuals and organizations advocating a transformation of society and the state to conform to Islamic rules.

Secularization, religious revival, and fundamentalism in the Christian world

The *secularization thesis* claims that religion is in decline due to general modernization processes. The central idea is that citizens have become wealthier over time and thereby more independent from the church, while scientific developments also seem to be at odds with religion – a conflict nicely illustrated by the evolutionary model for explaining the origin of species, which contradicts many religious creation narratives. In line with the secularization thesis, a secularization process has been taking place in many developed, Christian countries. To the extent that religious communities can provide a positive contribution to society, as argued in the previous section, secularization may have problematic consequences for these countries. Among other things, citizens may experience a weakening of their sense of purpose, identity, and meaning; they may become more socially isolated; and at the macro-level volunteering rates and social cohesion may suffer.

Table 13.1 provides statistics on church membership and frequency of church attendance for thirteen Western countries from 1981–2018. Looking at the statistics, it appears that both church membership and church attendance have decreased in most countries, in line with the secularization thesis. However, the magnitude of the decline varies considerably from one country to another. Moreover, for some countries we observe somewhat different trends for church membership than for church attendance. For example, in the Nordic countries church membership dropped significantly, whilst church attendance has remained fairly stable. Conversely, in Spain the decline in church membership has been relatively more pronounced than the decline in church membership.

As Table 13.1 demonstrates, there was a decline of more than 20 percentage points in church membership in Belgium, Canada, Denmark, Norway, Spain, and Sweden. In Germany, Ireland, Italy, the UK, and the US, on the other hand, church membership rates are still above 75 percent. With regard to the percentage of the population attending church at least once a week, Belgium, Ireland and Spain experienced a decline of more than 20 percentage points. Especially striking is the decline of 62 percentage points in Ireland: in 1981 more than 82 percent of the Irish population attended church at least weekly, but by 2018 this figure had been decimated to only 20 percent. The main reason why some countries experienced little decline in church attendance (and why France experienced no decline in church membership) is that these countries already started off from fairly low base levels in 1981.

If the percentage of churchgoers in a country remains stable, does that imply that there is no secularization taking place? As we have stated many times throughout the book, it is risky

Table 13.1 Church membership and attendance for a selection of countries, 1981-2018

	Percentage of population who are members of a church			**Percentage of population who attend church at least once a week**		
Country	**1981**	**2018**	**Change**	**1981**	**2018**	**Change**
Belgium	83	62	–21	30	6	–24
Canada	89	67	–22	30	20	–10
Denmark	94	70	–24	3	3	0
France	71	72	1	11	12	1
Germany	91	76	–15	18	10	–8
Ireland	99	85	–14	82	20	-62
Italy	93	81	–12	32	23	–9
Netherlands	62	51	–11	25	12	–13
Norway	96	57	-39	6	7	1
Spain	91	70	–21	40	15	-25
Sweden	93	58	–35	6	6	0
UK	90	77	–13	14	8	–6
US	94	77	–17	43	36	–7

Note: Data for 1981 are from the European Values Study; data for 2018 are from the Pew Research Center.

to draw conclusions from macro-level indicators alone. We can illustrate this with an example from the Netherlands. By way of background, church membership in the Netherlands began decreasing in 1849, but the decrease was very small until 1960. From 1930–1960, church membership decreased by only five percentage points. A clear fault line is visible around 1960. During the relatively short period from 1960–2009, the percentage of non-churchgoers increased from 18 to 45 percent. Interestingly, however, the percentage of Catholics only began decreasing in 1971 – about a decade later than for most other denominations. Indeed, between 1960 and 1971, the percentage of Catholics remained roughly the same, which is all the more surprising because this was a decade in which the Catholic Church underwent a considerable amount of turmoil in the Netherlands: a number of priests and religious leaders resigned, and many congregants left the church.

The apparent contradiction can be explained by the fact that there were substantial differences in fertility between Catholics and non-churchgoers. Because Catholics on average have more children than the rest of the population, disproportionally many Catholics have to leave the church for the percentage of Catholics in the population to go down over time. This is what happened during the 1960s: even though many Catholics left the church, the percentage of Catholics in the total population did not decrease because of the high fertility rate among Catholics (Need and De Graaf 1996). A corollary is that research based on repeated cross-sections of the population will usually underestimate the rate of church leaving. Indeed, higher rates of fertility among religious groups are the reason why the world as a whole still becomes more religious, despite powerful secularization trends (Norris and Inglehart 2004).

Secularization and fundamentalism among Catholics and Protestants

Here we discuss secularization and fundamentalism trends within three major Christian denominations: Catholics, Reformed Protestants, and Evangelical Protestants. For the sake of simplicity, we group both the Eastern Orthodox Church and the Anglican Church together with the Catholic Church.

Secularization is visible in the Roman Catholic Church both at the institutional and societal level. Although the Catholic Church fiercely rejected many aspects of modernity until the 1950s, it changed tack in the 1960s when confronted with a widespread loss of members due to secularization, and decided to soften its stance on certain aspects of modernity. During the *Second Vatican Council* (1962–1965) a range of far-reaching reforms were introduced. An example of such *institutional secularization* was that religious members and lower-ranked spiritual leaders were given a bigger say over the affairs of the church, thereby moving the church towards more democracy. More generally, the reforms introduced during the Second Vatican Council centred on defending democracy, human rights, and, as a clear indicator of secularization, the principle of freedom of religion.

However, in the 1970s, conservative cardinals initiated a counter-movement against the reforms of the Second Vatican Council, attempting to impede the progressive course of the church. According to the French political scientist Gilles Kepel (1994), this conservative stream became the dominant one within the Church after the appointment of Pope John Paul II in 1978. This new Pope reasserted the traditional Catholic doctrine on moral issues by re-emphasizing the monogamous heterosexual marital relationship and sexual abstinence for unmarried people.

He also provided strong opposition to homosexuality and artificial means of birth control. Furthermore, the church adopted a stalwart position against abortion and campaigned to outlaw such procedures in various countries. Its well-known argument is that, since all human life is holy, and the embryo is the beginning of a human individual, abortion is tantamount to murder.

The Roman Catholic Church has also steadfastly opposed the use of condoms in developing countries, although Pope Benedict XVI stated in 2010 that the use of condoms could be morally justified under certain circumstances – a claim reiterated by his successor Pope Francis. For a long time, Catholic officials in Latin America, Asia, and Africa have sought to block birth control programs that encourage the use of the condom or the contraceptive pill. This opposition runs counter to the great need for birth control among citizens of these regions. Consequently, the policies of the Roman Catholic Church have influenced the spread of the HIV/AIDS epidemic. The church has opposed campaigns for safe sex that recommend the use of condoms; instead, it prescribed for a long-time abstinence and marital faithfulness as the means of combating the spread of this disease.

Protestants, in turn, form the biggest religious community in the US. American Baptists, Episcopalians, Lutherans, and Presbyterians all belong to the Protestant mainstream derived from the churches that emerged in Europe during and after the *Reformation*. The Reformation emerged from resistance against the Pope in Rome, and ever since, Protestant churches have had a strong preference for democratic organization. This goes together with a highly decentralized organization, which means Protestantism is highly fragmented. Because the Reform Protestants believed that any given person is predestined to end up either in heaven or in hell, they did not see much use in trying to convert people through missionaries. It was only in the nineteenth century that churches began to pursue the goal of expansion.

Evangelical Protestant churches are derived from Reform Protestantism, but the content of their religious doctrines is markedly different in a number of ways. Reform Protestants believe that a human being is unable to affect whether or not they end up in heaven, because their fate is predetermined by God. However, in the nineteenth century, American Protestant preachers started to announce that human beings could, in fact, consciously decide to convert to Christ. The Evangelical Protestant churches that grew out of this movement thus place strong emphasis on conversion, on the emotional experience of one's faith, and on evangelization (that is, preaching the faith to others).

Fundamentalism within Protestant churches in the US was a reaction to churches becoming worldlier and adjusting their views to modernity. At the end of the nineteenth and the start of the twentieth century, fundamentalists viewed these adjustments as heresy and, as typical for fundamentalists, wanted to go back to the fundamentals of their faith. Hence, they advocated interpreting the Bible literally rather than symbolically, based on the belief that it contains the absolute truth about the word of God. From the 1920s to the 1960s, the fundamentalist Protestant streams were however still in the minority, meaning that the Protestant church's agenda was determined by mostly liberal Mainline Protestants.

Yet, at the same time as the Catholic conservative movement emerged, the fundamentalist Protestant movement became much more prominent. In 1976, Baptist minister Jerry Falwell started a series of "I Love America" rallies across the US. This became a movement known as the *Moral Majority*. The leaders of this movement were concerned about the moral decline of the country, and asked believers to rise up and help to reverse this trend. Similar to the Catholic conservative movement, they argued that mainstream Christian churches had lost members because they had neglected traditional values.

Among other things, the fundamentalists campaigned fiercely (and continue to do so) against abortion and Charles Darwin's theory of evolution. Regarding the latter, they have succeeded to legalize the teaching of *creationism* in some states – that is, the creation story described in the Old Testament of the Bible, which implies that God created all life on earth and that Darwin's theory is wrong. Similarly, it is widespread among Evangelical Protestant Christians to believe in the Biblical prophecy of the end of time. During the nineteenth century, Protestant preachers in the US started to espouse this belief, and it has since acquired a central place within the evangelical movement. One of the many versions of this belief states that, at the end of time, the rapture will take place: Christ will appear and take all true believers to heaven, leaving those who do not qualify behind. Then a seven-year period of tribulation follows, and a battle on earth between the powers of good and evil (known as Armageddon). Eventually, Christ will return again and establish a kingdom of peace and justice on earth.

To further illustrate the continuing relevance of religion in the US, an opinion survey by the Pew Research Center (Lipka 2015) found that, in 2014, 63 percent of all Americans believed in God and were absolutely certain about their faith, 20 percent believed in God and were fairly certain about their faith, six percent believed in God but were uncertain, and nine percent simply did not believe in God (with an additional two percent refusing to answer the question or reporting that they did not know). Moreover, although the proportion of "absolutely certain believers" came down from 71 percent in 2007, and the proportion of "non-believers" went up from five percent in that same year, it is important to note that some religious groups have been more resilient than others. For example, while the proportion of "absolutely certain believers" among Mainline Protestants was 66 percent in 2014, it equalled as much as 88 percent among Evangelical Protestants, with an additional ten percent of Evangelical Protestants being fairly certain about their faith. These disparities emphasize that belief in God remains more widespread among fundamentalist groups than among groups with more liberal doctrines.

The importance of fundamentalism in the American religious landscape is further stressed by surveys documenting that, anno 2017, around 40 percent of the US population believe in creationism (Swift 2017). Once again, there is significant variation in the prevalence of such beliefs among different religions groups. One mainly finds creationist views among followers of Evangelical Protestant churches like the Pentecostalists, Southern Baptists, and the Assemblies of God. Relatedly, the view that God created humans is shared by 65 percent of all people who attend church weekly, versus only 21 percent of those who attend church less than once a month. Once again, however, we do observe certain shifts towards a declining faith in God in recent years. In particular, while the proportion of Americans accepting the evolutionary account of human origin (with no role for God) remained stable at nine percent from 1982–2000, this number rose to 19 percent by 2017.

Why is the United States less secularized than Europe?

As indicated by Table 13.1, the process of secularization – measured as a decrease in church membership and the frequency of church attendance – has not occurred to the same extent in all countries. In this context, the fact that the US is the world's largest and most technologically advanced economy, combined with the fact that a large number of Americans are still affiliated to a church, exemplifies that there is no clear-cut relationship between measures of secularization and measures of economic development.

Figure 13.1, displaying trends in the population shares of different denominations in the US, shows in this respect that – although there has been a clear increase in the percentage of *religious nones* since 2000, mostly driven by a fall in Protestantism – almost 80 percent of all Americans still considered themselves as belonging to a religion in 2017. Furthermore, religion and politics are still closely intertwined in the US. Surveys show that very few Americans would consider voting for a president who identified as atheist. Republicans also often attack Democrats on the grounds that religion plays too small of a role in their political programme, and US presidents regularly make statements along the lines of "may God bless America". In short, religion is still very much alive and kicking in the US, contrary to what one would expect on the basis of the secularization thesis, and contrary to what we see in nearly all countries in Europe.

How can this "American exceptionalism" with respect to secularization be explained? One early theory (Herberg 1955) draws a link with acculturation processes among European immigrants, 35 million of which settled in the US in the nineteenth and early twentieth centuries. The idea is that the first generation of migrants had held onto the ethnic identity of their countries of origin for a long time, but that their children, the second generation, left their parents' identities behind and sought to assimilate into American society. However, their children, the third generation, supposedly returned to their religious family traditions.

Another, more recent theory by the sociologist Laurence Moore (1994) argued that American religion had become a "commodity" to be sold on the "cultural market". In particular, television had become an alternative to the pulpit, from where preachers could reach many thousands of people at once. After the Second World War, so-called "televangelists" tried to convert people

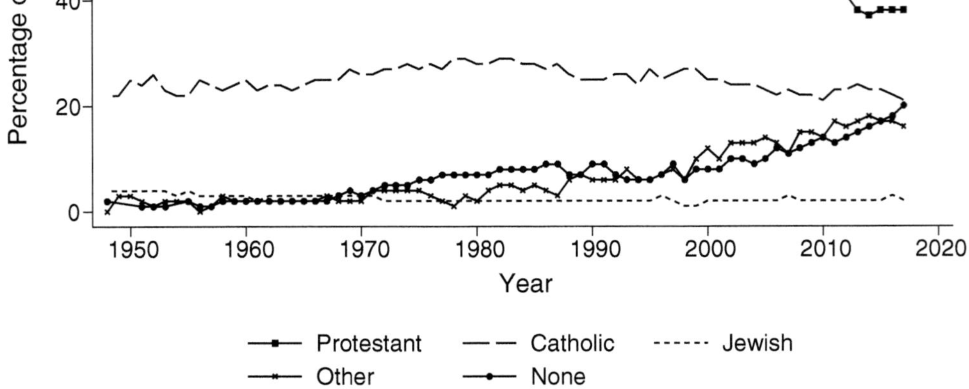

Figure 13.1 The population of the United States by religious denomination, 1948-2017

Note: Data are from the Gallup Religion Database.

through immersive programming and their own personal charisma. In the 1950s and 1960s, Time magazine described Fulton Sheen as the first televangelist. Later, in the 1980s, Jim Bakker, another televangelist, built a Christian theme park comparable to Disneyland. Moore's theory is that such marketing strategies may have made people stick to their faith.

A related, but more formalized theory, known as the *supply-side theory*, has attracted a lot of attention from social scientists since the 1980s. This theory was developed by the sociologist Rodney Stark and economist Laurence Iannaccone (1994; see also Stark and Finke 2000). The starting-point is that people can choose to join a religious organization or not, and that in making such decisions they act rationally. Religious organizations can subsequently make more or less effort to retain members. When a church has the monopoly position in a country, say because it is a state church (e.g., the Church of England), that church is expected to make much less of an effort to retain members than when it faces fierce competition from other churches. A key assumption of the supply-side theory is that the demand for religion remains constant over time. Whether or not people join a church is, therefore, entirely determined by the supply of religious organizations that compete with each other to win and retain followers.

Fierce competition implies that all organizations will make a big effort in this regard (because they have to), resulting in many people being won over to become and stay religiously affiliated (although they may switch between churches). Weak competition implies that religious organizations will take more of a back seat, resulting in lower recruitment and retention rates. Applying this logic, the supply-side theory argues that the reason for the high level of religiosity in the US is its particularly high degree of competition among churches.

However, the supply-side theory has been the subject of much criticism (De Graaf 2013). For example, it seems to imply that Americans who do not attend church are not religious. After all, every American with even a whiff of a religious inclination should be able to find a religious organization of their liking, given such a diverse and competitive religious market. Empirical evidence, however, suggests that Americans who do not go to church are more religiously inclined than do non-churchgoers in countries where the supply of religious goods is more limited (Kelley and De Graaf 1997). In addition, supply-side theory puts much emphasis on the idea that belonging to a certain church is an active choice. Yet, most believers report to identify with their religion purely because they were raised that way.

Another perspective on the question of American religious exceptionalism purports that American society is actually secularizing (see also Figure 13.1), and that the question of why the US is an exception is therefore misstated. In support of this argument, the sociologists David Voas and Mark Chaves (2016) show that religiosity in the US has already been declining for decades, and that this process is driven by the same forces as in Europe. That is, there is a clear pattern of cohort replacement in the US, whereby each successive birth cohort is more secular than the one that came before it.

That said, it still appears that secularization took off later, and/or at a slower pace, in the US than in other advanced countries. Sociologist Steve Bruce (2002) offers a potential reason for this, by noting that the US has had high rates of immigration from religious countries. Especially the inflow of Mexicans, who are generally socialized into religious belief, may have compensated for secularization among native-born Americans. This could also partly explain the relatively flat line for Catholics in Figure 13.1.

Moderate Islam, Muslim fundamentalists, and violent extremism

Indonesia is an example of a country where Muslims have become more conservative in past decades and where secularization hardly exists. Fundamentalist Muslims are gaining momentum, as illustrated by their successful bid in 2017 to have Jakarta's governor Basuki Purnama (a Christian of Chinese descent) put in prison for blasphemy. In addition, there has been an increase in intolerance towards other religions, in the proportion of women wearing a *hijab* (the Islamic veil), and in the strictness of fasting during the *Ramadan*. Finally, along the extremist spectrum, Indonesia witnessed a number of terrorist attacks in the name of radical Islam in 2018, including several by families with young children.

The re-Islamization in the Islamic world started in the 1970s, through a movement led by Saudi Arabia and other Gulf States. The massive increase of economic power commanded by these states, as a consequence of risen oil prices after the 1973 oil crisis, played a crucial role in establishing this movement. The ruling dynasties of the Gulf states invested heavily in promoting a fundamentalist version of Islam, known as *Wahhabism*. They funded the building of mosques (including abroad, such as in Europe), scholarships for Islamic study, hospitals in poor areas, and sent missionaries to Islamic countries in the developing world.

Core beliefs and key components of Islam

Islam and Christianity are both *monotheistic religions* (believing in one God) and share a common place of origin in the Middle East. However, there are also clear differences between them. Several of these differences relate to the rules by which both religions are governed. The community of Islamic believers (the *ummah*) is governed by divine laws. According to Islam, Allah revealed these laws to the Prophet Muhammad in the holy Quran. Stories about the actions and words of the Prophet are given in the *hadith*. The totality of prescriptions and prohibitions that form the content of the obligatory doctrine of Islam are known as the *sharia*, or Islamic law. A pious Islamic society is one that adheres to the guidelines of the *sharia* as closely as possible. The Islamic laws apply to both the public and the private sphere, covering both criminal and civil law. As such, they regulate all aspects of life: worship of Allah, religious obligations, marriage and divorce, inheritance, trade, etc. In practice, many interpretations of the Islamic laws have been derived over the course of fourteen centuries by different script scholars (*ulama*), so not all concrete prescriptions are fully agreed upon.

Another important difference between Christianity and Islam is that Christianity prescribes a code for individuals to live by, but contains few rules for the design of society as a whole – that is, it offers many micro-level laws but not that many macro-level ones. Islam, on the other hand, emphasizes public ethics and collective morality, rather than individual or private guidelines. Therefore, Islam is sometimes described as a political religion. While this is in practice often an appropriate characterization, Islamic laws are primarily meant to govern public order in general, not the state per se. That said, in traditional Islam, religion and politics were closely intertwined, which is why it is frequently asserted that Islam is incompatible with secular, liberal, democratic societies.

Especially since the beginning of the twenty-first century, Western societies have become acquainted with one of the core tenets of Islam, *jihad*, which means effort or struggle. In principle, every Muslim is obligated to engage in jihad – that is, to fight for the expansion of Islam. Moderate Muslims interpret this as a duty to respect the general lessons of Islam's holy scriptures and to conduct oneself piously. However, fundamentalist believers and especially Islamic extremists interpret jihad as a command to discriminate against non-believers, and even to wage war against them. Many extremists use the notion of jihad to justify terrorist attacks against Christians, Jews, Hindus, Buddhists, or even against moderate Muslims. In fact, over the past few decades, many more Muslims have been killed by their fellow believers than by adherents of other religions.

Although Islamic doctrine emphasizes the unity of all believers, there are actually many pronounced divisions and disparate factions and sects within Islam. The most important distinction is between *Sunnis* and *Shia*. This schism arose about 1,400 years ago following a conflict about the succession of the Prophet Muhammad. In *Sunni Islam*, there is no central organization or any hierarchy of clerics, whereas in *Shia Islam* there are such hierarchies. In this respect, Shia Islam can be considered more similar to the Roman Catholic Church. About 85 to 90 percent of all Muslims in the world are Sunnis, and Sunni Islam is therefore dominant in most Muslim countries, including Saudi Arabia, Egypt and Syria, to mention a few. In turn, roughly ten percent of all Muslims in the world are Shia, and they represent the majority in, amongst others, Iran and Iraq.

Islamic scholars are tasked with interpreting the Islamic doctrines and providing an answer to the question of what particular behaviour Islam prescribes in any given situation. In this context, related questions and answers together form a *fatwa*. However, as re-Islamization was getting underway in the Islamic world, Islam's religious and political leadership became further decentralized and fragmented, especially in the Middle East. This is illustrated by the fact that not only script scholars nowadays announce fatwas, but increasingly also religious teachers, military leaders, or lower-level clerics without extensive religious training. Examples are the proclamation of war against "Zionists and crusaders" by the late Osama bin Laden and the many fatwas spread by ISIS. Illustrative for the fragmentation is that nearly 70,000 Indian Muslim clerics in 2015 issued a fatwa against ISIS, al-Qaeda, the Taliban and other terror groups (Mortimer 2015).

Salafism, political Islam, and Islamism

The term *Islamism* denotes any movement that interprets Islam as a political ideology and becoming an Islamist thus is a political statement. According to the historian Michael Cook (2014), Islamists want to develop their politics from their Islamic heritage and Islamism is a fundamentalist programme for political and social activism. Islamism should not be confused with *Salafism*, which is the idea that the true Islam is found in the lived example of the early generations of Muslims, known as the *Salafi*, who were closest to the Prophet Muhammad. Salafists are regarded as fundamentalists, but they are less inclined towards active political engagement and, by and large, they try to avoid confrontations with state authorities.

In the 1970s, movements that could be characterized as Islamist arose in a number of Middle Eastern countries. The chief goal of these movements is to impose sharia law in all areas of society. Islamist groups put pressure on their fellow Muslims to abide by sharia law, and try to force governments to prohibit alcohol consumption, outlaw prostitution, proscribe women from walking the streets unaccompanied, and prescribe them to wear hijabs. Islamists believe that if all Muslims adhere to such rules, Islam will flourish and become a powerful force on the world stage. Islamism is a large and growing global movement. For example, the governments of Iran and Sudan are both avowedly Islamist. Globally, between ten and 50 percent of all Muslims can be considered Islamist, depending on the exact definition used (Lipka 2017).

Insofar as Islamism is an ideology, it should be distinguished from traditional Islam, even though the latter also places great emphasis on adherence to Islamic practices. The key difference derives from the fact that in traditional Islam sharia law is construed as a personal life regimen that applies to every Muslim, but not to non-Muslims. According to Islamism, by contrast, sharia law is construed as a territorial law, which applies to an entire territory, like that occupied by ISIS. This means, for example, that the prohibition to drink alcohol applies not only to Muslims, but also to non-Muslims who happen to live within the same territory.

In other words, Islamists interpret sharia law in the same way as state legislation is interpreted in Western countries. Additionally, they view the sharia as a system of eternal truths. This interpretation runs counter to the convictions of many moderate Islam scholars, who argue that Islamic law is the result of a process of historical development within Islamic societies, and that it therefore must be constantly reinterpreted. These scholars distance themselves from Islamist interpretations of the sharia, which they label as so-called ahistorical essentialism, whereby it is assumed that the meaning of particular laws is unchangeable, independent of concrete social contexts, and strictly fixed over time.

Within Islamism, there are extremist groups whose members are prepared to commit violence against their political enemies, whether those are Muslims or non-Muslims. Well-known examples of such groups are *Hamas* in the Palestinian Territories and *Hezbollah* in Lebanon. These organizations exercise violent resistance, including terrorism, against the ruling powers in their territories. As such, they are considered freedom fighters by their supporters. In addition to violent resistance, these organizations are also involved in social and political activities. However, there are also extremist groups that are driven solely by religious ideology, such as ISIS and al-Qaeda. These organizations are highly expansionist and have certain cult-like features. They strongly oppose Western countries, whom they view as colonizers intervening in what are rightfully Muslim lands. Their primary goal is to drive Christians and Jews out of Islamic territory.

Islamist movements

In the wave of decolonization after the Second World War, newly independent countries typically adopted the Western model of the secular, democratic state. Yet, several decades later, many of these countries were often not only poor, but also racked by war or ethnic conflict. In addition, various attempts to create a secular ideology for the Muslim world, such as *pan-Arabism*, consistently failed. Consequently, towards the end of the twentieth century, many intellectuals in the Islamic world became convinced that the Western model had failed, and turned against political leaders who blindly followed Western ideas. This development strengthened the revival of Islam since the 1970s.

We have already discussed the importance of the role of Saudi Arabia's oil revenues for the emergence and diffusion of the re-Islamization movement. Nevertheless, this was not the only force driving the re-Islamization of the Islamic world that started in the 1970s. The sociologist Mansoor Moaddel (2002) discusses in this context several families of theories: namely the crisis, the cultural duality, and the state culture theories.

If you take the *crisis theories*, they assert that fundamentalism is a response to a political, economic and cultural crisis in countries such as Egypt, Iraq and Syria before the turn of the century. These circumstances produced many dissatisfied people, who harboured a desire for political change. However, while it makes sense that persistently high unemployment would produce a large number of dissatisfied people, such a positive correlation between economic hardship and rising fundamentalism was not observed in all settings where the re-Islamization movement gained ground. Iran, for example, was on a path of steady economic development when the Islamic Revolution of 1978–1979 started.

According to Moaddel (2002), *cultural duality theories* have overcome these shortcomings. These theories maintain that the re-Islamization movement had its origin in the parallel cultural structures that had developed in many Muslim countries and that were difficult to reconcile with one another. In Iran before the revolution, for example, there was on the one hand the secular state, developing according to Western models, and on the other the Muslim tradition. In the 1970s, both structures were increasingly on a collision course. In particular, the Iranian political regime had become authoritarian, repressive and corrupt, and this was a driver for revolt, whereby the country's Muslim tradition was used as a vehicle to unite the revolting masses.

State culture theories do not presuppose a duality between the state and religion. They focus more singularly on the failure of secular states as the crucial driver behind the re-Islamization movement. Advocating a state culture theory, Kepel (2002) assumes a key role for what he calls the frustrated intelligentsia in explaining the rise of Islamism. Part of his logic is illustrated though a macro-micro-macro scheme in Figure 13.2.

The macro-level starting-point is that in the 1950s and 1960s many young people in Muslim countries entered tertiary education for the first time. This resulted in a growing class of

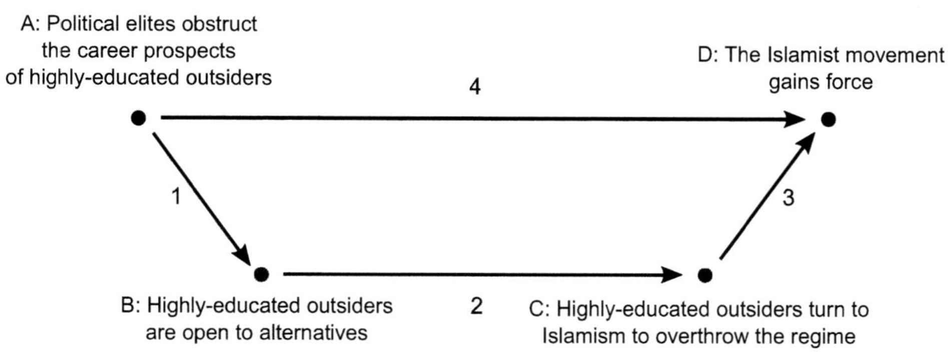

Figure 13.2 How Islamism can gain a foothold among a frustrated intelligentsia

highly-educated citizens. However, these intelligentsia had a hard time building successful careers in which they could take advantage of the knowledge and skills that they had accumulated. The reason was that the ruling political elites, feeling threatened by this growing class of highly-educated citizens, actively obstructed the career opportunities of these outsiders to the regime (point A in Figure 13.2). Among other things, only very few graduates were able to secure a place within the state apparatus, as the ruling elite guarded their own power and privileges closely, for example giving preferential treatment in accessing government jobs to friends and family. In this way, the elites checked the upward mobility of highly-educated outsiders.

Because the intelligentsia had no opportunities to rise within the existing political system, they became frustrated with the regime, and came to see the secular state according to Western model as a failed experiment. As such, they were susceptible to Islamists who favoured an alternative system, and promised more opportunities to highly-educated outsiders (point B in Figure 13.2). At the micro level, many highly-educated outsiders thus decided that it was a good idea to join the Islamist movement and to help them to overthrow the ruling elites (point C). Because many highly-educated outsiders followed this course of action, the Islamist movement became increasingly powerful at the macro level (point D).

According to Kepel (1994), the growth of the Islamist movement was further facilitated by a middle class of professionals, officials, and traders, who were also frustrated regarding the political regime and thus prepared to finance the movement. Moreover, the fact that many highly-educated individuals joined the movement had important multiplier effects. In particular, the intelligentsia played an important role in packaging and presenting the Islamist movement in an attractive and sympathetic way to potential new recruits to the movement, as well as foreign parties that could at some point also be of service in overthrowing the regime. With regard to the former, the Islamist movement managed to mobilize a large class of urban poor, who were susceptible to well-communicated recruitment messages, which for example emphasized that the ruling elites had ignored the interests of the urban poor for many years. The large numbers of urban poor that subsequently joined the Islamist movement were of great strategic importance, as they could fill the lower ranks of the movement.

Terrorism and suicide terrorism

Terrorism is the unlawful use of violence and intimidation to spread fear on a large scale in the pursuit of political, religious, or other aims. Typically, it involves indiscriminate violence aimed at civilians, meaning that everyone could in principle fall victim to it – a crucial element in ensuring that widespread fear is provoked. In recent decades, atrocious terrorist attacks have occurred almost everywhere in the world. At the time of writing, the large-scale terrorist attacks in Paris in 2015 are still in the minds of many in the Western world, and the same is true for the attacks in Brussels in 2016, the attack in Manchester in 2017, and many more. Many of these recent terrorist events are suicide attacks in which activists blow themselves up in an attempt to kill as many others as possible.

While the abovementioned attacks all occurred in Europe, similar attacks also very regularly occur – and often even more frequently – in places such as Israel, Indonesia, Sri Lanka, and Nigeria. What is more, while the abovementioned European attacks were committed in the name of radical Islam, terrorism is by no means exclusive to Islam. One could, for example, think of the extensive series of terrorist actions by separatist movements such as the IRA in Northern Ireland and the ETA in the Basque Country (Spain), both of which caused many casualties in the second half of the twentieth century and, in the case of the ETA, the first decade of the twenty-first century.

It is relatively straightforward to explain why extremist organizations utilize the weapon of suicide terrorism. Specifically, it allows them to inflict maximum damage prior to detection, and at a low cost. A martyr blowing themselves up also attracts the attention of the media, thereby bringing the relevant grievance to the attention of the public. Whereas recruiting, training, equipping, and sending out a suicide attacker is relatively cheap, public authorities must incur immense expenses to prevent such attacks (e.g., installing surveillance systems, putting up barriers, and hiring additional police officers), especially because it is virtually impossible to predict where the next terrorist attack will strike.

From the perspective of a relatively weak party fighting a comparatively strong enemy, suicide terrorism is hence a very efficient and effective weapon. A possible consequence, of course, is that a spiral of violence and counter violence is set into motion, which makes it very difficult for the opposing parties to ever reach a compromise that could serve as a solution to this problematic situation. However, a compromise is often exactly what violent extremists – with an unbendable all-or-nothing mentality when it comes to their fundamentalist views – are not interested in. Indeed, they generally prefer creating polarization over reaching a peaceful compromise.

Naturally, people find it difficult to grasp why terrorists carry out suicide missions, certainly also in cases when the attackers are still children, as for various recent terrorist actions for which ISIS claimed responsibility. However, the children involved in such actions are children without much future, who are vulnerable to indoctrination efforts and sensitive to promises of rewards in the afterlife. With respect to adult terrorists, interviews with failed attackers and family members of attackers have revealed that suicide terrorists are usually, in fact, not from impoverished backgrounds or afflicted by personality disorders (Atran 2003). Such interviews furthermore confirm that religious beliefs related to afterlife rewards play a key role, and that terrorists are frequently driven by a sense of anger about humiliation and oppression at the hands of a foreign occupier (Gambetta 2005).

Looking at the perspective of extremist organizations, sociological and psychological research shows that these organizations deliberately target young people, who are unmarried, deeply religious, and indignant about their personal situation (Atran 2003). They then apply specific propaganda techniques in order to activate the appropriate psychological dispositions of prospective attackers. These techniques are usually applied within small, isolated cells of three to eight members, where monitoring and sanctioning is relatively straightforward. Because of the intense interactions within the cell, and because of their relative isolation, bonds of brotherhood emerge between the members.

Regarding the creation of such bonds, it appears terrorist organizations are aware of the *theory of kin-selection*, which states that acts of *altruism* – whereby one individual incurs a cost in order to benefit another – tend to occur disproportionately among close relatives. Organizations that recruit and train suicide attackers, therefore attempt to inculcate a sense of brotherhood in them by fostering fictive kinship relations. The organization thereby redirects prospective attackers' evolved instinct for kin altruism toward unrelated co-ethnics. As noted by the anthropologist Scott Atran (2011), the internet and social media channels can be very effective in nurturing bonds of brotherhood, by enabling "would-be" jihadi martyrs to extensively exchange ideas with like-minded others in an anonymous setting. Such interactions can strengthen participants' commitments to certain means and causes, force intimate social ties, and instil a sense of community and kinship.

Coming to the end of this section, one may wonder what there is to expect from the future. It is impossible to answer this question without engaging in a certain degree of speculation, but one important factor may be what will happen in Saudi Arabia in the near future. As mentioned, Saudi Arabia has been an influential source of spreading a fundamentalist approach to Islam, making use of its oil revenues. In 2017, however, the crown prince of Saudi Arabia, Mohammad bin Salman, announced that the country should return to a more moderate interpretation of Islam.

If this means that Saudi Arabia's financial support for Islamic fundamentalists and extremists will dry up, this might lead to a more moderate version of Islam in many countries, especially if Saudi Arabia decides to turn its oil revenues to the purpose of actively spreading such an approach to Islam. Nevertheless, scepticism as to the good intentions of the crown prince is certainly warranted, among other things in light of the repressive violence that Saudi Arabia continues to employ in domestic affairs as well as its sustained aggression towards its much poorer neighbour Yemen.

Among other things, Human Rights Watch (2018:461–463) reports that, as recently as September 2017 (when Mohammed bin Salman had already been appointed as crown prince), "Saudi authorities carried out a wave of arrests of clerics and others in what appeared to be a coordinated crackdown on dissent. Saudi Arabia continued to repress pro-reform activists and peaceful dissidents. (. . .) Saudi Arabia does not tolerate public worship by adherents of religions other than Islam and systematically discriminates against Muslim religious minorities". Perhaps most strikingly, a series of royal decrees from 2014 re-defined atheists as terrorists, and in 2017 a man was reportedly sentenced to death because he renounced Islam and the Prophet Mohammed in videos on social media (McKernan 2017). From this perspective, Saudi Arabia has an incredibly long way to go before it can lead any shift in the Middle East to a more moderate version of Islam.

Religion and human rights issues

In her book *Islam and Human Rights*, the socio-legal scholar Ann Mayer (2013) describes the problematic relationship between human rights and certain interpretations of Islam. The UN's Universal Declaration of Human Rights (UDHR) stipulates that all human beings are born free and equal in dignity, and enumerates a number of rights to which all people are entitled, including freedom from oppression, torture, and persecution, and freedom of religion. However, various Islamic fundamentalists and extremists who strictly and literally adhere to the words of the Prophet Mohammed as they are revealed in the Quran, refuse to accept the authority of manmade laws, arguing that human reason cannot legitimately question divine commands. Accordingly, a number of Muslim countries have not endorsed the UDHR.

Saudi Arabia – one of the founding members of the UN in 1946 – rejected the UDHR at the time on the grounds of it being incompatible with the divine laws of Islam. Kuwait, Pakistan, and Turkey, amongst others, refused to sign later UN covenants pertaining to human rights. In 1981, a number of Muslim countries, together with various Sunni Muslim organizations, created a Universal Islamic Declaration of Human Rights (UIDHR), modelled on the earlier UDHR. The UIDHR obviously outlines various human rights, but severely limits their application by articulating certain principles that are derived from Islamic laws but incongruent with basic elements of international law. As such, the UIDHR represents a firm rejection of the UDHR.

Of course, it should be stressed that Islam is not the only religion for which we can observe tension with human rights issues. Tension also arises in relation to more extreme interpretations of other religions. This applies, for example, to the oppression of women that is common among many strict adherents to holy scriptures, including among certain groups of Christian fundamentalists. Indeed, in many fundamentalist religious communities, women are heavily monitored and subordinated to their male relatives. As noted in Chapter 8, such gender inequalities are problematic from a moral perspective, and imply that half of society cannot live up to its potential.

Another delicate matter concerning the relationship between religion and women's rights is the practice of female genital mutilation (FGM). FGM concerns the ritual cutting or removal of some or all of a girl's or a woman's external genitalia. The alleged aim is to keep women from losing their virginity. It is still practiced in many countries around the world, being particularly common in Africa, Asia, the Middle East, and elsewhere within migrant communities that originate from countries where FGM is common. UNICEF (2016) estimated that as many as 200 million girls and women from around 30 countries were subjected to FGM in 2015. Both Muslims and certain Christian groups are known to carry out the procedure, although neither the Quran nor the Bible contain any justifications for it.

Through a social science lens, the persistence of FGM can be explained using the concept of *conventions* and the mechanism of a *belief trap* – which describes how situations can exist in which a particular belief within society has very negative consequences for society as a whole or certain subgroups, but where this belief cannot (easily) be changed, because the costs associated with such a change are prohibitively high. The political scientist Gerry Mackie (1996) reasons in this context that, once there is a convention that women should be subjected to FGM, every high-ranking man will expect the woman he marries to have been subjected to it. This will, in turn, mean that every low-ranking family will subject their daughter to FGM, in order to leave open the possibility of her marrying a high-ranking man. FGM thus turns out to be a self-reinforcing convention: any family that departs from the convention, by not subjecting their daughter to FGM, will pay a high cost, by foregoing the opportunity of marrying her off. Families could accordingly come to believe that they would be depriving their daughters of the opportunity to marry by not subjecting them to FGM.

However, recent evidence suggests that FGM is actually not maintained via a belief trap, even if it did originally come about through the interactions and considerations that Mackie (1996) describes. To show this, the behavioural psychologist Charles Efferson and his colleagues (2015) went out and surveyed forty-five communities in Gezira, a state in Sudan where FGM is widespread. In each community, they measured the proportion of girls who had been subjected to FGM – a measure referred to as the cutting rate. They found that most communities had an intermediate cutting rate somewhere between zero percent and 100 percent. This is contrary to Mackie's theory, which predicts a so-called bimodal distribution of cutting rates, with most communities either having a cutting rate of zero percent (a non-cutting equilibrium) or a cutting rate of 100 percent (a cutting equilibrium). In light of these findings, Efferson and his colleagues speculate that the practice of FGM is maintained simply because some families have particularly firmly-held religious beliefs or a particularly strong desire to signal their daughter's chastity. Of course, the question then still remains why this is the case.

The practice of *honour killings* is another phenomenon that possesses a dominant role within certain religious communities, yet violates important human rights. Honour killings have been documented, amongst other places, in the Middle East, South Asia, and several countries around the Mediterranean Sea. The practice is derived from the belief that a man's honour depends on the chastity of his wife and other female family members. In communities where this belief prevails, girls must for example have no contact with men before marriage, while married women must be faithful to their husbands, and must ensure that their behaviour does not provoke gossip and accusations of infidelity. When rumours spread that a woman has not complied with such norms, family members are allowed – or according to certain interpretations even obliged – to punish her or kill her.

To conclude, it is crucial to emphasize that the troublesome relationship between religious fundamentalism and extremism on the one hand and human rights on the other, is by no means restricted to the specific human rights violations discussed in this section. In many places around the world, fundamentalists and extremists use their religious beliefs as justification for horrible actions towards other humans, from the discrimination and persecution of religious minorities or non-believers, to the assault of people with different sexual orientations, to involvement in wars and military conflict, and many other brutalities. Various international organizations, including ones linked to the UN and NGOs such as Human Rights Watch, are closely involved in the fight against such reprehensible acts, through keeping a strict record of transgressions and lobbying for reforms and sanctions. Realistically, however, it is likely that clashes between radical approaches to religion and human rights will continue to abound for the foreseeable future.

Recommended readings

- Eli Berman (2009) applies an economic approach to answer the twin questions of why religious terrorism is on the rise and why we have seen a shift towards the use of suicide attacks among religious terrorists. Berman argues that religious terrorists are often not primarily motivated by the promise of rewards in afterlife or by specific religious ideals, but rather by a combination of a rational desire to help their own community and an eagerness to make personal sacrifices to signal their commitment to the community.
- Michael Cook (2014) addresses the question of why Islam plays a larger role in contemporary politics than most other religions. For answering this question, Cook scrutinizes the history of Islam and compares the fundamental scriptures of Islam to the equivalents for other religions. Among other things, he concludes that Islamic scriptures tie up more closely

with contemporary political debates, and that Islamic fundamentalism leaves more space for involvement in political activism.

- Steve Bruce (2011) provides an accessible overview of secularization theory, which argues that phenomena such as modernization, religious diversity, and rising individualism threaten the power, popularity, and prestige of religion. Offering a wide array of evidence, Bruce investigates the nature of the secularization trend. He additionally analyzes the role of secularization in relation to themes such as the political influence of religion in the US, reactions to Islam in Europe, and recent controversies over the place of religion in public life.

Bibliography

Atran, Scott. 2003. "Genesis of Suicide Terrorism". *Science 299*:1534–1539.

Atran, Scott. 2011. "Who Becomes a Terrorist Today?". Pp. 45–58 in *The Ethics and Efficacy of the Global War on Terrorism*, edited by Charles P. Webel and John A. Arnaldi. New York, NY: Palgrave Macmillan.

Berman, Eli. 2009. *Radical Religious and Violent: The New Economics of Terrorism*. Cambridge, MA: MIT Press.

Bruce, Steve. 2002. *God Is Dead: Secularization in the West*. Oxford: Blackwell.

Bruce, Steve. 2011. *Secularization: In Defence of an Unfashionable Theory*. Oxford: Oxford University Press.

Cook, Michael. 2014. *Ancient Religions, Modern Politics: The Islamic Case in Comparative Perspective*. Princeton, NJ: Princeton University Press.

De Graaf, Nan Dirk. 2013. "Secularization: Theoretical Controversies Generating Empirical Research". Pp. 322–354 in *Handbook of Rational Choice Social Research*, edited by Rafael Wittek, Tom Snijders, and Victor Nee. Stanford, CA: Stanford University Press.

Efferson, Charles, Sonja Vogt, Amy Elhadi, Hilal E.F. Ahmed, and Ernst Fehr. 2015. "Female Genital Cutting is Not a Social Coordination Norm". *Science 349*:1446–1447.

Gambetta, Diego (ed.). 2005. *Making Sense of Suicide Missions*. Oxford: Oxford University Press.

Hammer, Olav, and Mikael Rothstein (eds.). 2012. *The Cambridge Companion to Religious Movements*. Cambridge: Cambridge University Press.

Hechter, Michael. 1987. *Principles of Group Solidarity*. Berkeley, CA: University of California Press.

Herberg, Wil. 1955. *Protestant, Catholic, Jew: An Essay in American Religious Sociology*. Chicago, IL: University of Chicago Press.

Human Rights Watch. 2018. *World Report 2018 – Events of 2017*. New York, NY: Human Rights Watch.

Iannaccone, Laurence R. 1994. "Why Strict Churches are Strong". *American Journal of Sociology* 99:1180–1211.

Kelley, Jonathan, and Nan Dirk De Graaf. 1997. "National Context, Socialization, and Religious Belief: Results from 15 Nations". *American Sociological Review 62*:639–659.

Kepel, Gilles. 1994. *The Revenge of God: The Resurgence of Islam, Christianity, and Judaism in the Modern World*. University Park, PA: Pennsylvania State University Press.

Kepel, Gilles. 2002. *Jihad: The Trail of Political Islam*. London: Tauris.

Lawrence, Bruce B. 1989. *Defenders of God: The Fundamentalist Revolt Against the Modern Age*. Columbia, SC: University of South Carolina Press.

Lim, Chaeyoon, and Robert D. Putnam. 2010. "Religion, Social Networks, and Life Satisfaction". *American Sociological Review 75*:914–933.

Lipka, Michael. 2015. "Americans' Faith in God May Be Eroding". *Fact Tank* (Pew Research Center). http://www.pewresearch.org/fact-tank/2015/11/04/americans-faith-in-god-may-be-eroding/.

Lipka, Michael. 2017. "Muslims and Islam: Key Findings in the U.S. and Around the World". *Fact Tank* (Pew Research Center). http://www.pewresearch.org/fact-tank/2017/08/09/muslims-and-islam-key-findings-in-the-u-s-and-around-the-world/.

Mackie, Gerry. 1996. "Ending Footbinding and Infibulation: A Convention Account". *American Sociological Review 61*:999–1017.

Mayer, Ann E. 2013. *Islam and Human Rights: Tradition and Politics*. Boulder, CO: Westview Press.

McKernan, Bethan. 2017. "Man 'Sentenced to Death for Atheism' in Saudi Arabia". *Independent*, 26 April.

Moaddel, Mansoor. 2002. "The Study of Islamic Culture and Politics: An Overview and Assessment". *Annual Review of Sociology 28*:359–386.

Moore, R. Laurence. 1994. *Selling God: American Religion in the Market Place of Culture*. Oxford: Oxford University Press.

Mortimer, Caroline. 2015. "70,000 Indian Muslim Clerics Issue Fatwa against Isis, the Taliban, al-Qaeda and Other Terror Groups". *Independent*, 10 December.

Need, Ariana, and Nan Dirk De Graaf. 1996. "'Losing My Religion': A Dynamic Analysis of Leaving the Church in the Netherlands". *European Sociological Review 12*:87–99.

Norris, Pippa, and Ronald Inglehart. 2004. *Sacred and Secular: Religion and Politics Worldwide*. Cambridge: Cambridge University Press.

Roy, Olivier. 1994. *The Failure of Political Islam*. London: Tauris.

Ruiter, Stijn, and Nan Dirk De Graaf. 2006. "National Context, Religiosity, and Volunteering: Results from 53 Countries". *American Sociological Review 71*:191–210.

Stark, Rodney, and Laurence R. Iannaccone. 1994. "A Supply-Side Reinterpretation of the 'Secularization' of Europe". *Journal for the Scientific Study of Religion 33*:230–252.

Stark, Rodney, and Roger Finke. 2000. *Acts of Faith: Explaining the Human Side of Religion*. Berkeley, CA: University of California Press.

Swift, Art. 2017. "In U.S., Belief in Creationist View of Humans at New Low". *Gallup Politics*. https://news.gallup.com/poll/210956/belief-creationist-view-humans-new-low.aspx.

UNICEF. 2016. *Female Genital Mutilation/Cutting: A Global Concern*. New York, NY: UNICEF.

Voas, David, and Mark Chaves. 2016. "Is the United States a Counter Example to the Secularization Thesis?". *American Journal of Sociology 121*:1517–1556.

INDEX